THE AEROSPACE ENCYCLOPEDIA OF

AIR WARFARE

Volume 1

1911 - 1945

THE AEROSPACE ENCYCLOPEDIA OF
AIR WARFARE
Volume 1
1911 - 1945

Editors:
Daniel J. March
John Heathcott

Aerospace Publishing Ltd
AIRtime Publishing Inc.

Published by
Aerospace Publishing Ltd
179 Dalling Road
London W6 0ES
UK

Published under licence in USA and
Canada by
AIRtime Publishing Inc.
10 Bay Street
Westport
CT 06880
USA

Aerospace **ISBN 1 874023 87 5**
AIRtime **ISBN 1-880588-25-0**

Distributed in the UK,
Commonwealth and Europe by
Airlife Publishing Ltd
101 Longden Road
Shrewsbury
SY3 9EB
Telephone: 01743 235651
Fax: 01743 232944

Distributed to retail bookstores in the
USA and Canada by
AIRtime Publishing Inc.
10 Bay Street
Westport, CT 06880
USA
Telephone: (203) 838-7979
Fax: (203) 838-7344

US readers wishing to order by mail,
please contact :
AIRtime Publishing Inc. toll-free at
1 800 359-3003

Publisher: Stan Morse

Editors: Daniel J. March
John Heathcott

**Production
Editor:** Claire Alexander

Authors: Francis K. Mason
Peter R. March
Daniel J. March
John Heathcott
Jim Winchester
Jon Lake
Brian S. Strickland

Designer: Charlotte Cruise

Artists: John Weal
Keith Woodcock
Keith Fretwell
Chris Davey
Iain Wyllie
Ichiro Hasegawa

Colour reproduction:
Universal Graphics Pte Ltd
Singapore

Printed in Italy

WORLD AIR POWER JOURNAL
published quarterly and providing
an in-depth analysis of
contemporary military aircraft and
their worldwide operators.
Superbly produced and filled with
extensive colour photography,
World Air Power Journal is
available by subscription from:

**(UK, Europe and
Commonwealth)
Aerospace Publishing Ltd
FREEPOST
PO Box 2822
London W6 0BR
Telephone: (0)181-740 9554
Fax: (0)181-746 2556
(no stamp needed within the
UK)**

**(USA and Canada)
AIRtime Publishing Inc.
Subscription Dept
10 Bay Street
Westport, CT 06880
USA
Telephone: (203) 838-7979
Fax: (203) 838-7344
Toll-free order number in USA:
1 800 359-3003**

CONTENTS

WORLD WAR I AND THE INTERWAR YEARS

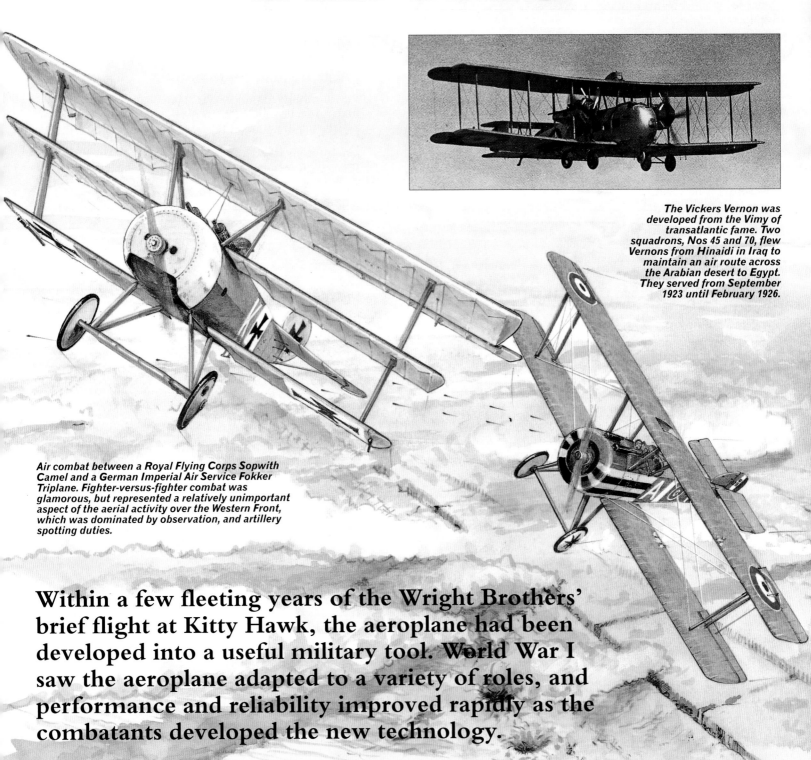

The Vickers Vernon was developed from the Vimy of transatlantic fame. Two squadrons, Nos 45 and 70, flew Vernons from Hinaidi in Iraq to maintain an air route across the Arabian desert to Egypt. They served from September 1923 until February 1926.

Air combat between a Royal Flying Corps Sopwith Camel and a German Imperial Air Service Fokker Triplane. Fighter-versus-fighter combat was glamorous, but represented a relatively unimportant aspect of the aerial activity over the Western Front, which was dominated by observation, and artillery spotting duties.

Within a few fleeting years of the Wright Brothers' brief flight at Kitty Hawk, the aeroplane had been developed into a useful military tool. World War I saw the aeroplane adapted to a variety of roles, and performance and reliability improved rapidly as the combatants developed the new technology.

The Italo-Turkish War

SEPTEMBER 1911 - SEPTEMBER 1912

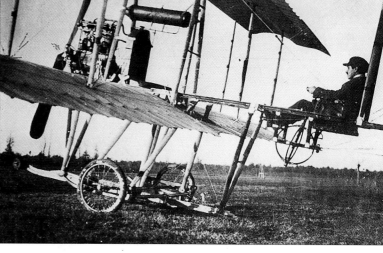

Gianni Caproni with his Ca-5 biplane at Malpensa, Italy in 1911. Several widely differing types of biplanes had been evolved during 1910 and 1911. The last, with variable tail-incidence and cambered wings, was not an effective machine.

Long before World War I the aeroplane was being considered as potential military equipment, the US Army calling for demonstration by Orville Wright of his aircraft as far back as 1908. It was during such a flight at Fort Myer that he crashed on 17 September that year, killing Lieutenant Thomas E. Selfridge, US Signal Corps, and injuring himself. Thus died the first military man in an aeroplane.

It was just three years later, on 25 September 1911, that Italy mobilised a special expeditionary Army Corps with an Air Flotilla for despatch to Libya to counter Arab-Turkish occupation of the town of Tripoli. Under the command of Captain Carlos Piazza, the Air Flotilla comprised five operational pilots, six reserve pilots and 30 ground crew; their aircraft were three Nieuports, two Blériots, two Farmans and two Etrich Taubes.

AIR RECCE

Tripoli was stormed on 5 October, and 10 days later work started to unload the crated aircraft from ships anchored offshore, the first being air tested a week later. In the meantime, the Turks had counterattacked and the Italian beachhead was becoming precarious. On 23 October, Piazza took off on a dawn flight in his Blériot with orders to discover the exact whereabouts of the enemy's main forces, a mission successfully accomplished when he discovered a number of Turkish encampments and reported his findings on landing after a 59-minute flight. Six reconnaissance flights were carried out during 23-25 October, a flight by Captain Ricardo Moizo in a Nieuport on the third day being met by rifle fire, three shots passing through his wings. The location of some 8,000 enemy troops opposing the Italian forces was vital in re-arranging the Italian line. Before the end of the month Lieutenant Guilio Gavotti and naval Lieutenant Ugo de Rossi had also

made ready their aircraft.

The next role undertaken by the Air Flotilla was artillery observation when Piazza and Moizo performed spotting duties for the Italian warship *Sardegna* bombarding the Zanzur Oasis, but this was handicapped by the pilots' inability to signal the effects of the gunnery until Piazza hit on the idea of dropping small tins containing messages to the gunnery officer. By the end of November successful artillery spotting was being carried out as a matter of routine.

On 1 November the first bombs ever dropped by an aeroplane on operations were released by Lieutenant Gavotti in his Etrich Taube. On that occasion he dropped three 4.4-lb (2-kg) Cipelli grenades over the Taguira Oasis and another at Ain Zara. Refinements in weapons followed when an engineer, Lieutenant Bontempelli, produced a cylindrical bomb containing explosive and shrapnel, of which 10 could be carried aloft in a box container which, after operation of a lever in the cockpit, would drop them singly or in a 'stick'.

Atrocious weather at the turn of the year did not prevent the Italian pilots from supporting the Italian advance towards Ain Zara, working out a system of flying manoeuvres to indicate the presence of threatening enemy forces. Occasional instances in which the ground forces would not believe the pilots' reports prompted Piazza to have a camera fitted to his Bleriot, the only

difficulty being that the aircraft had to land after taking each photograph as it was impossible to change plates in the air. The Italian aircraft were also used to drop propaganda leaflets among tribal groups in successful efforts to win their support for the Italian cause.

During the winter two replacement Farmans were received at Tripoli to allow maintenance on other aircraft which were beginning to show signs of considerable wear and tear. With them came Lieutenant Oreste Salomone, newly trained in Italy, who was to gain fame in World War I with the award of Italy's highest gallantry decoration, the Gold Medal for Valour.

At the end of 1911, as the campaign moved east and north into Cyrenaica, a new flotilla came into being at Homs, near Benghazi under the command of Captain Montu. It was in this theatre that the Turks began using anti-aircraft artillery, and it was in one of the

Above: When flying first became a recognised military sideline, the heavier-than-air 'specialists' grew into the Aviation Battalion during the Tripoli campaign with some Bleriot XIs in 1912, the floatplane being called 'Hydro-avion'. The lettering on the tail stands for 'Società Italiana Transaerea'.

Left: An Italian Caproni biplane of 1910 powered by an 18.63-kW (25-hp) Millen engine driving a pusher propeller. Aerodynamic experiments of all kinds were tried, including the effects of flexible surfaces.

first Bristol two-seaters to reach Africa that naval Lieutenant Roberti was flying a reconnaissance sortie when his aircraft was hit and his propeller struck by shrapnel; in a congratulatory gesture typical of the time, Roberti dived low over the enemy battery scattering his personal visiting cards (some of which he found on display in a Turkish museum 14 years later).

The first operational night flights were made by the Cyrenaica Flotilla, Captain Marengo making five night reconnaissance sorties between May and July 1912, and on 11 June he dropped several bombs on a Turkish camp in moonlight shortly before dawn, the first night bombing attack in history. Tragedy struck on 12 August, when the first Italian pilot was killed during an operational flight, although the accident was caused by loss of control (probably due to a severe thermal near the ground).

ITALIAN LEAD

As the Libyan campaign drew to an end the achievements of the Italian air flotillas were hailed by the international press as a new chapter in warfare, and certainly gained military attention throughout Europe. Though no evidence can be found to confirm the presence of any British observer with the Italians, one cannot be blind to the coincidence that it was in April 1912 that the formation of the Royal Flying Corps was announced, followed almost immediately by the opening of the Central Flying School; at this, reconnaissance, artillery spotting and night flying were the main constituents of the military flying training course, all of which were being practically demonstrated by the Italians in Libya with their tiny air flotillas.

The Opening Rounds

APRIL 1914 – APRIL 1915

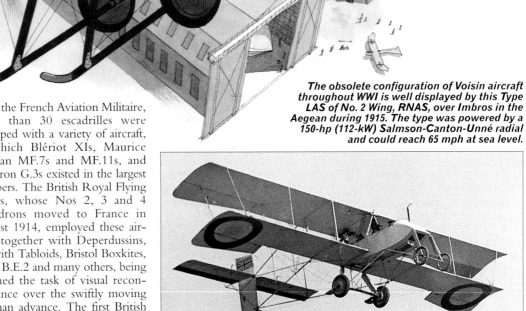

The first successful strategic air raid on Germany, on 8 October 1914, resulted in the destruction of the new German Army Zeppelin LZ25, which had been fully inflated inside its shed. Flt Lt 'Reggie' Manx, flying a Sopwith Tabloid, surveys the damage caused by his bombs.

To many of the pioneer air enthusiasts, the very concept of using aeroplanes as weapons of war was not only distasteful but a prostitution of a sporting machine. Such a perception ignored the fact that the Italo-Turkish War had ever been fought, and that soldiers and sailors of a score of nations had already become proficient in the skills of flying. In America five Curtiss A-1s had been employed for reconnaissance during the Vera Cruz incident in April 1914, and the French had employed aeroplanes during a colonial campaign in Morocco early that year.

In Europe alone, France, Germany, Russia, the UK, Turkey, Belgium, Italy and Bavaria already had military air arms, the purpose of which was almost exclusively reconnaissance, the two first-named nations being measurably the most advanced both in equipment and tactical concept. Even so, no aeroplane at the outbreak of war was equipped with a gun of any sort, it being generally thought unlikely that a rifle or pistol shot from one moving aircraft would prove fatal against another.

In the French Aviation Militaire, more than 30 escadrilles were equipped with a variety of aircraft, of which Blériot XIs, Maurice Farman MF.7s and MF.11s, and Caudron G.3s existed in the largest numbers. The British Royal Flying Corps, whose Nos 2, 3 and 4 Squadrons moved to France in August 1914, employed these aircraft together with Deperdussins, Sopwith Tabloids, Bristol Boxkites, RAF B.E.2 and many others, being assigned the task of visual reconnaissance over the swiftly moving German advance. The first British aeroplane to be lost to enemy action was an Avro 504, shot down by enemy small arms fire from the ground on 19 August.

FIRST BOMBS

The Germans, whose Military Aviation Service had formally existed since October 1912, went to war with 246 first-line aeroplanes of numerous types, of which the Taube monoplane, and Albatros and Aviatik biplanes predominated.

The obsolete configuration of Voisin aircraft throughout WWI is well displayed by this Type LAS of No. 2 Wing, RNAS, over Imbros in the Aegean during 1915. The type was powered by a 150-hp (112-kW) Salmson-Canton-Unné radial and could reach 65 mph at sea level.

The service possessed an established operational strength of 254 pilots and 271 observers, distributed among units deployed to support the defences of the great German fortress towns.

There was no specific organisation or plan in being to commit any of these air services to armed combat duties, so ,no attempt was made by either side in the early weeks of

The Blériot XI was one of history's significant aircraft. Before the beginning of WWI, the RFC and RNAS had taken delivery of a number of Blériots. At the outbreak of hostilities, five squadrons were equipped with the type.

the war to interfere with the enemy's use of the skies over the Western Front, other than the instinctive use of the infantryman's rifle. The employment of the aeroplane as a bomber had not been overlooked, however, and it was not long before individual pilots started out on what can only be regarded as courageous, if foolhardy ecapades: one Leutnant Franz von Hiddeson dropped (by hand) two light bombs from his Taube over Paris on 13 August. The first bomb to fall from an aeroplane on English soil was another such light bomb which dropped into a Dover garden on Christmas Eve, 1914. By

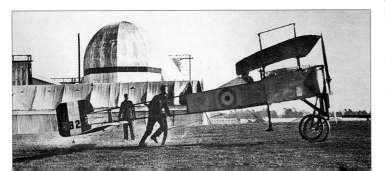

Modelled closely on the Aviatik B.I of 1914, the more efficient Aviatik B.II appeared in 1915. It had a lightened but stronger structure and a more powerful engine, though still no provision for the fitting of any armament.

then a number of planned bombing attacks had been executed, notably the attack on 8 October by two pilots of the British RNAS based at Antwerp who, in Sopwith Tabloids, bombed Cologne railway station and the airship shed at Dusseldorf; in the latter attack Flight Lieutenant R.L.G. Marix destroyed the brand-new German airship Z IX.

Inevitably, airmen of the opposing air services encountered each other in the air, and it soon became customary for the observers, if not the pilots themselves, to carry rifles and pistols with which to persuade

their opponents to vacate that particular part of the sky. The first aeroplane to be shot down (as distinct from being forced down by 'aggressive manoeuvres') was a German Aviatik, shot down by the French pilot Sergeant Joseph Franz in a Voisin over Reims using a free-mounted Hotchkiss gun on 5 October. (A British pilot, Lieutenant L.A. Strange, had fitted his Farman biplane with a Lewis gun in the very first days of the war, but had been ordered to remove it as it severely restricted the aircraft's performance.)

AIR COMBAT

Elsewhere, drastic means were being adopted to destroy enemy aircraft. Staff Captain Nesterov of the Imperial Russian Air Service, flying an unarmed Morane-Saulnier, rammed an

Austrian two-seater over Galicia flown by Leutnant Baron von Rosenthal; both pilots were killed. An even more unorthodox method was employed by another Russian, Staff Captain Kazakov, who trailed a grapnel below his Morane-Saulnier MS 5; with this he engaged the wing of an Albatross two-seater near Gusov and then struck the enemy aircraft with his landing gear.

Notwithstanding these primitive forms of combat, efforts were being made to fit guns in aeroplanes early in the war, rifles and machine-guns at first being mounted on makeshift pylons for use by the observer. In France, Roland Garros became the world's first pilot to destroy an opponent using a fixed, forward-firing machine-gun in his Morane Type L parasol monoplane. With steel deflector wedges bolted to the propeller blades to deflect bullets that would otherwise damage them, Garros shot down an Aviatik over the Western Front on 1 April 1915. The era of true air combat had opened.

The Bristol Boxkite was a refined copy of the Henri Farman biplane, with a 50-hp (37-kW) Gnôme rotary piston engine. Here Lt Eric Harrison receives congratulations from an Army official after a flight in a Boxkite on 1 March 1914.

Early warplanes

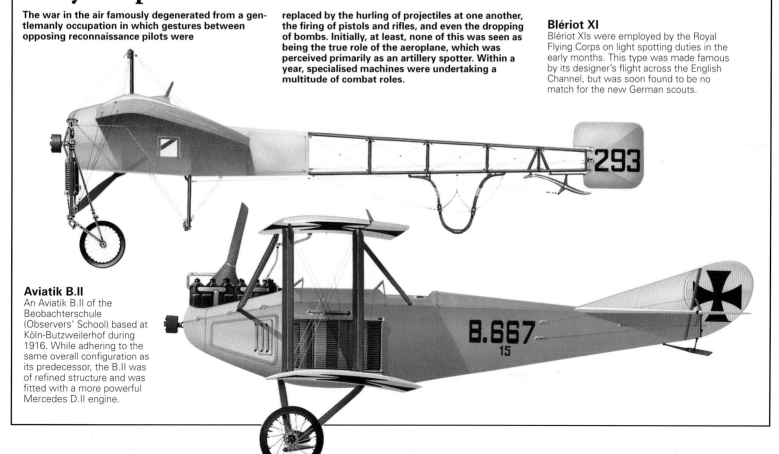

The war in the air famously degenerated from a gentlemanly occupation in which gestures between opposing reconnaissance pilots were

replaced by the hurling of projectiles at one another, the firing of pistols and rifles, and even the dropping of bombs. Initially, at least, none of this was seen as being the true role of the aeroplane, which was perceived primarily as an artillery spotter. Within a year, specialised machines were undertaking a multitude of combat roles.

Blériot XI

Blériot XIs were employed by the Royal Flying Corps on light spotting duties in the early months. This type was made famous by its designer's flight across the English Channel, but was soon found to be no match for the new German scouts.

Aviatik B.II

An Aviatik B.II of the Beobachterschule (Observers' School) based at Köln-Butzweilerhof during 1916. While adhering to the same overall configuration as its predecessor, the B.II was of refined structure and was fitted with a more powerful Mercedes D.II engine.

Battle of the Front Gun

APRIL 1915 - APRIL 1916

Fok. E.III 417/15

Left: The RFC's first dedicated fighting scout was the Airco D.H.2, this example being one of the first to be delivered to No. 24 Squadron at Hounslow, commanded by Major Lanoe Hawker VC, late in 1915.

Above: The Fokker E III monoplane was a compact and agile fighting machine. With a single synchronised machine-gun, it dominated the Western Front during the latter half of 1915, despite lack of numbers.

Although the idea of mounting a machine-gun in the nose of an aeroplane to fire forward through the propeller had been conceived before World War I, only the French had ordered such an aircraft (the Morane Type I) for service. This had proved unreliable and it was not until the Frenchman Roland Garros, flying a Morane Type L with Escadrille MS 23, shot down three German aircraft in April 1915, that the era of dedicated air combat opened. His aircraft was equipped with a machine-gun on the nose and steel deflector plates on the propeller blades to prevent the bullets shooting off the blades,

a device evolved by Saulnier. Garros was forced down behind the German lines on 19 April and taken prisoner, his Morane being closely examined by the enemy.

In the meantime, the German engineer Schneider had already developed an interrupter gear which mechanically prevented the gun from firing at the instant a propeller blade passed the gun muzzle, and this was being incorporated in a small monoplane fighting scout

Below: A B.E.2c on the Western Front. These aircraft gave good service in the reconnaissance role during early 1915, but they were extremely vulnerable in any form of air combat.

then being produced by Anthony Fokker for the Germans.

ALLIED LOSSES

When originally conceived, the Fokker E-type monoplane was not intended for offensive air combat but simply as an escort for reconnaissance aircraft which were becoming ever more widely used over the Western Front, and was initially issued in small numbers to the Fliegerabteilungen. It was when such men as Boelcke, Immelmann and Kastner came to fly the new scout that they appreciated the supreme advantage of the synchronised gun as an offensive weapon and quickly mastered the basic skills necessary to stalk and shoot down unsuspecting enemy pilots.

As more German pilots learned

Above: The Germans recognised the need to fire a gun directly forward along the aircraft's axis, through the propeller. Fokker produced his E-type monoplanes with suitable interruptor gear.

these rudimentary tactics with the Fokker E I, losses among British and French observation aircraft increased rapidly, with little in the way of immediate remedy in sight. The first French aircraft fell to the new German 'fighting scout' in June, and the following month two British B.E.2c aircraft were forced down. By November the depredations of the Fokker monoplanes had given rise to the 'Fokker Scourge', though in fact at that time there were probably fewer than 80 Fokkers in service over both Eastern and Western Fronts. Already the first Allied pilots were becoming known to the public for their prowess in air combat, the legendary Georges Guynemer having shot down his first victim while flying a Morane-Saulnier Type N on 19 July. He had survived being shot down once and, on his 19th birthday on Christmas Eve 1915, he was awarded the Cross of the Legion d'Honeur for having destroyed two enemy aircraft. During the next three months he shot down six more.

None of the Allied pilots attracted the adulation commanded by the German Max Immelmann, dubbed by his colleagues 'the Eagle of Lille'. Taught to fly the Fokker monoplane by Oswalde Boelcke, Immelmann was regarded with almost spectral awe by his enemies, and shot down 15 Allied aircraft before finally being killed near Lens on 18 June 1916. His mentor, Boelcke, was, however, the true originator of air combat tactics and, with his extraordinary gifts of patience and meticulous instruction, brought a new level of flying discipline to the pilots whom he personally coached. He, like

Unequal opponents

The Fokker E series monoplanes were introduced to counter Allied observation aircraft, which proved extremely vulnerable to the German scouts, with their forward-firing armament. The

Fokker's dominance was short-lived, however, with the introduction of British pusher scouts which had forward-firing guns manned by a dedicated gunner.

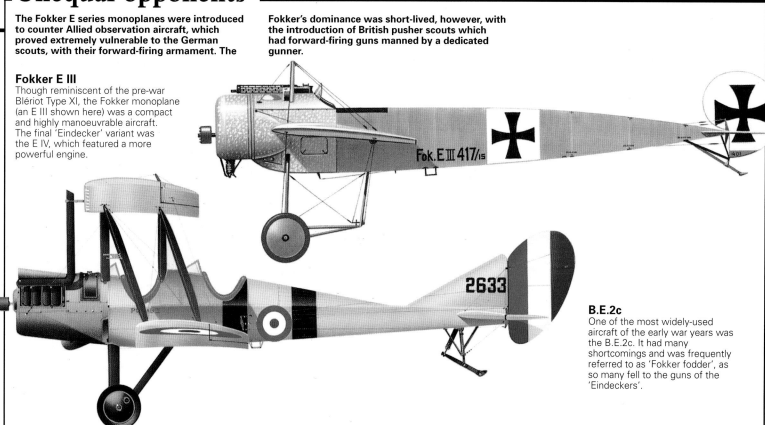

Fokker E III
Though reminiscent of the pre-war Blériot Type XI, the Fokker monoplane (an E III shown here) was a compact and highly manoeuvrable aircraft. The final 'Eindecker' variant was the E IV, which featured a more powerful engine.

B.E.2c
One of the most widely-used aircraft of the early war years was the B.E.2c. It had many shortcomings and was frequently referred to as 'Fokker fodder', as so many fell to the guns of the 'Eindeckers'.

Immelmann, was awarded the coveted Pour le Merite, before he met his death on 28 October 1916 with a score of no fewer than 40 victories. He has remained the father figure of German fighter aviation.

The British were slow to introduce the sychronised front gun and, unlike the French and Germans, cointinued to produce biplane designs. The merits of the biplane (maximising lifting area while retaining excellent agility, and structural integrity) should not be overlooked. The pusher layout was adopted so that a front gun could be mounted without the need for any interrupter gear. Thus it was that the Airco D.H.2 pusher biplane

The Morane-Saulnier Type N had a fixed 0.315-in (8-mm) Hotchkiss or 0.303-in (7.7-mm) Vickers or Lewis machine-gun. The RFC received 24 of the type, the principal operator being No. 6 Squadron.

equipped the Royal Flying Corps' first true fighter squadron, No. 24, commanded by Major Lanoe G. Hawker VC; it did not reach the Western Front from England until February 1916. The F.B.5 and F.E.2 pusher biplanes predated the D.H.2, but neither was as successul as a fighter.

Although initially delivered in 1915 to reconnaissance units, it was soon realised that the Fokker E-types possessed real combat potential. Thus began the 'Fokker Scourge' phase of the war in the air.

Losses among B.E.2c aircraft of the RFC over the Western Front had reached alarming proportions during the latter half of 1915, for this type of aircraft (a veritable forest of struts and wires) retained no more than a modest performance provided it was not encumbered by a defensive gun; when such a gun was fitted, perforce unable to fire through the propeller, the aircraft was so slow and cumbersome as to invite swift destruction should a German scout appear. Both this and the F.E.2b were in truth two years out of date when they reached the front, and it speaks volumes that Lanoe Hawker's pilots in their ungainly D.H.2s were able partly to redress the balance of superiority, first during the early stages of the

Battle of Verdun and, more important, during the great Battle of the Somme in 1916.

PUP APPEARS

In the fact that such aircraft as the B.E.2c and F.E.2b had taken so long to appear lay the reasons for the prolonged success of the Fokker E-types. Petty squabbling was rife in the British aircraft industry, and where the Royal Aircraft Factory at Farnborough should have provided guidance and leadership there was little but acrimony and jealousy, compounded by inter-service rivalry for aircraft contracts. It fell to the commercial firm of Sopwith Aviation to provide a remedy, but it was not until February 1916 that the first Pup appeared with its single front gun and Sopwith-Kauper interrupter gear, and even this had been ordered by the Admiralty. Moreover, not until September of that year did the Pups of RNAS squadrons finally put paid to the Fokkers' superiority.

The Year Of The Somme

FEBRUARY 1916 - OCTOBER 1916

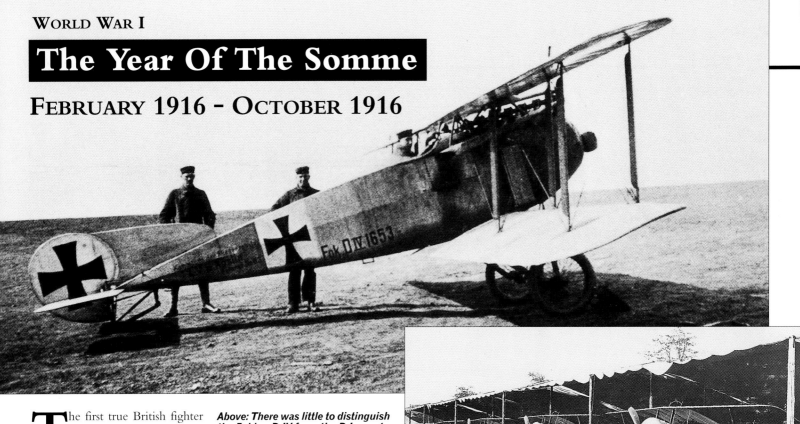

The first true British fighter Squadron was No. 24. Its commanding officer, Major Lanoe Hawker, had won the Victoria Cross on 25 July 1915 when, flying a Bristol Scout armed with a single-shot cavalry carbine, he forced down three machine gun-armed enemy two-seaters. The Bristol Scout was not a fighter in the true sense but had been supplied in small numbers for the protection of observation aircraft. In February 1916 Hawker took No. 24 Squadron to France equipped with the D.H.2, a single-seat pusher biplane armed with a free-firing front gun. The aircraft was manoeuvrable and sensitive on the controls. Although fitted with a movable gun in the nose, its pilots soon adopted the practice of fixing the gun to fire along the line of flight and aiming the aircraft directly at the target. Lieutenant Tidmarsh was the first to open the squadron's score with a victory near Bapaume on 2 April.

German ace Günther stands in front of his Albatross C I. The type was in service on the Western Front by the late summer of 1915, and was well liked by its crews as a reliable aircraft.

Above: There was little to distinguish the Fokker D IV from the D I, apart from slightly larger dimensions, a twin-gun armament and a 160-hp (119-kW) Mercedes D.III engine. Its performance was inadequate.

Thereafter No. 24 achieved a fast-growing reputation for determination and skill in countering the 'Fokker Scourge', being joined shortly after by two more D.H.2 squadrons, Nos 29 and 32.

FIGHTER REAPPRAISAL

The Germans, meanwhile, recognising that the superiority of the Fokker E-type monoplanes must soon be disputed by the Allies, were already early in 1916 introducing the Fokker D I and Halberstadt D II biplanes with single synchronised 'Spandau' (LMG 08/15) machine-guns. These were aircraft of neat but conventional appearance, and with better handling characteristics than the monoplanes. The whole concept of air fighting was undergoing reappraisal in the German air force, largely as a result of representations by Oswald Boelcke. He had demonstrated (with Immelmann) the superiority of the E-types in 1915, on return from a tour of the front early in 1916 was given command of a new fighting unit, Jasta 2 equipped with Fokker D Is and D IVs. This represented the beginning of the creation of a large number of dedicated air combat units (after the formation of the first RFC fighter squadrons, it should be noted). Notwithstanding the success of the relatively small number of D.H.2s, the French were the first among the Allies to introduce a truly successful fighting scout, the Nieuport 17, which arrived at the front late in March. It was faster by 10 mph (16 km/h) than any British aircraft and was

armed with a single synchronised front gun. It also served in large numbers with the RFC, and among the British pilots who gained their first victories in this excellent little aeroplane was Captain Albert Ball (later VC, DSO and MC), who destroyed an Albatros D I in May and a Roland C II on 2 July.

The prolonged Battle of Verdun had started late in February 1916, and was to drag on for many months. Inevitably, the increasing dependence on aircraft for artillery observation by both sides led to frequent air combats between opposing Fokkers, Halberstadts, Nieuports and D.H.2s, not to mention the widespread destruction of poorly-armed reconnaissance aircraft. By the start of the bloody Battle of the Somme in July there were dozens of dedicated fighter squadrons in action over the Western Front.

BEWARE THE STALKER

Operations by both sides took much the same form, with single observation aircraft sent to cover closely defined sections of the front line, their pilots seldom being instructed to penetrate more than a mile or so into enemy airspace. They would occasionally be escorted by a flight of fighting scouts, but more often a flight or even a squadron would patrol within sight of the reconnaissance aircraft, the pilots keeping watch for enemy

The Nieuport enjoyed high speed and superb manoeuvrability, making it an excellent biplane de chasse or 'destroyer'. These are French Nieuport 17s. Note the gun housing above the upper wing.

scouts. Some use was made of decoy aircraft, which it was hoped would lure the defending scouts away from their charges, after which the lumbering B.E., F.E., Voisin or Aviatik would be easy prey for prowling scouts.

This was the era of the lone 'stalker', of whom Ball in his Nieuport was one of the most deadly, while McCudden of No. 29 Squadron in a D.H.2 scored the first of his 57 victories on 6 September. The Frenchman Charles Nungesser had been flying Nieuports of various types since late 1915, and by the end of 1916 had destroyed 20 enemy aircraft, despite constant pain from unhealed wounds. In the German air service, Immelmann had been killed on 18 June, followed by Boelcke on 28 October, but a new star was in the ascendant. Rittmeister Manfred Freiherr von Richthofen, the greatest German flying name to emerge from the War, had joined Jasta 2 under Boelcke in September, and scored the first of 80 air victories on 17 September while flying an Albatros D II. It has been estimated that by the end of that year more than a dozen German scout pilots had gained at least a dozen victories.

Left: The Sopwith Pup entered service with both the RFC and RNAS in 1916. Here a Pup takes off from an improvised platform over the guns of a British warship off the Belgian coast.

Right: The American-manned Lafayette Escadrille received some examples of the Nieuport 21, powered by an 80-hp (60-kW) Le Rhône engine. This example is seen at Cachy on the Somme in 1916.

It was in September that German air superiority over the Western Front was first challenged, with the arrival in France of such excellent Allied fighting scouts as the Sopwith Pup which, though in no way radical, proved such a delightfully manoeuvrable aircraft that in even only moderately skilled pilots' hands it could outfly and outfight almost any German aircraft extant. Pups of the RNAS were in action over the Belgian and French coast in September, and the following month No. 8 (Naval) Squadron was formed in the Somme area; within 50 days 'Naval Eight' had destroyed 20 German aircraft.

Right: A Halberstadt D II of Kampfeinsitzer Staffel II, the type which began to replace the Fokker Eindecker in 1916. It was robust and popular but never achieved the success or status of the Albatros.

Fighters of 1916

1916 was a year of great change for Britain's Royal Flying Corps. Following his appointment as RFC commander in France, Trenchard reduced the reliance on inefficient Royal Aircraft Factory products by purchasing D.H.2s and Nieuport scouts, and introduced separate, specialised scout, reconnaissance and bombing squadrons. He also decentralised his force, assigning individual wings (one observation and reconnaissance, one fighting) to different armies on the ground. The resulting British air superiority over the Somme was briefly challenged by Germany's new fighter circuses.

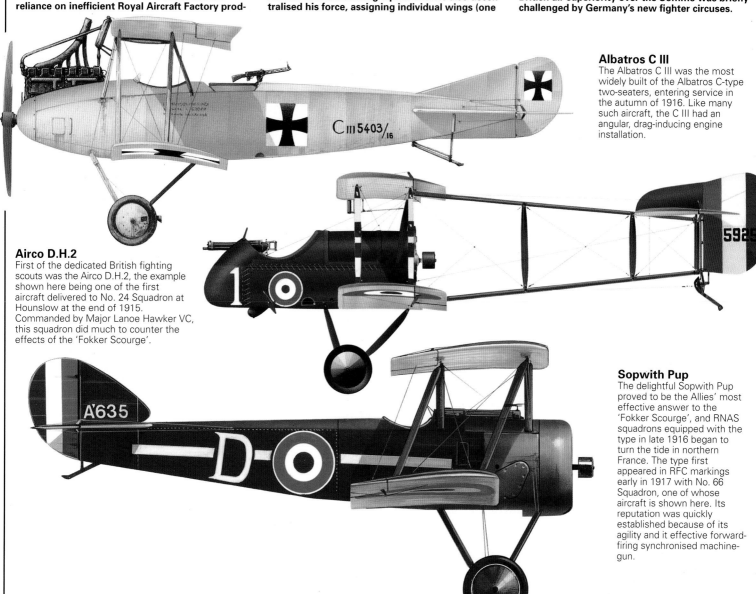

Albatros C III
The Albatros C III was the most widely built of the Albatros C-type two-seaters, entering service in the autumn of 1916. Like many such aircraft, the C III had an angular, drag-inducing engine installation.

Airco D.H.2
First of the dedicated British fighting scouts was the Airco D.H.2, the example shown here being one of the first aircraft delivered to No. 24 Squadron at Hounslow at the end of 1915. Commanded by Major Lanoe Hawker VC, this squadron did much to counter the effects of the 'Fokker Scourge'.

Sopwith Pup
The delightful Sopwith Pup proved to be the Allies' most effective answer to the 'Fokker Scourge', and RNAS squadrons equipped with the type in late 1916 began to turn the tide in northern France. The type first appeared in RFC markings early in 1917 with No. 66 Squadron, one of whose aircraft is shown here. Its reputation was quickly established because of its agility and it effective forward-firing synchronised machine-gun.

Hunters And Aces

DECEMBER 1916 - DECEMBER 1917

Above: No. 22 Squadron became a fighter squadron when it received its Bristol Fighters. These were used primarily for long offensive patrols into enemy territory. This F.2B is pictured at Agincourt in 1917.

The highly agile Sopwith Triplane proved deadly in the hands of the RNAS squadrons. These aircraft served with No. 201 Squadron, RNAS, at Bailleul in France.

The year 1917 brought home to the Western nations all the horrors of modern warfare, with the start of unrestricted submarine operations, the first major aeroplane raids against civilian targets and the first use of tanks on the Western Front. On that dismal front trench warfare ensured a continuation of bloody stalemate, while overhead the Allied air forces began the year with a tenuous possession of air superiority.

Both the British and the French were slow to exploit the limited tactical successes they had achieved in the air during the autumn of 1916, and persisted in using slow and vulnerable bombing and reconnaissance machines in the mistaken assumption that small numbers of fighting scouts, patrolling nearby, would be adequate to defend them. Air fighting tactics were not developed, other than by individual example, with the result that the Germans were able to gain the measure of such aircraft as the Sopwith Pup and Nieuport 17, and in so doing quickly evolved improved combat tactics which were embraced in the flying training programmes.

OBSOLETE FIGHTERS

The Royal Aircraft Factory R.E.8 was introduced before the end of 1916 and, despite shortcomings that immediately became apparent, was delivered in fast-growing numbers in the new year to the RFC. Other patently outdated aircraft, such as the B.E.2e, F.E.2b and F.E.8, con-tinued in service, while promising aircraft like the S.E.5a, Sopwith Camel and Sopwith Triplane suffered persistent delays before delivery got under way to the RFC, a situation that resulted in searching questions in the British parliament.

In the meantime, the German air force had set its sights on creating an impressive force of Jagdstaffeln (Jastas, or 'hunting squadrons'), aiming to establish 37 such units by April 1917, each with 14 aircraft of which the new Albatros D III was to provide the principal equipment. When this formidable force started concerted operations over the Western Front it achieved absolute

Fokker Dr Is of Jasta (abbreviation of Jagdstaffel, or fighter squadron) 12 at Marle in 1917. These bear the old-style Croix Pattée (so-called Maltese Cross) insignia on the tail and fuselage.

mastery and took the Allies totally unawares. The R.E.8 was to suffer terrible casualties for, having apparently learned from previous experience, its designers had so increased the aircraft's stability that its manoeuvrability suffered disastrously. Good fighters were too few in number to afford protection, with the result that April 1917 became known in RFC annals as 'Bloody April'. Squadron after squadron was decimated, and within the space of one month no fewer than 316 pilots and observers were lost. By the same token, an increasing number of German pilots achieved fame on account of their mounting victory

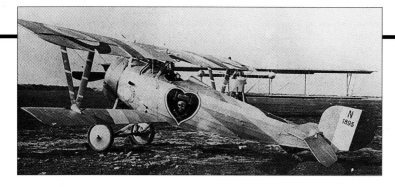

The Nieuport 17 from France was the personal mount of many World War I aces, this one belonging to French ace Charles Nungesser. It was in a Nieuport 17 that 'Billy' Bishop won his VC on 2 June 1917.

Below: The first successful landing on a ship underway was made on 2 August 1917, when Sqn Ldr E.M. Dunning touched down on HMS Furious. The straps helped the deck crew to bring the aircraft to rest.

tallies; there is no doubt that this period marked a summit of German achievement in the air that was not to be matched again until the advent of the Fokker D VII in 1918.

Forced by the events of April to take drastic action, the RFC now introduced the new scouts and, with commendable speed, the Sopwith F1 Camel, with 130-hp (97-kW) Clerget rotary, appeared over the Western Front. It was in time to join combat in July over the great 3rd Battle of Ypres which lasted until November, a battle which cost the Allies almost half a million

casualties, and gained little more than the capture of a ridge between Armentières and Dixmude. It did nevertheless serve to reduce the German pressure on the French after the collapse of their spring offensive.

This was the period of swiftly improving combat training in the RFC and, with such aircraft as the improved S.E.5a, the Camel and the Bristol F.2B Fighter, the balance began to swing back in the Allies' favour. Men like Mannock, Bishop, McCudden, Fullard and Collishaw became household names in the UK, no less than those of von

Opposing armed scouts

Trenchard had begun to replace his general purpose squadrons with dedicated bomber, observation and scout squadrons in 1916, and was

responsible for the introduction of a range of new fighters with which the RFC could take on the new German Pfalz, Fokker and Albatros scouts.

Albatros D V
This Albatros D V fighter was flown by Vizefeldwebel Clausnitzer of Jagdstaffel 4. Projecting above the upper wing centre-section is part of the radiator; this was offset to starboard to ensure that in the event of combat damage the pilot would not be drenched by a stream of scalding water.

SPAD VII
A good scout, the SPAD VII served in several air forces. This example of Escadrille SPA 81 is in the grey finish of the Aviation Militaire in 1917. The developed SPAD XIII gained much success with the American Expeditionary Force.

Sopwith Camel
The Sopwith Camel was a tricky and temperamental little aircraft to fly for a novice pilot, but was unequalled in agility and overcame its lack of speed with this vital asset. This example is from No. 65 Squadron, RFC in 1917, and the colours and markings are typical of the period.

Major Edward 'Mick' Mannock scored 73 victories, the highest tally of any RFC pilot. Awarded the DSO and two bars, and MC and one bar, he was posthumously awarded the VC post-war for his actions.

Above: The Sopwith Triplanes of Black Flight, No. 10 Squadron, RNAS, were led by the Canadian Flt Sub-Lt Raymond Collishaw, who eventually destroyed a total of 68 enemy aircraft.

Below: Major J. T. B. McCudden, DSO and bar, MC and bar, MM and Croix de Guerre, who flew (in particular) with No. 56 Squadron RFC was credited with 57 victories. He received the VC on 2 April 1918.

Above: Lt Col (later Air Marshal) W. A. Bishop DSO and bar, MC, DFC, Ld'H, C de G, of No. 60 Squadron, here with Nieuport Scout B1566, was credited with destroying 72 aircraft, gaining the VC on 2 June 1917.

British Aces

From 1917 Britain's Royal Flying Corps was well-equipped and well-led, and several of its pilots (and those of the RNAS) amassed large victory tallies. Several came within a whisker of matching Richthofen's record-breaking 80 victories.

USA Aces

The first American combat pilots in action entered the fray before their country joined the war, flying with the French Lafayette Escadrille. American aces included the legendary Rickenbacker and Frank Luke, most famous for the black art of balloon-busting.

Initially (and unhappily) equipped with Nieuports early in 1918, American squadrons changed to the SPAD XIII, one of the greatest exponents of which was Lt Frank Luke Jr, who achieved 21 victories.

Cpt Eddie Rickenbacker (the top American ace of WWI with 26 victories) became Commander of the 94th Aero Squadron, American Expeditionary Force. He is pictured with a SPAD XIII.

German Aces

Of all the fighting powers, Germany did most to encourage a 'cult' of aces, showering its most successful pilots with decorations, promoting them to lead their own units, and encouraging public interest in their exploits.

Below: The death of Hauptmann Oswald Boelcke on 28 October 1916 was a great loss to the Germans. It was primarily Boelcke's suggestion that specialist fighter units were established.

Above: 'The Eagle of Lille', Lt Max Immelmann, was one of the early German aces of WWI and his exploits captured the imagination of the German public. One of the first exponents of the Fokker E-type, he was killed in 1916.

French Aces

The French aircraft industry produced some of the finest scouts of the war, most notably in the Nieuport and SPAD families of fighters. Fittingly enough, it also produced some high-scoring individual pilots.

By mid-1916, famed French aerial fighter Georges Guynemer was a top scorer. He gained his first victory on 19 July 1915 and eventually achieved 54 victories, the second highest tally of all French aces. He was killed in September 1917.

Charles Nungesser was one of the legendary trio of French aces who scored heavily in 1917, achieving a total score of 45 in his Nieuport 17bis C1. An upward-firing Lewis gun enabled attacks to be made from below enemy aircraft.

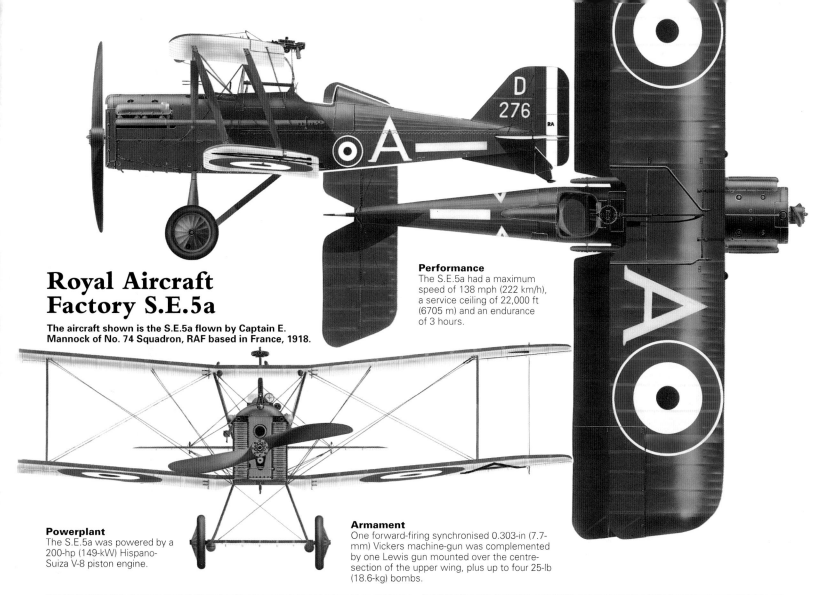

Royal Aircraft Factory S.E.5a

The aircraft shown is the S.E.5a flown by Captain E. Mannock of No. 74 Squadron, RAF based in France, 1918.

Performance
The S.E.5a had a maximum speed of 138 mph (222 km/h), a service ceiling of 22,000 ft (6705 m) and an endurance of 3 hours.

Powerplant
The S.E.5a was powered by a 200-hp (149-kW) Hispano-Suiza V-8 piston engine.

Armament
One forward-firing synchronised 0.303-in (7.7-mm) Vickers machine-gun was complemented by one Lewis gun mounted over the centre-section of the upper wing, plus up to four 25-lb (18.6-kg) bombs.

The Albatros scout introduced twin front guns, and was one of the aircraft with which the Germans sought to wrest air superiority from the Allies in late 1916. Here a trio of Albatros D Is of Jagdstaffel 2 are takes off on 28 October 1916.

Schleich, Manfred von Richthofen and Berthold in Germany. Against the new British scouts, and the French SPADs and Nieuports, were flown the new Albatros D Vs and Fokker Dr I triplanes (the latter flown by von Richthofen himself, and its most dashing exponent, Werner Voss). In the French air force, the legendary Georges Guynemer failed to return from combat in his SPAD on 11 September when his score stood at 54 victories, but the superb marksman René Fonck and the indomitable Charles Nungesser were already far along the road to stardom among fighter pilots. Yet for all these supreme individual

achievements, usually the product of the pilots' preference for lone patrol and single-handed combat, the pattern of air fighting was undergoing change, and the era of combat between formations of fighters had already dawned. The Germans in July had created a menacing new tactic with the formation of their first 'flying circus', in effect a wing of Jastas, commanded by Manfred von Richthofen. The purpose of this large fighting formation was to switch quickly from sector to sector of the front to achieve local air superiority. As much as anything else, this tactic convinced the RFC (and RNAS) of the importance of training for squadron combat. It was significant that many of the British high-scoring pilots were posted home to training units, where they could put their experience to good effect in the combat training of new squadrons.

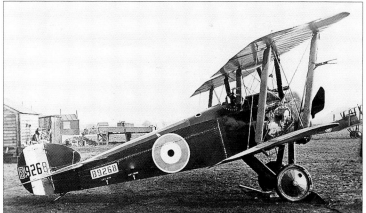

Above: The Sopwith Camel replaced the Pup in service on the Western Front and was arguably the finest British fighter of WWI, although it was tricky to fly. This is an early 1F.1 version.

Below: Known as the 'Harry Tate', the Royal Aircraft Factory R.E.8 entered RFC service at the end of 1916. The type suffered catastrophic losses during 'Bloody April' in 1917 under attack by German scouts.

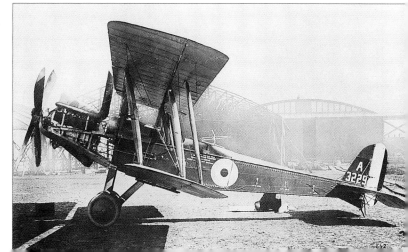

The Bloody Red Baron

The most successful fighter pilot of the Great War was Baron Rittmeister (Cavalry Captain) Manfred von Richthofen. An excellent shot, Richthofen was only an average pilot, but a good writer!

Known as 'The Red Baron', Manfred von Richthofen was World War I's most successful aerial fighter, shooting down 80 enemy aircraft in less than 15 months at the Western Front.

"Your opponent often slips downwards over one wing, or lets himself fall like a dead leaf in order to shake off an attack. In order to stick to him, one must on no account follow his tactics, since one has no control over a machine while falling like a dead leaf. Should one's opponent try to evade attack by such tricks, one must dive with him without losing sight of him....

"Looping the loop is worse than worthless in air fighting. Each loop is a great mistake. If one has approached one's adversary too close, a loop only offers him a big advantage. Change of speed should be relied upon to maintain the desired position, and this is best effected by adjusting the throttle.

"The best method of flying against the enemy is as follows. The officer commanding the group, no matter how large, should fly lowest, and should keep all machines under observation by turning and banking. No machine should be allowed either to advance or to hold back. The whole squadron should advance on a curved course: flying straight on above the front is dangerous, as even planes of the same type develop different speeds. Surprise can be avoided only when flying in close order.

"Many English airmen try to win advantages by flying tricks while engaged in fighting, but as a rule it is just these reckless and foolish stunts that lead them to their deaths.

"The second of April was a particularly warm day for my Jasta..... I was still in my bed when my orderly ran in exclaiming, 'Herr Leutnant, the English are here!' Half asleep, I looked out of the window and saw, circling over the airfield, my 'dear friends'.

"In spite of everything, I was the last to be airborne, and my comrades were already close to the enemy. Suddenly, however, one of the impertinent fellows dropped on me from above, hoping to force me down. Calmly I let him come at me, and then we began a merry dance. My opponent flew on his back, he did this, he did that. He was flying a two-seater, but I was superior to him, and he soon realised that he could not get away from me.

"It didn't take long. I squeezed below him and fired a burst, but without doing serious damage. We were some two kilometres behind the Front and I expected him to land, but I had misjudged my opponent: when he was only a few

This line-up of Albatros D IIIs is from von Richthofen's Jasta 11. The second aircraft in the line is the all-red machine flown by the Rittmeister himself, known to the RFC as le petit rouge (the little red).

metres from the ground he suddenly levelled up, flying straight ahead in an attempt to shake me off. Too bad for him! I attacked him again, flying so low that I was afraid I would hit the houses in the village below. The Englishman kept fighting back, and near the end I felt my machine being hit. I must not let up now: he must fall. He flew at full speed into a block of houses, and there wasn't much left. Once more, an example of splendid daring: he defended himself right to the end.

"By the end of April the English

Von Richthofen's Dreidecker

Conceived as a counter to the Sopwith Triplane, the Fokker Dr I was one of the most agile combat aircraft in history. Flown by such accomplished airmen as Manfred von Richthofen, the small number built shot down many times their own number of enemy aircraft on the Western Front.

Fokker Dr I
One of the most famous aircraft of all time, this is the Fokker Dr I flown by Rittmeister Freiherr von Richthofen at the time of his death. The Dr I was designed to emulate the success of the Sopwith Triplane but, apart from those flown by Richthofen and Voss, was never to achieve this, its performance being overshadowed by other German scouts.

Despite all that has been written about it, the Fokker Triplane was difficult to fly and was not as successful in service as is generally believed. Here von Richthofen is depicted downing an RFC S.E.5.

Production Fokker Dr Is reached JG 1 from 12 October 1917. The fame of the agile machine had spread and von Richthofen's pilots eagerly awaited their new aircraft. Here the 'Red Baron' lands after a raid.

had devised a fine scheme either to capture me or to shoot me down, and to this end they had set up a special squadron to patrol our sector. . . . [On 29 April] we flew up to the Front, hoping to find the enemy. After some 20 minutes the first arrived and really pounced on us.

"There were three Englishmen in SPAD single-seaters, who thought themselves superior to us because of the excellence of their

machines. Wolff, my brother and I were flying together: three against three, just as it should be.

"My opponent was the first to fall, his engine shot to pieces, I believe. He decided to try to land nearby but, as I gave no quarter, I attacked him a second time and his whole plane fell to bits. The wings dropped off like pieces of paper, and the fuselage fell like a stone, burning fiercely. It plunged into a marsh. It was impossible to dig out, and I never learnt my adversary's name.

"Wolff and my brother had attacked the opponents at the same time, and forced them to the ground not far from my victim."

Richthofen had now scored 52 kills. But on 1 May he went on leave to celebrate his 25th birthday – and Bloody April was over.

The simple black wooden coffin bearing Richthofen's body was carried with dignity, and he was buried with full military honours by No. 3 Squadron, Australian Flying Corps at Bertangles on 22 April 1918.

Below: Manfred von Richthofen, who flew this Triplane when he shot down his 60th victim on 1 September 1917, is seen on the right behind General von Lossberg, who is talking to the pilot.

The German Spring Offensive

NOVEMBER 1917 – JUNE 1918

After the end of the 3rd Battle of Ypres in November 1917 there followed a relative lull in the air fighting over the Western Front. The British, French and Germans set about strengthening their air forces, the Germans for their part preparing for a final great offensive to defeat the Allies before the arrival in France of the Americans who were expected to be ready to enter the fighting early the following summer.

As already mentioned, the German air force had created the first of its Jagdgeschwader (popularly known as the 'flying circuses', literally hunting wings) in July 1917 under Manfred von Richthofen, and such had been the success gained by this formidable fighting formation that two more (JG 2, initially comprising Jastas 12, 13, 15 and 19, and JG 3 with Jastas 2, 26, 27 and 36) were formed on 1 February 1918 under Rudolf Berthold and Bruno Loerzer respectively. Simultaneously another type of formation came into being: this was the Jagdgruppe, usually of no more than two or three Jastas. This unit was of a more transient nature and was created simply for convenience during a specific operation or offensive; a total of 12 such Jagdgruppen (Nos 1 to 12) being formed from time to time during 1918.

Elsewhere in Germany, trials were held in January 1918 to decide on new fighter equipment for the Jastas, and the choice fell on the Fokker D VII, one of the best German fighting scouts to achieve major production during the last year of the war. Unfortunately, it did not achieve significant deliveries in time for the beginning of the great German offensive in March.

The L.V.G C II was the first aircraft to drop bombs on London, when six light bombs were dropped near Victoria Station on 28 November 1915. It continued in a variety of roles throughout 1917.

Between July 1917 and November 1918, the Sopwith Camel destroyed 1,294 enemy aircraft, achieving more victories than any other type of aircraft in the war. Only the Fokker Dr I could match its agility.

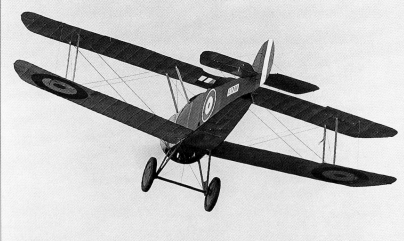

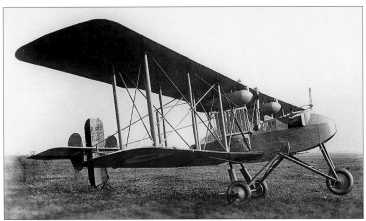

The Bréguet Biplane Type M.5 bomber was the winner of the competition for high-powered Avions in October 1915 and was much used for night-bombing in 1916-17. It was developed from the earlier Br M.4.

Right: In combat, the S.E.5a soon proved a formidable fighter and it quickly became associated with the foremost British pilots of the day. These are No. 1 Squadron S.E.5s at Clairmarais on 3 July 1918.

German scouts

The German Imperial Air Service used a bewildering array of fighters, with several different types often flying together within the same unit. Often streamlined, and usually powered by inline engines, the best German scouts were a match for the best machines operated by the Allies for long periods of the war. The best was the Fokker D VII, but it came too late to turn the tide.

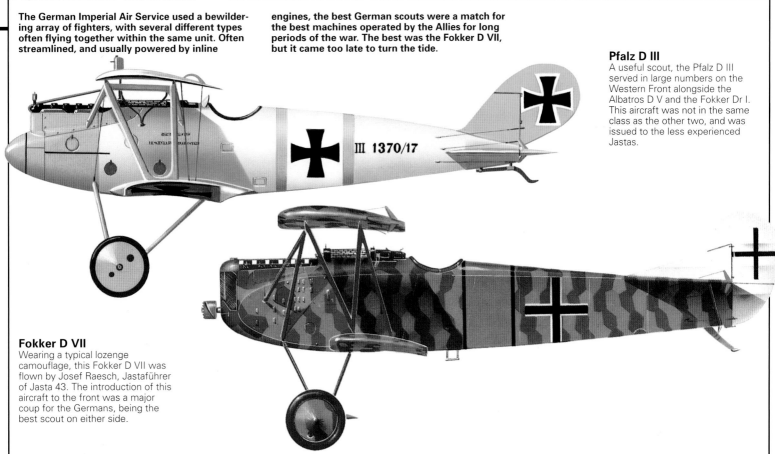

Pfalz D III
A useful scout, the Pfalz D III served in large numbers on the Western Front alongside the Albatros D V and the Fokker Dr I. This aircraft was not in the same class as the other two, and was issued to the less experienced Jastas.

Fokker D VII
Wearing a typical lozenge camouflage, this Fokker D VII was flown by Josef Raesch, Jastaführer of Jasta 43. The introduction of this aircraft to the front was a major coup for the Germans, being the best scout on either side.

III 1370/17

Instead, the majority of the 80 Jastas were equipped with Albatros D Vs and D Vas, Pfalz D IIIs and D IIIas, and Fokker Dr I triplanes.

At the time of the German offensive there were 2,047 aircraft facing the Allies, of which 1,680 were deployed on the British Front; of the latter, 475 were single-seat fighting scouts flying with 51 Jastas.

The RFC and RNAS, on the other hand, contented themselves with building up their strength of Camel, S.E.5a and Bristol Fighter squadrons, and by March there were in France nine squadrons with the Camel (151 aircraft), 10 with the S.E.5a (163 aircraft), six with the Bristol Fighter (79 aircraft) and nine with other miscellaneous fighting scouts (130 aircraft, including the excellent SPAD S.XIII, Nieuport 17 and Nieuport 27). These squadrons bore the brunt of the air combat over the British front, but were also assisted by a

A British S.E.5a (probably flown by Mannock or McCudden) on 21 June 1918, advertising the fact that 39 'Huns' had been shot down by his squadron within a two-week period.

number of French escadrilles on a short-term basis.

HEAVY FIGHTING

The German offensive opened on 21 March, by which time the establishment of RFC scout squadrons had been increased by 50 per cent to 24 aircraft each. Already heavy air fighting had broken out as the Germans sought to prevent Allied reconnaissance aircraft of V Corps from exposing the massive assembly of troops and artillery. As the enemy barrage opened on 21 March, Camels of No. 46 Squadron attacked the German gun batteries north of Bourlon Wood as No. 3 Squadron strafed enemy infantry. No. 54 Squadron was tasked with

escort of the corps reconnaissance machines. The following day Camels of Nos 73 and 80 Squadrons shot down six German scouts, and on 24 March Captain

J.L. Trollope of No. 43 Squadron set a new record by alone shooting down six aircraft in one day, a feat equalled by Captain H.W. Woollett of the same squadron on 12 April.

The French Nieuport 28 was the ultimate member of this famous line. It was initially intended to equip American scout units in France in 1918, but it was replaced in favour of the SPAD S.XIII.

Below: The Fokker D VII, ordered into immediate production in January 1918, was operational within three months. More effective than the D V series, it was only matched by the Sopwith Snipe and SPAD XIII.

Above: The best German single-seat fighter of World War I, the Fokker D VII was just too late to take part in the opening phase of the Kaiserschlacht (Emperor's Battle) on the Somme.

Left: Ground and aircrew sort out their gear at a hastily improvised airfield in France on 25 March 1918. The aircraft are R.E.8s of No. 15 Squadron RFC, one of the most widely used observation types.

The Pfalz D III was an unequal-span biplane fitted with a 160-hp (119-kW) Mercedes D.III inline engine. It first entered service on the Western Front in late 1917, and was much underrated by both of the opposing forces.

offensive Fonck's score was approaching 50, and he was to continue up to 75 to become the leading Allied ace by the end of the war.

TOP GUNS

By now air combats frequently involved more than 100 aircraft. These huge fights certainly accounted for the large individual victory scores being achieved by British, French and German pilots for the days were ending when

Nine days later fell the greatest of the war's legendary scout pilots when a Canadian Camel pilot, Captain A.R. Brown of No. 209 Squadron, shot down a Fokker Dr I triplane near Corbie; in it died Manfred von Richthofen, victor of 80 air combats.

Now fully aware of the serious nature of the German offensive, the RAF (which had formally come into being on 1 April) rushed eight more scout squadrons to France. The American squadrons, which had already started arriving in France, were not yet considered battle-ready.

On the French front the Aéronautique Militaire, facing 367 German aircraft (of which 168 were scouts in 18 Jastas), successfully denied the enemy unrestricted reconnaissance over the battlefield, and it was now that the French pilot René Fonck began his extraordinary spell of multiple victories, and on 9 May alone destroyed six of the enemy (dispatching three in 45 seconds). By the end of the German

Above: A wide arc of parked Albatros D III and D V aircraft of Jasta 12, with an A.E.G two-seat biplane Type C IV behind – a type used for observation and reconnaissance.

The Breguet 14, powered by a Renault 12F engine, was issued to a number of well-known reconnaissance Escadrilles and served with great distinction during a number of battles in 1917 and 1918.

Left: The Fokker Dr I triplane (103/17) in which the German ace Leutnant Werner Voss (with a total of 48 victories credited) was killed during combat on 23 September 1917.

Above: Pilots, now in their RAF uniforms, surrender the contents of their pockets before embarking on a patrol on 17 June 1918. The long leather coats were essential for operations in open cockpits.

pilots would be ordered off on lone patrols. The large formations could be sighted at long range and accordingly engaged by equally large formations of defending scouts. As the German offensive ground to a halt on 14 June it became clear that the enemy ground forces had run out of steam, possibly for good, and that, with the Americans now streaming into France in large numbers, it might require no more than one great 'push' eastwards to end the war.

Fighters for a new force

On 1 April 1918, the RFC and RNAS were amalgamated to form a new independent air arm, the Royal Air Force. Its new commander placed great faith in strategic bombing operations, but upon its formation the RAF was very much a tactical air force, with huge numbers of scouts whose primary purpose was to shoot down other aircraft. When the German offensive ran out of steam, these types carried the war to the enemy, undertaking fighter sweeps and strafing missions.

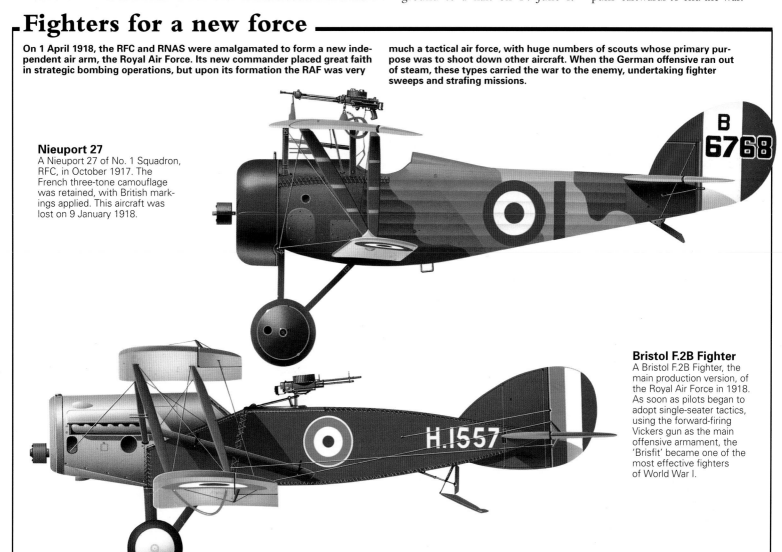

Nieuport 27
A Nieuport 27 of No. 1 Squadron, RFC, in October 1917. The French three-tone camouflage was retained, with British markings applied. This aircraft was lost on 9 January 1918.

Bristol F.2B Fighter
A Bristol F.2B Fighter, the main production version, of the Royal Air Force in 1918. As soon as pilots began to adopt single-seater tactics, using the forward-firing Vickers gun as the main offensive armament, the 'Brisfit' became one of the most effective fighters of World War I.

The Final Curtain

JUNE 1918 – NOVEMBER 1918

A Fokker D VII executes a loop. The D VII became operational from April 1918 and was soon in combat with the latest Allied aircraft. Faster than the Sopwith Camel, only the Snipe and SPAD XIII could match it.

If the defeat of the German offensive of March-June 1918 suggested that the energy of the enemy army had been catastrophically sapped, such was by no means evident in the air. A number of Jastas were certainly withdrawn from the front to re-man and re-equip for, by June, deliveries of the superb new Fokker D VII were well under way; by the end of that month no fewer than 270 had been received by the fighting units. Indeed, at the moment that Manfred von Richthofen was killed on 21 April, JG 1 was already scheduled to

Airco DH.4s of 'A' Flight, No. 27 Squadron RFC at Serny, Pas de Calais on 17 February 1918. No. 27 played an important role in the development of reconnaissance techniques and bad weather flying.

receive the new aircraft, and did so during the remainder of that month.

It was now that the first American scout squadrons took their place in the line. In fact, the 94th and 95th Squadrons (of the 1st Pursuit Group) had arrived at Villeneuve in February and March, and had carried out their first combat sortie on 15 March when Major Raoul Lufbery led an unarmed patrol over the lines in Nieuport 28s. The Americans disliked this aircraft (as they did the Camel), however, and opted to change to the SPAD S.XIII. During the summer and autumn of 1918 they began to accumulate an impressive score of victories. Their leading aces, Captain Eddie Rickenbacker and Lieutenant Frank Luke, gained scores of 26 and 21 respectively;

third in the list was Lufbery himself, with 17, but this pilot was killed on 19 May.

On 18 August the great British offensive ('the Big Push') opened in Flanders. In support, either directly or at longer range, were 13 squadrons with the S.E.5a, 17 with the Camel, six with the Bristol Fighter, four with the new Sopwith Dolphin, 14 with the R.E.8, four with the F.K.8, five with the D.H.4, 14 with the D.H.9/9A, seven with the F.E.2b/d and seven with the O/400 heavy bomber, for a total of 91 squadrons fielding almost 1,700 aircraft.

AIR SUPERIORITY

On the French front, where an initial counter-offensive had opened on 18 July, the Aéronautique Militaire had undergone continuous strengthening with almost complete standardisation among the scout escadrilles with the SPAD S.XIII, there being 49 subordinate escadrilles and 10 independent escadrilles thus equipped. In addition there were 23 bomber escadrilles flying Breguet 14s, Caproni 10s and Voisin 10s, the Breguets being used in the 'ground attack' role; there were also almost 140 artillery and army cooperation escadrilles, the majority of which flew Breguet 14s and Salmson 2s. By the beginning of August the Aéronautique Militaire possessed a front-line strength of over 2,800 aircraft, a total that would grow to 3,222 within four months.

From the beginning of this final phase of the air war, the Allies pos-

The Sopwith Snipe was designed around the new Bentley rotary engine, and was intended as the ultimate successor to the Camel. However, only around 100 Snipes reached France before the Armistice.

Just before the Armistice, No. 201 Squadron's second VC was awarded to Canadian Major William Barker DSO, MC, for shooting down four Fokker D VIIs on 27 October, while wounded and heavily outnumbered.

sessed air superiority, as much on account of excellent fighting aircraft as of the much improved standard of combat training, following the rotation of experienced pilots to training units in the rear. For their part the Germans formed a fourth Jagdgeschwader, this time under the command of Ritter Eduard von Schleich, the veteran Bavarian who had won the Pour le Merite a year earlier and gained a score of 35 victories. During those last months of the war the 'flying circuses' inflicted very heavy casualties among the

S.E.5as of No. 85 Squadron lined up at St Omer on 21 June 1918. The upper wing-mounted Lewis gun was in addition to the Vickers machine-gun fixed to the top of the fuselage, and fired through the propeller arc.

Final fighters

There was little to choose between the various fighter types in service at the end of the war, when newer aircraft were beginning to replace even the Fokker DVII, S.E.5 and Sopwith Camel.

Unfortunately for Germany, the war had already been lost on the ground, and, it must be said, on the home front as well as on the battlefield.

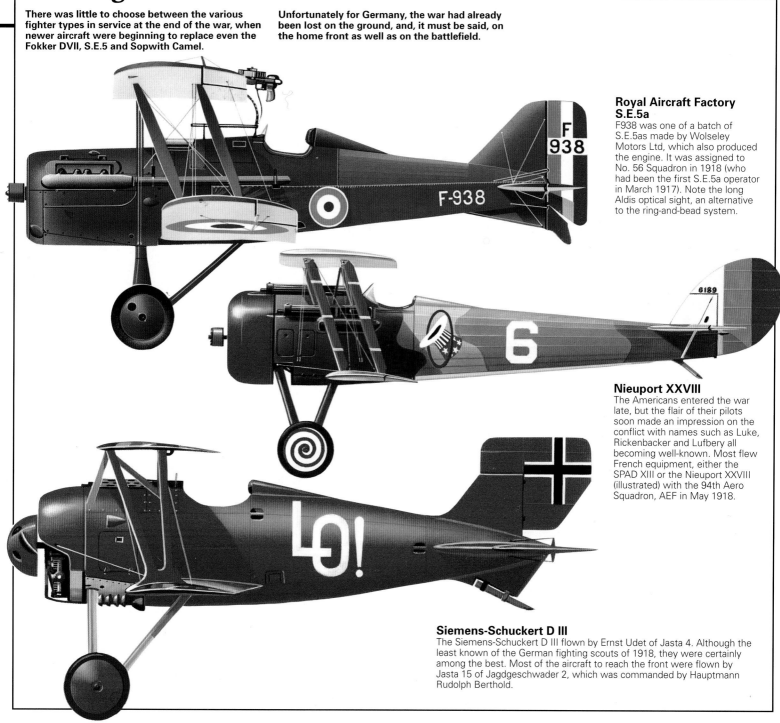

Royal Aircraft Factory S.E.5a
F938 was one of a batch of S.E.5as made by Wolseley Motors Ltd, which also produced the engine. It was assigned to No. 56 Squadron in 1918 (who had been the first S.E.5a operator in March 1917). Note the long Aldis optical sight, an alternative to the ring-and-bead system.

Nieuport XXVIII
The Americans entered the war late, but the flair of their pilots soon made an impression on the conflict with names such as Luke, Rickenbacker and Lufbery all becoming well-known. Most flew French equipment, either the SPAD XIII or the Nieuport XXVIII (illustrated) with the 94th Aero Squadron, AEF in May 1918.

Siemens-Schuckert D III
The Siemens-Schuckert D III flown by Ernst Udet of Jasta 4. Although the least known of the German fighting scouts of 1918, they were certainly among the best. Most of the aircraft to reach the front were flown by Jasta 15 of Jagdgeschwader 2, which was commanded by Hauptmann Rudolph Berthold.

Allied air forces, not least among the relatively inexperienced Americans. When the American land forces launched an attack west of Metz on 20 September, JG 2 alone destroyed 89 American aircraft in two days.

It was in September that the RAF began to receive the first examples of the new Sopwith Snipe fighting scout, a derivative of the successful Camel and one which was to survive in service for some years after the war. In the event, very few reached operational squadrons in France, and its place in the history of the war is almost entirely filled by the epic fight by a lone pilot. Major W.G. Barker, who was attached to No. 201 Squadron to gain experience in the new aircraft, was on patrol high above the Foret de Mormal on 27

October when he became involved in a prolonged fight with more than 15 enemy aircraft. Despite being severely wounded, he shot down at least four of the enemy (including three Fokker D VIIs) before crash-landing behind the British lines; he survived to be awarded the Victoria Cross.

Like the Snipe, the German Fokker D VIII parasol monoplane scout also failed to reach operational squadrons in significant numbers but, with a speed some 10 mph (16 km/h) higher than that of the Snipe, and much lighter on the controls, there is little doubt but

Originally known as the Fokker E V, the D VIII did not arrive at the front in any great numbers. It was the fastest scout to see service and possessed good agility, but suffered from structural problems.

that this aircraft would have otherwise given the Allied pilots a great deal of trouble. Be that as it may, it was the D VII that came to be most respected by the Allies, so much so that the terms of the Armistice specifically named this aircraft (*in erster Linie alle apparate D VII*, or 'particularly first-line aircraft known as D VII') to be handed over.

The fighting on the Western Front was the key to the war's outcome. With internal strife inside Germany, shortages of food and the loss of the Hindenburg Line in October, the strength and power of the German air force had become superfluous. On 11 November the war ended when armistice terms were negotiated in France.

The Russian Front

AUGUST 1914 - SEPTEMBER 1918

Left: One of the four-engined Sikorsky Ilya Mourometz heavy bombers that served so well from 1915. Type B used four Salmson-Canton-Unne radials of 200 hp and 135 hp (two of each). It could carry 1,102 lb of bombs.

Though not an exceptional aircraft in terms of performance or agility, the Fokker E III achieved results by means of its unique synchronised machine-gun, offset to starboard and firing straight forward through the propeller, making aiming easy.

The war between Germany and Austria-Hungary on the one hand and Tsarist Russia on the other lasted for three years before dying out with the onset of the Russian Revolution in October 1917. At the outbreak of war the frontier dividing the two empires stretched from midway between Riga and Danzig on the Baltic coast, running west of Warsaw south through Galicia (now southern Poland) and finally southeast to the mouth of the Danube on the Black Sea coast. Early air fighting predominated in Galicia and the north, the Germans at first deploying little air strength in the east, and the Russians pos-sessing even less of an air force in any case. When the war opened

An Ilya Mourometz G-9 heavy bomber used by the Imperial Russian Army during WWI. Few were identical, a result of continual improvement. Shortages led to a mix of powerplants on some aircraft.

the Imperial Russian Air Service had a total of 244 aeroplanes, 12 airships and 46 kite balloons, of which 145 aeroplanes were in the field; most were of French design, produced under licence by such companies as Duks, Russo-Baltic and Lebedev. Notable exceptions were the four-engined Sikorsky bombers which started bombing operations over the Eastern Front on 15 February 1915; no fewer than 73 of these huge aeroplanes were produced by the Russo-Baltic Wagon Works dur-ing the war.

Early combat was no less primi-tive in its tactics than in the West. The first Russian pilot to achieve fame was Piotr Nesterov (a pre-war pilot of renown), who was killed while gaining his only air victory near his airfield at Sholkiv by ram-ming a German aircraft in his Nieuport; Sholkiv was later renamed in his honour. Relentless pressure by the Central Powers

forced the Russian armies back in the Ukraine where constant opera-tions were flown in the Lutsk and Kovel regions, with frequent attacks being made to destroy the railway centre at Kovel. One of the great Russian pilots, Aleksandr Kazakov, spent most of his combat career in this area and became the top-scoring pilot on the front, some of his early victims being Fokker monoplanes when they arrived in the east late in 1915. In 1917 he commanded the newly-formed No. 1 Fighter Group, but this broke up at the time of the revolu-tion and Kazakov made his way north to Archangelsk to join the British who landed there in 1918; he died needlessly while practising aerobatics in a Camel the following year. His decorations included the British DSO, MC and DFC.

RUSSIAN EX-PATS

The bomber designer Igor Sikorsky was later to make his home in the USA. Another to do so was Alexander de Seversky, who had an outstanding combat record on the Eastern Front, much of it spent in the Riga region with the Imperial

Naval Air Service. During his first night bombing flight he was shot down into the sea and his bomb exploded, blowing off his right leg; despite this, he returned to com-mand fighter aviation in the Baltic area and went on to destroy 13 German aircraft. He was in the USA at the time of the revolution and so decided to apply for American citi-zenship, later creating the Seversky Aero Corporation in 1922.

There is no doubt that the Russian air forces possessed many fine pilots, no less courageous and skilled than their opponents in the German and Austro-Hungarian air services. And their aircraft, though generally lagging about six months behind those in the West (as was the German equipment), were ade-quate and well serviced. The weak-ness lay in the command structure, a failing that permeated all the forces of Tsarist Russia. The officer corps was treated with elitism far

Although the Anatra D had serious design faults, it was widely operated by the Russians. It became operational in mid-1916 and was powered by a 130-hp (97-kW) Clerget rotary engine.

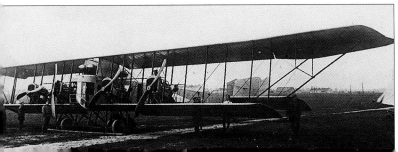

Powered by a 110-hp (82-kW) Le Rhone rotary engine, the Nieuport 17 was fast-climbing and highly manoeuvrable. It was flown by the Imperial Russian Air Service, and some survived in Bolshevik use.

beyond that of other nations, so that when setbacks and ultimate disaster faced the Russian forces, disintegration followed in numerous units, although the air force was probably less affected than the army.

Collapse of discipline, particularly in the Ukraine, immediately before the October Revolution literally cut the ground from under the air force. Despite orders forbidding the continuation of hostilities against the Germans, many Russians fought on. One such incident involved Lieutenant Commander Viktor Utgov of the Black Sea Fleet who, flying a Grigorovich M-9 seaplane from the

carrier *Imperator Nicolai Pervyi*, attacked a German U-boat with bombs, only to be summoned before the sailors' revolutionary executive to explain his conduct. (He also emigrated to the USA and joined Sikorsky, only to be killed in a flying accident with the US Marine Corps.)

Many Russian airmen served on the Western Front, and others learned to fly with the RFC in the UK. Likewise, a number of individual French pilots (as well as some French squadrons) served in Russia. The Imperial Russian air forces also numbered a few women among their pilots, the most famous (or

The Zeppelin-Staaken R IV – the first of the series to carry the 'R' (Riesenfugzeug, or giant aircraft) designation – had five 240-hp (179-kW) Maybach Mb.IV engines giving a top speed of 78 mph (125 km/h).

infamous) being Princess Eugine Shakhovskaya; one of the first women to learn to fly in Russia before the war, she became a reconnaissance pilot on the Riga front. After the revolution it is said that she was chief executioner in the Tcheka at Kiev.

OCCUPATION COMPLETE

By the summer of 1918 German forces occupied a gigantic area of Russia, including the entire Ukraine and almost all the territory to the west of the River Don.

The main fighter of the Austro-Hungarian air arm was the Aviatik (Berg) D I, seen here in modified form. The fighting on the Russian front was not as compeititive as on the Western front.

However, if Germany had 'killed herself by victories' (*Wir siegen uns zum Tod*), the skills and courage of the Imperial Russian air forces may have unwittingly contributed to the widespread popular appeal of revolutionary opportunism in the armed forces simply on account of the adulation the officer corps attracted.

Opposing Fighters

The Imperial Russian Air Service fought with courage, but was not well led, and operated in support of an army that was no match for the German army. When Revolution came, the Air Service disintegrated, with some factions going over to the Bolsheviks, and others to the White Russians.

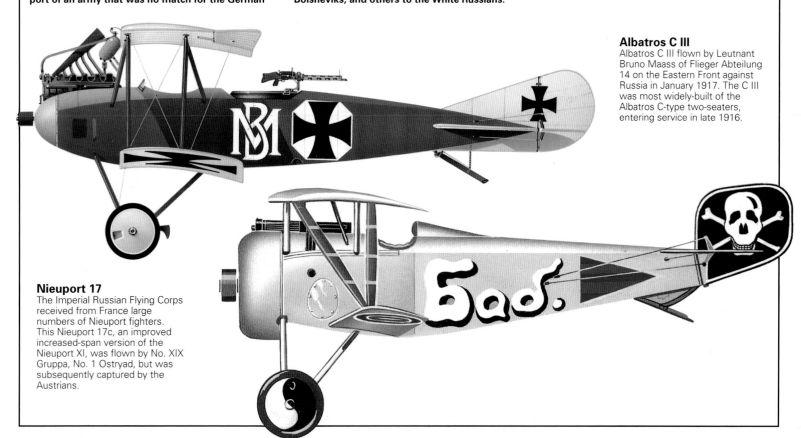

Albatros C III
Albatros C III flown by Leutnant Bruno Maass of Flieger Abteilung 14 on the Eastern Front against Russia in January 1917. The C III was most widely-built of the Albatros C-type two-seaters, entering service in late 1916.

Nieuport 17
The Imperial Russian Flying Corps received from France large numbers of Nieuport fighters. This Nieuport 17c, an improved increased-span version of the Nieuport XI, was flown by No. XIX Gruppa, No. 1 Ostryad, but was subsequently captured by the Austrians.

The Italian Front

MAY 1915 – NOVEMBER 1918

Originally known as the Caproni 600HP (the total horsepower of its three engines), the Ca 5 first flew in 1917. Although unpopular with its crews, 669 examples were built. Maximum bombload was 900 kg.

The outbreak of war in the south in May 1915 found the Italian army poorly prepared for action, despite fielding a total of 35 divisions against 25 Austrian. The frontier was largely Alpine, the four Italian armies being deployed in the Trentino, Cadore, Carnia and Isonzo sectors, of which the last-named absorbed 14 divisions, with seven in reserve. The Austrians, however, possessed a considerable superiority in artillery.

In the air, the Italian Aeronautica del Regio Esercito (Royal Army Air Service) was better prepared, with 14 squadriglie of Nieuports, Maurice Farmans and Blériots in the field. Faced with ineffective opposition by the Austro-Hungarian air force these squadriglie gave a good account of themselves, particularly in recon-

naissance duties, during the first general offensive which involved a combined advance by all four armies. Gradually the fighting concentrated on the eastern flank where the Isonzo plain provided the best opportunities for greatest gain, and it was in this sector that the Italians made their biggest gains in the early months. By the autumn, however, following Russian defeats in Galicia, Austrian forces had been freed for service on the Isonzo, incorpating increasing numbers of German aircraft including Rumpler and Aviatik C Is, which now provided the Austrian artillery with fairly effective spotting services. In this, the 2nd Battle of the Isonzo, the Italians had greatly reorganised their air force, greater emphasis being placed on bombing and reconnaissance. Capronis and Farmans were employed in the former tasks, and

Macchis, Farmans and Caudrons in the latter.

The Italians progressively reduced their fighting scout strength early in 1916, retaining two squadrons of Nieuport 11s for the defence of Santa Caterina and Aquileia. Successive battles were fought on the Isonzo front, as gradually the Austro-Hungarians built up their ground and air forces. As the Italian Capronis flew daylight bombing raids over the Alps a small

number of Fokker E I monoplanes became available to mount token opposition; increasing numbers of Lohner and Lloyd reconnaissance aircraft were introduced into service, together with Fokker B IIs and D IIs. The first aircraft to make its mark on the front was the Brandenburg D I, the famous 'Star-Strutter'. This was flown by the top-scoring Austrian, Godwin Brumowski, who led Fliegerkompanie (Flik) 12 and whose aim it was to create an elite fighting unit on the same lines as those beginning to appear on the Western Front. Opposite him the great Italian ace, Francesco Baracca (whose personal emblem, the Cavallino Rampante, or prancing horse, is to this day adopted in the Italian air force) had by November 1916 destroyed five enemy aircraft; before the end of the war, while flying Nieuports and SPADs, he was to top the Italian scout fighters with a score of 34 victories.

After the desperate battles of the winter of 1916-17, in which appalling weather conditions and hardships sapped the morale of Italian fighting personnel from the warmer south, the fortunes of Italy continued to deteriorate. However, the failure of the Austrian Bainsizza offensive also took its toll and Austria was forced to seek assistance from Germany, a massive build-up

Above: The Rumpler C I was one of the best German two-seaters in 1916, providing the Austrian forces with an effective spotting platform. Armament comprised one rear-mounted Parabellum machine-gun.

Left: Designed by Ernst Heinkel for Hansa und Brandenburgishe, the C I was built under licence in Austria and saw widespread use by the Austrian forces. Here pilots of Flik 7 have returned from a raid on Milan on 16 February 1916.

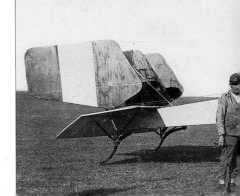

Air war over Italy

The Austro-Hungarian air forces primarily used German-designed aircraft, while the Italians used a mixture of French, British and indigenously-built machines. The Italian Aeronautica del Regia Esercito began the war enjoying a significant advantage over the smaller, less well-equipped Austro-Hungarians. By the end of the war, the combatants were more evenly matched in the air, although the Italians retained a slight edge.

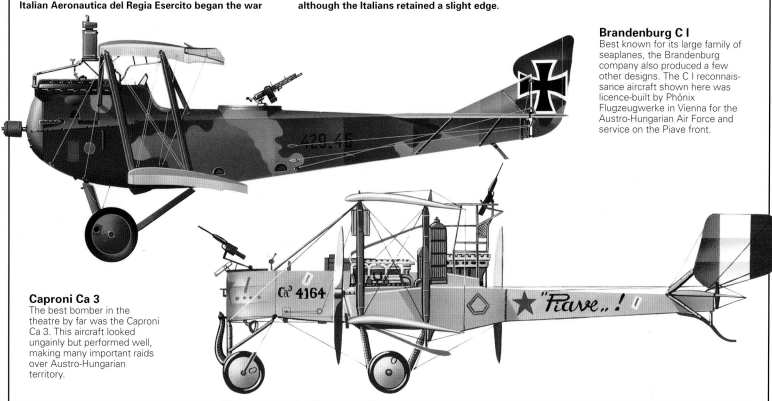

Brandenburg C I
Best known for its large family of seaplanes, the Brandenburg company also produced a few other designs. The C I reconnaissance aircraft shown here was licence-built by Phönix Flugzeugwerke in Vienna for the Austro-Hungarian Air Force and service on the Piave front.

Caproni Ca 3
The best bomber in the theatre by far was the Caproni Ca 3. This aircraft looked ungainly but performed well, making many important raids over Austro-Hungarian territory.

Among the top-scoring Italian pilots were Francesco Baracca (with 34 kills) and Silvio Scaroni (with 26 kills). The leading Italian pilots flew SPAD and Nieuport scouts.

that was to result in the crushing defeat at Caporetto in October 1917 of the Italians, who were utterly unprepared for the use against them of gas shells. As the entire front threatened to collapse under the weight of attack by five armies, the Allies rushed reinforcements to Italy, particularly from France; these included 11 British and French divisions, and four RFC squadrons (of Camels and Bristol Fighters) and three French escadrilles.

FIERCE BATTLES
By a supreme effort of bravery and sacrifice the Italians eventually mended the front and held the Austro-Hungarian assault on the Piave. Fighting in the air continued to rage furiously, the Italians having resurrected their fighting scout squadriglie such that by the time of Caporetto they possessed eight Hanriot HD 1 squadriglie, four of SPAD S.VIIs and three of Nieuports. Caproni bombers equipped 14 squadriglie, and the excellent Ansaldo light reconnaissance bomber entered service in January 1918, later performing a number of epic missions. Air combat in the theatre brought to the fore numerous great pilots, Baracca continuing to score heavily until his death on the Piave front on 19 June. Teniente Silvio Scaroni, who only opened his air fighting score in November 1917 and flew Nieuports and Hanriots, survived the war with 26 victories, and reached the rank of general.

In the Austro-Hungarian air force Brumowski had progressed from the Brandenburg D I to the two-gun Albatros D III, leading a 'flying circus' of these aircraft during the Caporetto campaign. Julius Arigi, whose victory score reached 32, also flew Albatros D IIIs, and survived beyond World War II having numbered among his flying students the Luftwaffe's Walter Nowotny and Hans-Joachim Marseille. Third highest-scoring pilot was the Polish-born Frank Linke-Crawford, commander of Flik 60, whose combat score increased rapidly over Caporetto but who was killed on 31 July 1918.

Following the great Italian victory at Vittorio Veneto on 30 October an armistice was signed between Austria and Italy on 4 November.

Left: A Caproni Ca 3, of which 299 were built. Powered by three 150-hp (112-kW) Isolta Fraschini V.4B engines, the Ca 3 proved to be the most successful Allied bomber of World War I.

Below: The Albatros C III began operations during the latter half of 1916. Its single rear-mounted defensive Parabellum machine-gun was supplemented by a Spandau machine-gun for forward attack.

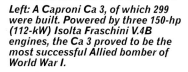

Zeppelins At War

SEPTEMBER 1914 - AUGUST 1918

Paradoxically, it was not the Germans but the French (or rather a Brazilian who lived in France) who first produced a practical airship: Alberto Santos-Dumont built some 15 non-rigid dirigibles by 1904 before being diverted to heavier-than-air craft. In Germany Count Ferdinand von Zeppelin, pursuing earlier theories of the Austrian engineer David Schwartz, began trials with a compartmented, rigid airship in 1900, the LZ 1, but it was not for several years that success attended his trials.

By the beginning of World War I, however, more than a score of very large airships had been produced in Germany, seven of them by Luftschifflbau Zeppelin for its associated airship-operating company Deutsche Luftschiffahrts AG (Delag), an airline that made 1,588 flights totalling 107,205 miles (172525 km) in the five years before the war and carried 32,722 passengers. As early as 1909 the German war ministry took over

two airships, the LZ 3 and LZ 5, for crew training, and it was Kapitan Kahlenberg of the 1st Prussian Airship Battalion who was in fact in command of LZ 7 *Deutschland* when it crashed in June 1910, though without loss of life.

The outbreak of war put an end to anything resembling commercial airship operation in Germany, although as late as 1917 a naval craft, the L 59, was called on to carry supplies to German forces in East Africa; it was recalled, when near Khartoum, having flown 4,200 miles (6760 km). Among the seven airships on army charge in August 1914 were the LZ 11 *Viktoria Luise*, taken over by the XVIII Corps, LZ 13 *Hansa* by the VII Corps (and used for training) and the LZ 17 *Sachsen* by the XIX Corps; in addition the LZ 25 (IX) was being completed to an army order. The Imperial navy had suffered catastrophe in 1913 when LZ 14 was lost at sea and LZ 18 exploded near Berlin, killing most of the service's trained crews. During the war Luftschifflbau Zeppelin built a total of 95 rigid airships, production of their giant craft (most of which were about 492 ft/150 m long) continuing at the

rate of about one every fortnight. German army and navy airship stations had been established before the war (some of which were taken over from Delag) at Baden-Baden, Berlin, Bremen, Brunswick, Dresden, Dusseldorf, Emden, Hamburg, Cologne, Leipzig, Mannheim, Nordholz, Potsdam and Stuttgart.

BOMBERS

Most of the early wartime operations by the German airships were navigation exercises, but on the night of 2/3 September 1914 LZ 17, flying from Cologne, dropped three bombs of about 200 lb (91 kg) on Antwerp before returning safely to base. Three months later this airship was transferred to the Eastern Front where it is said to have made half a dozen bombing raids before being handed over to the navy for training duties.

Of the two airships LZ 25 (IX) and LZ 26 (XII), the former was destroyed in its shed at Dusseldorf on 8 October in the epic bombing attack by Flight Lieutenant R.L.G. Marix, RNAS, in a Sopwith Tabloid. The latter, a 500-ft (153-m) airship, delivered to the army in December, was one of the

The Zeppelin airships were the most successful lighter-than-air aircraft of the war, performing patrol and bombing missions with equal facility. Their success led to civil versions after the war.

first to fly a sortie over the British Isles.

The first authenticated raids over the UK were by the naval Schutte-Lanz L 3 and L 4, flying from Hamburg and Nordholz on 19 January 1915; their bombs fell in the area of Great Yarmouth, Norfolk, causing numerous casualties. A third airship turned back following engine trouble. L 3 and L 4 were later wrecked on the coast of

Peter Strasser was the head of the airship detachment. Following the loss of the L 2 with the loss of all on board, Strasser chartered the privately-owned **Hansa** *and got his key personnel back in the air to help to restore confidence.*

The last Zeppelin raid on England took place on 5 August 1918. In the later raids, the Zeppelins tried to reach safety above 21,400 ft and for a while were able to evade the British fighters.

Above: On 11 August 1918, Lt S.D. Culley in a Camel spotted Zeppelin L 53 at 19,000 ft over Heligoland. Although at his aircraft's ceiling, he was able to fire at the airship which burst into flames and broke in two.

Cpt W. Leefe Robinson of No. 39 Squadron flying BE.2C 2092 shot down the German airship SL 11 at Cuffley on the night of 2/3 September 1916, for which action he was awarded the VC.

Jutland during a second raid attempt.

As explained elsewhere, all German air raiding policies at the beginning of the war were under tight political control, the Kaiser himself withholding sanction for indiscriminate bombing. Nevertheless, despite an almost total lack of black-out precautions in the UK, the German naval airships (soon followed by those of the army) began flights over East Anglia, southern England and northern France. The first bombs to fall on London were dropped by a German army airship on 31 May 1915.

A week later the first German airship, LZ 37 (captained by Oberleutnant Otto van de Haegen, and flying in company with LZ 38 and LZ 39), was destroyed in 'air combat' over Ghent, Belgium, on the night of 6/7 May when Flight

Bomb release switches on a Zeppelin. They had caused much alarm and a deflection of resources to defence, but the physical damage inflicted by the Zeppelins was in no way commensurate with the effort.

Sub-Lieutenant R.A.J. Warneford RNAS, flying a Morane-Saulnier parasol monoplane from Dunkirk, struck the craft's hull with a small bomb, an action fraught with hazard and one for which the British pilot was recommended for the Victoria Cross. Warneford, who had to force land after his successful exploit, lost his life in a flying accident a fortnight later, before his award was gazetted.

Further German airships were lost in action at an increasing rate as the frequency of attacks was stepped up, but it was not until the night of 2/3 September 1916 that one was shot down over British soil

German Naval Zeppelin LZ 53 leaving its hangar for a night attack on England during WWI. The biggest airship raid of the war was on the night of 2/3 September 1916, when 14 crossed the coast, although none reached London.

when Lieutenant William Leefe Robinson of No. 39 (Home Defence) Squadron, RFC, shot down SL XI at Cuffley, Hertfordshire; Leefe Robinson was also awarded the Victoria Cross.

LONDON HIT

By the end of 1916 the German airships, of which about 50 were in service, were carrying bombs of up to 600-lb (272-kg) weight, roughly twice the size of those capable of being carried by the early twin-engined bombing aeroplanes. On 27/28 November that year two German naval airships were destroyed in a single night over the English East Coast, the same night that six tiny bombs fell for the first time on London from an aeroplane. The airship raids continued throughout 1917, being launched wholly independently of the Gotha raids which started on 25 May. On 21 August the German naval airship L 23 was shot down off the Danish coast by a Sopwith Pup launched from a platform on the light cruiser HMS *Yarmouth* and flown by Flight Sub-Lieutenant B.A. Smart, RNAS.

It was perhaps ironic that it was the build-up of the UK's home defences against the aeroplane raids that eventually led to the discontinuation of the airship raids on the UK, the last to cause casualties being on 12 April 1918.

German Long-Range Bombing

MID 1915 - APRIL 1918

Although the origins of strategic bombing probably lie in the Russian use of the Sikorsky four-engined bombers early in 1915, the Germans sought to extend the operations by their growing fleet of airships with development of the large aeroplane, of whose manufacturers the Siemens-Schuckert, Gothaer-Waggonfabrik and Zeppelin-Staaken companies were actively engaged in producing experimental examples at that time. Origins of the German use of bombers lay in the so-called battleplanes which equipped the first Kampfstaffeln (battle squadrons) of mid-1915, and although such large aircraft were generically referred to as K-types, such as the AEG K I, the first operational bombing units

were codenamed Carrier Pigeon Units (Brieftauben Abteilungen), one of which was based at Ostend, ostensibly for attacks against south east England and the busy Channel ports. Because of delays in bringing the larger aircraft up to reliable service standard, these units continued to fly relatively small aircraft of the B- and C-type and were therefore capable of no more than nuisance raids with very small bombs.

On the Eastern Front the large multi-engined battleplanes, such as the Siemens Forssman (obviously inspired by the Sikorsky bombers), Siemens-Schuckert Steffen R I and Zeppelin-Staaken VGO (Versuchs Gotha Ost) had undergone operational trials over the front with both the army and navy, and although most were either found to be alto-

gether unsatisfactory or in need of further development, establishment of front-line Kampfgeschwader (battle wings) went ahead in 1916 for the purpose of launching worthwhile bombing raids on strategic targets well behind the Russian and French fronts. Such a policy of carrying the war to the rear areas, and the consequent endangering of civilian lives by premeditated acts of war, was the outcome of persistent pressure by the German military and naval staffs upon the Kaiser to permit military targets within cities remote from the battle theatres to be attacked from the air. Such a policy ignored the absence of any workable bomb-aiming equipment, so that any damage of a military value would be quite fortuitous.

The Brieftauben Abteilung Ostende was withdrawn to Bulgaria in mid-1916 and redesigned Kampfgeschwader Nr 1 (KG 1), three of its Staffeln (squadrons) being detached to form the basis of KG 3 (known as Kagohl 3). This

Above: The one-off DFW R I flew only a single mission (on the Eastern Front), crashing on landing when it aborted its second mission.

Top: The VGO II was the first successful R-plane, and the first in a long line of Staaken giant bombers.

was in turn moved to Ghent with the stated purpose of starting raids on the UK with Gotha and Friedrichshafen bombers under the command of Hauptmann Ernst Brandenburg, the first of which was launched on 25 May 1917. On that day 23 Gotha G IVs set out for London but, on finding the British capital obscured by cloud and haze, turned for home and dropped their bombs on Folkestone, killing 95 and injuring 260 – higher casualties than in any previous raid by airship or aeroplane.

OUTCRY IN BRITAIN

As an outcry erupted in the British Parliament at the defences' inability to counter this daylight raid, Brandenburg launched an attack on

Above: The best known of the R-planes was the Zeppelin-Staaken R VI, of which 18 were built. They formed the backbone of the heavy bomber squadrons on the Western Front, and at least two were shot down, one by anti-aircraft fire and one by a night-fighter.

Right: The SSW R VIII was the largest aircraft built during World War I. Too late to see operational service, the aircraft was examined as a possible carrier for wire- or radio-guided glide bombs of between 300 and 1000 kg. It taxied but never flew.

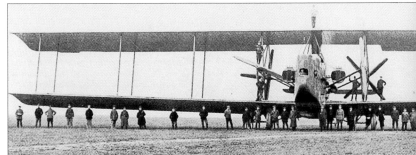

The German Giants

The Germans built only some 65 long-range Riesenflugzeug (giant aircraft or R-planes), and of these only about 30 reached the front, augmenting larger numbers of Gothas and Friedrichshafens. The R-planes saw service on the Eastern Front, where air supremacy could often be assumed. Following the withdrawal of the Zeppelin from bombing raids over England, Gothas and the later Staaken R-planes took over. None of the Staakens were lost to enemy action.

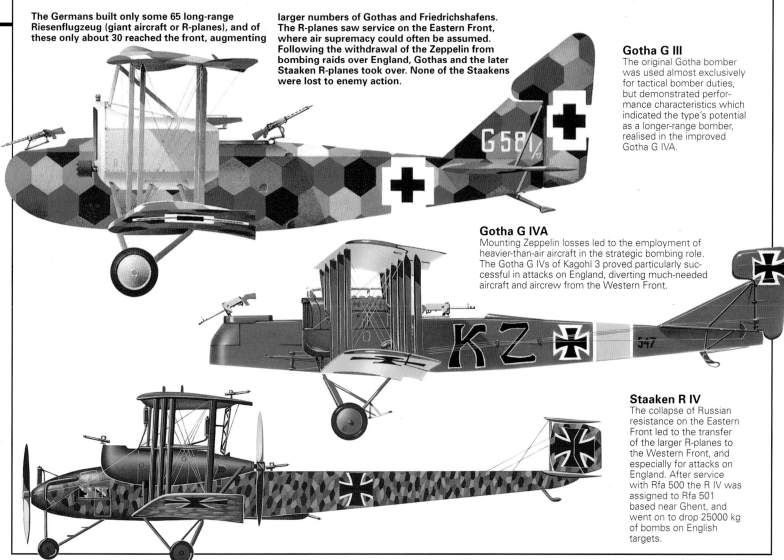

Gotha G III
The original Gotha bomber was used almost exclusively for tactical bomber duties, but demonstrated performance characteristics which indicated the type's potential as a longer-range bomber, realised in the improved Gotha G IVA.

Gotha G IVA
Mounting Zeppelin losses led to the employment of heavier-than-air aircraft in the strategic bombing role. The Gotha G IVs of Kagohl 3 proved particularly successful in attacks on England, diverting much-needed aircraft and aircrew from the Western Front.

Staaken R IV
The collapse of Russian resistance on the Eastern Front led to the transfer of the larger R-planes to the Western Front, and especially for attacks on England. After service with Rfa 500 the R IV was assigned to Rfa 501 based near Ghent, and went on to drop 25000 kg of bombs on English targets.

the naval town of Sheerness on 5 June by 22 Gothas; little damage was done, but 45 people were killed. One of the raiders was shot down by the ground defences. The next raid, flown on 13 June, marked the climax of Kagohl 3's fortunes: 20 Gothas set out for London, where the majority of bombs fell on the dock area and East End. One bomb fell on an infants' school at Poplar, killing 16 young children. Other bombs fell in the City, causing damage and casualties near St Paul's cathedral and Liverpool Street station. As Brandenburg brought his bombers home without loss, London counted 162 dead and 432 injured.

The clamour in the UK caused the defences to be strengthened by withdrawal of fighters from France and the establishment of gun and balloon belts around London and other Home County targets. The result in turn was to encourage the

The Gotha G IV mounted a daylight bombing campaign against England from 25 May 1917, and London from 13 June. Some 401 civilians were killed, two fighters were shot down, and six RFC aircrew were killed. The Gothas also forced new Sopwith Camels to be witheld from the front.

Germans to attack by night, and on the evening of 3 September 1917 four Gothas attacked Chatham, one bomb falling on a naval barracks, killing 131 ratings and injuring 90 others in the worst single bomb incident of the war. During the following 30 nights the Gothas flew 64 sorties over England, reaching London on six occasions.

Meanwhile, the Germans had been making ready a new weapon, the R-type bomber (Riesen-flugzeug, or giant aeroplane). These truly colossal aircraft, most of which were built by Zeppelin-Staaken, originated in the VGO 1 that had flown in 1915, and in various forms were powered by four (and sometimes five) Maybach or Mercedes engines. They formed the equipment of two units, Riesenflugzeug-abteilungen 500 and 501, and operated from the Ghent area both over France and south east England. With a wing span of over 138 ft (42 m) and a crew of at least seven, Rfa

501's R VIs carried out a total of 11 raids on the UK between 18 December 1917 and 20 May 1918. On 28 January an R VI, with the unit commander Hauptmann Richard von Bentivegni aboard (he was not himself a pilot), dropped a 661-lb (300-kg) bomb on a printing works in London, killing 38 and injuring 85. On the night of 16/17 February an R VI dropped a 2,205-lb (1000-kg) bomb on the Royal Hospital, Chelsea, the heaviest bomb to fall on the UK during the war.

The Gothas did not have it all their own way, and eight were shot down by fighters and AAA. Nine more were lost in an abortive raid which ran into severe headwinds, and 10 were written off after landing, most badly shot up by RFC fighters.

Allied Bombing

AUGUST 1915 - NOVEMBER 1918

It was not until 1915, when in August that year Colonel Hugh Trenchard assumed command of the RFC in France, that a single British squadron was specifically assigned the task of supporting the army by bombing operations. And with nothing better than the Royal Aircraft Factory B.E.2 available, such long-distance raids that could be undertaken fell to the French to launch. The only aircraft that existed in any numbers were Voisin IIIs which could carry a bomb load of 132 lb (60 kg); this archaic single-pusher biplane, of which no fewer than 2,162 were ultimately built in France alone, served on the Western Front as well as in Russia and Italy.

In December 1915 the first purpose-built heavy bomber made its maiden flight in the UK. This design had been ordered by the Admiralty, yet it was not until November of the following year that the first example reached an operational unit. In the meantime, little more than sporadic short-range bombing operations by B.E.2c and R.E.7 aircraft could be carried out by the RFC. The majority of bombs dropped were the 20-lb (9-kg) Hales weapon, but from early in 1916 an increasing number of 112-lb (50.8-kg) bombs became available and, on 30 June, six R.E.7s of No. 21 Squadron each dropped one of the new 336-lb (152.4-kg) RAF heavy-cased bombs over Lille railway station.

NAVAL BOMBERS

Meanwhile, the RNAS's 3rd Wing had assembled under Captain W.L. Elder, RN, with the intention that from bases in the Vosges its 35 Sopwith 1½-Strutters and Short bombers would be able to reach the Saar industrial area. However, demands for aircraft to support ground operations on the Western Front resulted in most RNAS 1½-Strutters being transferred to the RFC, and it was not until October 1916 that the 3rd Wing was strong enough to launch a powerful bombing raid, nine 1½-Strutters and six French Breguet bombers attacking the Mauser factory at Obendorf on 12 October.

It was the RNAS 5th Wing at Dunkirk that received the first Handley Page O/100 heavy bomber in November 1916, followed shortly afterwards by the 3rd Wing, then based at Luxeuil. It was the latter that carried out the first British night raid by a heavy bomber when a single O/100 bombed Moulin-les-Metz railway station on 16/17 March 1917. Four days later the RFC's first squadron (No. 100) formed and trained specifically for night bombing arrived in France, albeit without aircraft.

In October 1917 there was formed the RFC's 41st Wing under Lieutenant Colonel (later Marshal of the RAF Lord) C.L.N. Newall with the expressed purpose of mounting

Above: Designed and developed to make it possible for the RAF to mount attacks on German targets from the UK, the Handley Page V/1500 was the first practical strategic bomber, although too late to see service during WWI.

Over 400 Handley Page O/400 heavy bombers were built during 1917/18. In August 1918, Nos 97, 115 and 215 went to France equipped with O/400s and carried the brunt of the bombing offensive.

a strategic bombing campaign against German industrial targets. It was intended ultimately that this wing would operate independently of the tactical elements of the RFC so as to avoid its strength being squandered by local military commanders. The initial components of this wing were No. 55 Squadron (Airco/de Havilland DH.4 day bombers), No. 100 (Royal Aircraft

Above: Members of the 11th Squadron, American Expeditionary Force, pose by their Airco DH.4s at Maulan, France in 1918. The DH.4 was built in America with the Liberty engine, and by the time of the Armistice 3,227 had been built – 1,885 of which were shipped to France.

Right: One of France's best-known warplanes, the Breguet 14 was built in the A.2 class for reconnaissance, and B.2 class for bombing. It was widely used in the latter role, and was also supplied to the American Expeditionary Force.

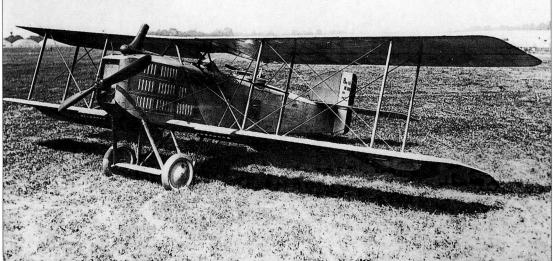

RFC bombers

Under the leadership of Major General Trenchard, the RFC, and then the autonomous RAF, built up a powerful bomber arm, and developed the theory and practice of independent strategic bombing as a means of actually winning a war. Trenchard's legacy shaped the inter-war and World War II RAF, and found its natural conclusion in the Bomber Command night offensive of World War II.

Airco DH.4
The Airco DH.4 bomber, known in the RFC as the 'Flaming Coffin' because the fuel tank was located between the two crew members, first went to France with No. 55 Squadron, RFC in March 1917. This Westland-built example is seen in the markings of No. 2 Squadron, RNAS at Bergues in 1918.

Handley Page O/400
At the time that the RAF was formed on 1 April 1918, the RFC's standard day bomber was the O/400, An aircraft from No. 207 Squadron at Ligescourt, France is shown here. This was the first British squadron used solely for long-range night bombing, and the first to operate Handley Page bombers.

Concerns about the effectiveness of night bombing were dispelled by the exploits of the Handley Page O/400 squadrons during 1918. Up to 40 O/400s could be airborne on good nights attacking German targets.

Factory F.E.2b night bombers) and No. 16 (Naval) (O/100 night bombers); in February 1918 the wing was reorganised as VIII Brigade and three months later Nos 99 and 104 Squadrons (both with DH.9s) were added.

During the period between October 1917 and May 1918 this force carried out 142 raids, of which 57 were over German territory and included such cities as Koblenz, Cologne, Mainz, Mannheim and Stuttgart.

With the creation on 1 April 1918 of the Royal Air Force by the amalgamation of RFC and RNAS, the way was clear to extend further the independence of VIII Brigade and, on 6 June, under the command of Major General Sir Hugh (later Marshal of the RAF Lord) Trenchard, was formed the

Structurally similar to its predecessor, the DH.9 used identical mainplanes and tail surfaces. It was not a successful aircraft in its intended role as a long-range bomber and was rapidly replaced by the DH.9A

Independent Force. This comprised Nos 55, 99, 100, 104 and 216 Squadrons (the last-named was previously No. 16 (Naval) Squadron), to which were added in August and September Nos 97, 115 and 215 Squadrons with Handley Page O/400 bombers and No. 110 Squadron with D.H.9a aircraft. No. 100 Squadron also converted to O/400s.

This force continued the bombing task, begun by the 41st Wing, right up to the Armistice. In the last five months of the war it dropped a total of 550 tons of bombs, of which 390 tons were delivered at night. Among the targets were Bonn, Darmstadt, Frankfurt, Kaiserslautern, Karlsruhe, Rombas, Saarburg, Wiesbaden and Zweibrucken, as well as further visits to the cities attacked by the 41st Wing.

That these bombing raids began to have a serious effect on the German morale, already severely strained by civil unrest, was evidenced by a rapid increase in the enemy fighter defences. To counter this it was proposed to add a squadron of Sopwith Camels as escort to the force. Casualties were high, with a total of 109 aircraft lost (of which 69 were the big Handley Pages).

During the last five months of the war the weight of RAF bombs increased dramatically, the most notable being the 1,600-lb (726-kg) (later increased to 1,800-lb/816-kg) bomb capable of being carried by

the O/400. Shortly before the Armistice, deliveries began of a new, much larger bomber, the Handley Page V/1500, capable of lifting the 3,360-lb (1524-kg) bomb, and it was intended that No. 166 Squadron with V/1500s would bomb Berlin. On the day the war ended three of these huge aircraft were bombed-up and ready for take-off from Bircham Newton.

The Short Bomber was produced only as a stop-gap until Handley Page aircraft became available. Basically a Short 184 seaplane conversion, it went into action on 15 November 1916 with the RNAS.

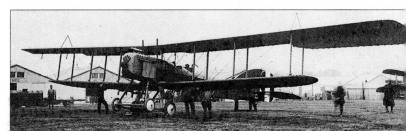

Colonial Operations

1918 – 1939

The UK's Royal Air Force emerged from World War I the most powerful air force in the world, having taken a major part in the air campaigns in the West. Within a couple of years of the Armistice the RAF was faced with a far more sinister fight for survival, as the generals and admirals squabbled to acquire for their own services the slender defence funds allowed by the British Treasury. Sir Eric Geddes, wartime First Lord of the Admiralty and for long an opponent of an autonomous RAF, achieved almost total emasculation of the RAF, reducing its squadrons

Above: Over a five-year period, 435 Bristol Fighters were issued to the overseas squadrons of the RAF, to help maintain law and order in Iraq, Baluchistan and the North-West Frontier of India.

from 188 to 25, and its personnel from 291,000 to 28,300, inclusive of overseas deployment.

It was indeed overseas that Sir Hugh Trenchard saw his opportunity to foster the survival of his service, first during the Chanak Crisis of 1920 in Turkey, when a small force of RAF personnel lent stability in a flashpoint situation, and then in the age-old trouble spots in the Middle East. Ever since the end of

hostilities with the Turks the British Army had waged a costly and exhausting campaign against warring factions in Iraq in efforts to stabilise the area. Trenchard's policy was to concentrate a major part of the surviving RAF in the Middle East (there was only a single fighter squadron left in the UK in 1920) and use his resources sparingly but firmly in a wide-ranging campaign of air policing. For this he deployed the Snipes of No. 1 Squadron, Bristol F.2Bs of No. 6

In 1928 the RAF evacuated over 500 British citizens caught up in a civil war in Afghanistan. Here Lord Irwin inspects No. 70 Squadron at Hinaidi on completion of the evacuation of Kabul on 2 February 1929.

Squadron and D.H.9As of Nos 8, 30 and 55 Squadrons in Iraq, all World War I aircraft but representative of the RAF's equipment until the mid-1920s. Faced initially with little more than inter-tribal strife, the RAF squadrons quickly evolved a pattern of 'benevolent policing',

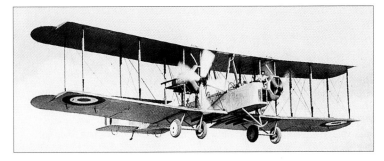

Above: The Vickers Vimy served from late 1918 until 1931. This example flew with No. 216 Squadron at Heliopolis from June 1922 to January 1926.

Right: At the end of September 1922, No. 25 Squadron was sent to Turkey with Sopwith Snipes for a period, returning in October 1923. Here two Snipes are at a field location at San Stefano during the Chanak crisis in 1923.

seldom firing a gun in anger and more often than not simply staging a demonstration. Frequently, however, the wear of sand and dust caused engine failures far out over the desert, and a burst of Lewis gun from a downed F.2B was sometimes needed to keep inquisitive tribesmen at a respectful distance until help arrived from the nearest British army post. Very soon relative peace reigned in the area, an achievement that had previously cost the army much time and money. The RAF proved itself a

The Vickers Vincent replaced the Wapitis and Fairey IIIFs that had served overseas for so long. This No. 47 Squadron Vincent near Khartoum in 1936 carries a varied array of wing-mounted bombs.

A formation of Fairey Flycatchers of No. 405 Flight from HMS Glorious flies over Malta in the late 1920s. This much-admired fighter served with every aircraft-carrier of the period during its 10 years' service.

highly cost-effective force and gained a fine reputation, on which Trenchard played heavily to acquire new aircraft. The big Vernons of No. 70 Squadron gave excellent service, moving units around the Middle East, and in 1926 these were replaced by Victorias at Hinaidi; two years later they evacuated 500 British nationals caught up in the Afghan civil war. Also in 1928 the old DH.9A began giving place to the Westland Wapiti, a process that continued until 1932.

In Egypt and India the pattern

had been much the same. To provide defence for the Suez Canal a total of eight squadrons served in Egypt during the 1920s, while No. 14 Squadron was based in Palestine until the outbreak of World War II, latterly co-operating with the Palestine Police in maintaining some semblance of peace between Jew and Arab and re-equipping with Fairey Gordons in 1932.

NORTH-WEST FRONTIER

Deployment of the RAF in India was more extensive throughout the inter-war period, most squadrons

serving some time on the North West Frontier; stations such as Risalpur, Peshawar and Kohat became familiar postings for RAF flying personnel. The majority of squadrons in India were on permanent deployment, Nos 5, 20, 28 and 31 taking out Bristol F.2Bs in 1919-20, and keeping them until 1929-30 when they received Wapitis. No.5 continued to fly

1933 saw the widespread adoption of the Hawker Osprey by ships of the Royal Navy. This Mk III is from No. 447 Catapult Flight with the 1st Cruiser Squadron, Mediterranean Fleet.

Desert patrollers

The RAF's light bombers were able to reinforce British control of its more troublesome colonies very cheaply, proving adaptable, versatile, and capable of quickly reacting to any crisis, uprising or banditry. Rebel villages were occasionally bombed to provide an example, but seldom until the inhabitants had been warned. The use of aircraft proved much more economical than using Army units.

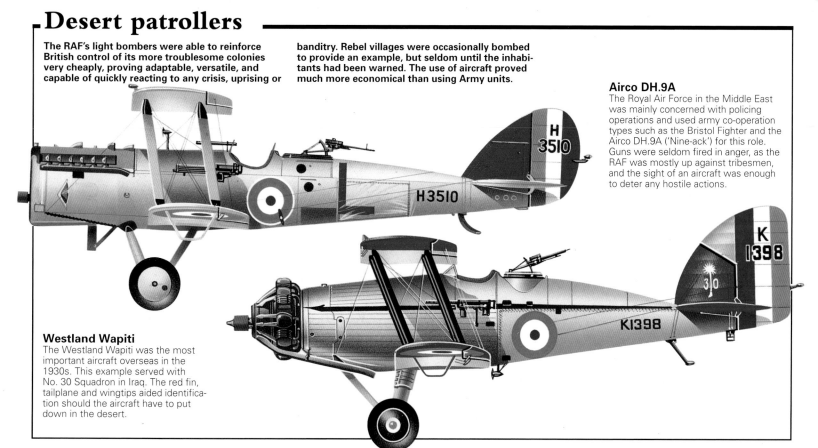

Airco DH.9A
The Royal Air Force in the Middle East was mainly concerned with policing operations and used army co-operation types such as the Bristol Fighter and the Airco DH.9A ('Nine-ack') for this role. Guns were seldom fired in anger, as the RAF was mostly up against tribesmen, and the sight of an aircraft was enough to deter any hostile actions.

Westland Wapiti
The Westland Wapiti was the most important aircraft overseas in the 1930s. This example served with No. 30 Squadron in Iraq. The red fin, tailplane and wingtips aided identification should the aircraft have to put down in the desert.

Vickers Vimy

The Vickers FB.Mk 27 Vimy bomber arrived in RAF service just too late to see action in World War I. It continued in production, however, and became the standard heavy bomber for the beginning of the 1920s. Several aircraft were sold for civilian use and were used for trail-blazing long-distance flights – across the Atlantic and from England to Australia were just two such feats. Those in RAF service were used mainly in the Middle East, with Nos 45, 58, 70 and 216 Sqns and No. 4 Flying Training School, while Nos 7 and 9 Sqns in the UK together with 'D' Flight of No. 100 Sqn also flew them until re-equipped with Virginias. The aircraft shown, F3184, served in Egypt with No. 70 Squadron.

Dimensions
The Vimy spanned 68 ft 1 in (20.75 m) and had a length of 43 ft 6.5 in (13.27 m). Its height was 15 ft 7.5 in (4.76 m) and its wing area totalled 1,330 sq ft (123.56 m²).

Armament
The Vimy defended itself with two or four 0.303-in (7.7-mm) Lewis Mk III machine-guns (with up to 12 97-round ammunition drums) in nose, dorsal and ventral positions, and carried a normal bombload of up to 2,476 lb (1123 kg).

Performance
Maximum speed of the Vimy Mk IV was 103 mph (166 km/h) at sea level. It could climb to 5,000 ft (1525 m) in 22 minutes and had a service ceiling of 7,000 ft (2135 m). At 81 mph (130 km/h), the Vimy had a range of 910 miles (1464 km).

Powerplant
The Vimy Mk IV was powered by two 360-hp (269-kW) Rolls-Royce Eagle VIII V-12 water-cooled engines.

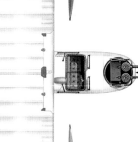

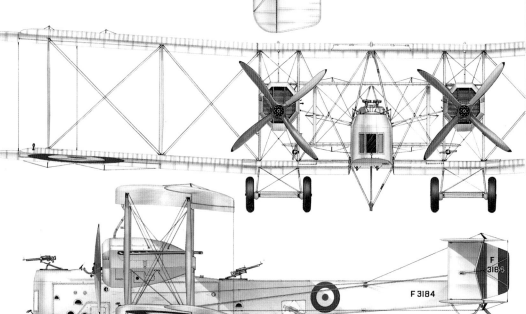

Below: Four Fairey IIIFs of No. 47 Squadron made the 11,000-mile Cairo-Cape-Cairo flight. The aircraft left Heliopolis near Cairo on 30 March 1927, reached Cape Town on 21 April and returned on 22 May.

Right: The Hawker Hardy was produced as a replacement for the Westland Wapitis of No. 30 Squadron engaged in policing duties in Iraq. The first aircraft that went to Iraq joined No. 30 Squadron at Mosul.

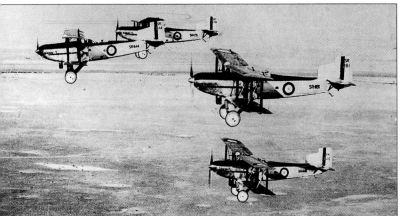

these until the beginning of World War II, but Nos 20 and 28 changed to Audaxes in the mid-1930s, and No. 31 became a transport squadron with Valentias in 1939. No. 60 Squadron was equipped in turn with DH.10s, DH.9As and Wapitis. As the strength of the RAF increased perceptibly during the late 1920s, Nos 11 and 39 Squadrons, both with Wapitis, were sent out to India so that by the mid-1930s there were 13 RAF squadrons serving on the sub-continent.

DEPLOYMENTS

A minor crisis in China threatened the safety of the international settlement at Shanghai and prompted the despatch of No. 2 Squadron with Bristol Fighters from Manston in April of 1927, but it was returned later that year to re-equip with Atlases.

The continued presence of the RAF in Iraq (on aerodromes at Mosul, Baghdad, Hinaidi, and elsewhere) prompted the construction of a single large, centralised base at Habbaniyah in 1934. This became

Entering service in 1937, the single-engined Vickers Wellesley bomber served mainly in the Middle East. These aircraft, flying over an area of Transjordan in 1938, are from No. 14 Squadron.

Right: The RAF in the Middle East was on the alert during the invasion of Abyssinia by Italy in 1935. This Fairey Gordon Mk I of No. 47 (General purpose) Squadron is flying over Kassala in Sudan.

in effect the focal point of the British military presence in the country, not only providing maintenance and training facilities but also becoming the base of No. 30 Squadron equipped with Hardy aircraft, developed specifically for the air policing role.

The last major Imperial deployment of the RAF overseas before World War II was undertaken when the Italian adventure in Abyssinia threatened the security of the sea route through the Red Sea. Accordingly, so as to reinforce the British presence in the Canal Zone and at Aden, Nos 12 (Harts) and 41 (Demons) Squadrons were sent to

Aden, No. 45 (Harts) to Kenya, No. 35 (Gordons) to the Sudan, and Nos 29 (Demons) and 33 (Harts) to Egypt; No. 22 Squadron with Vildebeests was based on Malta to cover any hostile move-

ment by the Italian fleet. The following year, with the subjugation of Abyssinia, the crisis passed and these squadrons returned home where preparations for possible world war were now under way.

Left: Fairey IIIF Mk IVMs of No. 47 Squadron moored on the Nile at Khartoum. The IIIFs were operated on floats for three months of the year. Note the original squadron badge on the tail fin.

Above: No. 33 at RAF Eastchurch became the first Hawker Hart day bomber squadron in February 1930. A wing of Hart squadrons was sent to reinforce the RAF in the Middle East after Italy invaded Abbysinia.

American Flashpoints

1922 - 1935

Above: Upon the outbreak of war in Leticia, the Colombian air force was ordered to purchase a single warplane. This Curtiss Falcon, 'Ricaurte', transported Benjamin Mendez Rey on a sensational flight from New York to Bogota in 1928.

Aviation had come early to South America. One of the early pioneers of flight was the Brazilian Alberto Santos-Dumont, who had contributed so much to European flying in the first decade of the 20th century. Military air forces had, before World War I, been created in Argentina, Brazil, Chile and Peru, to which Uruguay was added in 1916. It was not long before the age-old abrasive politics arising from contentious border demarcation, arbitrary ethnic divisions and external industrial exploitation involved the Central and South American states in self-imposed strife, though relatively few of the coups and revolutions were staged by more than a few troops. Military aircraft were scarcely in

Above: A Curtiss Wright Osprey general-purpose biplane, of which Bolivia received 20. With the aircraft is General R. Martinez Pitar of the Commission de Neutrality at Villa Montes in June 1935.

evidence during the continuous internal strife that existed in Mexico between 1922 and 1926, or during the bloodless coup in Guatemala of 1924, or the Cuban revolution of 1930.

In 1932, however, conflict between Peru and its neighbour, Colombia, broke out when the border territory of Leticia (previously awarded to Colombia in a

One of the two Dornier C29s of the Colombian air force. This particular aircraft is believed to be the one flown by Von Karl Maringer.

Below: The Breda Ba 44 was a six-passenger cabin biplane powered by two 200-hp de Havilland Gipsy engines, and a small number were acquired by the Paraguayan air force from Italy in 1934 for use as transport aircraft.

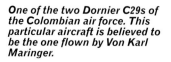

1922 treaty) became a source of disputed sovereignty. Peruvian forces entered Leticia in 1932 and ejected Colombian officials, installing their own provincial administration. Colombia at that time possessed a small air force comprising a handful of Curtiss Hawk biplane fighters, Curtiss O-1 Falcon reconnaissance biplanes and a small number of other American and European air-

craft. Peru, on the other hand, had been strengthening its air force, the Cuerpo de Aeronautica del Peru (CAP), since 1929, and already possessed Curtiss Hawk and Nieuport 121 fighters, Vought 02U-lE Corsair observation aircraft, Douglas M-4 bombers and Boeing 40B-4 transports; orders had also been placed in the UK for Fairey Fox II bombers and some Fairey Gordon general-purpose aircraft.

Flying proficiency was generally lacking on both sides, though there were a number of incidents involving air combat. While the Colombian air force was handicapped by the lack of established aerodromes within 200 miles (320 km) of the disputed border territory, the CAP contrived to use its fighters and observation aircraft in support of the ground forces to some effect; its bombers, being sea-

planes and based on the coast some 600 miles (960 km) from the war zone, were not used. When in April 1933 the Peruvian president Luis Sanchez Cerro was murdered, Peru became more conciliatory and hostilities died down; a year later Leticia was formally returned to Colombia.

While the Peruvian-Colombian conflict was at its height a major war was raging between Bolivia and Paraguay. Both nations had for many years been disputing sovereignty of the Chaco Boreal, a dispute fuelled by the belief by foreign interests that large oil deposits lay undeveloped in the territory. In 1928 Paraguayan forces had seized a Bolivian fort, and immediately a series of isolated but bloody clashes followed. A truce had been negotiated by the Pan American Conference and League of Nations, but this failed to hold and in 1932 all-out warfare between the two states erupted.

MERCENARIES

The small Paraguayan air force possessed a number of Italian Fiat CR.30 biplane fighters, Bergamaschi AP.1 monoplane fighters, Caproni Ca 101 three-engine bombers and Breda Ba 44 transports, while the larger Bolivian Cuerpo de Aviacion flew about 60 Curtiss Wright Osprey general-purpose aircraft, Curtiss Hawk IA fighters and Junkers W.34s converted as bombers. From 1933 onwards both sides made considerable use of their air forces. A high proportion of the aircrews were foreign mercenaries although, with the assistance of an Italian military aviation mission, the standard of training among Paraguayan flying personnel quickly improved. Numerous air combats took place, particularly when both sides began flying bombing raids, and it has been suggested that each air force lost about 30 aircraft. Best known pilot of the war was undoubtedly Major Rafael Pavon

War over the Chaco Boreal

From 1932 Paraguay and Bolivia were at war over the sovereignty of the undeveloped territory of the Chaco Boreal, believed to include significant oil and mineral deposits. The war raged until 1935, and some 88,000 men lost their lives.

The fighting on the ground was accompanied by fierce fighting in the air, with intensive bombing raids and sporadic fighter engagements accounting for some 60 aircraft losses.

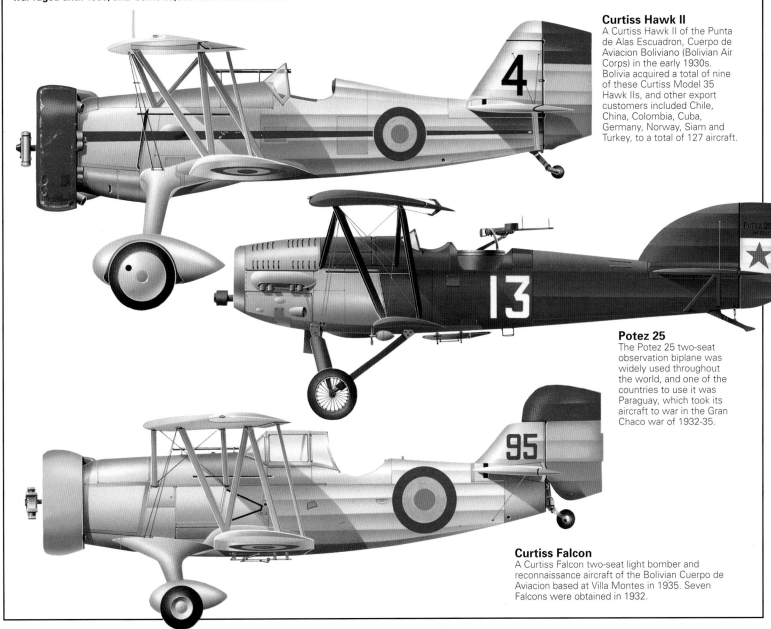

Curtiss Hawk II
A Curtiss Hawk II of the Punta de Alas Escuadron, Cuerpo de Aviacion Boliviano (Bolivian Air Corps) in the early 1930s. Bolivia acquired a total of nine of these Curtiss Model 35 Hawk IIs, and other export customers included Chile, China, Colombia, Cuba, Germany, Norway, Siam and Turkey, to a total of 127 aircraft.

Potez 25
The Potez 25 two-seat observation biplane was widely used throughout the world, and one of the countries to use it was Paraguay, which took its aircraft to war in the Gran Chaco war of 1932-35.

Curtiss Falcon
A Curtiss Falcon two-seat light bomber and reconnaissance aircraft of the Bolivian Cuerpo de Aviacion based at Villa Montes in 1935. Seven Falcons were obtained in 1932.

Left: During the conflict there was a sudden need to acquire further Curtiss Falcons that could serve as light bombers and reconnaissance aircraft. These new Falcons for export had better engines and a different fuselage.

Below: A Curtiss Triplane Type 18T, powered by a 400-hp Curtiss 12-cylinder water-cooled Vee engine with a maximum speed of 163 mph. Designed for the US Navy, one was imported into Bolivia in 1919, and was known as the Wasp.

who, in Curtiss Hawks, was credited with three combat victories and came to be dubbed the Bolivian 'ace of aces'.

A further truce was arranged in 1935 and the Chaco Treaty was signed at Buenos Aires dividing the Chaco Boreal between the two belligerents, Paraguay gaining by far the greater area. Both sides had suffered heavy casualties (Paraguay 36,000 men and Bolivia 52,000), and both were rendered economically exhausted by the Chaco War which achieved precious little, as the oil interests that had led to such bitter jealousies were not to be realised for many years to come.

The Nomonhan Incident

MAY – SEPTEMBER 1939

A formation of Nakajima Ki-27s on patrol. This type held air superiority for the Japanese throughout the conflict, largely on account of the superior training of the Japanese pilots, many of whom had previously fought Polikarpov aircraft over China.

Fought over the remote steppelands of Mongolia, the conflict now usually known as the Nomonhan Incident occupied 129 days just as World War II was breaking out in Europe in 1939. Despite the involvement of tens of thousands of troops and hundreds of aircraft, the incident is scarcely recorded in the history books of the West. Moreover, like the Spanish Civil War, it provided practical experience for combatant nations that were to be involved in World War II.

At a point where the Khalkha river formed the border between the Soviet-Mongolian province of Doronod and Japanese-administered Manchukuo, a band of nomadic tribesmen strayed into Soviet territory on 10 May 1939 and were pursued back by Mongolian border guards. *Ad hoc*

The Mitsubishi Ki-30 Army Type 97 Light Bomber was introduced into active service in China in 1938. The Ki-30 was the first Japanese light bomber to possess such modern features as an internal bomb-bay and a variable-pitch propeller.

Japanese air reconnaissance disclosed an unexpected build-up of military forces on the west bank of the Khalkha river and, smarting from previous humiliations by the Soviet Union, the Kanto-gun (the Japanese defence command in China) forthwith created a local detachment comprising about 50 aircraft in the area, with its headquarters at Hailar, some 100 miles (160 km) behind the border; the majority of these aircraft were Type 97 (Nakajima Ki-27) fighters.

AIR BATTLES

The Soviet forces comprised a cavalry division, a rifle corps and an armoured brigade, supported by three air regiments, also of about 50 aircraft, of which about 40 were Polikarpov I-15 biplane and Polikarpov I-16 monoplane fighters. Following the shooting down

The Mitsubishi A5M was the forerunner of the 'Zeke'. The model shown here has an enclosed cockpit but was succeeded by an open cockpit version, which in turn gave place to the A5M4 (known to the Allies as 'Claude'). It featured a fixed spatted undercarriage.

of a V-VS reconnaissance aircraft by the Japanese, a number of isolated air combats took place during May, in which the Type 97 fighters confirmed their superiority by shooting down a score of Soviet aircraft without loss to themselves.

The Soviets replied by sending a further fighter regiment of I-16s to the war zone, and at the same time established a group of airfields (little more than strips cleared on the steppeland) around the township of Tamsag Bulag. On 22 June the V-VS staged a number of sweeps and raids on the Japanese ground positions lining the Khalkha river, and fierce air battles developed. The Soviet attacks stung the Kanto-gun into retaliation, and on 27 June 30 Japanese bombers with an escort of 74 fighters twice raided the V-VS airfields around Tamsag Bulag.

Opposing fighters

Air battles over the battlefront provided invaluable combat experience for the participants. While the Japanese returned to their units to pass on the lessons they had learned, many of the Russians fell victim to Stalin's purges. Both air staffs learned valuable lessons. The Japanese continued development of new fighters, which were ever more agile, and also continued the development of close support tactics, using air power to support ground forces. The Russians realised that the era of the biplane fighter was over, and pressed on with monoplane fighters.

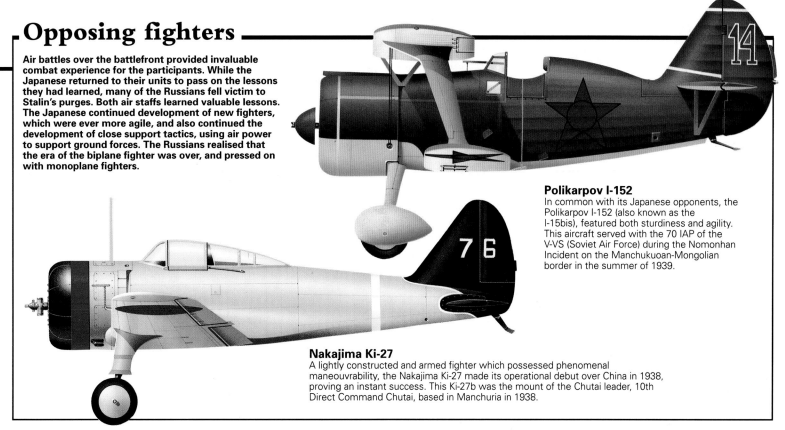

Polikarpov I-152
In common with its Japanese opponents, the Polikarpov I-152 (also known as the I-15bis), featured both sturdiness and agility. This aircraft served with the 70 IAP of the V-VS (Soviet Air Force) during the Nomonhan Incident on the Manchukuoan-Mongolian border in the summer of 1939.

Nakajima Ki-27
A lightly constructed and armed fighter which possessed phenomenal maneouvrability, the Nakajima Ki-27 made its operational debut over China in 1938, proving an instant success. This Ki-27b was the mount of the Chutai leader, 10th Direct Command Chutai, based in Manchuria in 1938.

On 2 July two Japanese divisions attacked across the Khalkha and came under heavy air attack by up to 60 Tupolev SB-2 bombers. Air combats between the opposing air forces were now frequently involving up to 100 fighters on each side, but still the Japanese proved superior, their fighters taking heavy toll of the I-15 biplane fighters opposing them. At the end of July the V-VS introduced 20-mm cannon-armed I-16 Type 17 monoplane fighters, and these to a large extent redressed the balance.

As Japanese losses in the air began to mount during August (particularly among their more experienced pilots), the Soviets, now commanded by Komkor Georgi Zhukov, mounted a large-scale attack by 100,000 troops and 800 tanks across the Khalkha, aiming to trap the Japanese forces in a giant pincer movement. Supporting this offensive were more than 500 aircraft, including a

The Polikarpov I-16 was the main fighter employed by the Soviets over Nomonhan, and the best. It was a good match performance-wise for the Nakajima Ki-27 (Type 97) but its pilots were not as well trained as the Japanese.

half regiment of Tupolev TB-3 four-engined heavy bombers which began night raids on Japanese supply lines in the rear. Through sheer tenacity and skill the Japanese managed to cling to a slender air superiority, although the SB-2s and TB-3s started making raids from 19,685 ft (6000 m) which gave them some immunity. When the Soviet fighters began strafing attacks on the forward Japanese airfields, losses among the Type 97 fighters increased rapidly.

HEAVY LOSSES

Just as it seemed that the Soviet forces were poised to destroy the two Japanese divisions on the eastern side of the Khalkha, the first heavy snow of the winter began falling on 11 September, effectively halting all activity on the ground. Air combat continued until 16 September, when peace negotiations between Tokyo and Moscow brought the conflict to an end.

The small war had been extraordinarily vicious, involving 120,000 Soviets and 80,000 Japanese on the ground, while each side lost upwards of 200 aircraft. The fighting had demonstrated unequivocally to the Soviets that the age of the

Above: The Tupolev SB-2bis was the bomber version produced during 1938. It had a crew of three and had a maximum speed of 450 km/h. Armament consisted of four machine-guns, and normal bombload was 600-kg. Some 60 were in service during this period.

Below: Japan acquired a number of Fiat BR.20 Cicognas from Italy and used them along the Manchurian border on bombing raids. The BR.20s also fought with the Nationalist forces in the Spanish Civil War.

biplane fighter was at an end (although the I-15 continued in service for almost two more years), and it also confirmed the SB-2 as an efficient light bomber by the standards of the day. The Japanese could take comfort in the excellence of their pilots, while the Type 97 fighter had continued to dominate the skies in the absence of really modern fighters.

The real lesson was missed. Foreign correspondents and observers were forbidden access to the war front, with the result that Western staffs remained blissfully ignorant of the high standard of training and equipment in the Imperial Japanese Army Air Force. This standard was to enjoy further progressive improvement, so that when the Pacific war broke out two years later the Japanese proved immeasurably superior to the Allied forces ranged against them.

Spanish Civil War JULY 1936 - MARCH 1939

Left: *By far the most capable fighter in the Spanish Civil War was the Messerschmitt Bf 109. Most were Jumo-powered Bf 109Bs, Cs and Ds, although a few DB 601-powered Bf 109Es arrived at the end.*

Below: *The Dornier Do 17 was one of the modern types evaluated in combat by the Legion Condor. The Do 17E-1 bomber served with 2.K/88 while the Do 17F-1 camera-carrying reconnaissance platform flew with 1.A/88. Both proved able to evade Republican fighters with some ease.*

Years of international antagonism between extremist socialism and fascism throughout continental Europe sparked into bloody civil war in Spain on 18 July 1936, when right-wing army officers rose against an ineffective and corrupt socialist administration. The government (Republican) air force was poorly equipped with a hotch-potch of obsolete Nieuport-Delage NiD.52 fighters, Breguet 19 reconnaissance bombers, some Vickers Vildebeest torpedo-bombers and a handful of other old foreign aircraft.

Sensing that the Nationalist forces were even more badly equipped, Nazi Germany quickly assembled a force of modern aircraft and volunteers for support of General Francisco Franco, and within a week the first Junkers Ju 52/3m bomber-transports were on their way to Morocco to airlift large numbers of troops from Africa to bolster the Nationalists. Some of the

Nationalist fighters

The Spanish Civil War provided Luftwaffe and Italian fighter pilots with invaluable combat experience. Initially they flew biplane fighters against Russian-flown Polikarpov I-15s operating in support of the Republican cause. Later, monoplane fighters were introduced, combatting Republican Polikarpov I-16s.

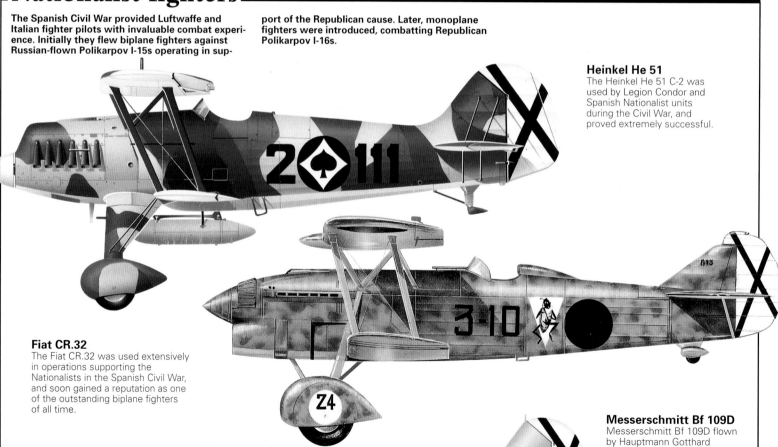

Heinkel He 51
The Heinkel He 51 C-2 was used by Legion Condor and Spanish Nationalist units during the Civil War, and proved extremely successful.

Fiat CR.32
The Fiat CR.32 was used extensively in operations supporting the Nationalists in the Spanish Civil War, and soon gained a reputation as one of the outstanding biplane fighters of all time.

Messerschmitt Bf 109D
Messerschmitt Bf 109D flown by Hauptmann Gotthard Handrick, Gruppenkommandeur JG 88, Legion Condor, Calamocha, in February 1938. The *zylinder Hut* (top hat) identified 2.Staffel, JG 88, and the motif on the spinner recalls Handrick's Modern Pentathlon Gold Medal at the 1936 Olympic Games in Berlin.

Fighters for the Republic

Republican air forces inherited aircraft from the pre-Civil War air force, and augmented these with aircraft supplied (and often manned) by the USSR. The Republicans also took into service aircraft captured from the Nationalists. The Republican pilots were from a similarly diverse range of backgrounds, and included International Brigade volunteers, front-line Soviet pilots and loyal Spaniards.

Hawker Fury
Three Furies were delivered to Spain powered by 700-hp (522-kW) Hispano-Suiza 12Xbrs engines, and featuring a single strut undercarriage in common with contemporary types such as the Gloster Gladiator. These aircraft originally flew in aluminium colour schemes with red panels on the fuselage.

Polikarpov I-16
The 'Double Six' emblem on the fin identifies this Spanish I-16 as a Super Mosca operated by the 3ª Escuadrilla de Mosca based at Albacete during 1937.

Left: A dozen Savoia-Marchetti S.M.81 bombers, together with a similar number of Fiat CR.32 fighters from Fascist Italy, took part in the Civil War. As in the early Heinkel He 111s, the S.M.81 carried its bombs vertically stowed, resulting in an untidy trajectory which did not help the aiming accuracy.

Below: One of the first of the new types to see operational service with Legion Condor was the Heinkel He 111B-1, in action with 3./K 88 (3rd Staffel of Kampfgruppe 88). They carried a variety of individual markings including this Scottie dog on the fin of one aircraft.

NiD.52 pilots had also joined the Nationalists and one of these, Teniente Miguel Guerro Garcia, shot down half a dozen Republican aircraft in the first fortnight of the war. In August the nationalist air force quickly gained strength with six Heinkel He 51 fighters and further Ju 52/3m bomber transports from Germany, and a dozen Savoia-Marchetti S.81s and a similar number of Fiat CR.32s from Fascist Italy. The S.81s went into action on 5 August, bombing a Republican warship; soon after, their initial trooping completed, the Ju 52/3m aircraft started bombing raids in support of Franco's northward advance.

The Republicans had also appealed for foreign assistance, and during August about 60 French aircraft (Dewoitine D.371s, D.372s, D.501s and D.510s, Potez 54s, Loire-Nieuport LN.46s and Blériot-Spad S.510s) arrived.

By the end of the year the flow of foreign aircraft to both sides was well established, the German con-

In the autumn of 1936, Polikarpov I-16 Type 5 fighters were delivered to the Spanish government at the start of the Civil War. A total of 278 were delivered, including this Type 10, known as the 'Super Rata'.

Below: A crashed Nieuport-Delage NiD.52 C1 of the Republican Forces. A French-designed aircraft, 91 were licence-built by Hispano Aviation at Guadalajana. At the outbreak of the war, six squadrons were still equipped with NiD.52 C1s and these were flown by both Republican and Nationalist pilots.

tingent having been organised into the Legion Condor, under General Hugo Sperrle, with Ju 52/3ms, He 51s, He 45s, He 46s, He 59s, He 70s and Henschel Hs 123s. The Italians, now formed into an autonomous Aviazione Legionaria, had added Meridionali Ro 37bis reconnaissance bombers to further CR.32s and S.M.81s. The Soviet Union, demanding full payment in gold, had supplied the first of a large number of Polikarpov I-15 biplane and I-16 monoplane fighters and some Tupolev SB-2 twin-engined bombers.

Enter the Bf 109

Most of these aircraft were deployed on the Madrid front in October where the Nationalists threatened the capital. It was the superiority of the I-15 and I-16 fighters that frustrated Nationalist air operations around Madrid, and it was the failure by such aircraft as the He 51 and CR.32 to secure air superiority that prompted the despatch of 45 Messerschmitt Bf 109B monoplane fighters early in 1937, as well as 30 Heinkel He 111B and 15 Dornier Do 17F bombers, from Germany.

Stalemate around Madrid in 1937 was followed by a Nationalist offensive in the north. Many of the He 51s and CR 32s were handed over to the Spaniards upon the arrival of the Bf 109Bs, and delivery of the new SM.79 allowed the more vulnerable Ju 52/3m aircraft to confine their operations to night bombing, while a shipload of Czech Aero

Left: The Fiat G.50 had all the modern features of a late-1930's fighter. The prototype flew in January 1937, and it entered production in 1938. Together with the Bf 109E, it effectively dominated the skies over Spain.

A.101 bombers, intended for the Republicans, was captured and put into service with Franco's forces. It was during the Nationalist drive in the north that an air attack on the small fortified town of Guernica was seized on by the socialist propagandists to point to the supposedly indiscriminate bombing by the fascists, yet neither side was innocent of such lapses.

Three main Republican counter-offensives in 1937 gained only limited success and did not succeed in diverting Nationalist air strength from the northern front, which crumbled in August. However, licence-production of the excellent I-16 fighter had contributed to a numerical superiority in Republican aircraft during the summer and led to yet further acceleration of German aircraft deliveries to the Legion Condor, including Junkers Ju 87 dive bombers and further Bf 109s, and Fiat BR.20 bombers to the Aviazione Legionaria.

During the spring of 1938, heartened by their victory in the north, the Nationalists succeeded in reaching the Mediterranean coast between Barcelona and Valencia, thereby cutting Republican-held

MAIN OFFENSIVES

Santiago
Santander
Bilbao
Guernica
FRANCE
Leon
Nationalist Offensive March-June 1937
Victoria
Logrono
Zaragossa
Republican Offensive July 1938
PORTUGAL
Republican Offensive penetrates Nationalists Front, May 1937
Barcelona (falls to Nationalists 25th January 1939)
Salamanca
Madrid falls to Nationalists, 27th March 1939
Madrid
Getafe
MAJORCA
Toledo
Nationalists reach coast, April 1938
Republican Offensives, July 1938
Nationalist Checked, October 1936
Nationalist Offence, February 1937
Valencia
Italian raids by S.79 bombers
Merida
Badajoz
IBIZA
NATIONALIST SWEEP AUGUST 1936
Cordoba
Murcia
Seville
NATIONALIST SWEEP AUGUST 1936
Principal airfields
Granada
Jerez
Rota
Malaga
MEDITERRANEAN SEA
Tetuan
Airlift of Nationalist forces from Morocco

This map of Spain during the Civil War shows the key offensive moves of both Nationalist and Republican forces from July 1936 to March 1939. The Nationalists cut through from south to north, enabling east and west points to be taken.

territory in two. That April the first Bf 109Cs replaced the last of the German-flown He 51s and, led by the great German pilot Werner Mölders, succeeded at last in mastering the I-16. As the Republican forces desperately fought to avoid defeat, the majority of Soviet volunteer pilots melted away and returned home. All the while, the Nationalist air force grew in strength, taking over German equipment as newer aircraft arrived in the country. On the central front in particular the Legion Condor proved almost invincible, and in November Franco crossed the Ebro and soon after was driving toward

Below: Three modified DH.89Ms were delivered to the Spanish government in December 1935 for police duties in Morocco. When the Civil War began they were formed into Grupo 40 and operated on the Nationalist side.

The Nationalists captured one of the Republican Hawker Furies after it shot off its own propeller, when its interruptor gear failed. The Hawker Fury was more than a match for Nationalist Fiat CR.32s and Heinkel He 51s, but only three were acquired.

Barcelona. Early in 1939 the Germans introduced the first cannon-armed Bf 109Es and the Italians delivered a few Fiat G.50s, and these (together with the earlier Bf 109Bs and Bf 109Cs) effectively dominated the air, Mölders himself becoming the highest-scoring German with 14 victories.

On 27 March the Nationalists

fought their way into the centre of Madrid and on the next day the war ended. Whatever the wider ramifications of the Spanish Civil War, it had proved the ideal testing ground for the infant German Luftwaffe, conceived as it was as an aerial support arm for the German army, and the success of close-support aircraft was classically demonstrated. German propagandists were quick to point to the devastating power of the dreaded Ju 87 dive-bomber, soon to terrorise half of Europe.

Bombers at War

Both sides made extensive use of bombers during the Spanish Civil War, ushering in a terrible new era of air warfare. If the much-hyped attack on Guernica was created as much by propaganda and deliberate demolition by the Republicans as by the Nationalist's bombers, there were plenty of less well-known examples of the awesome destructive potential of the modern bomber.

Savoia Marchetti S.M.81
Among the first Italian aircraft supplied to Franco's Nationalist forces were Savoia Marchetti S.M.81 Pipistrellos. These operated as bombers with a secondary transport role.

Junkers Ju 52/3mg4e
This Junkers Ju 52/3mg4e was flown by the Grupo de Bombardeo Nocturno 2-G-22 of the 1a Escuadra, Nationalist Arma de Aviacion. The Ju 52 made an effective bomber when out of the way of fighters, and carried a gunner in a ventral dustbin which was swung into position after take-off.

Tupolev SB-2
A handful of Tupolev SB-2 light bombers were supplied to the Republicans. The USSR demanded full payment for all the aircraft it supplied, whereas Italy and Germany gladly contributed aircraft and crew free in order to gain combat experience, and to support a political ally.

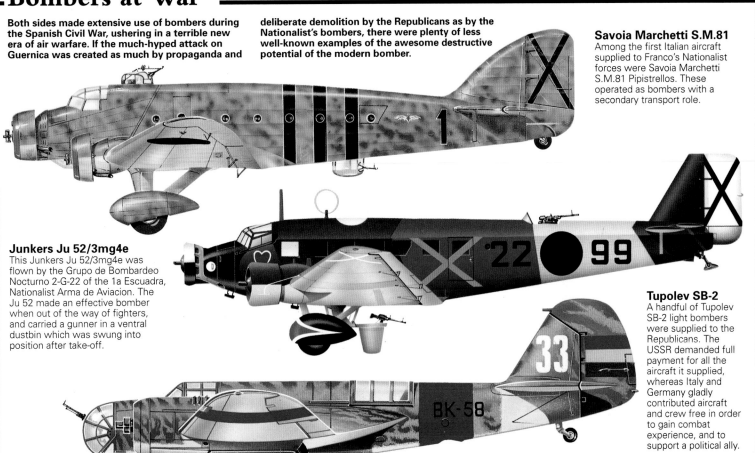

WORLD WAR II IN EUROPE

The Blitzkrieg on Poland opened on 1 September 1939 with raids by fleets of Ju 87 dive-bombers and He 111 and Do 17 medium bombers. They smashed the essential war factories, airfields and vital lines of communications. The flames of Warsaw and the whine of the Stukas were to be the harbingers of a hell that was to last for nearly six years. World War II had begun.

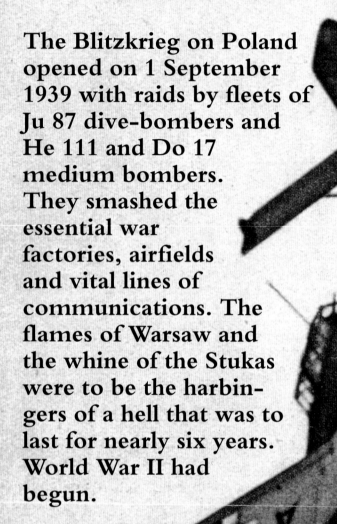

A Junkers Ju 87B Stuka in a classic pose, with its load of one 250-kg (551-lb) SC250 and four 50-kg (110-lb) SC50 bombs dropping away, just before the aircraft pulls out of its steep dive. The terrifying wail of the 'Jericho trumpet' sirens, mounted at the top of their main undercarriage legs, was to become a trademark of the Blitzkrieg.

On 1 September 1939, Poland's capital, Warsaw, was heavily bombed by Luftwaffe Heinkel He 111s. Their principal target was the PZL aircraft factory, but as this photograph shows, a considerable amount of damage was inflicted on civilian property.

Blitzkrieg on Poland

SEPTEMBER 1939

At 04.15 on 1 September 1939, World War II shattered an uneasy European peace as the German 3rd, 4th, 8th, 10th and 14th Armies burst across Poland's western frontiers as the components of two army groups embarking on a huge pincer movement designed to close successively at Kutna, Warsaw and Brest Litovsk, thereby encircling the ill-prepared Polish armies under General Smigly-Rydz. From the first moments of the crushing attack, the young Luftwaffe hurled some 2,000 modern aircraft into the battle with scant worry from the opposing Lotnictwo Wojskowe (Polish air force), which was quickly seen to be not only poorly equipped but badly organised and deployed; the Poles could field fewer than 200 obsolete PZL P.7 and P.11 fighters and a similar number of light bombers.

Over the battlefields themselves roared nine Gruppen of Junkers Ju 87 dive-bombers (some 366 aircraft), spearheading and supporting the devastating Blitzkrieg tactic whose theory had been proved in the Spanish Civil War. As aircraft and armour blasted its way through the Polish defences, the German bomber force ranged far afield against vital lines of communication, against the Polish war factories and against airfields in the rear. Three Kampfgeschwader of Heinkel He 111 heavy bombers (about 300 aircraft) and four of Dornier Do 17s (400 aircraft) were active on the first

day: 60 He 111s of I and III/KG 4 bombed Krakow airfield as 30 similar aircraft of II/KG 4 dropped 22 tons of bombs on Lemburg airfield, destroying six Polish fighters on the ground. The Putzig/Rahmel naval base was heavily hit from the air by I/KG 1, and the all-important PZL fighter factory was badly damaged in

a raid by II/LG 1 on Warsaw/Okecie airport.

The main fault in the Polish air force deployment lay in the rigid affiliation of fighter and bomber squadrons, bound tightly into autonomous regiments, to specific armies themselves regionally deployed. There was thus no

Left: Polish air force PZL P.37 Los bombers of the 1st Air Regiment based near Warsaw. Many were lost in September 1939 as they attacked the German troops and armour without any effective fighter escorts.

Above: Henschel Hs 123As carrying four 50-kg (110-lb) SC50 bombs on racks under their wings. These retain the sling under the fuselage for a single 250-kg (551-lb) SC250 bomb.

Opposing fighters

The greatly superior Messerschmitt Bf 109E 'Emil' equipped the Jagdverband in September 1939. It was faster, more manoeuvrable, had better armament and was generally more versatile than the best the Polish air force had available.

PZL's P.11 first flown in 1931, was powered by a Bristol Mercury VI engine, giving it a top speed of 390 km/h (243 mph) compared to the Bf 109E's 578 km/h (359 mph). Most P.11s only had two 7.7-mm machine-guns; a few had four guns.

Messerschmitt Bf 109E
The Luftwaffe had 850 Bf 109E-1 fighters and Bf 109E-1B fighter-bombers equipping 12 Gruppen on the eve of the invasion of Poland. This 'Emil' is painted in the 1939 markings of III/Jagdgeschwader 27, with dark-green upper surfaces and light-blue/grey undersides. Five of the Gruppen of Bf 109Es with 200 aircraft, actually took part in the invasion, of which 67 were lost, mainly to Polish ground fire.

PZL P.11c
The Polish air force received 175 examples of the all-metal P.11c fighter in 1935/36. These equipped 12 squadrons when the German army invaded Poland in 1939. They faced overwhelming odds, but still managed to claim 126 Luftwaffe aircraft in early air battles. This P.11c carries the markings of 121 Eskadra, 111 Dyon of the 2nd Air Regiment, based at Krakow.

Left: The Luftwaffe had 400 He 111Hs in September 1939. Heinkels of KG 2, KG 4, KG 26, KG 27 and II/LG 1 were in daily action. At first, raids went far beyond the front line, but as the Poles fell back towards Warsaw, bombing concentrated on the beleaguered capital.

Above: A triumphant Messerschmitt Bf 110 crew is seen during the short Polish campaign. Having learned at an early stage not to engage the nimble PZL P.11 fighters in close-in combat, the Bf 110s were highly successful when using dive and climb tactics. Most of the missions were flown as top cover for He 111 bombers.

flexibility in air defence, more than half the air force being withheld from battle until imminently threatened by the German advance. The Poles' trouble was that the Luftwaffe recognised no such parochial niceties and was frequently free to attack its targets with scarcely any opposition. Quickly realising the fatal flaw in their organisation, some of the Polish fighter squadrons abandoned their assigned bases and sought to attack the German bomber formations wherever they were reported.

Unfortunately the aged P.7 and P.11 fighters on which Poland's air defence rested almost exclusively, were no match for the German Messerschmitt Bf 109Es, whose

Below: Eleven Polish air force squadrons operated PZL P.23b Karas tactical bombers in 1939. They suffered heavy losses. The remains of this crashed example are being examined by the crew of a Luftwaffe Fieseler Fi 156C Storch.

pilots were given free rein to hunt the Polish skies. Nevertheless, there were numerous instances of reckless courage by the defending pilots who, with scant heed of appalling odds, waded into the big German formations.

POLAND CRUSHED

By the end of the third day the Luftwaffe had a total of 55 aircraft destroyed, 71 aircrew killed, 39 wounded and 94 missing. Polish casualties, on the other hand, had reached the loss of 46 fighters and about 60 light bombers; roughly a quarter of the entire air force in just three days. The light bomber force (the only arm of the Polish air force to be tightly reined within its

Right: The Luftwaffe's Ju 87 Stuka received a formidable reputation in the Blitzkrieg. This was on the basis of its tactical rather than general bombing success. Here armourers are priming 250-kg (551-lb) bombs before another attack.

regional deployment) had carried out several setpiece raids against German armour assembly areas with some success, but with crippling losses to flak and fighters. In one memorable attack by 28 P.23 light bombers in the Radomski-Piotrków area more than half the aircraft failed to return.

After 10 days the invading armies had virtually isolated a dozen Polish divisions in the Kutno area, and the Poles attempted to mount a concerted counter-attack against the German forces, now nearing Warsaw itself. This proved to be the last fully sustained resistance by the

Polish army in the field, now desperately handicapped by the surging masses of civilian refugees seeking escape from the ravaged towns and villages. No more than about 100 Polish fighters and bombers remained airworthy, and these were flown into battle piecemeal, their pilots seldom briefed as to the strength or presence of the enemy's air force. By 13 September German aircraft losses had risen to 150 aircraft destroyed, but as the German army closed its ring of steel around the capital, resistance by the Polish air force dwindled to nothing. Those pilots who could, made good

Tactical bombers

A total of 210 three-seat PZL P.23b army support bombers were built for the Polish air force, equipping 11 squadrons. By September 1939 the slow, inadequately-armed aircraft was nearing obsolescence and was an easy target for German gunners.

Specifically designed as a 'Sturzkampfflugzeug' (dive-bomber) the Junkers Ju 87 was very successful against Polish forces, destroying all but two of the Polish surface warships and virtually wiping out an entire infantry division at Piotrków station.

PZL P.23b Karas
Numerically the most important Polish bomber/reconnaissance aircraft in service in September 1939, the Dispositional Air Force and the Armies' Air Force had a total of 118 P.23s. Illustrated is a P.23b of No. 42 Squadron, attached to the Pomorze Army.

Junkers Ju 87B
This Ju 87B-1 wears the markings of the Gruppenstab of IV (Stuka) Gruppe of Lehrgeschwader 1, commanded by Hauptmann von Brauchitsch. This operational training, evaluation and demonstration unit saw extensive service as a combat formation – notably in Poland.

Left: A PZL P.11c fighter, riddled with bullets, after a crash landing. The Polish air force had 12 squadrons flying this mid-1930s fighter against the overwhelming might of the Luftwaffe.

Above: Every effort was made by the Polish army and air force to prepare for the threat of invasion by Germany and Russia. Here a pair of balloon barrage/observation blimps are being prepared.

their escape to neighbouring countries, and thence to the West, later joining the French and British air forces to continue their fight.

With tacit agreement on partitioning rights with Germany, the Soviet Union invaded Poland from the east on 17 September and, although Warsaw continued to resist until 27 September, the last concentration of Polish forces in the Modlin fortress was defeated on the following day and the campaign ended.

TOTAL WAR
The short Polish campaign sparked World War II, with the UK and France siding with Poland against Germany on 3 September, though neither country was in any position,

militarily or geographically, to offer any assistance during the four short weeks needed by Germany to crush all opposition. Those weeks witnessed a demonstration of total war. If the world had thus far been indifferent to the portents of Spain, the flames of Warsaw and the whine of Stukas were to be the harbingers of hell that would not be quenched or quelled for six long years to come.

Right: A Messerschmitt Bf 109E-1 with the markings of 1/JG 20 (later redesignated 8/JG 51). This was the first version powered by the 821-kW (1,100-hp) DB 601A and had four MG 17 machine-guns (two in the nose and one in each wing). This enabled it to eclipse its opponents for the first eight months of the war.

The Winter War

SEPTEMBER 1939 – MARCH 1940

Left: During the early part of the war, the Fokker D.XXI represented the Finnish fighter force (in addition to a handful of obsolete Bristol Bulldogs). They performed admirably, scoring many victories until the odds became too great. The Finnish air force shot down more than 50 Russian aircraft, almost all falling to the D.XXIs.

Below: Despite its biplane configuration, the Gloster Gladiator proved a handful for the Russian fighters. Thirty Gladiator Mk IIs, all of them ex-RAF aircraft, were supplied for use by the Finnish air force between December 1939 and February 1940. Most were fitted with a ski landing gear.

Opportunist intervention by the Soviet Union in the latter stages of Poland's rape by Germany was to be expected following the Ribbentrop-Molotov Pact of August 1939. The Winter War between Finland and the USSR, which broke out on 30 November that year, was the outcome of the Soviet Union's failure to steamroll Finland into giving her the use of land and bases to safeguard her approaches to Leningrad through the Gulf of Finland in the event of an attack by Germany.

The conflict, which lasted for 14 weeks, was fought largely on the shores of the huge Lake Ladoga and on the vital Karelian Isthmus in the south. The Finns, conscious of the hazards implicit in resistance to Soviet demands, had built a formidable line of defence, the Mannerheim Line, across the

Karelian Isthmus, this neck of land constituting the direct line of approach to Viipuri and the capital itself, Helsinki. In the air the Finns possessed a small but well-trained air force of some 145 aircraft, of which 114 were operational when war broke out. These comprised three squadrons of Fokker C.X reconnaissance biplanes and two squadrons of Bristol Blenheim Mk Is which constituted the bombing force. Two fighter squadrons were equipped with Fokker D.XXIs, although one squadron still had a flight of aged Bristol Bulldogs. Obsolete Blackburn Ripons and Junkers K.43s were employed for coastal duties.

SOVIET FORCES

Against Finland was ranged a total of 696 Soviet aircraft in support of ground forces, plus some 20 aircraft operating from Estonian bases. Main

equipment consisted of Tupolev SB-2 and Ilyushin DB-3 medium bombers, Tupolev TB-3 heavy bombers and about 230 Polikarpov I-15bis biplane fighters, deployed along virtually the length of frontier from north to south.

Air attacks against targets in

southern Finland by Estonia-based bombers on the first day found the defences unprepared but when repeated on the following day, met a spirited defence by the D.XXIs, whose pilots destroyed 10 of the raiders; a Bulldog was lost and a D.XXI was shot down by Finnish

Fighters in winter

With a strong family resemblance to the earlier I-15 biplanes, the I-16 flew in prototype form in December 1933. Its fuselage, of monocoque construction, was skinned with plywood. The

Gladiator represented the pinnacle of more conventional biplane design of the 1930s. Although it featured such advances as an enclosed cockpit, it was soon outclassed by the new monoplanes.

Gloster Gladiator
Halfway through the battle, help arrived from Britain in the shape of Bristol Blenheim Mk IVs, Gloster Gauntlets and Gloster Gladiators. One of the latter is illustrated, equipped with skis for operation from snow during the winter conditions and appropriately camouflaged.

Polikarpov I-16
Polikarpov fighters equipped all the fighter regiments facing Finland. Most were I-15s, but some I-16 monoplanes were employed. In winter camouflage, this aircraft served with the 4 IAP in the Lake Ladoga region.

Opposing bombers

Eleven 'long-nosed', Mercury XV-powered Blenheim Mk IVs were made available from Britain in late-1939, along with a number of Gauntlet and Gladiator fighters. Tupolev's SB-2 was produced in large numbers and was to remain operational throughout World War II, armed with four machine-guns and able to carry up to 600 kg (1,323 lb) of bombs. The first Finnish kill of the Winter War was an SB-2.

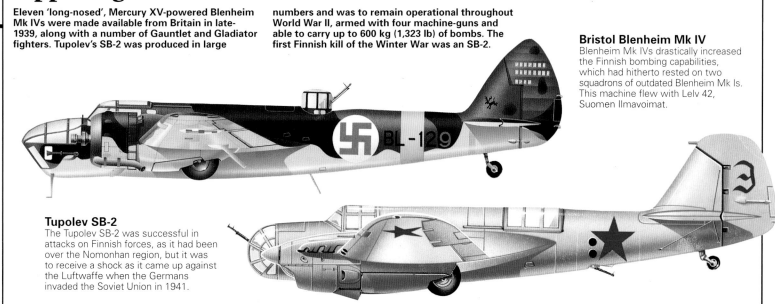

Bristol Blenheim Mk IV
Blenheim Mk IVs drastically increased the Finnish bombing capabilities, which had hitherto rested on two squadrons of outdated Blenheim Mk Is. This machine flew with Lelv 42, Suomen Ilmavoimat.

Tupolev SB-2
The Tupolev SB-2 was successful in attacks on Finnish forces, as it had been over the Nomonhan region, but it was to receive a shock as it came up against the Luftwaffe when the Germans invaded the Soviet Union in 1941.

ground defences in error. Atrocious weather now set in, preventing any further air action for three weeks, a period spent by both sides in building up their strength. On the ground the Finnish army, better-equipped to fight in the fierce snowstorms, held the Soviet attacks almost everywhere, small infiltrating forces inflicting enormous losses on Soviet convoys moving up to the Karelian Front. In the Soviet air force, Polikarpov I-16 monoplane fighters started arriving at the front, and early in the New Year the total number of Soviet aircraft in the Finnish theatre grew to around 1,500.

By the end of 1939 the Finnish air force had been credited with destroying more than 50 enemy aircraft, almost all falling to the D.XXIs, but also two or three to the ancient Bulldogs. On 6 January, as the Finns counter-attacked fiercely in Karelia and to the north of Lake Ladoga, eight DB-3s raided the Utti area; all were shot down by D.XXIs, six of them by one pilot.

It was at this point in the war that help arrived from Finland's Allies. Eleven Blenheim Mk IV bombers. 24 Gloster Gauntlets and 30 Gloster Gladiators were sent from the UK; 30 Morane-Saulnier MS.406 fighters arrived from France and, from Sweden, a volunteer force of four Hawker Harts and a dozen Gladiators arrived to fight in the north. Some Italian Fiat G.50s had also arrived in December.

FACING DEFEAT

As the Finnish counter-attack stabilised the front line, the Soviets stepped up the air attacks to cover a big build-up on the ground. On 17 January D.XXIs destroyed nine SB-2s, on 19 January five and on 20 January 13. Despite these significant successes, there were signs that the Soviets were beginning to avoid combat with the Finnish fighters, preferring to attack the bombers; in three weeks during January about half the Blenheims were lost.

In the first week of February the Soviet army launched a massive and ultimately decisive offensive towards Viipuri. As the Finnish fighters, now including Gladiators and G.50s, which first entered combat service on 2 and 26 February respectively fought desperately to prevent the large Soviet bomber formations from interfering in the ground battle, air combat became perceptibly less one-sided than hitherto. There were still

outstanding successes for the Finnish pilots, but their losses were mounting rapidly as when on 29 February, a large formation of I-16s attacked one of the Gladiator bases, destroying five Gladiators and a D.XXI while they were taking off.

Despite defending Viipuri successfully right up to the end, the Finns recognised the war situation as hopeless. By the end of the first week in March the strength of the opposing Soviet air force was estimated at 2,000 aircraft, whereas that of the Finns was dwindling rapidly. Some 44 Brewster Buffalo fighters were on their way from the United States, but arrived too late. On 13 March the Finns agreed to an armistice, being forced to cede a large part of Karelia and other tracts in the north to the Soviet Union. It was perhaps strange, however, that Finland was permitted to retain her air force in which the tardy Buffaloes were to form an important element.

Below: The Polikarpov I-15bis (or I-152) biplane was a later version of the I-15 with a conventional strut-braced upper wing centre-section, to remedy Soviet air force complaints of poor pilot visibility. Power was provided by a 559-kW (750-hp) M-25V radial engine.

Above: Lt Jorma Sarvanto of the Finnish air force in his Fokker D XXI. He became the first fighter airman to shoot down six enemy aircraft during a single combat in World War II when he attacked a force of seven DB-3 bombers on 6 January 1940.

Right: The Ilyushin DB-3F was widely used on the Finnish front by the Soviets. It featured a lengthened glazed nose, with a machine-gun at the front. This captured example force-landed behind Finnish lines.

The Scandinavian Conquest

APRIL 1940

Motivated as much by concern for the continuing supply of Swedish iron ore along the Norwegian coast to the furnaces of the Ruhr as for the security of his left flank in his planned attack on the Soviet Union, Hitler decided to eliminate Norway as a potential enemy foothold in the north. Because of the long distances involved, the Junkers Ju 87 dive-bomber was scarcely to be used, ground support being provided by some 70 Messerschmitt Bf 110C heavy fighters and only 40 Ju 87Rs. A bomber force of 290 Heinkel He 111Hs and Junkers Ju 88As possessed the range to reach central

Norway, and to the extreme north once Norwegian bases had been captured. In the likely absence of serious fighter opposition, no more than a single Gruppe (30 aircraft) of Bf 109Es was deployed.

By far the largest element of the air arm was to comprise about 500 Junkers Ju 52/3m transports, and these aircraft were to be employed to deliver waves of assault forces during the first 10 days of the campaign.

NORWAY INVADED

The UK for her part had been planning an occupation of northern Norway with the very object of denying German use of the port of Narvik and when, on 9 April, the German blow fell on Denmark and southern Norway, the Royal Navy was already at sea and an RAF

squadron of Gloster Gladiators (No. 263) in the process of preparation for service in Scandinavia.

RAF aircraft were also already active in the German Bight as German naval forces were approaching the Norwegian coast but, as no troop transports were sighted, the sailing of British convoys was delayed. Such was the extent to which the Germans were able to conceal their preparations that Denmark was effectively over-run in a single day, paratroops being dropped on the airfields of Aalborg-Ost and Aalborg-West, followed by the arrival of further airborne infantry brought in by the swarms of Ju 52/3m transports. Denmark's handful of Gloster Gauntlets, Hawker Nimrods and Fokker D.XXIs had no chance to oppose

Above: German Fallschirmjäger (paratroopers) come down in Norway. This campaign marked the first use of such troops, whose shock value proved to be high, but at the cost of significant casualties.

the lightning attack.

Meanwhile, as German warships steamed up Oslo Fjord and seaborne landings were carried out along the south Norwegian coast, the Bf 110s strafed the airfields of Oslo-Förnebu and Stavanger-Sola, easily disposing of the small number of Norwegian Gladiators which rose in defence. The following day the airfield at Trondheim-Vaernes fell and with the constant arrival of men, guns, fuel and ammunition, brought in by the transport aircraft, it seemed that the whole of Norway would be quickly

Left: One of a small number of sturdy Heinkel He 115 floatplanes flown by the Royal Norwegian Air Force. Together with three others, it made bombing attacks on the invading German forces, before being flown to Scotland.

Obsolete fighters

The Danish Hawker Nimrod Mk II stood little chance against the invader's modern fighters. It had a top speed of just 315 km/h (196 mph) and was armed with two Vickers Mk III machine-guns.

Similarly the Norwegian Gladiator Mk IIs were little better with four Colt 7.7-mm (0.303-in) machine-guns and a top speed of 414 km/h (257 mph). All 12 aircraft were lost in the defence of Oslo.

Hawker Nimrod Mk II
This Nimrod, designated L.B.V. by the Danish Naval Air Service, was operated by 2 Luftflotille. Two aircraft were originally supplied by Hawker and a further 10 built under licence by the Orlogsvaerftet. At the time of the German invasion they had been due for replacement by Italian Macchi C.200s.

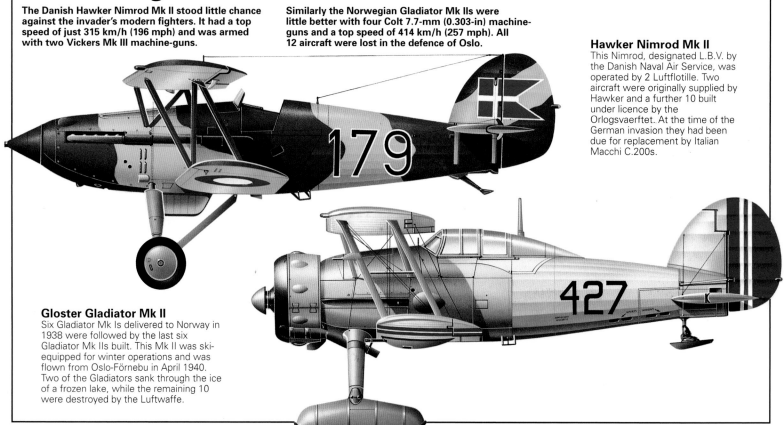

Gloster Gladiator Mk II
Six Gladiator Mk Is delivered to Norway in 1938 were followed by the last six Gladiator Mk IIs built. This Mk II was ski-equipped for winter operations and was flown from Oslo-Förnebu in April 1940. Two of the Gladiators sank through the ice of a frozen lake, while the remaining 10 were destroyed by the Luftwaffe.

Luftwaffe supreme

The latest Messerschmitt Bf 109E-3s had two MG 17s in the nose and two in the wings, plus an MG FF/M firing through the propeller shaft, ensuring the Luftwaffe's air supremacy over Scandinavia.

Although soon replaced by the superior three-engined Do 24, the Dornier Do 18 served well in the air-sea rescue role, proving particularly useful during the invasion of Denmark and Norway.

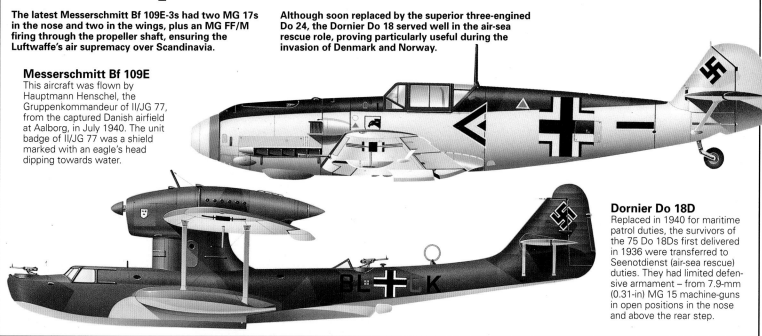

Messerschmitt Bf 109E
This aircraft was flown by Hauptmann Henschel, the Gruppenkommandeur of II/JG 77, from the captured Danish airfield at Aalborg, in July 1940. The unit badge of II/JG 77 was a shield marked with an eagle's head dipping towards water.

Dornier Do 18D
Replaced in 1940 for maritime patrol duties, the survivors of the 75 Do 18Ds first delivered in 1936 were transferred to Seenotdienst (air-sea rescue) duties. They had limited defensive armament – from 7.9-mm (0.31-in) MG 15 machine-guns in open positions in the nose and above the rear step.

Left: The view through the glazed nose of a Heinkel He 111 sweeping in towards a small Norwegian port. Operating against minimal fighter opposition, the German Kampfgruppen provided ground forces with essential tactical support as the invasion proceeded.

over-run within the next few days.

After the initial delay, however, British forces were quickly on the scene. A German advance force which had sailed to Narvik in the far north was isolated by the destruction of its supporting naval force.

Fleet Air Arm Blackburn Skuas of No. 803 Squadron dive-bombed and sank the *Königsberg* at Bergen, and the similar *Karlsruhe* was torpedoed by a British submarine. British land forces were put ashore at Narvik on 15 April, at Namsos on 16 April and at Andalsnes on 18 April. At once the Luftwaffe retaliated with its Ju 87s, bombing the ports so heavily as to render them virtually unuseable.

Five days later 18 RAF Gladiators of No. 263 Squadron landed on the frozen Lake Lesjaskog near Andalsnes, having flown off the carrier HMS *Glorious*. The Luftwaffe was again ready for them and, as a result of the extreme cold, difficulty was experienced in getting the Gladiators into the air, most of them being destroyed on the ice in raids which started the next day. Although about half a dozen raiders were claimed shot down in 36 hours, the frozen lake was unuseable by 25 April. The surviving aircraft were destroyed where they stood, and the wrecked ports of Andalsnes and Namsos were evacuated on 30 April and 2 May respectively. The members of No. 263 Squadron returned to the UK to re-equip with a fresh complement of Gladiators.

COUNTER ATTACK
The British now decided to concentrate an attack on the port of Narvik, despite the rapid and relatively simple build up of German forces in the south. No. 263 Squadron with its new Gladiators embarked on HMS *Furious*, this time accompanied by No. 46 Squadron with Hawker Hurricanes, arriving at Bödo and Bardufoss on 26 May. An assault by British, Norwegian, French and Polish forces on 28 May succeeded in eliminating the German forces at Narvik, but such were the distances involved that it became all too obvious that to sustain what could be little more than an isolated garrison was out of the question. German air attacks were increasing daily, despite the RAF pilots' success in downing some 20 of the enemy raiders. In an effort to bring their aircraft home, the pilots volunteered to land aboard HMS *Glorious* for passage home but within 48 hours the ship, the aircraft and all but two of the pilots were at the bottom of the ocean, sent there by salvoes from the German warships *Scharnhorst* and *Gneisenau*.

On 7 June King Haakon of Norway left his shores aboard HMS *Devonshire* and on the following day Allied forces were extricated from Narvik. The campaign was over. Once more the overwhelming superiority of the Luftwaffe had contributed a vital weapon, this time the use of massive delivery of airborne infantry proving decisive. It was moreover but a dress rehearsal for worse to come.

Left: The German Fallschirmjäger, here preparing to board a Junkers Ju 52/3m three-engined transport aircraft, were fully air-mobile Luftwaffe paratroops. They could be delivered into the battlefield by parachute, glider or tactical transport aircraft.

Right: A formation of Luftwaffe Junkers Ju 88A-4s heading for a bombing raid over northern Norway in April 1940. This, the first longer wing-span version, had more powerful Jumo 211J engines and greater range than earlier versions of the bomber.

Blitzkrieg in the West

10 May 1940 – 22 June 1940

Following a massive and not wholly unobserved build-up of land and air forces along her frontiers with France and the neutral Low Countries, Germany on 10 May 1940 launched an overwhelming offensive westwards. Recognising the futility of a frontal assault on the established Maginot Line, Hitler chose to attack through the Netherlands and Belgium, and strike directly at the Channel ports, thereby isolating the British army in the north, before striking south at Paris, so outflanking the French army concentrated on the border facing Germany.

Supporting the attack by some 75 divisions were Luftflotten II and III, comprising 4,000 front-line aircraft, of which more than 400 were Junkers Ju 52/3m transports, recently redeployed from the Norwegian campaign, as well as the full panoply of Blitzkrieg, the Ju 87s, Ju 88s, Dornier Do 17s, Heinkel He 111s, Messerschmitt Bf 109s and Bf 110s. Opposing this array of might were some 130 Dutch, 150 Belgian, 1,600 French and 450 British aircraft based in northern France; however, not only were the Allied airmen outnumbered by odds of about two to one, but two-thirds of their aircraft were at best obsolescent.

DUTCH COLLAPSE

Moreover, the element of surprise enabled the Luftwaffe to concentrate its strength where needed, so that within a matter of four days, during which Rotterdam suffered a catastrophic raid by Heinkel He 111s, the Netherlands had

Above: Although they only carried a small bombload, these Dornier Do 17Zs of the Kampfgruppen performed with credit when the German Blitzkrieg was launched in May 1940. However, they were easy prey when intercepted by Spitfires.

Right: A German fallschirmjäger (paratrooper) leaving a Junkers Ju 52/3m three-engined transport at low-level, during the invasion of the Low Countries. He is using a static line for quick parachute deployment. Some 400 of these aircraft were transferred to the region after the Scandinavian conquest.

Above: Crew walking out to a Fairey Battle of No. 218 Squadron, somewhere in France, where it was part of the Advanced Air Striking Force. This unit, along with most of the RAF's Battle squadrons, was wiped out within a few days of the start of the German Blitzkrieg at the beginning of May 1940.

Right: On 10 May 1940, nine Fokker D.XXIs of the Dutch air force, including '241' seen here, took part in a battle with a similar number of Messerschmitt Bf 109s. '241' was the only Dutch aircraft lost, the German formation losing half their number. This was an unrepresentative victory, however, as the Bf 109 was a superior machine.

Left: Invasion of the Netherlands on 10 May 1940. German paratroops being dropped from a trio of Junkers Ju 52/3ms during the opening offensive. Operation 'Fall Gelb' was the swift assertion of German air superiority, the support of ground forces and the launch of a series of parachute operations.

Below: An aerodynamically refined and structurally robust fighter, this French air force Dewoitine D.520 could not match the Luftwaffe's Messerschmitt 109s for level speed, but had a marked edge in manoeuvrability.

Below: The Belgian air force acquired 22 Gloster Gladiators, five of which are seen here on delivery. The Belgian Aéronautique Militaire could muster just 15 surviving Gladiators to fight against the invading German forces in May 1940. They were quickly overwhelmed.

capitulated. Belgium, now the scene of powerful German armoured thrusts, quickly lost the key defence positions vital to its survival, the great Fort Eben-Emael falling to a dawn attack by glider-borne troops on the first day. Key crossing points on the Albert Canal were captured intact by the Germans and, despite frantic efforts by RAF Fairey Battle and Bristol Blenheim bombers to destroy them, this enabled the German columns to continue their swift advance, reaching Abbeville long before the end of the month.

Within 10 days the Belgian air force had virtually ceased to exist, while losses among the RAF Battle squadrons had reached about 70 per cent. In the RAF only the Hawker Hurricane succeeded in matching the modern German aircraft, and it was estimated that around 200 of the enemy fell to their guns in the first fortnight.

BELGIUM FALLS

In the French Armée de l'Air the Dewoitine D.520 fighter was of roughly equal quality to the British Hurricane, but only some 150 of

Lowly defenders

The Dutch air force had a total of just 132 aircraft, including 28 Fokker D.XXI and 23 Fokker G.1a fighters to face more than 1,000 Luftwaffe fighters. Likewise the Belgian air force only had a handful of fighters and light bombers, including Hurricanes, Gladiators and Fairey Battles. The strongest air force was the French Armée de l'Air, with 278 MS. 406s, 98 Curtiss Hawks and 36 Dewoitine D.520s.

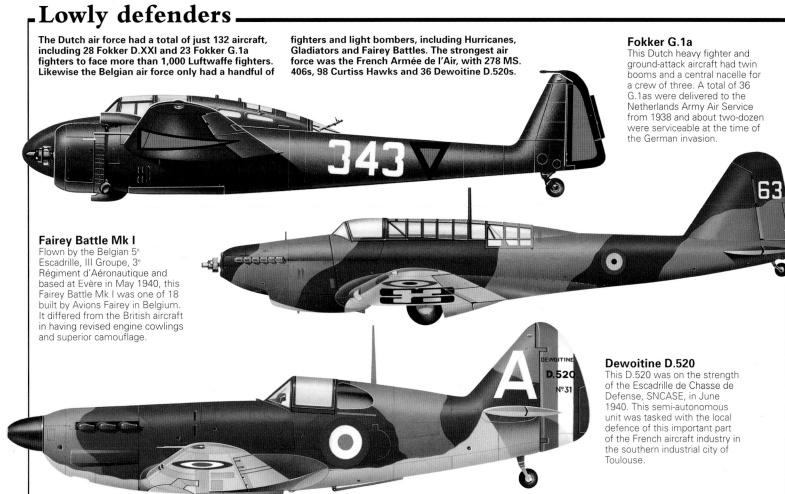

Fokker G.1a
This Dutch heavy fighter and ground-attack aircraft had twin booms and a central nacelle for a crew of three. A total of 36 G.1as were delivered to the Netherlands Army Air Service from 1938 and about two-dozen were serviceable at the time of the German invasion.

Fairey Battle Mk I
Flown by the Belgian 5ᵉ Escadrille, III Groupe, 3ᵉ Régiment d'Aéronautique and based at Evère in May 1940, this Fairey Battle Mk I was one of 18 built by Avions Fairey in Belgium. It differed from the British aircraft in having revised engine cowlings and superior camouflage.

Dewoitine D.520
This D.520 was on the strength of the Escadrille de Chasse de Defense, SNCASE, in June 1940. This semi-autonomous unit was tasked with the local defence of this important part of the French aircraft industry in the southern industrial city of Toulouse.

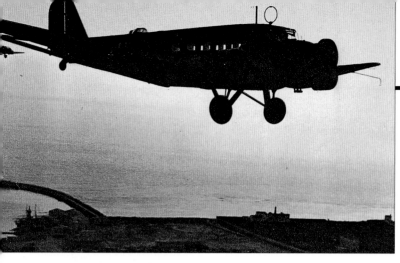

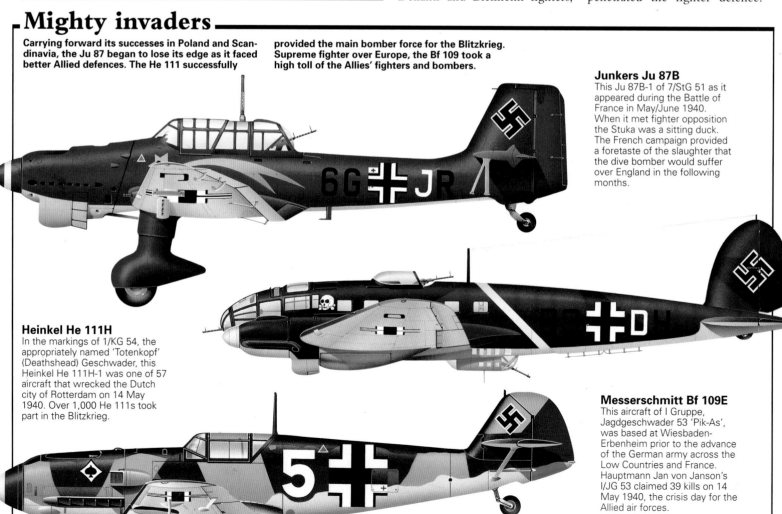

Above: The Junkers Ju 52/3m was the workhorse of the Blitzkrieg, dropping paratroops in Norway, Greece and the Low Countries, towing gliders and keeping the armies re-supplied as they scythed their way through Europe.

Below: Spitfires were in action day after day over the Dunkirk beaches, trying to establish air superiority and so enable the troops to escape across the Channel. This Spitfire Mk I was shot down on 6 June 1940.

these aircraft were available during the Battle of France. However, until the RAF's Supermarine Spitfire was committed to battle in the later stages, the German Bf 109 was the supreme fighter in French skies and this, together with highly effective mobile flak which accompanied the advancing German columns, took tremendous toll of British and French light bombers.

The latter, when not being clawed out of the smoke-filled skies over the land battle, were pulverized on their bases.

By 26 May the Belgian front had collapsed and almost 400,000 British and French soldiers were falling back on the port of Dunkirk. At this point Hermann Goering prevailed on Hitler to allow his air force to annihilate the Allied armies trapped with their backs to the sea. As orders were issued in the UK to evacuate these forces by sailing an armada of small vessels to Dunkirk, Spitfires, Hurricanes, Boulton Paul Defiants and Blenheim fighters,

Above: A formation of Bristol Blenheim Mk IVs of No. 139 Squadron over France in 1940. This unit deployed in September 1939 and flying from Plivot lost the bulk of its aircraft attacking German columns as the invasion advanced westward towards the Channel ports.

hitherto reserved for defence of the British Isles, were ordered to protect the great evacuation. Numerous heavy attacks by German He 111s, Ju 87s, Ju 88s and Do 17s were launched against the port and beaches during the following week, some of which inevitably penetrated the fighter defence.

Mighty invaders

Carrying forward its successes in Poland and Scandinavia, the Ju 87 began to lose its edge as it faced better Allied defences. The He 111 successfully provided the main bomber force for the Blitzkrieg. Supreme fighter over Europe, the Bf 109 took a high toll of the Allies' fighters and bombers.

Junkers Ju 87B
This Ju 87B-1 of 7/StG 51 as it appeared during the Battle of France in May/June 1940. When it met fighter opposition the Stuka was a sitting duck. The French campaign provided a foretaste of the slaughter that the dive bomber would suffer over England in the following months.

Heinkel He 111H
In the markings of 1/KG 54, the appropriately named 'Totenkopf' (Deathshead) Geschwader, this Heinkel He 111H-1 was one of 57 aircraft that wrecked the Dutch city of Rotterdam on 14 May 1940. Over 1,000 He 111s took part in the Blitzkrieg.

Messerschmitt Bf 109E
This aircraft of I Gruppe, Jagdgeschwader 53 'Pik-As', was based at Wiesbaden-Erbenheim prior to the advance of the German army across the Low Countries and France. Hauptmann Jan von Janson's I/JG 53 claimed 39 kills on 14 May 1940, the crisis day for the Allied air forces.

Five Fairey Battles of No. 12 (Bomber) Squadron attempted to destroy the road bridges over the Albert Canal that had been taken intact by the Germans and over which the invading columns were passing. All the Battles were lost and only one of the bridges hit.

Casualties were very high on both sides, but by 3 June some 336,000 men of the British and French armies, though with scarcely any of their equipment, had been evacuated to safety.

RETREAT

As the German army closed swiftly on the Channel ports, which fell in rapid succession despite all possible support by RAF aircraft based in England, the remaining elements of the British air forces that had been deployed across the Channel fell back westwards through France, giving what cover they could to the ragged remains of the BEF and French force until eventually evacuated from Cherbourg, Brest, St Nazaire and other ports. The German army now swung south towards Paris, the first massive air raids on the capital being launched on 3 June; French fighter pilots claimed the destruction of 26 aircraft in the first attack, but lost almost as heavily. Despite great

gallantry by the men of the Armée de l'Air, however, German air superiority was never threatened, and the final land assault opened on 5 June. On 14 June Paris fell, and eight days later an armistice was signed.

The campaign that had lasted just six weeks had cost the Luftwaffe the loss of 1,254 aircraft, but most of those aircrew who survived being shot down were now released by the French to return to their units. Much of the surviving French air force escaped to the unoccupied zone in France under a

Above: A formation of six Hurricanes from No. 73 Squadron, that flew with No. 1 Squadron in the AASF over France. As their outline resembled the French Dewoitine D.520 and they were operating with the Armée de l'Air, the Hurricanes were painted with distinctive rudder stripes.

Left: Two Junkers Ju 87B-2 dive bombers returning to their temporary bases in France after a successful attack. The VIII Kliegerkorps, the main tactical strike force, had some 380 Stukas for the Low Countries' Blitzkrieg.

puppet government in Vichy, or to French territory in North Africa; some pilots made their way to the UK, where they joined the RAF.

The RAF itself had lost a total of 944 aircraft, of which 386 were Hurricanes and 67 Spitfires, fighters whose loss was to be sorely felt in the summer months to come. More important were the many professional pilots lost, whose peacetime training could never be matched by that of the men now rapidly filling the depleted ranks of RAF Fighter Command.

Left: Messerschmitt Bf 110C-2 'Zerstörer' over Dunkirk in June 1940. The heavy, twin-engined fighter met its match when it came up against RAF Hurricanes and Spitfires by day. It later had a much more distinguished career as a night fighter.

Battle of Britain: The Assault

JULY – OCTOBER 1940

BRITAIN ON ITS KNEES
A pair of Junkers Ju 88A-5s; the first of the improved version with increased wingspan. These aircraft shown approaching the English coast are from I/KG 54. In 1940 Ju 88s made up a large proportion of the 2,800 aircraft that bombarded Britain.

Following the invasion of Norway and the fall of France and the Low Countries in May and June 1940, and as the RAF set about dressing its wounds, the Luftwaffe moved up to bases lining the coasts facing the British Isles. For the all-out air attack, intended to eliminate RAF Fighter Command in preparation for an invasion of the islands, the Luftwaffe disposed its forces in three air fleets, Luftflotte III based in north-west France, Luftflotte II in north-east France and the Low Countries, and Luftflotte V in Norway and Denmark.

By early July the German air forces facing the UK fielded about 2,800 aircraft comprising 1,300 Heinkel He 111, Junkers Ju 88 and Dornier Do 17 bombers, 280 Junkers Ju 87 dive-bombers, 790 Messerschmitt Bf 109 single-seat fighters, 260 Messerschmitt Bf 110 and Junkers Ju 88C heavy fighters and 170 reconnaissance aircraft of various types, of these totals roughly half were immediately combat-ready. Facing them, RAF Fighter Command possessed 640 fighters, the great majority of them Hawker Hurricanes and Supermarine Spitfires.

THE BATTLE BEGINS

The daylight Battle of Britain opened at the beginning of July with relatively scattered raids by small formations of German bombers against coastal targets in southern England and against

Above: A Messerschmitt Bf 110C-4 operated by Zerstörergeschwader 52, provides a fighter escort for Heinkel and Dornier bombers on their raids over Britain. Bf 110s received a severe mauling by the RAF during the Battle of Britain.

Below: Palls of smoke fill the sky over London, silhouetting Tower Bridge and the Tower of London, after massive Luftwaffe bombing raids on the East London docks area on 7 September 1940. This was a month of heavy German losses.

"...denn wir fahren gegen Engeland!"

Heute wollen wir ein liedlein singen;
trinken wollen wir den kühlen Wein
und die Gläser sollen dazu klingen,
denn es muß, es muß geschieden sein.

Kommt! die Kunde, daß ich bin gefallen,
daß ich schlafe in der Meeresflut;
Weine nicht um mich, mein Schatz, und denk:
für das Vaterland, da floß sein Blut.

Unser Flagge, und die wehet auf dem Maste.
Sie verkündet unsres Reiches Macht;
Denn wir wollen es nicht länger leiden,
daß der Englischmann darüber lacht.

Gib mir deine Hand, deine weiße Hand,
leb wohl, mein Schatz,
Weine nicht um mich, mein Schatz, leb wohl, mein Schatz, leb wohl.
Leb wohl, denn wir fahren, denn wir fahren,
denn wir fahren gegen Engeland Engeland!
H. LÖNS

AUS D SAMMLG., DER KL. ROSENGARTEN, VERL. v. EUGEN DIEDERICHS, JENA.

Above: During the early days of the Battle of Britain German morale was extremely high due to their successful conquest of France. This postcard depicts three Ju 87 Stuka bombers accompanied by a comical song predicting an easy conquest of the British Isles. Three months later the mood of the Luftwaffe had dramatically changed.

Right: A flight of Luftwaffe Messerschmitt Bf 109Es flying along the French coast early in 1940. With their superior performance and more experienced pilots, the 16 Gruppen of Bf 109s wreaked havoc on the RAF's Spitfires and Hurricanes during the long summer of 1940.

shipping in the English Channel, the initial object being to test the defences and to discover the extent to which they relied upon the coastal radar chain, known to have existed since before the war. As the month wore on the anti-shipping attacks increased in ferocity, as did German losses, and it became clear that the British radar was not only highly efficient but gave substantial warning of approaching raids.

LUFTWAFFE LOSSES

German losses in July amounted to some 220 aircraft and, as the Germans finalised plans for the all-out assault, scheduled for mid-August, there followed a lull in the fighting. The first heavy raids, against shipping in the Channel, were launched on 8 August by large formations of Ju 87s escorted by Bf 110s but, as was to be confirmed during the next few days, both these aircraft were found to be extremely vulnerable in the face of attacks by the Hurricanes and Spitfires, and losses were exceptionally heavy. Further shipping attacks were carried out on 11 August, but now the raiders were more adequately protected by Bf 109 single-seaters. This phase continued until 18 August, particularly severe fighting taking place on 12, 13, 15, 16 and 18 August. As a result of heavy losses suffered, the Ju 87 was

Left: A Luftwaffe Messerschmitt Bf 109E after crash landing with battle damage in a cornfield at Berwick near Eastbourne. It is painted in the standard 1940 colour scheme, with only the upper surfaces of its wings and fuselage camouflaged.

Below: The remains of a Junkers Ju 88A-1 of KG 30, the first Luftwaffe unit to operate the bomber, after it had been shot down while on a raid over the Home Counties in 1940.

largely withdrawn from the battle after 18 August.

By now raids were penetrating further inland, and on 15 August the aircraft of Luftflotte V attempted to attack targets in northern England,

but suffered so badly that such raids were not repeated during the Battle.

A reappraisal of the tactics being employed led to a marked shift during the next phase of the attack which began at the end of August.

Fighters of the Reich

The Messerschmitt Bf 109E proved generally superior to the Hurricane and the Spitfire except in the critical area of turn performance. The potentially fatal weakness of the 'Emil' was its fuel capacity.

While the Messerschmitt Bf 110Cs were virtually immune to the Hurricanes and Spitfire Mk Is above 6700 m (21,980 ft), they were cut to pieces at medium-level, unable to out-turn the RAF's fighters.

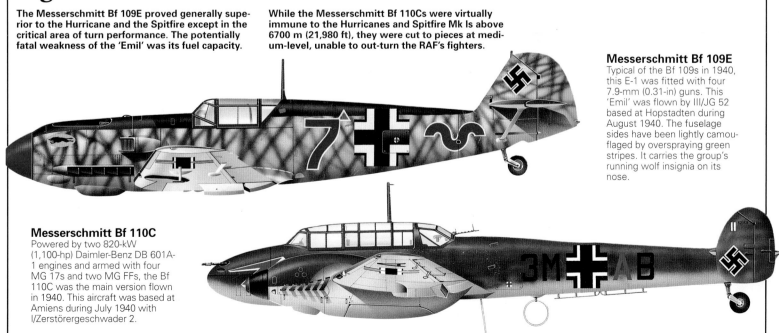

Messerschmitt Bf 109E
Typical of the Bf 109s in 1940, this E-1 was fitted with four 7.9-mm (0.31-in) guns. This 'Emil' was flown by III/JG 52 based at Hopstadten during August 1940. The fuselage sides have been lightly camouflaged by overspraying green stripes. It carries the group's running wolf insignia on its nose.

Messerschmitt Bf 110C
Powered by two 820-kW (1,100-hp) Daimler-Benz DB 601A-1 engines and armed with four MG 17s and two MG FFs, the Bf 110C was the main version flown in 1940. This aircraft was based at Amiens during July 1940 with I/Zerstörergeschwader 2.

Following complaints by the Bf 109 pilots that they were badly handicapped when employed in the bomber-escort role, the Jagdgeschwader were allowed to resume the 'free chase' tactics over southern England, frequently catching the RAF fighters either during take-off or landing, or as they returned short of fuel and ammunition after combat.

This was unquestionably the most successful phase from the Luftwaffe's viewpoint and would have quickly brought the defences to their knees had the Germans persisted. However, exasperated at continuing losses, Göering ordered the attack to switch from the RAF to the British civilian population with a sudden massive attack on East London in the late afternoon of 7 September.

Below: A camera gun photograph from a Bf 109E showing an RAF Hurricane Mk I on fire after a dog-fight. The Luftwaffe fighter was particularly successful against the slower, British fighters flown by less experienced pilots in 1940.

SCREAM OF THE STUKA
A Stuka releases its load of bombs – a single 250-kg (551-lb) SC250 and four smaller 50-kg (110-lb) SC50s during its vertical dive. Entry into the dive and the 6g pullout were fully automatic, leaving the pilot with the task of steering the aircraft to put his bombsight reticule over the target.

This marked the turning point of the whole battle, and the easing of pressure on the fighters allowed them a much-needed respite. In the course of further heavy daylight attacks on London, particularly on 15 September and on south-east England at the end of the month, the Germans took a heavy beating; the British fighter pilots no longer

Below: Armourers with a 500-kg (1,102-lb) SC500 bomb that was carried externally on the Heinkel He 111H is shown here. These bombs began to feature prominently during the latter part of the Luftwaffe's assault on Britain.

had to fight over their airfields and could concentrate on the great armadas making their way ponderously towards some unfortunate town or city.

The very heavy losses of September constituted the Luftwaffe's first major setback of the war; survival of the British fighter defences led to postponement of the invasion (and its eventual abandonment), and the final phase, which occupied most of October,

consisted of no more than nuisance raids by high-flying aircraft (usually Bf 109s) carrying single bombs, which were dropped with little hope of causing significant damage.

The daylight Battle of Britain cost the Luftwaffe a total of 2,020

Right: The legendary Oberstleutnant Adolf Galland flying his Messerschmitt Bf 109E-3 with Jagdgeschwader 26 in France during the autumn of 1940. His personal 'Mickey Mouse' emblem is carried below the cockpit and the unit Schlageter badge behind the engine's supercharger intake.

aircraft destroyed, and more than 200 aircrew killed or missing. As with the RAF's losses in France, a high proportion of these men were the most experienced in the German air force and had been responsible for evolving and proving the battle tactics employed. Nevertheless, whereas the British could regard the final outcome of the Battle of Britain as a resounding victory, it was by no means the end of the air assault, which now continued (with very different results) under cover of darkness.

Above: A mass formation of Heinkel He 111Hs forms up over France before climbing to cross the English Channel and another heavy raid, in July 1940. The He 111H, with its 435 km/h (270 mph) top speed, proved a difficult aircraft for the RAF to shoot down, compared with the Dornier Do 17.

Right: A high-flying Heinkel He 111H-2 photographed as it headed across London on 7 September, to drop its eight 250-kg (551-lb) bombs onto the Surrey and West India Docks. The better-armed H-2 version carried its weapons in the fuselage either side of a central gangway.

Bombers over Britain

The Junkers Ju 87 dive-bomber's almost legendary reputation from the first year of the war was shattered during the Battle of Britain, with severe losses. The Luftwaffe's most successful bomber, the Heinkel He 111H, was relatively fast and often survived heavy battle damage. The Dornier Do 17's defensive armament was inadequate, but it could outrun RAF fighters in a shallow dive.

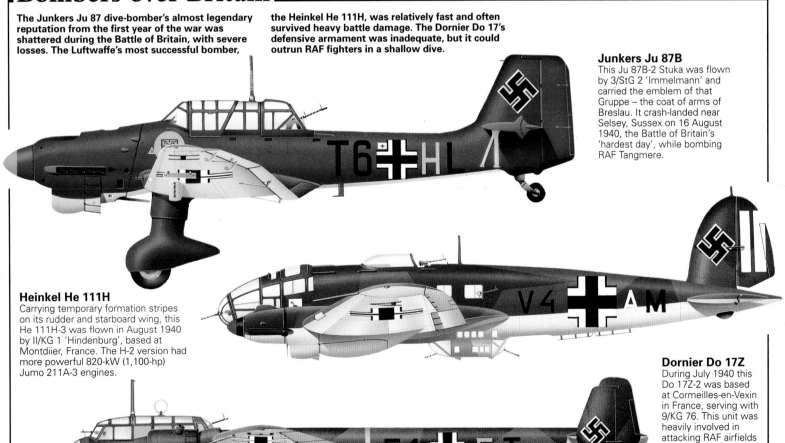

Junkers Ju 87B
This Ju 87B-2 Stuka was flown by 3/StG 2 'Immelmann' and carried the emblem of that Gruppe – the coat of arms of Breslau. It crash-landed near Selsey, Sussex on 16 August 1940, the Battle of Britain's 'hardest day', while bombing RAF Tangmere.

Heinkel He 111H
Carrying temporary formation stripes on its rudder and starboard wing, this He 111H-3 was flown in August 1940 by II/KG 1 'Hindenburg', based at Montdiier, France. The H-2 version had more powerful 820-kW (1,100-hp) Jumo 211A-3 engines.

Dornier Do 17Z
During July 1940 this Do 17Z-2 was based at Cormeilles-en-Vexin in France, serving with 9/KG 76. This unit was heavily involved in attacking RAF airfields in Kent during the Battle of Britain.

Battle of Britain: The Defence

JULY – OCTOBER 1940

A Spitfire I breaks to starboard during a head-on attack on a Messerschmitt Bf 109E. The Spitfire's superior agility made it more than a match for the Bf 109, although the more experienced Luftwaffe pilots tended to use better tactics. Many downed Spitfire pilots were able to return to the battle, bailing out over friendly territory. Britain's aircraft industry also proved better at replacing the aircraft which were lost in action.

The unexpected month-long respite after the Dunkirk evacuation allowed RAF Fighter Command time to rest and re-equip most of its weary squadrons, and to some extent broadcast among its pilots vital information regarding German fighting tactics.

At the head of Fighter Command, Air Chief Marshal Dowding divided his air defences into three groups: No. 11 in the south under Keith Park, No. 12 in the Midlands under Trafford Leigh-Mallory and No. 13 in the north under Richard Saul. A fourth group, No. 10 under Quintin Brand, would shortly be added to cover the southwest.

Dowding disposed a total of 640 fighters at the beginning of July 1940, including 347 Hawker Hurricanes, 199 Supermarine Spitfires, 69 Bristol Blenheim night-fighters and 25 Boulton Paul Defiants; slightly over half his strength was deployed in the south. The key airfields of Biggin Hill, Kenley, Croydon, Hornchurch, Manston and Tangmere constituted a defensive ring round London and the Thames estuary. To provide early warning and a degree of fighter control, the south and east coasts were covered by a network of radar stations which could detect approaching raids at a distance of about 100 miles (160 km).

RAF STRETCHED

The German attacks of July, aimed principally at shipping and coastal targets in the south, proved something of a strain on the British pilots. They were obliged to fly standing patrols over the convoys until the German tactics were recognised for what they were, and orders given

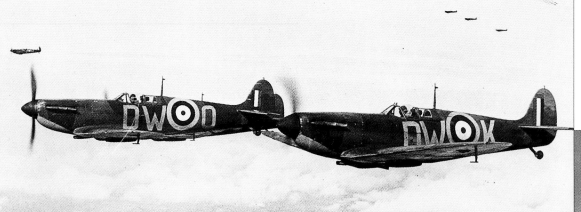

Above: Supermarine Spitfire Mk IAs of No. 610 (County of Chester) Squadron, Royal Auxiliary Air Force, on patrol over Kent in the summer of 1940. During August No. 610 played a vital role in the defence of Biggin Hill, before being withdrawn to Acklington at the end of the month for the defence of Newcastle.

Right: High above the clouds, Hurricanes of No. 1 Squadron. After fighting previously with the AASF in France, the squadron returned to the UK and re-equipped with factory-fresh Hurricane Is. During the Battle of Britain, the squadron flew from Northolt, Hawkinge, Tangmere, Manston, North Weald and Heathrow before returning to Wittering on 9 September 1940.

Above: A Spitfire I returns to base over the Kent coast during the Battle of Britain. Though it played a smaller role in the Battle of Britain compared to the less glamorous Hurricane, the Spitfire was arguably the most important Allied aircraft of WWII.

Below: Taken at Gravesend in August 1940, this group photgraph shows Hurricane pilots of No. 85 Squadron. The CO is Sqn Ldr Peter Townsend, seen leaning on a stick, necessitated by the loss of a toe during combat over Croydon.

not to engage enemy fighters unnecessarily. British losses in the July combats amounted to 77 fighters, of whose pilots roughly half survived. A particularly savage combat on 19 July had shown the two-seat Defiant to be unsuitable for day fighting, and it was temporarily withdrawn out of harm's way.

HEAVY LOSSES

The onset of the main assault on 8 August was competently countered by Park's squadrons, whose pilots

quickly spotted the weaknesses of the Junkers Ju 87 and Messer-schmitt Bf 110, and set about developing effective tactics to deal with them. The appearance of large formations of Messerschmitt Bf 109s, which were superior in most respects to the Hurricane, caused the British controllers, where possible, to order their Spitfires against the enemy fighters, while the Hurricanes fought the slower, lower-flying bombers.

The resumption of 'free chase' sorties by the Bf 109s at the end of

ACES FROM THE BATTLE OF BRITAIN

In 1940, Fighter Command had a mix of RAF regular, auxiliary and reserve pilots, borrowed Bomber and Coastal Command, test and Fleet Air Arm pilots – with British, Commonwealth and foreign nationalities, all of whom fought in the Battle of Britain. As with so many of the Few, not all could be aces; pen-portraits of six of them are illustrated below. The Battle of Britain instilled a brand of camaraderie that will forever be associated with the wearing of air force blue.

Sqn Ldr Douglas Bader

This tin-legged hero shot down 22 aircraft – a remarkable score considering that he became a POW less than a year after the Battle of Britain. A crash in a Bristol Bulldog in 1931 cost him both his legs. A key figure in No. 12 Group, Bader was perhaps the leading supporter of the theoretically superior but tactically inferior 'Big Wing' formation advocated by the commander of No.12 Group, Sir Trafford Leigh Mallory.

Sqn Ldr Peter Townsend

Peter Townsend was commanding officer of No. 85 Sqn at Martlesham and Debden during the battle. He was shot down by the gunner of Do 17 on 11 July and baled out into the sea, where he spent some time before rescued. Later wounded near Croydon, Townsend evened the score by destroying six German aircraft. He achieved further success as a night-fighter pilot. He retired from the RAF as Group Captain Peter Townsend DSO,CVO,DFC in 1956.

Sgt James Lacey

Having learned to fly in the RAFVR in 1937, at the outbreak of war 'Ginger' Lacey joined No. 501 Squadron flying Hurricanes. In the Battle of France he shot down five enemy aircraft and was awarded the Croix de Guerre. Shot down or forced to land nine times, he achieved a score of 23, most of them during the Battle, including on 13 September an He 111 which had just bombed Buckingham Palace.

Flt Lt 'Sailor' Malan

Adolph 'Sailor' Malan, a South African, was commissioned into the RAF in 1935 from the Merchant Navy. He flew with No. 74 Squadron, one of the first to receive the Spitfire in January 1939. An outstanding shot, he ordered his guns harmonised at only 250 yards, from the usual 400 yards. Appointed CO of No. 74 Sqn at the height of the Battle, his final tally probably exceeded 35 but many kills he gave to inexperienced wingmen.

Flt Lt Bob Stanford Tuck

Bob Stanford Tuck was another Battle of Britain pilot whose career was cut short over France when he was shot down in January 1942 with an accredited tally of 29 victories. Commissioned in 1935, by 1940 he was a squadron leader in command of No. 257 Squadron, flying Hurricanes. One of the Battle's best practitioners of deflection shooting, he owed much to his pre-war skills as a shot. Stanford Tuck was a superb fighter leader, and an inspiration to those he led.

Sqn Ldr 'Paddy' Finucane

Brendan Finucane (with 32 victories credited) commanded No. 452 Squadron RAAF, with Spitfires, operating from RAF Kenley and Redhill. An outstanding pilot, and leader of the Hornchurch Wing, he was forced to ditch his Spitfire on 15 July 1942 when a flak hit drained the coolant from his engine. Finucane died when he hit the water near Le Touquet.

RAF FIGHTER COMMAND GROUPS & FIGHTER STATIONS

The size, nature and disposition of Fighter Command in 1940 was entirely the result of Hugh Dowding's efforts in building it up before the war, in the face of considerable opposition, and a prevailing doctrine which placed the emphasis on offensive operations by bombers. Dowding argued the case for the importance of fighter defences, and the necessity of defending the home base. During the belated rush to expand the RAF in the late 1930s he pressed for a minimum of 45 fighter squadrons and took a close interest in the development of new aircraft, weapons and tactics, as well as in new equipment and technologies, including radar. He oversaw the formation of Fighter Command's groups and ensured that its assets were well distributed to meet all potential threats.

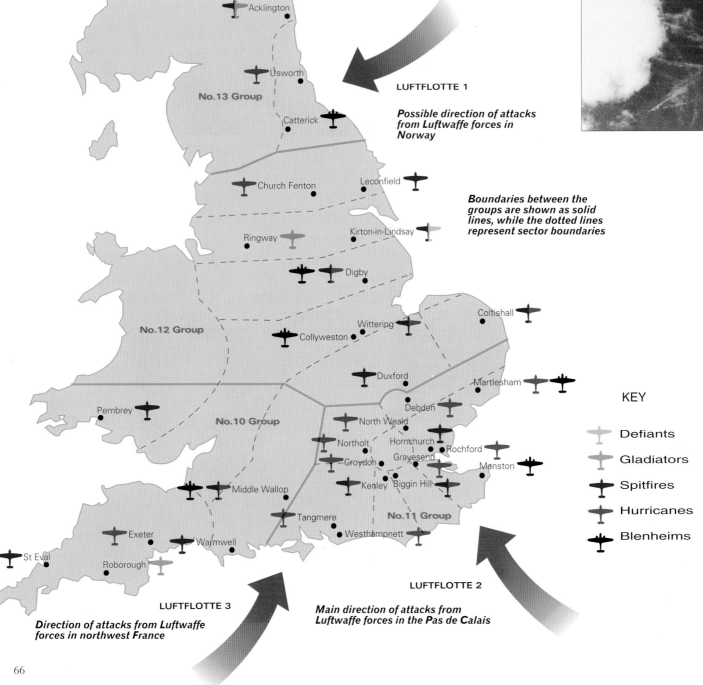

LUFTFLOTTE 1

Possible direction of attacks from Luftwaffe forces in Norway

Boundaries between the groups are shown as solid lines, while the dotted lines represent sector boundaries

LUFTFLOTTE 2

Main direction of attacks from Luftwaffe forces in the Pas de Calais

LUFTFLOTTE 3

Direction of attacks from Luftwaffe forces in northwest France

No.13 Group — Acklington, Usworth, Catterick

No.12 Group — Church Fenton, Leconfield, Ringway, Kirton-in-Lindsay, Digby, Coltishall, Wittering, Collyweston, Duxford

No.10 Group — Pembrey, Middle Wallop, Exeter, Warmwell, St Eval, Roborough

No.11 Group — Martlesham, Debden, North Weald, Hornchurch, Rochford, Northolt, Gravesend, Manston, Croydon, Kenley, Biggin Hill, Tangmere, Westhampnett

KEY

- Defiants
- Gladiators
- Spitfires
- Hurricanes
- Blenheims

Below: For Londoners and residents of Southeast England, the Battle of Britain was an unforgettable sight – a display of aerial strategy marked out in white condensation trails against the deep blue sky of the summer of 1940.

Right: With the onset of the Battle, controllers in the operations rooms at Fighter Command, groups and sectors were able to follow the progress of operations visually with the help of plotters who moved pieces representing all friendly and hostile forces.

August certainly posed a serious threat to Dowding's defences, so much so that by 5 September Fighter Command's losses were running at the rate of an equivalent of two whole squadrons every day. Moreover, there was little the RAF pilots could do to combat them.

Losses during the past four weeks had deprived many squadrons of their most experienced members, and very young men with no more than two or three months' squadron service were being promoted to command; the aircraft themselves were now showing severe wear and tear, despite frantic efforts by their manufacturers and repair organisations. Bowing to the inevitable, Dowding was forced to withdraw some of his finest squadrons to the relative quiet of the north to rest and re-equip, bringing to the south newly-formed and inexperienced squadrons, among them the first Canadian, Polish and Czech squadrons of the RAF.

NEW APPROACH

It was at this time that the differing tactics favoured by Park and Leigh-Mallory came into sharp focus, the former advocating use of single squadrons (because of the short time available in the south to assemble larger forces) and the latter favouring the committing of whole fighter wings to battle. Both men were probably justified in their own combat environments, and it must be said that, given adequate warning, Park himself tried to employ two or three squadrons simultaneously. There were, however, occasions when Leigh-Mallory's wing tactic failed to operate efficiently as

RAF Fighters

Merlin-engined fighters formed the bulk of RAF Fighter Command. Great things were expected of the Defiant, but it proved slow and cumbersome, and vulnerable to belly and head-on attacks. The

Hurricane was altogether more successful and destroyed more enemy aircraft than all the rest of the defences put together.

Defiant Mk 1
This aircraft, of No. 264 Squadron, entered service with the squadron in June 1940 and was used for the disastrous day combat role. The Germans thought the aircraft were Hurricanes and attacked from behind, but once the Defiant formation was broken the RAF aircraft – with no forward-firing guns – was easy prey. N1535 was lost in action on 24 August 1940 on a day operation.

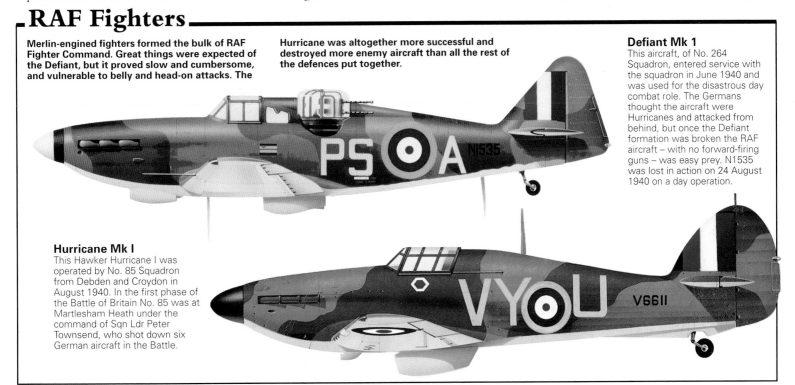

Hurricane Mk I
This Hawker Hurricane I was operated by No. 85 Squadron from Debden and Croydon in August 1940. In the first phase of the Battle of Britain No. 85 was at Martlesham Heath under the command of Sqn Ldr Peter Townsend, who shot down six German aircraft in the Battle.

Supermarine Spitfire Mk I

This Spitfire I served with No. 74 Squadron during the Battle. Among its pilots was the officer commanding, Squadron Leader 'Sailor' Malan.

Armament
The Spitfire I was armed with eight rifle-calibre 0.303-in Browning machine guns. This represented a lighter punch than was packed by the Bf 109E, whose armament included two 20-mm cannon. Therefore, the Spitfire pilot had to register more hits than the Bf 109 pilot in order to down his prey. Some 30 examples of the Mk IA were delivered for operational trials during the Battle of Britain, these carrying two 20-mm cannon and four 0.303-in machine-guns.

Canopy
This Spitfire Mk I has the original sliding canopy section, which was soon replaced by a bulged hood which gave more headroom and a better all-round view.

Powerplant
The Spitfire Mk I was powered by a 1,030-hp Rolls-Royce Merlin II or Merlin III engine. This had fuel delivered by conventional carburettors, rather than a fuel injection system. The pilot was prevented from bunting into a dive, a tactical disadvantage when pursuing a Bf 109.

Spitfire improvements
By the time the Battle of Britain began the basic Spitfire I had received a host of modifications. The original fixed-pitch two-bladed wooden propeller had been replaced by a de Havilland three-bladed variable-pitch prop. A constant-speed airscrew would arrive before the Battle ended. The tailskid had been replaced by a tailwheel, and ejector exhausts were added.

Pilots and ground crew of No. 310 (Czech) Squadron, based at Duxford during the Battle. The shortage of RAF pilots was critical, and Royal Navy, Commonwealth, Empire, Czech, Polish and Free French pilots helped to swell Fighter Command's ranks.

No. 92 Squadron received Spitfire Is in March 1940 at Tangmere and flew patrols over France before being sent to south Wales for defensive duties. In early September, it transferred to Biggin Hill within No. 11 Group, to play a part in the Battle raging over Kent.

a result of the time taken to assemble.

Be that as it may, the victory gained by RAF Fighter Command was achieved as much by the courage, resilience and skill of the RAF pilots and their ground crews as by the extraordinarily close-knit organisation that existed within the command, and there is no doubt that the extent to which the radar chain had been integrated into the fighting processes came as an unpleasant surprise to the enemy.

The cost of victory in the daylight Battle of Britain was heavy. Considerable damage was suffered at many of the key airfields, some of which were temporarily abandoned for operational purposes. The cost in aircrew lives was heavy, more than 500 men being posted killed or missing, yet on the last day of the Battle (31 October) Fighter Command possessed eight more squadrons in the front line than on the first day, and replacement pilots were arriving from the training schools twice as quickly as they had in July, to continue a tradition that would for ever be remembered by a grateful nation: survival had been achieved through the prowess in combat of just 3,030 airmen, forever remembered as The Few.

A view from one of the Few

Flight Lieutenant D.M. Crooke flew Spitfire Is with No. 609 'West Riding' Squadron, an Auxiliary unit which flew from Northolt, Middle Wallop and Warmwell during the Battle of Britain. Here he describes his first kill.

During the month of July the two air forces tested one another out, examining each others' tactical weaknesses and strengths. The RAF, for instance, gradually learnt to give up its tactics of attacking in fixed V formation, and evolved the use of pairs of aircraft or 'finger four' detached sections.

THE SECRET OF SUCCESS

As Flight Lieutenant D. M. Crook of No. 609 Squadron later wrote of those July days: "We had not yet learnt that it did not pay to go out to sea to meet the enemy, but to let them come to us. Also we did not realise the importance that height meant. Afterwards we used to get as high as possible before going into action. This is the whole secret of success in air fighting."

The chief test pilot of Supermarine was (then) Flying Officer Jeffrey Quill, who fought for a time with No. 65 Squadron from Hornchurch: "When the battle heated up, the job of the Spitfire squadron was to climb up, engage the German fighter escort, and let the bombers go by . . . We'd see a bloody great formation of Dorniers coming in at 12,000 ft. We'd be told to ignore them. Up above were their fighter escorts.

"Our job was to get up and engage those fighters, get a good old dogfight going, get everything milling around, during which time the bombers would be groaning inexorably along. With any luck,

by the time they got anywhere near their target, we'd have forced all their fighter escorts out of position and down would come our Hurricanes to get at the bombers. These two aircraft together – plus the radar – those were the things that won the Battle of Britain."

The Germans began by attacking convoys in the Channel. Meanwhile, bombing attacks were also mounted on naval installations at Portland, on 4 and 9 July. In the first raid, defending British fighters arrived too late, but on the second occasion long-distance radar gave sufficient warning, and Spitfires from No. 609 Squadron were ordered into the air.

Crook and two companions were patrolling over Weymouth. "I saw one or two Huns appear, and recognised them as Junkers 87 divebombers. I immediately turned on my reflector sights, put my gun button on to 'fire' and settled down to enjoy a little slaughter of a few Ju 87s, as they are rather helpless machines. . . when I happened to look round behind. To my

intense surprise and dismay, I saw at least nine Messerschmitt 110s about 2,000 ft above us.

"This completely altered the situation. We were now hopelessly outnumbered, and in a very dangerous position. I immediately called up Peter and Michael and shouted desperately, 'Look out behind!' I have never felt so desperate or so helpless in my life as when, in spite of my warnings, these two flew steadily on, apparently quite oblivious of the fact that they were going to be struck down from the rear in a few seconds.

"At that moment the leading Messerschmitt opened fire at me and I saw his shells and tracer bullets going past just above my head. They were jolly close too. I immediately did a very violent turn to the left and dived through a layer of cloud just below.

"I saw dimly a machine moving in the cloud on my left and flying parallel to me. I stalked him through the cloud, and when he emerged into a patch of clear sky I saw that it was a Ju 87.

"I was in an ideal position to attack, so I opened fire and put the remainder of my ammunition – about 2,000 rounds – into him at very close range. Even in the heat of the moment I well remember my amazement at the shattering

effect of my fire. Pieces flew off his fuselage and cockpit covering, a stream of smoke appeared from the engine, and a moment later a great sheet of flame licked out from the engine cowling and he dived down vertically. The flames enveloped the whole machine and he went straight down, apparently quite slowly, for about 5,000 ft, until he was just a shapeless burning mass of wreckage . . . I followed him down, and saw him hit the sea with a great burst of white foam."

FIRST KILL

The victim of Crook's first kill was Hauptmann Freiherr von Dalwigk, holder of the Knight's Cross. Sai Crook: "I had often wondered what would be my feelings when killing somebody like this, and especially when seeing them go down in flames.

"I was rather surprised to reflect afterwards that my only feeling had been one of considerable elation – and a sort of bewildered surprise because it had all been so easy."

Early British Bombing

SEPTEMBER 1939 – DECEMBER 1940

Left: The Air Component of the British Expeditionary Force in France had two squadrons of Bristol Blenheim Mk IVs (Nos 53 and 59). Both squadrons were based at Poix for long-range tactical reconnaissance and bombing.

Above: A rare photograph of No. 50 Squadron aircrew lined up in front of one of their Handley Page Hampdens at RAF Waddington. The squadron participated in the RAF's first raid on enemy land targets on the night of 19/20 March 1940.

Below: A Blenheim Mk IV of No. 226 Squadron from RAF Wattisham en route to its target over France in 1940. No. 2 Group Blenheims took heavy losses in their low-level attacks on enemy targets in France and the Low Countries.

The Royal Air Force went to war against Germany steeped in the Trenchard tradition that the heavy bomber was its principal weapon, yet the aircraft with which it was equipped (the Vickers Wellington, Armstrong Whitworth Whitley and Handley Page Hampden) proved to be wholly inadequate to impose any significant pressure upon the enemy. It was not only poorly equipped to navigate and bomb accurately at night but disastrously vulnerable by day. Nor was the British Air Staff single-minded as how best to employ its so-called heavy bombers.

In September 1939 the RAF possessed 10 squadrons of Wellingtons, 10 of Hampdens and nine of Whitleys, of which the Wellington was undoubtedly the best. It was in the mistaken belief that it could defend itself in the presence of enemy fighters, however, that the Wellington was first committed to daylight attacks during the first four months of the war. In deference to government restrictions on endangering the enemy's civilian population, the targets were German naval forces in or near their home ports. From the outset, German radar gave notice of the bombers'

approach so that flak and fighters were able to take a heavy toll. The last such raid, on 18 December, cost the loss of 12 out of 24 Wellingtons of Nos 9, 37 and 149 Squadrons. Scarcely any damage was inflicted on German ships, and thereafter the Wellingtons were confined to bombing at night.

If the efforts of the Wellington crews were disappointing, those of the RAF light bombers, the Bristol Blenheim Mk IVs, were more promising and from the first day of the war the type performed a

Left: The crew of a Wellington Mk IC of No. 149 Squadron take a last minute look at the map before boarding their aircraft. By the end of 1940 Wellingtons equipped no fewer than 19 squadrons of RAF Bomber Command.

Early twin-engined types

Without a power-operated gun turret the twin-engined Hampden had inadequate defence against enemy fighters. Although slower than the Hampden, the Whitley could carry a useful load over a good range and was used to drop leaflets during the propaganda war. Both took part in the first bombing raid in March 1940. Blenheims were far more successful as low-level coastal attackers.

Handley Page Hampden Mk I
A No. 5 Group Hampden Mk I (P1320) flown by No. 106 Squadron based at RAF Finningley in April 1940. The Mk I carried a crew of four, was armed with three 7.7-mm (0.303-in) Vickers machine-guns and had a bombload of 1814-kg (4,000 lb).

Armstrong Whitworth Whitley Mk V
This all-black painted Armstrong Whitworth Whitley Mk V was flown by No. 78 Squadron for night operations from RAF Dishforth and RAF Linton-on-Ouse between September 1939 and April 1941.

Bristol Blenheim Mk IV
Built by the Rootes shadow factory at Speke, Liverpool, this Blenheim Mk IV had rear defence guns fitted under the nose in December 1940 while serving with No. 40 Squadron at RAF Wyton.

Left: The rear gunner emerging from the tail turret of an Armstrong Whitworth Whitley. This aircraft (K8942) served with Nos 51 and 166 Squadrons before being relegated to training duties with 10 OTU, 7 BGS and finally 7 AGS in 1943.

over German towns at night, the bombing restrictions preventing the delivery of high explosive. Night after night these lumbering, angular aeroplanes set course from the UK to discharge their paper bundles with scarcely any interference from German defences, their worst enemy being bad weather. Early in 1940 Whitleys of No. 77 Squadron, flying from Villeneuve in France, dropped leaflets over Prague, Vienna and cities in Poland.

BOMBING STARTS
The third of the heavy trio was the Hampden – nicknamed the 'flying suitcase' on account of its deep, narrow fuselage. This was the only British bomber not to be armed with a power-operated gun turret, and was indeed appallingly vulnerable to enemy fighter attack. Fortunately the Germans possessed scarcely any night-fighter defence during the first eight months of the war.

Following the dropping of German bombs on British soil on 16 March 1940, which killed a civilian in the Orkneys, the RAF attacked an enemy land target four nights later when 26 Whitleys and 15 Hampdens attacked the seaplane base at Hörnum-on-Sylt. In the following month Wellingtons joined the attack with a raid on Stavanger airfield in Norway.

It was not until after the German offensive had opened in the West on 10 May that Bomber

Above: Packets of propaganda leaflets are loaded onto a Whitley for a night-time 'Nickelling' raid over Germany in the autumn of 1939. Whitley squadrons were given this thankless task, starting on the night of 3/4 September 1939.

Command aircraft were permitted to attack the German mainland, although their targets were still strictly confined to military objectives. Moreover, because of inadequate navigation equipment and outdated bombsights, few bomber crews attacked their briefed targets.

number of outstanding raids, although the small number and size of their bombs (the largest of which was the 227-kg [500-lb] weapon), severely limited the damage caused. Yet the numerous attacks against targets off the north German coast, carried out with great gallantry and often in poor weather, probably achieved more than all the raids by the heavy bombers combined.

The Whitley was the slowest of all the British bombers – though a rugged weight-lifter – and was assigned the nebulous task of dropping loads of propaganda leaflets

Right: A Whitley Mk V of No. 58 Squadron taking off from RAF Linton-on-Ouse at sunset for a night bombing raid over Germany in May 1940. The Whitley had a good range that enabled it to reach Poland, but at the expense of a significant bombload.

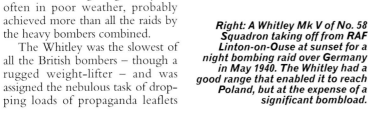

Vickers Wellington Mk IC

Vickers' Type 415 Wellington Mk IC, had a redesigned hydraulic system, a 24-volt electrical system and the substitution of beam guns in the midship position for the unsatisfactory ventral turret. The Pegasus XVIII-powered bomber set the standard for subsequent marks in the early war years.

Construction

With its unique geodetic 'basket weave' method of construction, the first prototype was flown on 15 June 1936, with the first production Mk I following on 23 December 1937. Aircraft were built at Chester and Blackpool, as well as Weybridge.

Powerplant

The Wellington Mk IC was equipped with two 783-kW (1,050-hp) Bristol Pegasus XVIII nine-cylinder radial engines, giving a maximum speed of 378 km/h (235 mph) at 4724 m (15,500 ft).

Armament

Two 7.7-mm (0.303-in) Browning machine-guns in each of the power-operated nose and tail turrets; two manually operated 7.7-mm (0.303-in) beam guns (replacing a single-gun ventral turret). The normal maximum internal bombload was 2041 kg (4,500 lb).

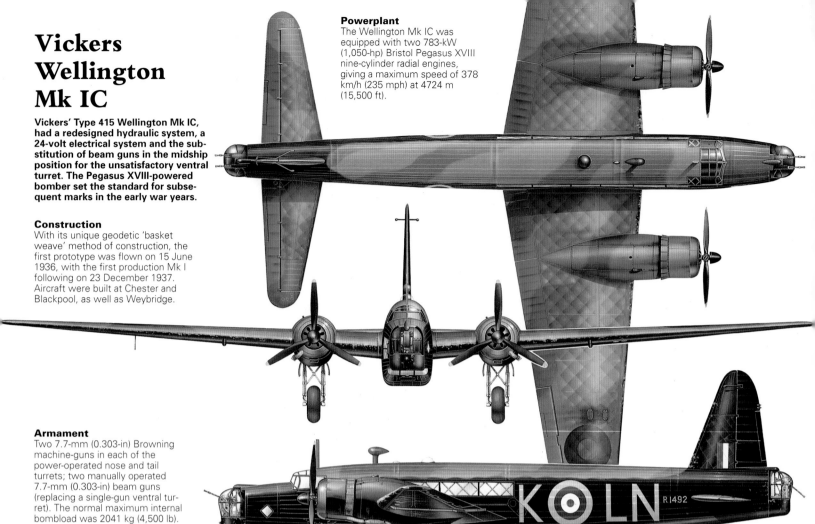

Left: The Handley Page Hampden Mk I equipped 10 squadrons in September 1939. By the end of the year, following heavy losses, they had been switched from day to night operations. The last of 500 aircraft was delivered in July 1940.

25/26 August 81 Wellingtons, Whitleys and Hampdens set out for the first time for Berlin, and 29 of their crews claimed to have bombed the German capital.

Despite these very modest beginnings, Bomber Command was aware of its own shortcomings and before the end of 1940 the first true heavy bombers, the Avro Manchester, Short Stirling and Handley Page Halifax, were arriving in the RAF. The new year would see a significant strengthening of bombing muscle, though its aim would still be suspect.

When eventually the War Cabinet lifted the restrictions on British bombing over Germany on 15 May and 99 Wellingtons, Whitleys and Hampdens opened Bomber Command's strategic bombing offensive with attacks on oil and steel targets in the Ruhr, fewer than 30 crews claimed even to have identified their target. Bomber Command was further restricted in its attacks on Italian targets (when that nation entered the war on 10 June), and although Wellingtons deployed to the south of France the French government curtailed their attacks for fear of reprisal raids on their territory.

During the Battle of Britain a number of RAF bomber bases were attacked by the Luftwaffe and some bombers (mostly Whitleys) were destroyed. However, three achievements marked the climax (if such it can be called) of this stage of British bombing. On 11/12 June 36 Whitleys flew from the UK, refuelling in the Channel Islands, to attack targets in northern Italy and, although only 12 crews claimed to have bombed Turin or Milan, the long flight over the Alps in poor weather represented something of an epic of endurance. On 1 July a Hampden, flown by Flying Officer Guy Gibson (later Wing Commander, VC) dropped Bomber Command's first 907-kg (2,000-lb) bomb over Kiel, the heaviest bomb thus far carried by the RAF in World War II. Additionally, on

Left: Sgt John Hannah (left) who, at 18, was awarded the Victoria Cross for putting out a serious fire on Hampden Mk I P1355 while over Antwerp. With him is P/O C.A.H. Connor who received the DFC for bringing the aircraft back to base.

A Battle Lost

On that fateful day, 18 December 1940, a daylight raid on enemy warships by Wellington Mk IAs of No. 9 Squadron resulted in a massacre at the hands of Luftwaffe Messerschmitt Bf 109 and Bf 110 fighters. Five of the squadron's aircraft were lost.

"The first thing I knew was that I felt cold around my feet and legs. I looked down, and saw only water beneath me! The guns refused to fire, too, and when I looked up I saw both barrels had been blown off. Then a hail of cannon shells passed in front of me and blew the Perspex out of the turret."

On 18 December 1940, 24 Wellington Mk IA bombers left England for a major daylight bombing raid on German warships at Wilhelmshaven. Only 12 of the aircraft survived as the formation was mauled by German fighters. One of the lucky ones amongst them – for surely luck it was – was WS-G, No. 9 Squadron's 'G for George', piloted by Sergeant John Ramshaw and with Charlie Driver, an 18-year-old fitter/rigger in the front turret.

Driver's position was precarious,

Below: In June 1939 a New Zealand Flight was formed to train with these Wellington Mk IAs. In April 1940 it was redesignated No. 75 Squadron at RAF Feltwell and began night bombing operations, moving soon afterwards to RAF Mildenhall.

to say the least. The turret had been demolished around him, and as he turned to make his way back into the body of the fuselage he found his way blocked by smoke and flame. He tore off one of his big leather outer gauntlets and used that to beat out the flames. When he got back and up to the cockpit, he found Ramshaw sitting calmly at the controls, whistling a popular tune, apparently unconcerned that the entire Luftwaffe seemed intent on shooting them out of the sky.

"You okay, Charlie?" he asked, and Driver stuck up both thumbs in acknowledgement. Sergeant Hewitt, the second pilot, couldn't believe that Driver had emerged alive from the wreckage of the turret.

FIGHT TO SURVIVE

G-George's rear turret had fallen silent too, its guns jammed, and the surrounding Messerschmitts knew it. One turned in for the kill, cannon shells smashing into the tail of the aircraft. Rear-gunner Walter Lilley was struggling in silence to clear his weapons when he was hit, and died there, far from help or comfort.

Lilley had downed one and perhaps two of the attacking aircraft and now, as if his life were sufficient restitution, the fighters fell away, ammunition and fuel running low. Somehow G-George was still in the air but Driver, looking out of the astrodome, couldn't imagine how.

"As I looked out, I saw all the fabric flapping on the wings. The

insides were all exposed and it was as though someone had taken a great knife and carved all along the leading edge of the wings. The nose of the aircraft was sheared away, but I'd closed the bulkhead doors behind the front turret when I'd got out, to keep the air blast from the rest of the fuselage. The engines looked like someone had used a sledgehammer and a great chisel on them."

Worse was still to come – the fuel tanks had been perforated. Driver was told to work the hand pump that sucked petrol from the reserve fuel tank. For 30 long minutes he pumped as hard as he

could and then, inevitably, felt the pump sucking air. First one engine died, and then the other.

They all knew that they would not make land but, instead, would have to ditch their stricken aircraft in the cold December sea. Then, in the distance, Ramshaw made out an alien shape – a Grimsby trawler! "I can see a ship!" he shouted excitedly over the intercom. "I'm going to try and make for it." The rest of the crew braced themselves as best they could.

The Wellington hit hard, within a quarter of a mile from the fishing boat, the impact tearing away more

of its torn fabric. Ramshaw smashed his head into the windscreen and, only half-conscious, could barely help himself. It was young Charlie Driver who released the rubber dinghy from its stowage in the aft part of the port engine nacelle, and then he and the wireless operator, Leading Aircraftman Conolly, made their way out onto the wing. Ramshaw, too, had struggled out through the cockpit top and fell into the sea. Driver and Conolly grabbed him as best they could and bundled him into the dingy. Then they and Hewitt clambered in too, just as G-George put her nose down and took Lilley

Above: Crews of Wellington Mk IAs of No. 149 Squadron walking out to their aircraft. Although the Wellington's geodetic construction made it very strong, its inadequate defensive guns left it vulnerable to critical damage by Luftwaffe fighters.

to a watery grave.

Quarter of an hour later they were picked up by the trawler and taken on the 16-hour journey back to Grimsby.

It took the sacrifice of the aircraft and crew on missions like this to wake up Bomber Command to the suicide of unescorted daylight bombing.

The Night Blitz

SEPTEMBER 1940 - MAY 1941

German defeat in the daylight Battle of Britain frustrated plans to invade the British Isles in the early autumn of 1940. Instead, Goering believed that his bomber force could impose a military solution to the war by repeated heavy attacks on London and other cities by night. The first such major attack was launched against the dock area of East London on the night of 7/8 September just as the Battle of Britain was reaching its decisive phase. Moreover, German bombers continued to visit London for more than 50 consecutive nights, creating infinitely greater damage and casualties than in the whole of the daylight assault.

LIMITED DEFENCE

Seldom more than 100 Heinkel He 111s, Dornier Do 17s and Junkers Ju 88s operated on any single night in this savage attack on the British capital yet, despite being without any form of fighter protection, they were able to escape any significant loss, such was the poor state of the British night-fighter defences. Up to this stage the obsolescent Bristol Blenheim, flying with extremely rudimentary airborne radar, backed up by a few single-seat Hawker Hurricanes had constituted the

Above: Junkers Ju 88A-4s are seen en route to their targets. Main force Luftwaffe bombers were all able to find their targets using Knickebein radio beams, while the elite and expert pathfinders of Kampfgruppe 100 used the more accurate X-Gerät to mark targets with incendiaries.

Right: The Heinkel He 111 was the mainstay of the Luftwaffe's night bombing force. This one shows a typical over-painted night camouflage colour scheme, with toned-down national insignia.

fighter defence at night. In September the first purpose-designed night-fighter, the heavily armed Bristol Beaufighter, started arriving in service with more effective radar, together with some Boulton Paul Defiant turret-equipped two-seaters (discarded as day fighters), but it would be many months before these aircraft would achieve noticeable results against the night raiders.

INDUSTRY TARGETED

Although the Nazi leadership espoused no pretence at achieving military damage in the night assault on London, the Luftwaffe itself recognised that worthwhile results from the night assaults could be gained only by striking at British industrial centres much farther afield, and had thus been developing navigation aids to enable its bombers to reach into the heart of the nation. Employing narrow radio beams transmitted from continental stations across the British Isles, the Germans started flying pathfinder He 111s of Kampfgruppe 100 specially equipped with radio receivers that enabled them to fly accurately towards distant targets, which they would mark with incendiary bombs to guide the crews of the main bombing force.

Above: A market trader in the East End of London continues his fruit-selling among the ruins of the Blitz. The Luftwaffe deliberately targeted London's East End, hoping that attacks on the densely packed population might lead Britain to sue for peace.

Right: Although devoid of any interception aids, the Hawker Hurricane was widely used as a night-fighter throughout the winter of 1940-41. This No. 85 Squadron Hurricane was used in the battle against night raiders over southern England.

Despite the existence of this equipment being discovered by the British, the defences were caught unawares when, on 14/15 November, KGr 100 led 437 bombers against Coventry, causing enormous damage, killing 380 civilians and seriously injuring 800 others. In the final week of November further heavy raids were launched against London, Southampton, Bristol, Plymouth and Liverpool. In December, Manchester and Sheffield were added to the list of stricken cities. Much in line with the growth of British bombs at this stage of the war, German weapons were in the main the 1,102-lb (500-kg) high explosive bomb, although huge numbers of 4.4-lb (2-kg) incendiary bombs were showered over British towns and cities during the Blitz. However, growing numbers of 2,205-lb (1000-kg) bombs were carried by the He 111s to short-range targets, as well as highly-destructive parachute 'mines', the latter being adaptations of the German sea mine fitted with a barostatic fuse to give maximum blast effect.

FIRE BOMBS

The year ended with a particularly vicious incendiary raid on the City

An early Ju 88A-1 runs up its engines at night. As a bomber, the type could carry a useful load at a reasonable speed. The Ju 88 owed much of its success to its high speed and concentrated defensive armament, and it survived far longer than its contemporaries.

of London which, carried out when the Thames was at low tide and during a weekend when few fire watchers were in their offices, caused grievous damage among centuries-old churches and other treasured buildings.

The second half of the Blitz brought about marked improvements in the British defences. Gradually the RAF night-fighters began to take a noticeable toll of the bombers: three in January, four in February, 22 in March, 48 in April and 96 in May. During the same five months the guns and balloons claimed a total of about 120 enemy aircraft. Meanwhile, Nottingham, Avonmouth, Merseyside, Swansea, Belfast, Clydeside, Hull, Sunderland and Newcastle were all heavily raided, in addition to still further attacks on the previous victims. Not only were the night-fighter crews becoming proficient in operating their airborne radar in collaboration with the new ground-control radar stations, but the gun

defences were also being steadily strengthened throughout the country. In February the first massed batteries of ground-to-air rockets went into action for the first time.

By May Hitler was completing his plans for the great assault on the Soviet Union, which the Luftwaffe

Left: Flying above the cloud tops, this Do 17Z-2 of 9./KG 76 is approaching the English coast. Previously criticised for being underpowered with a full bombload, the Do 17Z-2 had the 746-kW (1,000-hp) Bramo 323P engines that featured two-speed superchargers, which restored the bombload to 1000 kg (2,205 lb).

Right: A Luftwaffe Ju 88 bomber crew adjusts their parachute harnesses before departing on a night raid over England.

Luftwaffe night bombers

Attacks on Britain's centres of population were in part a reaction to the RAF's night raids against German cities. Although targets like docks, rail centres and factories were attacked where

possible, the primary aim of the campaign was to dislocate industry by exhausting and sapping the morale of the workers, to terrorise the civilian population and bring England to the negotiating table.

Junkers Ju 88A-1
Losses by day forced the RAF and the Luftwaffe to turn to nocturnal bombing. This Junkers Ju 88A-1 served with II/KG 52 'Edelweiss' from Melun-Villaroche in the winter of 1940 during the night Blitz against Britain. National markings were obscured and lamp-black distemper applied to the undersurfaces.

Heinkel He 111H
This Heinkel He 111H-3 flew with 2./KGr 100 from Vannes in Britanny. It is equipped with *X-Gerät* pathfinder gear which allowed the Gruppe to mark targets with extraordinary accuracy for other 'main force' bombers. It was widely used during the night Blitz.

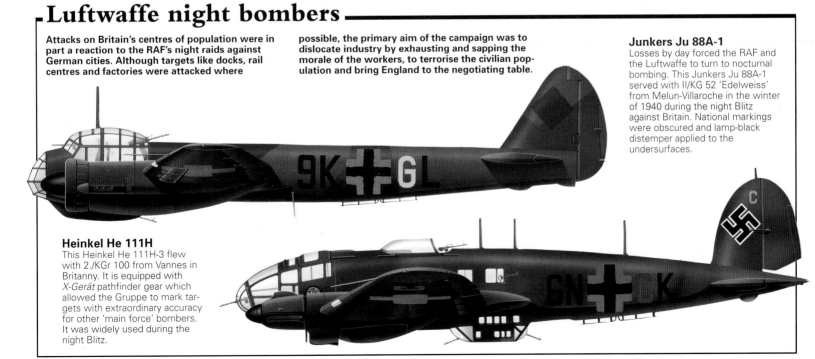

would be called on to support. With no appearance of a crack in British morale, the bulk of German bomber forces was moved from Western Europe eastwards, and the night Blitz on the UK petered out.

CIVILIANS KILLED

The bombing had indeed done little lasting damage to the UK's ability to wage war. Most serious was that caused in the aircraft industry, the output of which was reduced by about 20 per cent for almost six months (at the Supermarine, Short, Bristol, Avro and Vickers factories). In addition, 70,000 tons of food stocks had been destroyed. However, no more than 0.5 per cent of the nation's oil stocks were destroyed and most of the damage caused to the railways was quickly repaired. On the other hand, no fewer than 52,000 civilians had been killed and almost 80,000 severely injured, not to mention well over 120,000 rendered temporarily homeless.

Above left: The Bristol Blenheim Mk IF was the RAF's only practical night-fighter at the beginning of WWII, when it was already operational with Nos 25 and 29 Squadrons.

Above: A Boulton-Paul Defiant Mk II night-fighter of No. 256 Squadron at RAF Squires Gate, responsible for the night defence of Liverpool. The Defiant was relegated to the night-fighter role following its disastrous showing in daylight.

Left: As the battle continued, the RAF was fortunate to be able to call on increasing numbers of skilled aircrew of foreign origins, mostly refugees from occupied Europe, such as this group of Polish airmen.

Above: The view from the nose of a Dornier Do 17, dubbed 'The Flying Pencil', in daylight formation over southern England. The extensively glazed nose offered no armour protection to the machine-gunner/bomb-aimer.

Night defenders

In late 1940 and early 1941, night-fighter technology was in its infancy, and little more than a token effort could be made to combat the Luftwaffe's night bombers. One of the reasons for the replacement of Dowding as C-in-C Fighter Command was the perception that he had failed to make even this token effort, and had not assigned single-seat fighters to night defence.

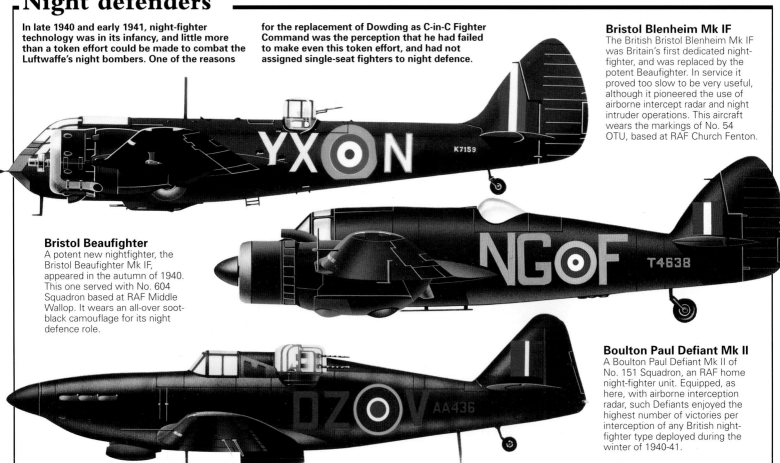

Bristol Blenheim Mk IF
The British Bristol Blenheim Mk IF was Britain's first dedicated night-fighter, and was replaced by the potent Beaufighter. In service it proved too slow to be very useful, although it pioneered the use of airborne intercept radar and night intruder operations. This aircraft wears the markings of No. 54 OTU, based at RAF Church Fenton.

Bristol Beaufighter
A potent new nightfighter, the Bristol Beaufighter Mk IF, appeared in the autumn of 1940. This one served with No. 604 Squadron based at RAF Middle Wallop. It wears an all-over soot-black camouflage for its night defence role.

Boulton Paul Defiant Mk II
A Boulton Paul Defiant Mk II of No. 151 Squadron, an RAF home night-fighter unit. Equipped, as here, with airborne interception radar, such Defiants enjoyed the highest number of victories per interception of any British night-fighter type deployed during the winter of 1940-41.

*With overpainted **Hakenkreuz** and with the white sections of the **Balkenkreuz** obscured, this Ju 88A-1 from 1./KG 51 was used in the night Blitz against British cities.*

Night Attacker

Peter Stahl flew the Ju 88 on night bombing missions over England, and here describes a typical mission.

"The sudden howling of the port engine shocks me awake. Next to me, Hans, my navigator, hangs in his harness, his head resting against the cabin glazing. I call Theo and Hein over the intercom. Asleep! Our Ju 88 has climbed from take-off to 4200 m. The engine temperatures are much too low because the engine flaps are still open; the fuel service tanks are nearly empty. None of us is wearing oxygen masks – had we continued in our sleep we would have passed cleanly and quietly into the next world.

"Fly, sleep, eat, and fly again – that is how it has been for weeks. Ahead are the outlines of the coast. The searchlights grope for us but there is no AA fire. The enemy gunners are not asleep, so that means night-fighters. Some of the lights have been grouped in fives. As a result our path is accurately marked by a pyramid of lights that wanders along with us.

"Frequently our aircraft is hit full-on by a beam that temporarily blinds me. The beam wanders with us for endlessly long moments before slipping away again, which shows that, when flying at high altitude, our matt-painted bombers can no longer be optically traced from the ground.

"I glimpse one twin-engined night fighter as it crosses my path 100 m ahead, but he is up-moon and misses us. Then, as if reporting nothing more unusual than a shooting star, of which we see hundreds every night, my gunner reports calmly over the intercom, 'Night-fighters to port behind.'

"I pull the Ju 88 into a steep half-roll to port and let it fall upside down into the night. I have just levelled off when Hein repeats his warning. The Devil! Once more we shoot like a stone into the pitch blackness below. Then a third time! By now we are just 800 m high, dragging our 2000 kg of explosives and with a long climb ahead of us to reach a decent altitude for attack. That we have escaped the night-fighter is due to the excellence of our aircraft, and I find myself stroking the control column in gratitude.

"As I climb back to our attack altitude we meet cloud and the aircraft develops slight icing-up. At 6000 m the temperature has dropped to -30°C, but the icing-up has stopped.

"The cloud clears and almost immediately the anti-aircraft guns pick us up. The shells burst ahead of and behind us and any attempt at evasion seems pointless. Nevertheless, I force myself to try every trick in my book, every anti-aircraft evasion manoeuvre I know, but in vain. Things are so bad that I catch myself several times wanting to drop my weapons blind into the night.

"Suddenly, a red reflection is visible beyond the horizon. There is no need for navigation now and I vary my approach route in an attempt to avoid areas with particularly massed anti-aircraft fire.

"As we get nearer, the anti-aircraft fire becomes thicker and it seems as if thousands of searchlights are in action. The approach flight through this blazing inferno, punctuated by the explosions of anti-aircraft shells, seems endlessly long and I am forced to fly evasive manoeuvres time and again.

"But what we experience over the target surpasses anything one could possibly imagine. The whole city seems to be ablaze. In addition the target is lit up by flare-bombs that flash at irregular intervals.

"With throttled-back engines I begin a glide towards my allocated target. Suddenly my Ju 88 is met by accurate anti-aircraft fire that forces me to turn away. I mark time until the exploding shells concentrate around another aircraft, and then use that moment to go into a steep incline at high speed towards my release point.

"Our targets are locks in the dock area. Hans has an easy task aiming our mines. I fly over the burning port in accordance with his instructions. We can recognise every detail shown to us on aerial reconnaissance photographs as if it were daytime. My stopwatch is running, and exactly on the second we see two fiery explosions in our area – our mines.

FRIENDLY COAST AHEAD

"Suddenly a string of parachute flares burst into blinding light just to the left of us and exactly at our altitude. I immediately bank away to starboard. Continually and at irregular intervals I vary my flight direction and my engine revs, changing their sound. The minutes drag endlessly until we finally see the coast. My nerves are ready to give up. Without further ado I throttle back to 'noiseless' running and nose down into high speed flight knowing that this will bring me into range of the light AA coastal batteries. I don't care any more, and rely on luck to avoid areas of massed anti-aircraft fire.

"Then it happens! A blinding flash. We are hit. I pull up our Ju 88 and cast a quick glance over the instruments. Everything seems normal and there are no injuries among the crew.

"I pull back on the throttle levers but the port engine continues to run at full revs. A shell splinter must have severed the throttle controls. I switch it off and the Ju 88 flies slanting in the dark night.

"Ahead of us the searchlights that finger the sky are our own, and we are glad to see them. We fire the identification flares but the searchlights continue beaming in our faces. Suddenly light AA guns open up on us. I am forced to fly a series of dangerous evasive turns over my stopped engine.

"This deadly game of searchlight and light AA guns follows us along the coast. Already exhausted with fear and lack of sleep, my crew give way to fury, firing back with their machine-guns at our own men.

"As we approach our base I prepare my crew for the peculiarities of a one-engined landing. Visibility is excellent, so, contrary to accepted practice, I let down my undercarriage rather than make a belly landing. This takes time as I have only half the normal hydraulic pressure. Aboard the aircraft nobody says a word.

"I estimate my height as we glide in for touch-down on the flare path. Too low! We hit with the port wing and crash onto the ground in complete darkness. The scraping slide along the ground seems endless. The starboard engine howls up and can not be stopped. Terrified of fire, we are desperate to get out and away from the aircraft but the cabin roof has jammed. Soldiers smash at the cabin and we tumble clear.

"The fire-fighters and doctors are quickly on the scene. The soldiers tell the doctor, a young one fresh to the front, that none of us is badly hurt. We watch him crawl into the Ju 88. He reappears with the aircraft clock as a souvenir.

"For Hans, the doctor's conduct is the straw that finally breaks the camel's back. Calmly he walks up to the doctor, takes the clock and hits him in the face with such force that the medicine man slithers over the wing and falls flat on the grass below.

"So ends another flight over London."

The Balkans and Crete

OCTOBER 1940 – MAY 1941

Left: Hs 126s served widely in the east on army co-operation duties. Their service in Greece was notable, this aircraft being seen over Athens. The yellow theatre bands were worn as the campaign was in mainland Europe. Aircraft on operations outside Europe wore white bands.

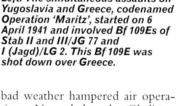

Left: The simultaneous assaults on Yugoslavia and Greece, codenamed Operation 'Maritz', started on 6 April 1941 and involved Bf 109Es of Stab II and III/JG 77 and I (Jagd)/LG 2. This Bf 109E was shot down over Greece.

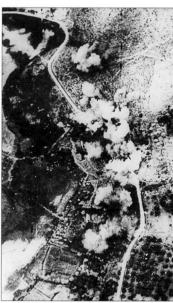

bad weather hampered air operations. Nevertheless the Gladiator pilots were credited with the destruction of around 30 Italian aircraft by the end of December, for the loss of 10 aircraft.

BALKANS INVADED

Fearing that the RAF might use Greek airfields from which to bomb the Romanian oil fields, Hitler began his move into the Balkans on 1 March 1941, with German troops entering Bulgaria. Within seven days three more RAF squadrons, including one of Hurricanes, were sent to Greece,

Above: Luftwaffe attack on Greece on 10 April 1941. The Greek army surrendered on 20 April and one week later the fall of Athens brought the campaign to a conclusion. Within less than a year, the British and Commonwealth armies had been forced to evacuate the continent in extremis.

Despite the eventual voluntary alignment by the other Balkan powers with the Axis, Hitler was aware that both Yugoslavia and Greece represented weak spots in his southern flank for his forthcoming attack on the Soviet Union. After weeks of little progress by the Italians in their own attack on Greece through Albania, Hitler accordingly decided to eliminate these potential Allied footholds in the Balkans.

Italy had struck at Greece on 28 October 1940, and in answer to appeals by the Greek government an RAF squadron of Blenheims was immediately sent from North Africa for the defence of Athens, and by the end of November two more Blenheim squadrons and two of Gladiators followed. Before the year was out the Gladiators were operating patrols over the Albanian frontier, though contact was seldom made with the Régia Aéronautica. Wellingtons, flying from Egypt, carried out occasional raids against Italian supply ports, but in general

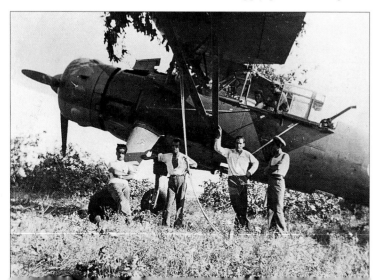

Left: In addition to its traditional role of army co-operation, the Henschel Hs 126B-1 was also used for battlefield reconnaissance and artillery spotting in 1940-41. Following the introduction of the Fw 189, the Hs 126 was relegated to second-line duties.

Above: Junkers Ju 87B Stukas and their lethal bomb-loads on a Greek airfield. As with other invasions, Stukas played a major role in the Wehrmacht's campaign in Greece and the Balkans.

Below: The Savoia-Marchetti SM.79 Sparviero (Sparrowhawk) medium bomber of the Régia Aéronautica was well respected by its antagonists and lauded by its crews for its handling qualities and sturdiness. This formation of five SM.79s is seen over typical Balkan terrain.

which were opposed by fewer than 500 Yugoslav, British and Greek aircraft, all but a few of them (the Hurricanes and Blenheims) being hopelessly outdated.

Despite all that these few aircraft could do, assisted by the long-range Wellingtons, the Germans had gained their first objectives (the occupation of Yugoslavia and the capture of Salonika) by 14 April. The previous day an entire formation of Blenheims had been shot down north of Monastir, and on 15 April enemy aircraft virtually wiped out a Blenheim squadron (No. 113) on the ground at Niamata.

EVACUATION

Development of the German two-prong advance southwards decided the fate of Greece, and with overwhelming enemy air superiority quickly eroding the RAF's resources capable of supporting the British and Greek armies, the only question remaining was how much of the air forces could be evacuated? In the event the three fighter squadrons, Nos 33, 80 and 208, now equipped with Hurricanes, remained until the last moment. In

one of the final air combats over the Piraeus the South African Squadron Leader M.T.St J. Pattle, the war's highest-scoring RAF pilot, was shot down and killed on 20 April. Four days later the last British fighters left Greek soil for the last time.

Some of the surviving aircraft from the Greek campaign landed on the island of Crete, and this soon became the next subject of German attention. On 20 May Luftwaffe Ju 52/3ms started dropping paratroops

Above: An early Macchi MC.200 Saetta, with the relatively low-powered Fiat A.74 RC.38 engine. The Régia Aéronautica first used the MC.200 in action against Malta and then Greece, but it was no match for later fighter types.

Below: The camouflage of this Dornier Do 17Z-2 does little to conceal it against the blue of the Mediterranean. A participant in the spring 1941 offensive against Greece, this particular aircraft belonged to Kampfgeschwader 2.

followed by two more shortly after this. Before the end of the month a military coup in Yugoslavia threatened that country's ties with the Tripartite Pact and on 6 April the German army and air force attacked both Greece and Yugoslavia, launching a devastating and ruthless air attack on Belgrade. Supporting the Balkan campaign, Luftflotte IV fielded some 1,200 modern aircraft,

Bombers over the Adriatic

Blenheim Mk Is had been superseded by the Mk IV in the bomber role at home by 1939. Those that remained saw use as night fighters. In Greece, however, they were used in their intended role. Fairey

Battles were similarly outdated, but were pressed into service with the Greeks. The Ju 88 was one of the most modern bombing types available, while the Cant Z.1007 suffered from a lack of top speed.

Bristol Blenheim Mk I
Bristol Blenheim Mk I of No. 113 Squadron, RAF, operational over the Macedonian Front (northern Greece) in the early part of 1941. Such bombers could have performed a useful role in North Africa, but were definitely outclassed by the German aircraft deployed against them in the forthcoming campaign.

Fairey Battle Mk I
Fairey Battle light bomber of the 33rd Mira Vomvardismou (bomber squadron), Royal Hellenic Air Force, operational over the Albanian front in 1940-41.

Junkers Ju 88A
Junkers Ju 88A-4 of III/Kampfgeschwader 30 'Adler Geschwader', on detachment from X to VIII Fliegercorps as from 24 May 1941 (hence the mixture of white Mediterranean and yellow Crete theatre markings). The scoreboard on the tail indicates successes over Malta and Crete.

CRDA Cant Z.1007bis
Cant Z.1007bis of the 210ª Squadriglia, Régia Aéronautica, operating in support of the Italian army on the Greco-Albanian front in early-1941. The Z.1007bis was produced in both single- and twin-finned versions.

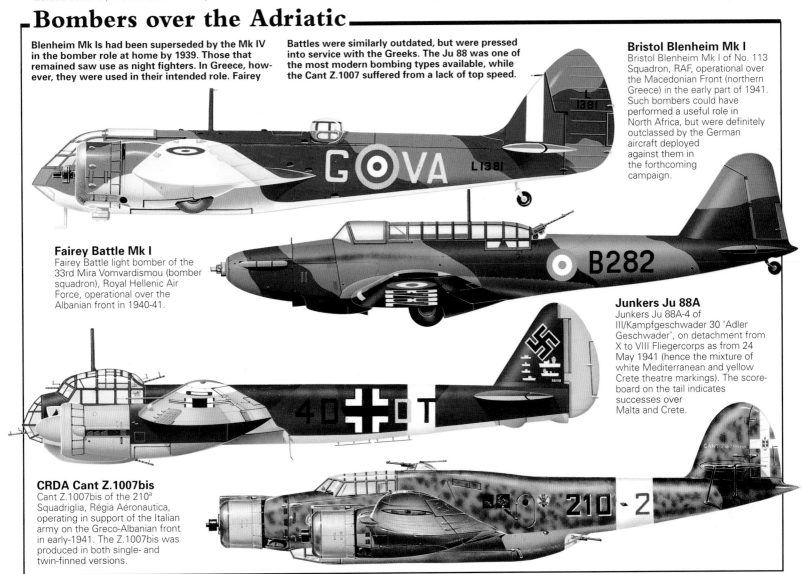

Left: Hawker Hurricane Mk Is were supplied abroad in small quantities in 1939, with 25 delivered to Yugoslavia. They were the best fighters available to the Yugoslavs, but could do little more than dent the Axis effort.

as gliders delivered infantry with the object of securing the island's landing grounds. To support the invasion the German air force mustered 650 first-line aircraft, 700 transports and 80 gliders. Opposing them were no more than a dozen Hurricanes, a handful of Fleet Air Arm Fulmars and some Gladiators dispersed on the two airfields and single rudimentary landing strip, although further limited support could be summoned from far-off Egypt. Since 14 May the Germans

had made clear their intention to invade Crete, with constant air attacks on the airfields, which the Hurricane pilots did their utmost to counter. By the eve of the invasion only seven fighters remained airworthy, and these were reluctantly evacuated to Egypt.

Despite the elimination of the island's fighter defence, the invasion certainly did not go according to plan, and the paratroops dropped initially at the two airfields were either wiped out or beaten off, and the glider landings were effectively contained. It was only after repeated waves of paratroops had been dropped that the airfields were eventually captured, after which the hosts of Ju 52/3ms started landing.

Fighters over the Adriatic

While aircraft like the Hawker Hurricane were available to Allied forces in the Balkans and Mediterranean, their limited numbers meant that they made little impression on the Luftwaffe.

Aircraft like PZL P.24s were out-classed and presented a negligible threat to Bf 110s and MC.200s that in other circumstances would have been at a severe disadvantage.

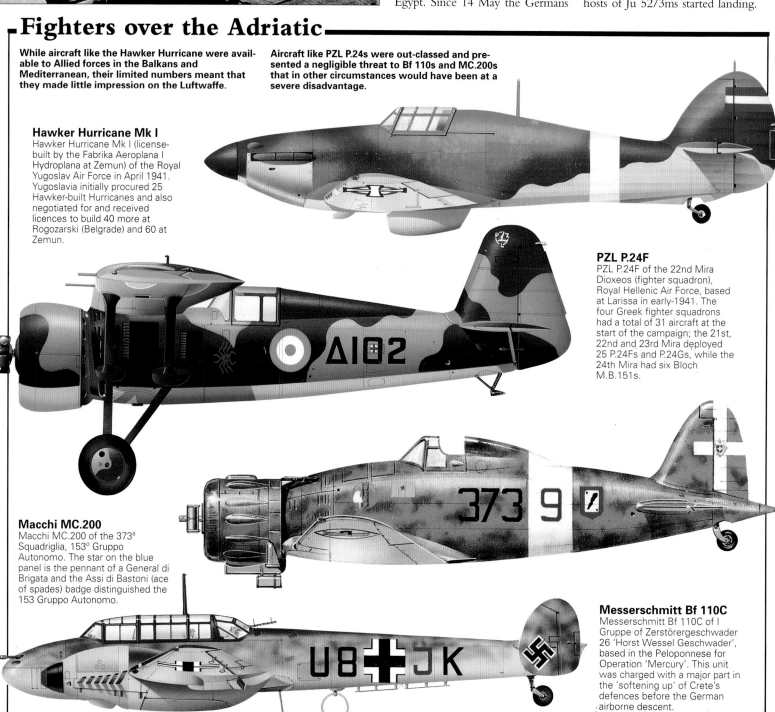

Hawker Hurricane Mk I
Hawker Hurricane Mk I (license-built by the Fabrika Aeroplana I Hydroplana at Zemun) of the Royal Yugoslav Air Force in April 1941. Yugoslavia initially procured 25 Hawker-built Hurricanes and also negotiated for and received licences to build 40 more at Rogozarski (Belgrade) and 60 at Zemun.

PZL P.24F
PZL P.24F of the 22nd Mira Dioxeos (fighter squadron), Royal Hellenic Air Force, based at Larissa in early-1941. The four Greek fighter squadrons had a total of 31 aircraft at the start of the campaign; the 21st, 22nd and 23rd Mira deployed 25 P.24Fs and P.24Gs, while the 24th Mira had six Bloch M.B.151s.

Macchi MC.200
Macchi MC.200 of the 373ª Squadriglia, 153° Gruppo Autonomo. The star on the blue panel is the pennant of a General di Brigata and the Assi di Bastoni (ace of spades) badge distinguished the 153 Gruppo Autonomo.

Messerschmitt Bf 110C
Messerschmitt Bf 110C of I Gruppe of Zerstörergeschwader 26 'Horst Wessel Geschwader', based in the Peloponnese for Operation 'Mercury'. This unit was charged with a major part in the 'softening up' of Crete's defences before the German airborne descent.

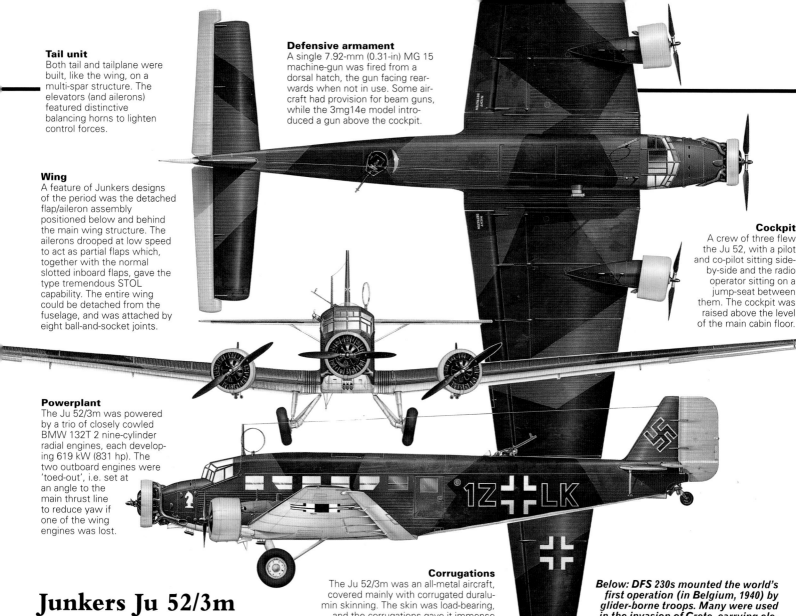

Tail unit
Both tail and tailplane were built, like the wing, on a multi-spar structure. The elevators (and ailerons) featured distinctive balancing horns to lighten control forces.

Wing
A feature of Junkers designs of the period was the detached flap/aileron assembly positioned below and behind the main wing structure. The ailerons drooped at low speed to act as partial flaps which, together with the normal slotted inboard flaps, gave the type tremendous STOL capability. The entire wing could be detached from the fuselage, and was attached by eight ball-and-socket joints.

Defensive armament
A single 7.92-mm (0.31-in) MG 15 machine-gun was fired from a dorsal hatch, the gun facing rearwards when not in use. Some aircraft had provision for beam guns, while the 3mg14e model introduced a gun above the cockpit.

Cockpit
A crew of three flew the Ju 52, with a pilot and co-pilot sitting side-by-side and the radio operator sitting on a jump-seat between them. The cockpit was raised above the level of the main cabin floor.

Powerplant
The Ju 52/3m was powered by a trio of closely cowled BMW 132T 2 nine-cylinder radial engines, each developing 619 kW (831 hp). The two outboard engines were 'toed-out', i.e. set at an angle to the main thrust line to reduce yaw if one of the wing engines was lost.

Junkers Ju 52/3m

This aircraft, a Ju 52/3mg7e, belonged to 2. Staffel, KGzbV 1, based at Milos, Greece, in May 1941 immediately prior to the invasion of Crete.

Corrugations
The Ju 52/3m was an all-metal aircraft, covered mainly with corrugated duralumin skinning. The skin was load-bearing, and the corrugations gave it immense strength for little weight penalty. Corrugation was a feature of many early Junkers designs.

Below: DFS 230s mounted the world's first operation (in Belgium, 1940) by glider-borne troops. Many were used in the invasion of Crete, carrying elements of the FJStR. Arriving too high, they had to circle and sideslip their way into the valleys.

Left: The three-engined Junkers Ju 52/3m 'Tante Ju' or 'Iron Annie' was by far the most common transport on all German fronts; an Axis equivalent to the C-47. Here one is dropping paratroops during the invasion of Crete.

Below: While Messerschmitt fighters hound the defences with strafing runs, Ju 52/3m transports, one on fire after being hit by AA guns, unload the men of 1 Fallschirmjäggeregiment over Heraklion, Crete.

In spite of some fighter cover, provided at long range from Egypt, the Germans landed almost 30,000 troops and by the end of the month Crete was in enemy hands.

HEAVY LOSSES
The campaign had cost the British forces dear. Apart from the loss of 38 RAF aircraft, the Royal Navy lost three cruisers and six destroyers sunk, and a battleship, carrier, six cruisers and eight destroyers damaged. About 15,000 Imperial troops were either killed or taken prisoner.

On the other hand the Luftwaffe suffered the loss of more than 200 aircraft, of which about half were Ju 52/3m transports. Of far greater significance, however, was the fact that the Balkan campaign had taken six weeks longer than planned and effectively delayed the opening of the great assault on the USSR. Apart from the severe losses among the vital transport aircraft, those six weeks may have been decisive in the conduct of Operation 'Barbarossa' before the onset of the dreaded Russian winter.

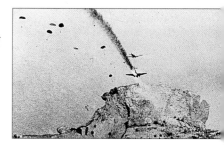

Into North Africa

JUNE 1940

Left: Two Bf 109E-4 Trops of JG 27 patrol over the Western Desert. White codes identify the aircraft as belonging to the 1st Gruppe. The Bf 109E enjoyed great success in North Africa, although it was rapidly replaced by later versions.

Below: On return from an operational sortie, the pilot of a Gladiator is rushed to debriefing at a desert location. Gladiators continued to serve in the Western Desert throughout 1941.

Believing that he would be deprived of the spoils of war when German forces burst into northern France, Benito Mussolini entered the war alongside Hitler on 10 June 1940. At a stroke the balance of naval power in the Mediterranean swung in favour of the Axis, even more heavily after the French fleet refused to continue operations on the Allied side and was accordingly attacked by the Royal Navy in its North African ports.

Three immediate threats to British strategic interests were posed by Italy's entry into the war: the naval base at Malta would be threatened by Italian air forces in Sicily; Italian forces in Cyrenaica were uncomfortably close to the vital Suez Canal and the British naval base at Alexandria; and a large Italian colonial army (and air force) threatened British bases in East Africa and the Arabian peninsula at the southern end of the Red Sea.

Little could be done to strengthen Malta's defences immediately and the island was left much to its own devices, recourse being found in a handful of obsolete Gloster Sea Gladiators and some Hawker Hurricanes with which to provide a measure of air defence. Fortunately, the Italians underestimated the strategic value of Malta and did little to attack the naval base from the air, at least for a month or so.

GLADIATORS

In the Western Desert, however, the position was more critical and in the face of considerable Italian numerical air superiority the RAF possessed an extraordinary mix of obsolescent aircraft with which to defend an enormous expanse of territory. Nevertheless, by dint of ingenious deployment and careful use of the resources available, the two Gladiator squadrons managed

to exact a considerable toll of Italian aircraft during the early months of the desert war, while General Wavell was able to set about his brilliant campaign which took his army far into Cyrenaica. Gradually,

the RAF was able to send a trickle of reinforcements to the Middle East, at first by convoy through the Mediterranean and later to Takoradi in the Gold Coast for overland flight to the Canal Zone.

Left: L5857 was the last of 50 Bristol Bombay Mk Is built and flew out to join No. 216 Squadron in the summer of 1940. It served its entire career with the squadron as a transport aircraft, being finally destroyed in an air raid on Kufra on 25 September 1942.

Left: The RAF created havoc with the Italian Air Force during the Battle of the Western Desert and Libya. This Fiat CR.42 crashed and burned out near Bandia in January 1941 after attempting a landing with one of its wheels shot away.

Above: Italian Air Force Savoia-Marchetti SM.79s. A total of four Stormi with 125 SM.79s was available in support of Marshal Graziani's land forces, based at Castel Benito, Bin el Bhera, Benina and El Adem.

Above: Frustrated by the Italians' inability to gain a decisive victory in North Africa, the Germans moved a major force of aircraft to the Mediterranean including Ju 87s such as this Ju 87D-1 Trop belonging to the 1st Staffel of I/StG 3 in late 1941.

Right: Bombing up a Blenheim Mk I for a sortie over the Western Desert in 1940 is this crew of No. 113 Squadron at a desert strip in Egypt. The Blenheim Mk I was almost entirely replaced by the Blenheim Mk IV in the desert campaign during 1941-42.

Vickers Wellingtons and Lockheed Hudsons were flown out directly from the UK, and Hurricanes and Bristol Blenheims arrived by the Takoradi route; other aircraft were crated and shipped out by the sea route round the Cape of Good Hope.

In East Africa the Italians gained early successes by invading and overrunning British Somaliland, and by doing so posed a threat to Aden.

However, in support of another brilliant counteroffensive by Commonwealth forces, RAF Vickers Wellesleys and Gladiators operating alongside aircraft of the South African Air Force succeeded in defeating elements of the Italian air force in East Africa. In due course the Italian presence in the horn of Africa was eliminated.

It was at the moment of triumph for Wavell's forces, which reached

Bombers in the Desert

Most of the bombing missions in the early desert air war were performed by light and medium bombers. This was primarily due to the fluid nature of the war, and to the fact that the targets were small and scattered. Most of the 'heavies' were desperately needed in the European theatre.

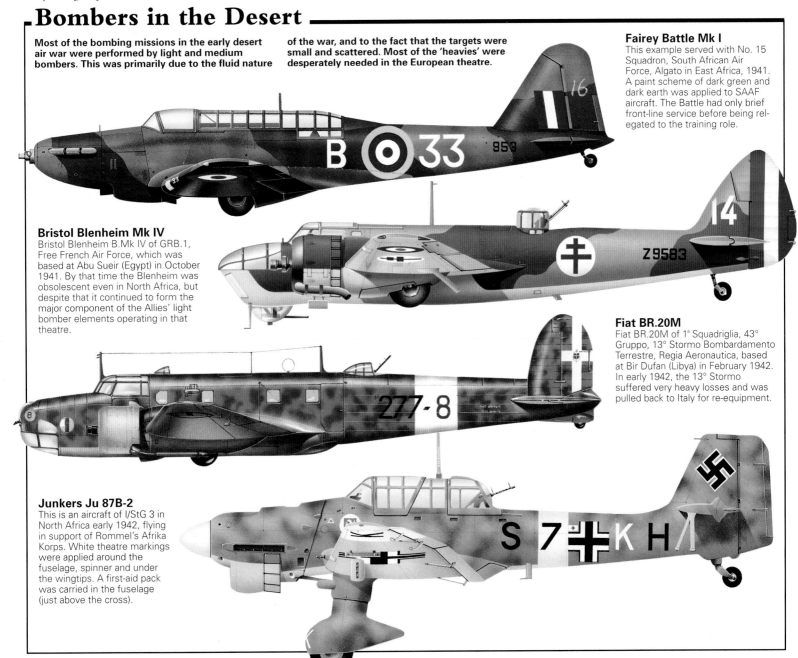

Fairey Battle Mk I
This example served with No. 15 Squadron, South African Air Force, Algato in East Africa, 1941. A paint scheme of dark green and dark earth was applied to SAAF aircraft. The Battle had only brief front-line service before being relegated to the training role.

Bristol Blenheim Mk IV
Bristol Blenheim B.Mk IV of GRB.1, Free French Air Force, which was based at Abu Sueir (Egypt) in October 1941. By that time the Blenheim was obsolescent even in North Africa, but despite that it continued to form the major component of the Allies' light bomber elements operating in that theatre.

Fiat BR.20M
Fiat BR.20M of 1ª Squadriglia, 43° Gruppo, 13° Stormo Bombardamento Terrestre, Regia Aeronautica, based at Bir Dufan (Libya) in February 1942. In early 1942, the 13° Stormo suffered very heavy losses and was pulled back to Italy for re-equipment.

Junkers Ju 87B-2
This is an aircraft of I/StG 3 in North Africa early 1942, flying in support of Rommel's Afrika Korps. White theatre markings were applied around the fuselage, spinner and under the wingtips. A first-aid pack was carried in the fuselage (just above the cross).

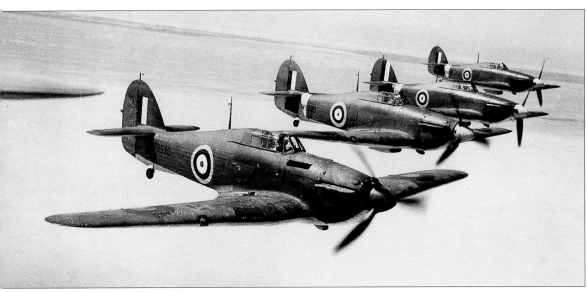

Benghazi in the first North African desert offensive, that RAF units were called on to go to the assistance of Greece (a campaign described elsewhere), a critical weakening that was to be compounded by events in Iraq in 1941.

Following a rebellion in support of the pro-Axis Rashid Ali, the large RAF base at Habbaniyah in Iraq came under attack supported by German and Italian aircraft, a threat only countered (and eventually overcome) by the deployment of ill-afforded Wellingtons, Blen-

Fighters of the Desert War

With the air conflict in Europe at full swing during 1940/41, the state-of-the-art fighters such as the Spitfire could not be spared for the North African campaign during the early phase of the desert action.

Nevertheless, the Tomahawks and Hurricanes were sufficiently capable to gain ascendancy over the Italian opposition. All this changed in the spring of 1941 with the arrival of the Messerschmitt Bf 109E.

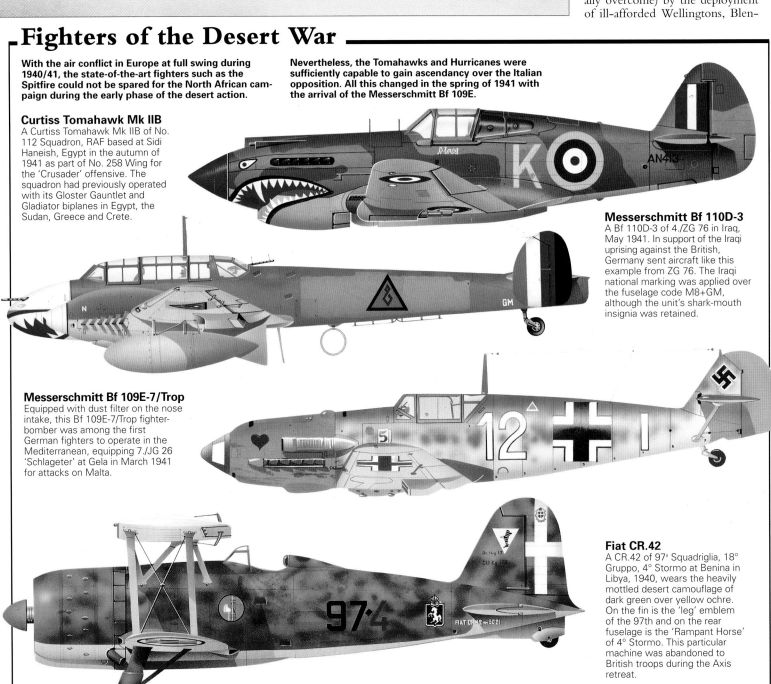

Curtiss Tomahawk Mk IIB
A Curtiss Tomahawk Mk IIB of No. 112 Squadron, RAF based at Sidi Haneish, Egypt in the autumn of 1941 as part of No. 258 Wing for the 'Crusader' offensive. The squadron had previously operated with its Gloster Gauntlet and Gladiator biplanes in Egypt, the Sudan, Greece and Crete.

Messerschmitt Bf 110D-3
A Bf 110D-3 of 4./ZG 76 in Iraq, May 1941. In support of the Iraqi uprising against the British, Germany sent aircraft like this example from ZG 76. The Iraqi national marking was applied over the fuselage code M8+GM, although the unit's shark-mouth insignia was retained.

Messerschmitt Bf 109E-7/Trop
Equipped with dust filter on the nose intake, this Bf 109E-7/Trop fighter-bomber was among the first German fighters to operate in the Mediterranean, equipping 7./JG 26 'Schlageter' at Gela in March 1941 for attacks on Malta.

Fiat CR.42
A CR.42 of 97ª Squadriglia, 18° Gruppo, 4° Stormo at Benina in Libya, 1940, wears the heavily mottled desert camouflage of dark green over yellow ochre. On the fin is the 'leg' emblem of the 97th and on the rear fuselage is the 'Rampant Horse' of 4° Stormo. This particular machine was abandoned to British troops during the Axis retreat.

Right: The establishment of Fliegerführer Afrika in Cyrenaica for the support of General Feld-Marshall Rommel's Afrika Korps in early February 1941 resulted in the recapture of El Agheila, and the subsequent advance to Sollum on the Egyptian frontier in April 1941. Here Ju 52/3m transports, with Bf 110 fighter escorts, are on a resupply operation to a forward area.

Below: This is a Bf 109E-7/Trop of 7.Staffel of Jagdgeschwader 26 operating from Aia El Gazala in June 1941 under Fligerführer Afrika.

heims, Gladiators and Hurricanes for defence of the base.

No sooner had the danger in Iraq been eliminated in the spring of 1941 than the Vichy French presence in Syria posed a threat to the Suez Canal (by possible defection to the Axis) as well as to important oil pipe lines, and it was decided to invade the country. This campaign, successfully completed in mid-July, involved the use of some 60 Hurricanes, Curtiss Tomahawks, Gladiators, Blenheims and Fairey Fulmars of the RAF, RAAF and the Fleet Air Arm.

Frustrated by the Italians' inability to gain a decisive victory in North Africa, the Germans moved the advance elements of a major force of aircraft to the Mediterranean (notably a Geschwader, JG 27 of Messerschmitt Bf 109Es) early in 1941, and these were quickly followed by Junkers Ju 87 and Junkers Ju 88 bombers. It was the arrival of this Fliegerkorps in the theatre that first posed a major threat to Malta; for a period its use as a naval base was severely restricted, and it was only sustained by sailing aircraft-carriers into the Mediterranean and

flying off fairly large numbers of Hurricanes to land on the island's airfields.

GAINING STRENGTH

Meanwhile, RAF strength in the Middle East was growing steadily. By November 1941, on the eve of the British 8th Army's second offensive into Cyrenaica against Erwin Rommel's Afrika Korps (Operation Crusader), RAF, Middle East Command comprised 29 squadrons of Hurricanes, Tomahawks, Curtiss Mohawks, Morane-Saulniers, Blenheim fighters and Fulmars, and 11 squadrons of Wellingtons, Blenheim bombers, Wellesleys, Douglas Bostons and Martin Marylands, as well as a dozen second-line squadrons, a total of almost 1,000 aircraft.

One of the most successful American bombers to enter the fight with the RAF was the Martin Baltimore, used exclusively in the Middle East, serving as a medium day-bomber and on anti-shipping reconnaissance. This is a Mk II version over the Western Desert.

Ranged against them were some 600 German and 1,200 Italian first-line aircraft.

At sea both the Royal Air Force and Fleet Air Arm were at work seeking out and attacking enemy supply vessels bringing troops and equipment from Europe to North Africa, a task carried out with increasing success, particularly between the Italian ports and Tripolitania. The theatre had assumed the status of a major war theatre.

Above: The Macchi MC.200 Saetta (lightning) proved adequate over Yugoslavia and Greece, but was soon outclassed in North Africa. This example is in the colours of 371ª Squadriglia, 22° Gruppo in 1940.

Right: The Curtiss Tomahawk served the RAF well in the desert, these shark-mouthed examples operating with No. 112 Squadron at Sidi Hanneish in late 1941. The type could master the Italian fighters with ease, but was outclassed by the Bf 109E.

Taranto

11/12 NOVEMBER 1940

On the night of 11/12 November 1940, 21 British Fairey Swordfish torpedo-bomber biplanes struck at the Italian fleet in Taranto harbour and in the first major and successful strike by naval aircraft, effectively redressed in British favour the balance of sea power in the Mediterranean.

Italy's entry into the war in June 1940 and the subsequent elimination of the French fleet had given the Axis superiority at sea in the Mediterranean; a situation that seriously threatened British convoys sailing to the UK with vital food, forces and munitions from the dominions east of Suez. Moreover, following Italy's attack on Greece in October that year, undisputed use of the Aegean and Adriatic by the Axis powers posed considerable difficulties in the support of any British foothold in the Balkans that might be considered.

Below: The Swordfish was designed to be flown at the very slow speeds required in carrier operations. With a single 45.7-cm (18-in) 730.3-kg (1,610-lb) torpedo under the fuselage it had a range of 879 kilometres (546 miles) and proved ideal for the Taranto attack.

Key to any operations in the central Mediterranean by the Royal Navy lay in the continued use of Malta, both as a naval and air base and it was with a fine sense of history that it had been intended to bring the Italian fleet to battle on 21 October (Trafalgar Day) with a British fleet of four battleships and battle-cruisers, two carriers (*Eagle* and *Illustrious*), 10 cruisers and four destroyer flotillas. Despite the

sailing of two convoys through the Mediterranean, the Italian fleet (comprising five battleships, 14 cruisers and 27 destroyers) declined to leave its base at Taranto; moreover, following a number of near misses from Italian bombers, the carrier *Eagle* was suffering mechanical troubles, necessitating the transfer of her Swordfish aircraft to the *Illustrious*.

FLEET LOCATED

The action was accordingly postponed and as a preliminary step a reconnaissance of Taranto was ordered on 10 November. A Maryland of No. 431 Flight, RAF, flown by Pilot Officer Adrian Warburton, was despatched from Malta that day and following an epic wave-top tour of the enemy port carried out in the face of intense flak, full details

Above: Shore-based, carrier-based and even catapulted from naval ships, the Fairey Swordfish was a very effective torpedo-bomber, although it was already obsolete and ready for replacement at the outbreak of World War II.

of the Italian fleet's dispositions were brought back and reported to Rear Admiral Lumley Lyster, the flag officer aboard *Illustrious*. The same evening the crew of an RAF flying-boat reported that a sixth Italian battleship had also entered Taranto.

Encouraged by the survival of the Maryland, Lyster decided to launch a strike against the Italian ships where they lay. On the evening of 11 November two waves of Swordfish flew off *Illustrious* at a position 274 kilometres (170 miles) south-east of

Below: HMS Illustrious, the carrier that launched the Swordfish aircraft that carried out the devastating attack on the Italian ships at Taranto on 11 November 1940. She is seen here in the Mediterranean with full war paint and Swordfish on the flight deck.

Right: Martin Marylands were used for aerial reconnaissance of enemy ports and to report on shipping movements in the Mediterranean. A Maryland flown from Malta by P/O Adrian Warburton spotted the Italian fleet at Taranto in November 1940.

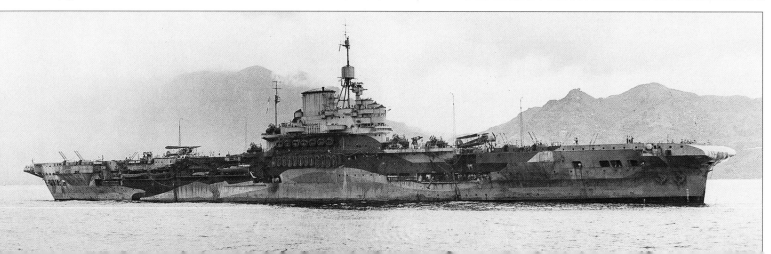

Anti-shipping aircraft

The Martin Maryland, designed as a light bomber, had its greatest success as a Fleet Air Arm reconnaissance aircraft, locating the Italian fleet at Taranto in November 1940.

The Swordfish, affectionately nicknamed the 'Stringbag', was able to use its slow speed and manoeuvrability to advantage, weaving in through the balloon barrage to attack the Italian ships.

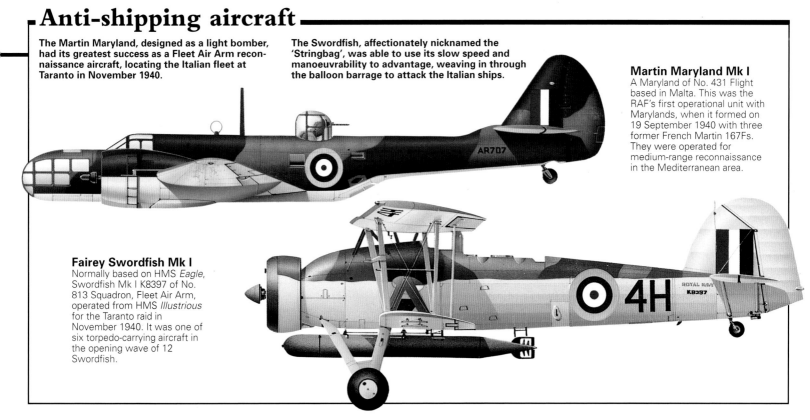

Martin Maryland Mk I
A Maryland of No. 431 Flight based in Malta. This was the RAF's first operational unit with Marylands, when it formed on 19 September 1940 with three former French Martin 167Fs. They were operated for medium-range reconnaissance in the Mediterranean area.

Fairey Swordfish Mk I
Normally based on HMS *Eagle*, Swordfish Mk I K8397 of No. 813 Squadron, Fleet Air Arm, operated from HMS *Illustrious* for the Taranto raid in November 1940. It was one of six torpedo-carrying aircraft in the opening wave of 12 Swordfish.

Taranto. The first formation, led by Lieutenant Commander Kenneth Williamson, comprised 12 aircraft (six with torpedoes, four with bombs and two with bombs and flares), the second wave of nine aircraft (five with torpedoes, two with bombs and two with bombs and flares) followed 40 minutes later, led by Lieutenant Commander John Hale.

Despite the obvious significance of the Maryland's appearance over the naval base on the previous day, the Italians were evidently caught completely unaware when Williamson's aircraft swept into Taranto harbour; added to this was the fact that the balloon barrage, which had been expected to cause some embarrassment during the attack, had been almost wholly destroyed by storms the day before. Moreover, the Italians had decided against the use of anti-torpedo nets on the pretext that they restricted the movement of their ships.

Two flares quickly disclosed the position of the new battleship *Littorio* (35562 tonnes/35,000 tons) and this was promptly sunk at her moorings by three torpedoes. Two older battleships, *Conte di Cavour* and *Caio Duilio* (both of 23979 tonnes/23,600 tons) were also hit, the former never to sail again and the latter, beached to prevent her sinking, severely crippled. In the inner harbour a heavy cruiser and a destroyer were also hit.

SWORDFISH LOSS

In due course the gun defences came into action and two Swordfish were shot down, including that flown by Williamson himself although he and his crewman survived to be taken prisoner. Another Swordfish failed to release its torpedo.

At a single blow half of Italy's battle fleet had been put out of action, a blow from which the Italians never fully recovered. On numerous occasions during the following three years their fleet declined battle with the Royal Navy, having been deprived of capital ship superiority. In the naval Battle of Cape Matapan on 28 March 1941, when a powerful force of Italian battleships might otherwise have crippled Admiral Cunningham's Mediterranean Fleet, the two enemy capital ships (albeit one of them damaged) sought safety by flight, leaving three cruisers and two destroyers to be sunk by Royal Navy. In the subsequent evacuation of Greece and Crete by British forces, losses among ships of the Royal Navy were grievous, being in the main inflicted from the air. Had the bulk of the Italian battlefleet been intact at that time, they would have been immeasurably worse.

TARANTO STRIKE
On the night of 11 November 1940 two waves of Swordfish flew 274 km (170 miles) from the new aircraft carrier HMS *Illustrious* and descended on the unsuspecting Italian battle fleet, causing so much damage that it changed the course of the whole war in the Mediterranean. For the first time a naval battle fleet had been destroyed by aircraft alone, without the fire-power of warships.

Malta

JUNE 1940 – JULY 1943

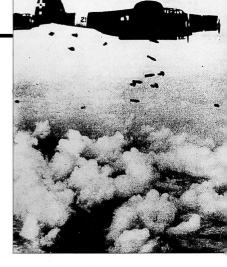

Left: HMS Indomitable *en route to Malta in 1942 with its mast head pennants flying. Hawker Hurricanes and Fairey Albacores are arranged on the flight deck. Photo taken from HMS* Victorious *with Hurricanes and Fairey Fulmars in the foreground.*

Right: An Italian Air Force three-engined Cant Z.1007bis 'Alcione' (Kingfisher) heavy bomber, releasing its bombload during a raid on Grand Harbour, Valetta in mid-1941.

Of all the British strategic bases overseas during World War II, the tiny rocky island of Malta, athwart the central Mediterranean, was probably the most important and accordingly, the most savagely assaulted from the air. At the time of Italy's entry into the war on 10 June 1940 Malta served two purposes: a British naval replenishment base on the maritime route through the Mediterranean to and from the Suez Canal and the Far East, and as a limited staging point for long-range flights from the UK to the Middle East.

Despite the completion of four air bases (at Hal Far, Luqa, Takali and a flying-boat station at Kalafrana), there was no organised fighter defence and only a naval gunnery flight in June 1940. When the Italians began somewhat desultory air attacks in that month, however, four Sea Gladiators were hurriedly uncrated and used to fly patrols against the raids (three of them ultimately being dubbed 'Faith', 'Hope' and 'Charity', though more with one eye on legend than with historical accuracy); before a fortnight was out four Hurricanes on their way out to North Africa were commandeered by the island for its defence.

These slender forces proved adequate to discourage the Italians from increasing their pressure on the island for several weeks, but it soon became obvious that, with major land operations imminent in North Africa, the need to reinforce both sides in Egypt and Cyrenaica

Left: The first 'Hurribombers' – Hurricane Mk IIBs fitted with bomb racks – went into action from Malta on 20 October 1941. This aircraft, about to scramble at Hal Far air-field, carries a 113-kg (250-lb) bomb under each wing.

would impose on Malta a vital role, lying as it did directly across the Italian supply route to Tripoli.

HURRICANES ARRIVE

On 2 August 12 Hurricanes were flown off the carrier *Argus* to the island, where they formed No. 261 Squadron and with adequate fighter defence now established, three reconnaissance Marylands of No. 431 Flight arrived from the UK. A second instalment of 12 Hurricanes, flown off the *Argus* on 17 November, was overtaken by tragedy, eight of them being lost at sea after running out of fuel. Meanwhile, Wellingtons – which had been staging at Malta on their raids from North Africa against targets in Italy – were now allowed to remain on the island to form No. 148 Squadron. It was also a Maryland of No. 431 Flight that carried out the superb reconnaissance of Taranto harbour before the epic raid by Fleet Air Arm Swordfish on the night of 11/12 November.

Throughout General Wavell's brilliant offensive in Egypt and Cyrenaica during the winter of

Carrier fighters

The Fairey Fulmar was the Fleet Air Arm's first carrier-borne monoplane fighter with the same level of fire-power as the Hurricane and Spitfire, when it was introduced in June 1940.

About 100 Gloster Sea Gladiators, the last of the Fleet Air Arm's biplane fighters, saw service from 1938. Four aircraft were borrowed from the RAF in June 1940 and fought in the defence of Malta.

Fairey Fulmar Mk I
Powered by a 805-kW (1,080-hp) Rolls-Royce Merlin II engine, the Fulmar had a top speed of 458 km/h (284 mph). It first saw action with the Fleet Air Arm defending the Malta convoys against the Italian Air Force. A good match for the Italian fighters, they were, however, out-classed by the Luftwaffe and were replaced by Seafires during 1943.

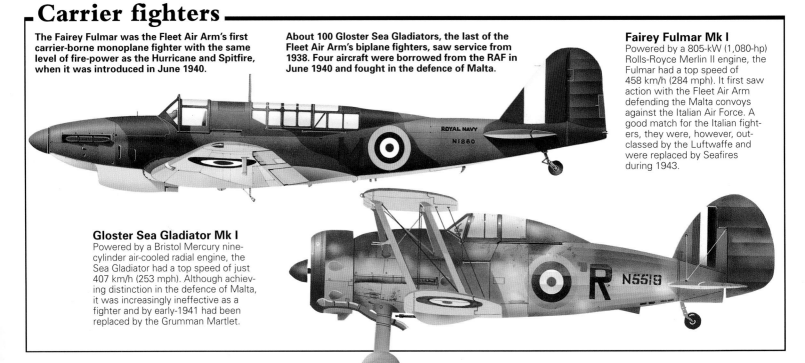

ROYAL NAVY   N1860

Gloster Sea Gladiator Mk I
Powered by a Bristol Mercury nine-cylinder air-cooled radial engine, the Sea Gladiator had a top speed of just 407 km/h (253 mph). Although achieving distinction in the defence of Malta, it was increasingly ineffective as a fighter and by early-1941 had been replaced by the Grumman Martlet.

R   N5519

Malta bombers

The Italian Régia Aéronautica flew German-built Junkers Ju 87B-2s carrying up to 1000 kg (2,205 lb) of bombs for attacks on Malta. Flown by inexperienced pilots, many were lost to defending fighters.

Junkers Ju 88A-5s were flown from Sicily by the Luftwaffe on very effective day and night raids against strategic targets in Malta and shipping convoys in the Mediterranean on a daily basis.

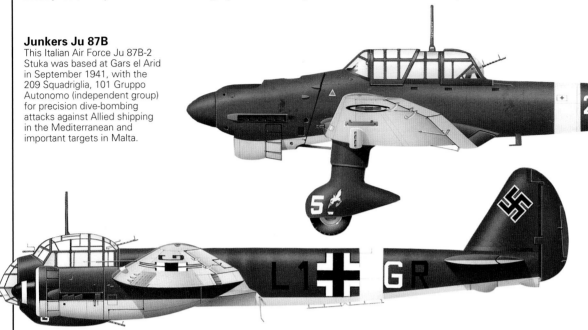

Junkers Ju 87B
This Italian Air Force Ju 87B-2 Stuka was based at Gars el Arid in September 1941, with the 209 Squadriglia, 101 Gruppo Autonomo (independent group) for precision dive-bombing attacks against Allied shipping in the Mediterranean and important targets in Malta.

Junkers Ju 88A
This Ju 88A-5 was used by the III Gruppe of Lehrgeschwader 1 for operations against Malta during early-1941, when the unit was based at Catania, Sicily, as part of Fliegerkorps X. The strengthened undercarriage of the A-5 made it more suitable for operations from the poorly prepared Sicilian airstrips.

Above: One of the three famous Sea Gladiators, named 'Faith', 'Hope' and 'Charity'. The three were in crates on the island en route to Egypt, when they were hurriedly assembled and flown by RAF pilots in the initial fighter defence of Malta, until the arrival of the first Hurricanes.

1940/41, the Wellingtons from Malta constantly raided Tripoli and Castel Benito, operations that brought swift reaction by the Axis with the arrival in Sicily late in December of the advance units of the German Fliegerkorps X; a force that within a month had grown to some 250 modern aircraft. On 10 January, 60 Ju 87s and He 111s attacked a British convoy in the Sicilian narrows, severely damaging the carrier *Illustrious* and the cruisers *Southampton* and *Gloucester*. The carrier limped into harbour at Malta where she became the target of heavy and repeated attacks by the Luftwaffe and Regia Aéronautica for more than a week. With losses increasing among the Hurricanes, the Wellingtons now had to be withdrawn to North Africa and, with Malta thus largely disarmed, the Germans were able to send about half of Fliegerkorps X to Cyrenaica to support Rommel's counter-offensive in the Western Desert.

CONVOYS GET THROUGH
The relief of pressure on Malta now allowed the British to sail a large convoy almost unscathed through the Mediterranean to Alexandria in May, by which time a second Hurricane squadron (No. 185 with Mk IIs) had been formed on the island. In June Fliegerkorps X was moved to Greece, Crete and the Dodecanese, a move that coincided with the arrival of Air Chief Marshal Sir Arthur Tedder to take over Middle East Command. At once the Wellingtons returned to Malta, together with Blenheims and further Marylands, and these aircraft renewed the attacks on the Italian ports and convoys, sinking over 71100 tonnes (70,000 tons) of enemy shipping in the last two months of 1941.

When two convoys reached Malta without loss Hitler resolved to eliminate the island once and for all, ordering Luftflotte II from the USSR to Italy before the end of the year under Albert Kesselring. There now started a four-month nightmare for Malta. Throughout January and February 1942 attacks by several dozen bombers were commonplace with never a day without raids, the targets in the main being the airfields. On 7 March 15 Spitfires reached the island from a carrier, but within a week the number of Hurricanes was down to 30, and at this point Kesselring started raids using 150 aircraft or more. The Wellingtons were withdrawn once more and April found the island seriously short of food, fuel and fighters, three out of four supply ships having been sunk. At the height of the assault, on 20 April, 47 more Spitfires arrived, followed by 62 on 9 May (having flown off the American carrier *Wasp*). Amidst rumours that the Germans were preparing to invade the island, Malta was awarded the George Cross for its sustained resistance.

It was now that Hitler stepped in with changed priorities (the first being the recapture of Cyrenaica) and Kesselring moved a large proportion of his aircraft to North Africa to support Rommel. The following month two convoys were sailed to Malta from east and west, of which one from Alexandria was forced to turn back. Two supply ships managed to reach the beleaguered island and the German offensive ran out of steam at El Alamein.

Following Montgomery's famous victory in November 1942, the aircraft on Malta, which had been preying on the supply convoys to North Africa, were further reinforced. For the next six months they took an increasing toll of Axis shipping in the central Mediterranean which was at first seeking to sustain the hard-pressed Axis forces and later desperately trying to extricate the beaten German and Italian forces from North Africa. The final irony of Malta's monumental achievement was reached when her fighter squadrons, numbering 12, provided air cover for the invasion of Sicily that was launched in July 1943.

Below: Spitfire Mk Vc being loaded on to the carrier USS Wasp at Glasgow in April 1942, to reinforce Malta. Fitted with four 20-mm cannon, tropical filters and 90-gallon slipper tanks, the Spitfires were flown north of Algiers.

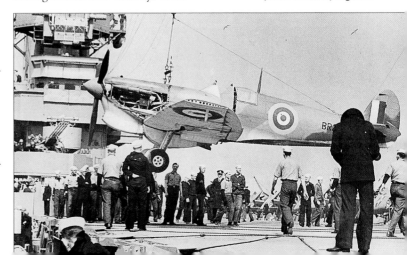

Operation 'Barbarossa'

JUNE 1941 – JANUARY 1942

Eclipsing all other German strategic planning during the first two years of the war was Hitler's determination to attack and defeat the Soviet Union. To do so it was necessary to eliminate any potential threat from the West to avoid the age-old German nightmare of war on two fronts. Following Italy's inability to impose a decisive solution in the Mediterranean and Balkans, Germany eventually launched her massive offensive in the East with the enemy still undefeated in the West and South and, as it transpired, with inadequate time to reach Moscow before the onset of the first Russian winter.

INVASION

The assault on the Soviet Union was launched before dawn on 22 June 1941 along a front that stretched from the Baltic to the Black Sea, the three army groups (under Leeb, Bock and Rundstedt) advancing 80 km (50 miles) in the

Above: A pair of Polikarpovs, armed with two synchronised machine-guns over the top of a powerful M-25V engine, operating on the Eastern Front in the summer of 1941. Initial losses in Operation 'Barbarossa' decimated the I-16 inventory, but it was still the most common V-VS fighter to oppose the Luftwaffe until October 1942.

Left: Ju 87D-1 Stuka of II/JG 77, Luftflotte 4 on a sortie over the Eastern Front near Kuban/Krymskaja. The revival in the fortunes of the Stuka was evident in the battles of 1941-42. This rugged aircraft gave invaluable support to German ground forces.

Below: During a break between sorties, Soviet pilots have a nerve-steadying cigarette and play dominoes. The Polikarpov I-16 is on an airfield in the region of the Khalkhin-Gol river in Barga province in July 1941.

first 24 hours. Supporting the huge offensive were four Luftflotten (air fleets) which between them deployed 19 Jagdgruppen of Bf 109Es and Bf 109Fs (600 aircraft), seven Stukagruppen of Ju 87 dive-bombers (more than 200 aircraft) and 24 Kampfgruppen of He 111s, Do 17s and Ju 88s (about 850 aircraft), as well as more than 1,000 other transport and reconnaissance aircraft.

Despite warnings from the West and the impossibility of concealing the German preparations for the attack, the Soviet Union was taken by surprise and when, on the first day, the Luftwaffe set out to destroy

Luftwaffe in the East

Hs 123s were originally intended as dive-bombers, though their careers were short-lived as the Stuka became available from 1937. The last examples were withdrawn in 1944. The STOL (short take-off and landing) Storch saw service on several fronts as an army co-operation and reconnaissance aircraft. The Do 17Z was the major production version of this medium bomber.

Henschel Hs 123A
On the Eastern Front the Hs 123 proved its worth in the close support role. During bad weather, when airfields were turned into mudbaths, the Hs 123s continued to operate by the simple expedient of removing the wheel fairings. This example wears the markings of 4. Staffel/Schlachtgeschwader 2, on the southern sector of the Russian Front in the winter of 1942-43.

Fieseler Fi 156C Storch
This Fi 156C Storch carries the codes of the Geschwaderstab of Lehrgeschwader 2, and was used on the Don sector of the Eastern Front during August 1942, operating as part of the Kurierstaffel Oberkommando der Luftwaffe.

Dornier Do 17Z
Dornier Do 17Z-2 of the Croatian-manned 10. Staffel of Kampfgeschwader 3 on the Central Sector of the front in December 1941: the Croatian Ustachi emblem is carried below the flight deck. The whole of KG 3 was committed to Operation 'Barbarossa' in June 1941, under II Fliegerkorps.

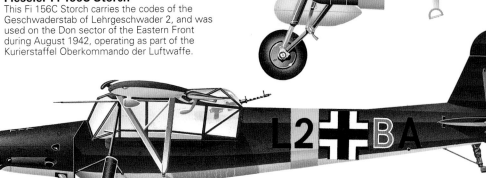

Above: As the position in the East worsened for the Soviets, production of the LaGG-3 fighter was stepped up, and although underpowered, it was available in quantity. Its design eventually led to the excellent La-5 and La-7 fighters.

the Soviet air force the German pilots found the enemy still on the ground. So widely dispersed were the Soviet airfields that the Luftwaffe was only able to send three or four aircraft against each, yet, by use of large numbers of 2-kg and 10-kg (4.4-lb and 22-lb) fragmentation bombs, they were able to devastate the grounded aircraft.

The relatively small numbers of outdated I-16 fighters which rose to defend their bases were swatted like flies by the experienced Luftwaffe pilots in their superb Bf 109s. During that first day the Soviets admitted the loss of more than 1,200 aircraft.

MOSCOW HIT
The airfield strikes were quickly followed by an attack by 127 He 111s and Ju 88s on Moscow, 104 tons of HE and 46,000 incendiary bombs being dropped; this was followed within 48 hours by two further raids by 115 and 100 aircraft. The massacre of Soviet aircraft

continued to occupy the Luftwaffe throughout July and August, and not unnaturally huge personal victory tallies were amassed by individual pilots; by mid-August four of the Jagdgeschwader (JG 3, JG 51, JG 53 and JG 54) had each passed a score of 1,000 enemy aircraft destroyed. On the ground it

Below: Widespread aerial reconnaissance during the preceding months had pinpointed every forward V-VS base and these came under sustained attack by Luftwaffe Ju 88s.

Tyrkowo attacked the Soviet fleet at Kronstadt, and a single bomb dropped by Oberleutnant Hans Rudel sank the Soviet battleship *Marat*. By the end of that month the front stretched from the Crimea in an almost straight line north to Leningrad.

Despite the weather the German armies managed to struggle forward and by early December reached Rostov, Voronezh and the outskirts of Moscow itself just as the first snows fell. This effectively brought air operations to a halt, as well as catching the Germans hopelessly ill-prepared for the rigours of the

seemed likely that the German army would be in Moscow before Christmas. The Soviet capital had not been Hitler's primary objective, however, and his orders to first secure the grain-rich Ukraine (which resulted in the capture of 650,000 Soviet troops) placed the entire campaign in jeopardy. In September the Finns advanced down the Karelian isthmus thereby helping to complete the investment of Leningrad. Not until October did Hitler renew the advance towards the Soviet capital, but by then it was too late.

Despite the widespread use of the incisive Blitzkreig tactics, which had hitherto overwhelmed so many armies in the previous two years, the German offensive slowed as autumn rains clogged the lengthening supply roads and organised partisan operations took their toll behind the German front. Increasing use was made of Ju 52/3m transports to bring up

supplies, but serviceable landing grounds were few and far between.

On 23 September Ju 87s of Stukageschwader 2 based at

Allies on the Eastern Front

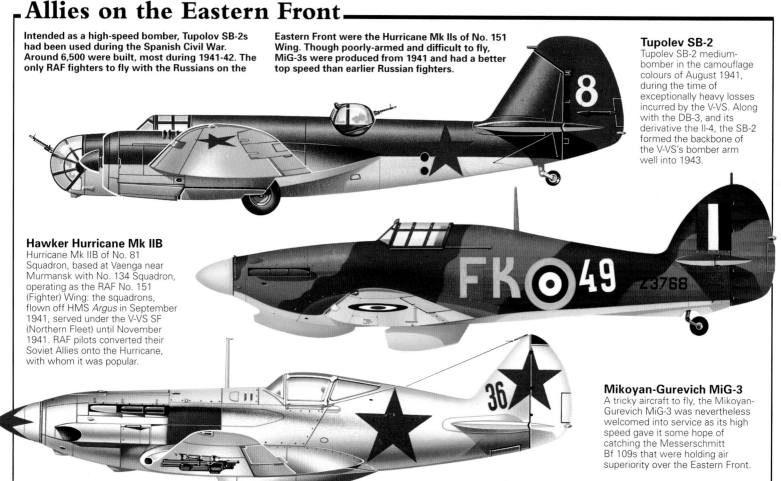

Intended as a high-speed bomber, Tupolev SB-2s had been used during the Spanish Civil War. Around 6,500 were built, most during 1941-42. The only RAF fighters to fly with the Russians on the Eastern Front were the Hurricane Mk IIs of No. 151 Wing. Though poorly-armed and difficult to fly, MiG-3s were produced from 1941 and had a better top speed than earlier Russian fighters.

Tupolev SB-2
Tupolev SB-2 medium-bomber in the camouflage colours of August 1941, during the time of exceptionally heavy losses incurred by the V-VS. Along with the DB-3, and its derivative the Il-4, the SB-2 formed the backbone of the V-VS's bomber arm well into 1943.

Hawker Hurricane Mk IIB
Hurricane Mk IIB of No. 81 Squadron, based at Vaenga near Murmansk with No. 134 Squadron, operating as the RAF No. 151 (Fighter) Wing: the squadrons, flown off HMS *Argus* in September 1941, served under the V-VS SF (Northern Fleet) until November 1941. RAF pilots converted their Soviet Allies onto the Hurricane, with whom it was popular.

Mikoyan-Gurevich MiG-3
A tricky aircraft to fly, the Mikoyan-Gurevich MiG-3 was nevertheless welcomed into service as its high speed gave it some hope of catching the Messerschmitt Bf 109s that were holding air superiority over the Eastern Front.

Ju 52/3m were starting to arrive at the front. Among the Soviet aircraft the I-15 and I-16 were being withdrawn at last as deliveries of modern LaGG-3s, MiG-3s and Yak-1s were frantically stepped up. Production of the Il-4 bomber (which had first raided Berlin on 8 August 1941) and Il-2 close-support aircraft was accelerating, and the first British convoys bringing Hurricane fighters had been arriving at Murmansk

since September. Hitler's dream of a speedy victory in the East was being shattered as his fighting men struggled to survive the frosts and snows of their first Russian winter.

cruel winter. Loathe to waste Luftwaffe resources where they would be useless, the Germans started moving some of their fighters and dive-bombers to the Mediterranean in December to support operations against Malta and the British forces in North Africa.

COUNTER ATTACK

Then on 6 December the Soviet commander Georgi Zhukov (of Nomonhan fame) launched a counter-attack with a fresh, well-equipped army in the Moscow area and, without the means to provide adequate air support for the ground forces, the Germans were forced to pull back. The bid to capture the Soviet capital was at an end.

At this time, however, both the Luftwaffe and V-VS were hurriedly introducing improved aircraft. The Bf 109E was now finally being replaced on all units by the Bf 109F; the Do 17 had almost disappeared from front-line service, being replaced by the Do 217, while new versions of the He 111, Ju 88 and

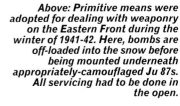

Channel Dash

FEBRUARY 1942

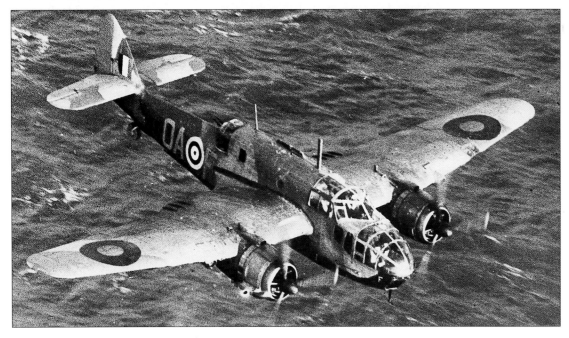

Above: Hudsons of Coastal Command patrolled the western end of the English Channel to detect and report any attempt by the German warships to sail through. However, on the crucial night of 11/12 February, two Hudsons failed in this task.

Left: Seen over choppy Channel waters is a Bristol Beaufort of No. 22 Squadron. F/O Campbell from No. 22 was awarded the Victoria Cross for damaging the Gneisenau during a daring raid on Brest harbour from which he did not return.

In February 1942 there occurred what was for the Royal Navy and the Royal Air Force one of the most humiliating events of the entire war. Three German warships, *Scharnhorst*, *Gneisenau* and *Prinz Eugen*, escaped an elaborate blockade in Brest harbour, sailed through the Dover Straits in daylight and reached their German ports despite all the British could do to prevent them.

Since early-1941 the powerful battle-cruisers *Scharnhorst* and *Gneisenau* had lain in Brest, where they had put in after destructive forays in the Atlantic and where they were joined by the heavy cruiser *Prinz Eugen* on 1 June. Thereafter this trio posed a considerable threat to British convoys not only crossing the North Atlantic but sailing to and from Gibraltar and further afield. Accordingly, at the insistence of the British Admiralty, they had attracted the constant attention of RAF Bomber and Coastal Commands; however, in the first two months of attacks on Brest with over 1,100 sorties flown

against the port, only four bombs damaged the ships, and it was decided to 'sew them in' using sea mines. On 6 April a single Beaufort, flown by Flying Officer Kenneth Campbell of No. 22 Squadron, managed to torpedo the *Gneisenau*, causing damage that took six months to repair. Throughout the remainder of 1941 an enormous tonnage of British bombs fell on Brest but caused little more than superficial damage to the warships, and in February 1942 the Germans decided on a bold bid to sail them back to Germany through the English Channel (Hitler being convinced that the UK was about to launch an invasion of Norway). The maritime operation was to be codenamed 'Cerberus', while 'Thunderbolt' covered the elaborate plans to provide air cover

Right: Six Swordfish of No. 825 Squadron, led by Lt Cdr Eugene Esmonde (who was awarded a posthumous Victoria Cross for his leadership and supreme gallantry), attacked the German ships, but all six were shot down.

during the voyage. The breakout from Brest was scheduled for the late-evening of 11 February.

NIGHT ESCAPE

To counter the threat of such an escape a British submarine lay off Ushant and the RAF covered the port with reconnaissance by day and operated radar watches ('Stopper') with Hudsons at night.

Delayed by a Bomber Command raid on the port itself that night, the German ships slipped their moorings shortly before midnight and sailed out unseen by the submarine and set course north-east up the Channel. Unfortunately at that critical moment the radar in the patrolling Hudson had become unserviceable and the German ships escaped undetected. By first light the following morning they had passed the Cherbourg peninsula. A further routine Coastal Command precaution, a patrol between Boulogne and Le Havre ('Habo'), had been recalled owing to the forecast of fog.

It was at this point that the first German day fighters arrived over the German ships to provide cover against the expected RAF attacks,

and these were spotted on British coastal radar at 08.30 but were dismissed by Fighter Command (under Air Vice-Marshal Leigh-Mallory) as being some sort of German air-sea rescue exercise. Two hours later the pilots of two Spitfires on an *ad hoc* sweep over the Channel spotted the German fleet and, under orders not to break radio silence, sped back to their base at Kenley to report, landing at 11.10. Thus it was not until 11.25 that the British air and naval authorities were fully aware that the enemy ships were at large in the Channel. By then they were entering the Dover Straits under the protection of numerous destroyers and E-boats, as well as swarms of Fw 190As and Bf 109Fs of Adolf Galland's JG 2 and JG 26.

BREAK-OUT SUCCEEDS

To counter such a break-out from Brest, the RAF (as part of Operation 'Fuller') had earmarked 100 Bomber Command aircraft and three squadrons of Beaufort torpedo-bombers, while the Fleet Air Arm had stationed a squadron (No. 825) of Swordfish at Manston. None of the Bomber Command aircraft were in the south of England and were only at four hours' standby; only seven of the Beauforts and the Swordfish were ready and loaded up with torpedoes.

As the German ships passed through the Dover straits the heavy guns on the Kent coast opened up, but their shells all fell wide of the mark. Three fighter squadrons were ordered off to escort the Manston Swordfish which, at 12.20, took off

and made for the enemy. Only one of the Spitfire squadrons, No. 72, arrived on time and was heavily engaged by the German fighters. Beset all around by Focke-Wulf Fw 190s and Messerschmitt Bf 109s and faced by a veritable wall of flak, Lieutenant Commander Eugene Esmonde led his old torpedo biplanes into the attack. All were shot down and none of their torpedoes found their mark. Esmonde himself was awarded a posthumous Victoria Cross.

As the German ships passed out of British coastal radar cover a few Beauforts attacked with torpedoes, but again without success, as did a group of British destroyers. Between then and darkness on the evening of 12 February 242 RAF bombers set out to attack but fewer than 40 crews claimed even to have seen their targets. The enemy ships did not escape unscathed, however, the *Scharnhorst* exploding a mine off Walcheren in the early afternoon

and another off Terschelling late that evening before limping into Wilhelmshaven; the *Gneisenau* also struck a mine but made Cuxhaven safely.

The bold Operations 'Cerberus' and 'Thunderbolt' had succeeded beyond all expectations, while 'Fuller', 'Stopper' and 'Habo' failed dismally. Ironically Bomber Command alone reaped an ill-earned reward: it no longer had the tiresome task of raiding Brest.

Above: The escape of the Scharnhorst, Gneisenau and Prinz Eugen was a tragic episode for the Swordfish. All six of the attacking aircraft were shot down, losing 13 crew. The Swordfish was subsequently used mainly on anti-submarine duties.

Below: The German warships Gneisenau, Scharnhorst and Prinz Eugen during the Channel dash. Torpedo attacks failed to inflict any damage, although in the event the Scharnhorst was partially crippled by mines previously dropped by the RAF.

Adversaries over the Channel

Only in service since mid-1941, Focke-Wulf Fw 190s of JG 26 were called upon to provide air cover for the break-out. Their first clashes with RAF Spitfire Mk Vs in 1941 had demonstrated its superiority; something that was not addressed until the

Spitfire Mk IX appeared in July 1942. Bristol's Beaufort was Coastal Command's standard torpedo-bomber from 1940 to 1943, until superseded by the Beaufighter. Early examples had Bristol Taurus engines; Mk IIs used Twin Wasps.

Focke-Wulf Fw 190A
One of the earliest Fw 190s to get into action was this A-2 flown by the Kommandeur of 1/JG 26 in early-1942 from St Omer in France. This was in the year that the formidable nature of the Fw 190 could no longer be doubted by the RAF's senior officers.

Bristol Beaufort Mk I
The Bristol Beaufort was used for a number of torpedo attacks on the German ships. This No. 22 Squadron aircraft had managed to score a single hit on the *Gneisenau* in April 1941.

Dieppe

19 AUGUST 1942

Left: The Hawker Typhoon saw its first action during the ill-fated Dieppe raid. These early aircraft tried desperately to hold off the Luftwaffe bombers, but other air cover for the landings was insufficient to support them. Two aircraft lost their tails in high speed dives trying to escape from Spitfires!

Below: By the time the RAF introduced its Spitfires and Typhoon fighter over the Dieppe landings, the Luftwaffe had some 200 Fw 190As in opposition. The RAF was unaware that a bomb-carrying version, the Fw 190A-3/U1 seen here, was in service.

Since the moment of French capitulation in June 1940 and the loss of the UK's last foothold in continental Europe, the cornerstone of possible eventual victory against Germany was assumed to be a return in force by British forces across the English Channel. Such a major amphibious landing on a hostile coast was an unknown venture, particularly in the age of the military aeroplane.

It was therefore decided in 1942 to mount a major operation across the Channel as something of a rehearsal for the eventual invasion, then believed to be a practical possibility in 1943; the objective chosen was the French port of Dieppe. The opportunity was to be taken to test the enemy's reaction to such a landing in force particularly in the air, and a major object was to attract the Luftwaffe in France into the air where it was hoped it could be decisively beaten. By mid-1942 it was hoped to be able to deploy as many as 60 fighter and fighter-bomber squadrons plus 10 reconnaissance and light bomber squadrons in the area of the landings, to counter the estimated German force of 250 fighters and 220 bombers based in France and the Low Countries. More important, it was hoped to field a dozen squadrons of the new 644-km/h

(400-mph) Typhoons and Spitfire Mk IXs which were calculated to be more than a match for the new German Fw 190A. Command of the air operations was in the hands of Air Vice-Marshal Leigh-Mallory.

DOOMED

From the outset matters went wrong with the British plans. After a couple of postponements (which are thought to have given the Germans an inkling of a pending attack), the operation was finally launched at first light on 19 August. The large number of Spitfire Mk V fighter squadrons took off before dawn to cover the landing areas and indeed provided powerful cover for the troops on the beaches as the Blenheims and Bostons attacked targets in and around Dieppe itself, and laid smokescreens over the beaches. Further afield Defiants with jamming equipment attempted to blind enemy radar as American B-17s carried out a raid on the important German fighter base at Abbeville.

At first the Luftwaffe reacted with only single Staffeln of Bf 109Fs and Fw 190As, and these were heavily engaged by the patrolling Spitfires. By mid-morning, however, enemy air activity was quickly increasing with the appearance of formations of Do 217 bombers and

a number of low-level bombing attacks by Fw 190A-4s which managed to penetrate beneath the RAF fighter cover and escape unscathed.

On the ground the Canadian and commando forces proved unable to capture vital enemy positions overlooking Dieppe, while the Churchill tanks were inadequately armed to knock out enemy strongpoints as they floundered up and down the shingle beaches. Garbled communications suggested that the Canadians were well established in the town so that support by the Hurricane fighter-bombers was called off at a critical point in the battle, resulting in heavy casualties among these troops.

There is no doubt that the huge armada of covering fighters prevented the German bombers from carrying out their attacks accurately on the ships and only two vessels were hit by enemy bombs. However, while the Spitfire Mk V pilots had been briefed not to continue combat too far from Dieppe, the Spitfire Mk IXs and Typhoons were allowed free rein. Unfortunately

Above: Dieppe was an occasion fraught with all manner of unknowns for the RAF. The fatal assumption was made that they would gain superiority over their German counterparts. It was realised too late that newer versions of the Fw 190A were superior to the current RAF fighters.

Left: The brunt of the fighting was borne by the outclassed Spitfire Mk Vb, like this formation of No. 122 Squadron here scrambling to intercept enemy raiders. The RAF was unable to provide adequate close support so numerous enemy aircraft succeeded in penetrating the air umbrella over Dieppe.

persistent development trouble with the latter had limited its entry into service and only a single wing was available for action at the time of the Dieppe operation and even then only with a number of flying restrictions. The only occasion on which Typhoons were in action was when they were accidentally attacked by a squadron of Canadian-flown Spitfire Mk IXs. Two Typhoons were lost when their tail units broke off as their pilots attempted to escape by diving away.

By late afternoon the assault ships were withdrawing across the Channel, still covered by the Spitfire Mk V squadrons. At first it was thought, by examination of the RAF pilots' combat reports, that the RAF had indeed won a signal victory. Early estimates suggested that more than 100 German aircraft had been shot down, compared with the loss in combat of 106 RAF aircraft in addition to 32 others written-off at base. German records later revealed that the Luftwaffe aircraft losses totalled no more than 48.

LESSONS LEARNT

The tactical lessons learned at Dieppe were indeed sobering. Ground support by the fighter-bombers and light bombers had been wholly inadequate, and there had been little or no effective communication between the landing forces and the supporting pilots.

Overall the ratio of fighters to support aircraft had been far too great, and the supposed superiority of the latest RAF aircraft proved illusory, while control of the fighters had been conducted at land-based radar stations too remote from the actual battle.

Ironically the value of the Dieppe landing lay in one vital piece of information: that the Allied forces, their tactics, equipment and training in 1942 fell far short of the standard obviously required for a successful invasion of Europe. There was, alas, no means of persuading the Soviet Union (which had been pressing the UK to open a 'second front' without delay) of this unpalatable fact.

Below: A German soldier surveys the tragic sight of Allied troops killed in battle and their abandoned equipment on the beach at Dieppe. It was to be almost two more years before the Allies succeeded in landing and holding the Channel coast of Europe. Then, ground support by Allied aircraft was properly planned and much more effective.

Combat fighters

The Spitfire Mk V, of which some 6,500 were built, proved to be underpowered when it came face-to-face with the Fw 190. The supercharged Merlin 60 engine with a four-blade propeller and other refinements was introduced as the improved Mk IX.
The Fw 190 first appeared over northern France in mid-1941 and immediately won the respect of Allied aircrew who quickly suffered at its hands. Superior to the Bf 109 in almost every respect, the Fw 190 had a major impact over Dieppe.

Focke-Wulf Fw 190A

In 1942, the Focke-Wulf Fw 190 factories switched to the A-4 model, with methanol/water boost for the engine and a better radio (with small aerial mast on the fin). The A-4 was flown by the adjutant of Stab III/JG 2 'Richthofen', one of the top-scoring fighter wings of all time. Its base in September 1942 was Poix.

Spitfire Mk VB

This Spitfire VB is in the colours of No. 340 Squadron, a Free French fighter unit. At the time of Dieppe it was operating from RAF Hornchurch and involved in fighter sweeps over northern France. The Cross of Lorraine emblem is carried under the cockpit.

Cross-Channel Operations

OCTOBER 1941 - JUNE 1943

Above: Early Hawker Typhoon IBs of No. 56 Squadron based at RAF Manston on an operational sortie across the Channel in early 1943. At this time, No. 56 was using the Typhoon for small-scale fighter or fighter-bomber attacks on ground targets of opportunity.

When viewed against events elsewhere, the scale and objectives of operations conducted by the Luftwaffe and RAF across the English Channel after the end of the Battle of Britain were minor. The principal difference lay in the fact that the British (and later the American) attacks were continuous and increasing in tempo, whereas those of the Germans were sporadic and, in general, of strictly limited effort.

The RAF's aims were threefold: to deny access by enemy coastal shipping to ports along the French coast; to disrupt all military (but particularly air) operations in northern France; and to defeat the relatively small German air force in France and the Low Countries in the air. To do this Fighter Command set about increasing its strength in 1941 by introducing the excellent Supermarine Spitfire Mk V, a version that eventually equipped no fewer than 71 squadrons. The Spitfire Mk VC variant was capable of carrying up to 500 lb (227 kg) of bombs. Hawker Hurricane Mk IIs, of which the four-cannon Hurricane

Mk IIC fighter-bomber was the outstanding version, equipped a further 42 squadrons; they eventually carried up to 1,000 lb (454 kg) of bombs.

From the beginning, the light bombers of No. 2 Group (Bristol Blenheims and Douglas Bostons) were tasked with Operation

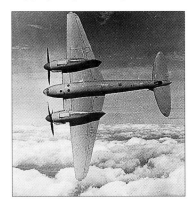

Above: In the mid-war years, the de Havilland Mosquito joined the Spitfire for longer-range photo-reconnaissance missions. This Mosquito PR.Mk IV was based at RAF Benson in early 1943 with a detachment of No. 540 Squadron, and used for photographic flights over occupied France.

Above: This Bf 109G-6/R6 was serving in the summer of 1943 with II/JG 26, one of the crack fighter units in northern France.

Below: A Westland Whirlwind I of No. 263 (Fighter) Squadron before modification to carry bombs under the wings. Operating from Warmwell in Dorset, No. 263 was involved in offensive sweeps over France.

Taking the war to the enemy

Offensive sweeps over occupied France began soon after the Battle of Britain (initially with Spitfires). These differed from the Luftwaffe's post-Battle of Britain nuisance raids in having ambitious and extensive aims: the disruption of all military operations in France, the denial of French Channel ports to coastal shipping, and the defeat of the Luftwaffe in the air, winning local temporary air superiority.

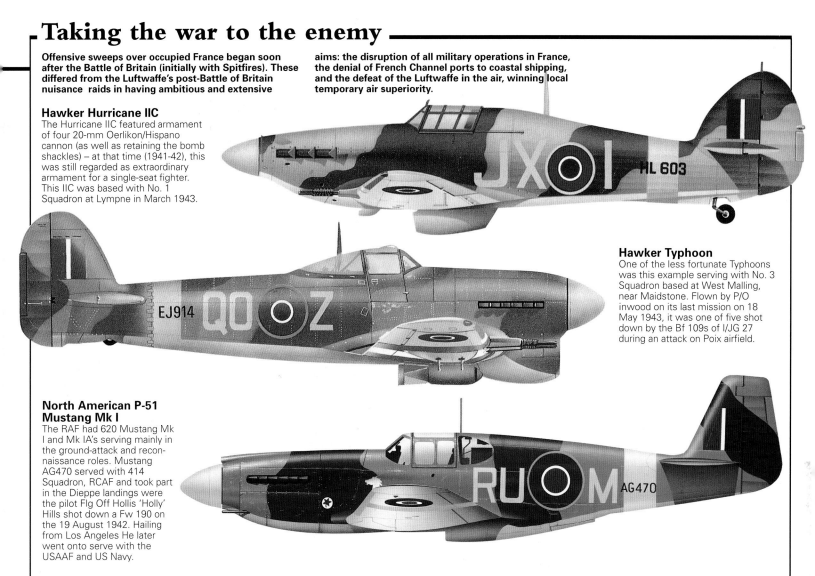

Hawker Hurricane IIC
The Hurricane IIC featured armament of four 20-mm Oerlikon/Hispano cannon (as well as retaining the bomb shackles) – at that time (1941-42), this was still regarded as extraordinary armament for a single-seat fighter. This IIC was based with No. 1 Squadron at Lympne in March 1943.

Hawker Typhoon
One of the less fortunate Typhoons was this example serving with No. 3 Squadron based at West Malling, near Maidstone. Flown by P/O inwood on its last mission on 18 May 1943, it was one of five shot down by the Bf 109s of I/JG 27 during an attack on Poix airfield.

North American P-51 Mustang Mk I
The RAF had 620 Mustang Mk I and Mk IA's serving mainly in the ground-attack and recon-naissance roles. Mustang AG470 served with 414 Squadron, RCAF and took part in the Dieppe landings were the pilot Flg Off Hollis 'Holly' Hills shot down a Fw 190 on the 19 August 1942. Hailing from Los Angeles He later went onto serve with the USAAF and US Navy.

Channel Stop', a constant offensive against enemy coastal shipping in the Channel. Upon the arrival of the fighter-bomber Hurricanes this task was taken over by Fighter Command on 30 October 1941, while the light bombers concentrated on land targets under heavy Spitfire protection. The Spitfires

The Focke-Wulf Fw 190, which first appeared over France in October 1941, dominated the skies for many months. RAF intelligence could not believe that this squat, angular fighter had the measure of the sleek and slender Spitfire V.

An unusual view of an RAF Boston Mk III, over Charleroi in France. The bulged twin-gun packs can be seen on each side of the nose, with the open bomb doors beyond. Normal bombload of the Boston was four 500-lb (227-kg) bombs.

themselves had initiated the first of the offensive sweeps, known as Rhubarbs, as early as 20 December 1940, and these continued to grow in scope until by 1942 as many as 500 aircraft would sweep along the French coast, trailing their coat in an effort to lure the Luftwaffe into the sky. Occasionally (and particu-

larly when German radar reported British light bombers approaching key fighter airfields), the Messer-schmitt Bf 109Fs of JG 2 and JG 26 would come up to intercept, and heavy air fighting would ensue; by and large, however, air combats tended to involve only the smaller formations.

SUPERIOR FOCKE-WULF
This pattern changed dramatically with the introduction of the Focke-Wulf Fw 190A, an excellent fighter that quickly proved superior

Early in 1941, the Hurricane IIC entered service with the RAF, and many were used on Channel sweeps and bomber escorts over France. Attrition was comparative-ly high and combat with Bf 109s was viewed with some apprehen-sion by Hurricane pilots.

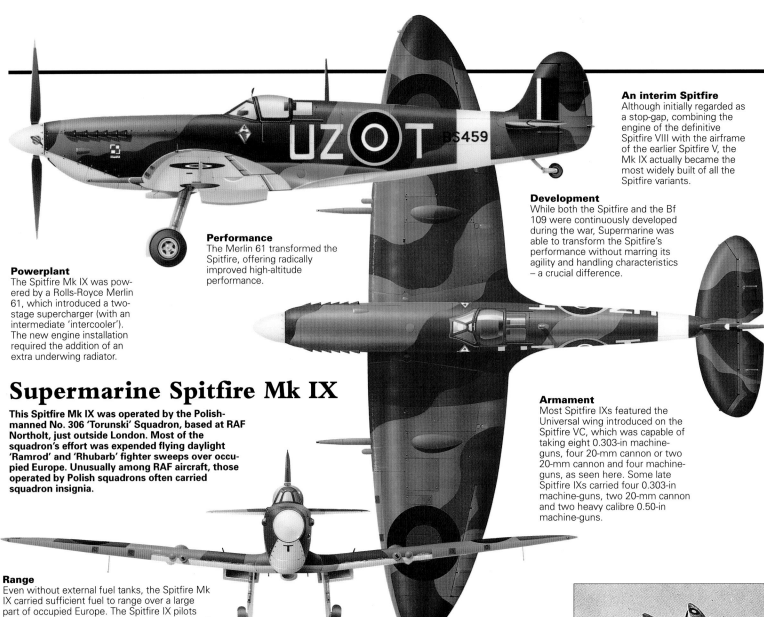

Although initially regarded as a stop-gap, combining the engine of the definitive Spitfire VIII with the airframe of the earlier Spitfire V, the Mk IX actually became the most widely built of all the Spitfire variants.

Development
While both the Spitfire and the Bf 109 were continuously developed during the war, Supermarine was able to transform the Spitfire's performance without marring its agility and handling characteristics – a crucial difference.

Performance
The Merlin 61 transformed the Spitfire, offering radically improved high-altitude performance.

Powerplant
The Spitfire Mk IX was powered by a Rolls-Royce Merlin 61, which introduced a two-stage supercharger (with an intermediate 'intercooler'). The new engine installation required the addition of an extra underwing radiator.

Supermarine Spitfire Mk IX

This Spitfire Mk IX was operated by the Polish-manned No. 306 'Torunski' Squadron, based at RAF Northolt, just outside London. Most of the squadron's effort was expended flying daylight 'Ramrod' and 'Rhubarb' fighter sweeps over occupied Europe. Unusually among RAF aircraft, those operated by Polish squadrons often carried squadron insignia.

Armament
Most Spitfire IXs featured the Universal wing introduced on the Spitfire VC, which was capable of taking eight 0.303-in machine-guns, four 20-mm cannon or two 20-mm cannon and four machine-guns, as seen here. Some late Spitfire IXs carried four 0.303-in machine-guns, two 20-mm cannon and two heavy calibre 0.50-in machine-guns.

Range
Even without external fuel tanks, the Spitfire Mk IX carried sufficient fuel to range over a large part of occupied Europe. The Spitfire IX pilots could create as much mayhem as they liked and still have fuel to get home.

Spitfire vs Bf 109

Despite the arrival on both sides of more modern fighters designed in the light of combat experience, the Spitfire and Messerschmitt Bf 109 met in combat over Europe from the first months of the war to the last days. The late-mark Spitfires and 109s that battled over Berlin, however, were far different beasts than those that first encountered each other at Dunkirk in May 1940. The Bf 109 was a slightly older design, having first flown in

September 1935, six months before the Spitfire, and had undergone considerable development, not to mention a combat blooding in Spain, by the outbreak of war in September 1939. In comparison with the Spitfire Mk I, the Bf 109E was higher-powered, faster-climbing (at lower altitudes) and better-armed. Conversely, the Spitfire was more manoeuvrable at all speeds and altitudes. Weights, range and maximum speed were all very similar. After

After its return from the USSR, No. 81 Squadron became part of the Hornchurch wing, equipped with Spitfire Mk VBs.

the Battle of Britain the Luftwaffe and RAF introduced new fighters, specifically the Fw 190 and Typhoon, but recognised the soundness of the Bf 109 and Spitfire design and developed them almost beyond recognition. In early 1942, the two main versions in

service were the Spitfire Mk V and Bf 109F. The 'Friedrich' introduced the more powerful DB 601E engine and the Spitfire Mk V, the similarly-uprated Merlin 45, boosting the maximum speeds and climb rates. The increase in weight affected the manoeuvrability and handling of both types – more detrimentally in the case of the Messerschmitt.

The next developments were the Spitfire Mk IX and Bf 109G, both of

No. 222 Squadron moved to RAF Coltishall in November 1940, from where it began to fly offensive operations early in 1941. The Spitfire Mk VB, seen here, equipped the squadron from August 1941.

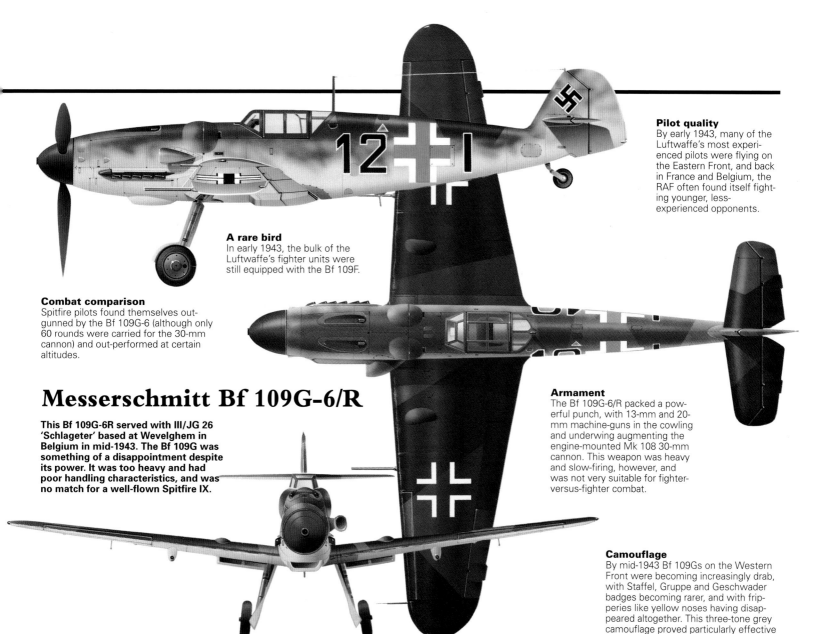

A rare bird
In early 1943, the bulk of the Luftwaffe's fighter units were still equipped with the Bf 109F.

Combat comparison
Spitfire pilots found themselves out-gunned by the Bf 109G-6 (although only 60 rounds were carried for the 30-mm cannon) and out-performed at certain altitudes.

Messerschmitt Bf 109G-6/R

This Bf 109G-6R served with III/JG 26 'Schlageter' based at Wevelghem in Belgium in mid-1943. The Bf 109G was something of a disappointment despite its power. It was too heavy and had poor handling characteristics, and was no match for a well-flown Spitfire IX.

Armament
The Bf 109G-6/R packed a powerful punch, with 13-mm and 20-mm machine-guns in the cowling and underwing augmenting the engine-mounted Mk 108 30-mm cannon. This weapon was heavy and slow-firing, however, and was not very suitable for fighter-versus-fighter combat.

Camouflage
By mid-1943 Bf 109Gs on the Western Front were becoming increasingly drab, with Staffel, Gruppe and Geschwader badges becoming rarer, and with fripperies like yellow noses having disappeared altogether. This three-tone grey camouflage proved particularly effective over the North Sea.

Right: A Polish pilot with No. 303 Squadron looks at his tally of 'kills' on the side of his Spitfire VB at RAF Kirton-in-Lindsey, Lincolnshire on 15 August 1942.

Below: The availability of the DB 601E engine at the beginning of 1942 resulted in the Bf 109F-3.

Below: A Spitfire VB in service with No. 92 Squadron at RAF Biggin Hill in late 1941. A total of 6,479 Spitfire Vs was built.

which entered service in 1942 to general acclaim. The Spitfire Mk IX was a hasty lash-up, a means of getting the new two-stage Merlin 60 series engine into a Spitfire as soon as possible to counter the threat of the Focke-Wulf Fw 190A. The airframe was that of the Mk V, but the result became the most numerous of all Spitfire variants, and in widespread use right to the end

of the war. Messerschmitt responded with the Bf 109G, driven by a DB 605 engine to give increased speed. This, too, became the most numerous variant, although it was built in a plethora of sub-variants.

One of the triumphs of Supermarine's design team was maintaining the excellent flying qualities of the Spitfire while constantly improving

the performance, a philosophy not adopted by Messerschmitt, who took the path of improving outright performance and adaptability at the expense of handling. Even so, the later Spitfires were less pleasant to fly than the earlier marks and had trickier ground handling characteristics than the lower-powered early models. From a pilot's point of view, the mid-series Spitfire Mk IX and Bf 109F models were generally regarded as the best of their respective breeds. The ultimate marks of the two great fighters to see combat in this war were the Griffon-engined Spitfire F. Mk 21 and the DB-605 (with water-methanol injection)-powered Bf 109K

The Spitfire Mk 21 had nearly double the engine power of the Mk I and 25 per cent greater maximum speed as did the Bf 109K compared to the E. Whereas the Spitfire's loaded weight increased by 75 percent between the Mk I and the much larger F. Mk 21, the Bf 109 grew little and a loaded K was 27 per cent heavier than an E.

Defending Fortress Europe

Although the introduction of the Fw 190 and Bf 109G gave the Luftwaffe an aircraft superior to the RAF's Spitfire V, the RAF maintained the initiative, accepting heavier casualties but remaining on the offensive. The introduction of the Spitfire IX

helped, but later Fw 190s (like the A-4 illustrated below) proved a match for the best of the Merlin Spitfires. At the end of the day, there were too few Luftwaffe fighters in France to stop the RAF's offensive.

Focke-Wulf Fw 190A-4

Far more heavily armed than the Messerschmitt Bf 109F and early Bf 109G, the Focke-Wulf Fw 190A-4 and close relatives multiplied in 1942. In the hands of the outstandingly skilled and experienced pilots in JG 2 and JG 26, the aircraft scored on average 5:1 against the RAF. This A-4 served with 2./JG 2 at Abbeville in May 1943.

Messerschmitt Bf 109G

From early 1942 the Messerschmitt Bf 109G became the standard production variant of the Luftwaffe's most numerous fighter, production building up to over 14,000 in 1944 alone. One of the early versions with light armament (one cannon and two machine-guns) was the G-4; this example operated from Poix with I/JG 27.

kampfgeschwader 10 (SKG 10) fighter-bomber wing began a series of daylight hit-and-run attacks with Fw 190A-4s, the RAF was forced to deploy disproportionately large forces of fighters to counter the

Below: In the European Theatre the first P-47 Thunderbolts and P-51 Mustangs in action were given white bands across the tail and around the nose to stop them being mistaken for 190s and 109s.

In February 1941, No. 601 Squadron based at RAF Northolt began taking part in offensive sweeps over northern France and flew the early sorties with Hurricane IIBs, before Spitfires began to dominate day offensive operations.

bomber, capable of carrying a 1,102-lb (500-kg) bomb, was serving with JG 2 in France. Thirty of these aircraft launched a vicious attack on Canterbury, Kent, on 30 October. Moreover, misled into believing that the Fw 190A-3 was the latest variant in service when an example landed intact in south

Wales on 23 June 1942, the British received an unpleasant surprise when confronted by the more powerful Fw 190A-4 which could outrun both the Spitfire Mk IX and Typhoon (the latter initially beset by restrictions).

When, during the winter of 1942-43, the newly-formed Schnell-

to the RAF's Spitfire Mk V. Fortunately for Fighter Command not more than about 60 of these aircraft were operational by February 1942 and, although losses among British aircraft began to increase, there was a breathing space in which to find a remedy.

FIGHTER-BOMBERS

As told elsewhere, the Hawker Typhoon was introduced into service before all its problems had been solved and, together with the Spitfire Mk IX, was entering service by the time of the Dieppe operation of August 1942. By then, though, the Fw 190A-3 fighter-

A Mustang I of No. II(AC) Squadron. Army Co-operation Command's Allison Mustangs were superb at low level and were used for the longest range cross-channel missions, even flying over Germany itself from October 1942.

The Westland Whirlwind was the first single-seat twin-engined fighter to see RAF service. Its existence was a closely guarded secret in the early days of the war, and problems with the Rolls-Royce Peregrine engines meant that only two RAF squadrons – Nos 263 and 137 – received Whirlwinds.

threat. Heavy damage was inflicted in a raid on London on 20 January 1943; in March SKG 10 struck Ashford, Eastbourne and Hastings, and the following month returned to Eastbourne and destroyed a ball-bearing factory at Chelmsford in Essex.

NEW SPITFIRE

Excellent though the stop-gap Spitfire Mk IX was, its performance at low altitude was inadequate to match that of the Fw 190A-3 and Fw 190A-4 fighter-bombers, and a new variant was hurriedly introduced: the Spitfire Mk XII with Griffon engine and clipped wings. (At low levels the Spitfire Mk VB with its single-stage low-blown Merlin 45, 46 or 50 was the equal of a Mk IX, especially in LF.Mk VB form with clipped wings which provided for a greater rate of roll.) Together with the Typhoon, whose snags had been largely cured and which was fast and adequately reliable at low level, the Spitfires grad-

Right: No. 601 Squadron, an Auxiliary Air Force Squadron, operated the Hurricane I from RAF Northolt, seen here in January 1941. The following month it received the later Hurricane IIB and made offensive sweeps over northern France until August, when it re-equipped with Bell Airacobras.

ually got the measure of the snap raids and, by late spring 1943, these had tailed off. In any case, with pressure mounting on other fronts, most Fw 190 fighter-bombers were being moved elsewhere.

By mid-1943 the Americans had arrived in the UK in sufficient numbers for the fighters and fighter-bombers of the US Army Air Force to make a significant contribution to the cross-Channel air

Right: No. 310 Squadron was formed at RAF Duxford in July 1940 as a fighter unit with Czechoslovak personnel. It received Spitfire VBs in November 1941 and flew them on operations from RAF Perranporth in Cornwall until May 1942.

offensive. On 13 April the Republic P-47s of the 56th Fighter Group entered combat for the first time with a sweep in the St Omer area, being followed into action in

later months by the 55th, 78th, 353rd 358th, 359th and 361st Fighter Groups of the 66th Fighter Wing, VIII Fighter Command. By the end of the year the Allies had at their disposal more than 2,200 Spitfires, Hurricanes, Typhoons, P-47 Thunderbolts, Lockheed P-38 Lightnings and North American P-51 Mustangs based in the UK. Their operations were divided between cross-Channel sweeps and escort missions with the British and American medium and heavy bombers which were by then mounting a devastating offensive against German-occupied Europe.

Showing the distinctive white identification bands, these P-47D-I-RE Thunderbolts are from the 62nd Fighter Squadron, 56th Fighter Group. At altitudes below 15,000 ft, the new Fw 190 proved to be more than a handful for the big American fighter, although above that height the P-47 could out-run and out-turn the Fw 190.

British Night Bombing

1941–1942

Left: Handley Page Halifax B.Mk II of No. 35 (Madras Presidency) Squadron, operating from RAF Linton-on-Ouse, North Yorkshire in May 1942. The bulbous Boulton Paul Mk III turret, with its raised fairing on top of the fuselage, created a great deal of drag.

Below: A morale boosting newspaper photograph that showed "the crew of the bomber 'MacRobert's Reply' all ready to take off for a raid over enemy territory". The Short Stirling Mk I of No. 15 Squadron at RAF Wyton, carried the coat of arms of the MacRobert family, the cost of the aircraft being donated by the family.

"We'll do our job – if you'll do yours"

As the German night blitz reached its climax at the beginning of 1941, RAF Bomber Command was beginning the long process of building a force of truly heavy bombers with which to carry the war back to the German people. The first landmarks in this process were reached when four-engined Short Stirlings of No. 7 Squadron bombed Rotterdam in the Netherlands on 10/11 February, Avro Manchesters of No. 207 Squadron attacked Brest on 24/25 February, and Handley Page Halifaxes of No. 35

Squadron raided Le Havre on the French coast on 10/11 March; two nights later Manchesters and Halifaxes made their first attack on German soil with a raid on Hamburg. It was, however, the twin-engined Vickers Wellington that dropped the RAF's first 1814-kg (4,000-lb) bombs when

Below: An Avro Manchester Mk IA, that flew with No. 207 Squadron from RAF Waddington in 1941. Incessant problems with the two Vulture engines made operations difficult and it was replaced by the Lancaster in 1942.

aircraft of Nos 9 and 149 Squadrons attacked Emden on the last night of March. Emden was again attacked on 27 April, this time in daylight by the Stirlings of No. 7 Squadron. On the night of 8/9 May Bomber Command assembled the largest force to date for raids on Germany when 360 aircraft of all types attacked Bremen and Hamburg.

By the end of 1941 Bomber Command possessed three

operational squadrons of Stirlings, three of Manchesters and three of Halifaxes, in addition to 21 Wellington squadrons, seven of Handley Page Hampdens and five of Armstrong Whitworth Whitleys, a total of about 420 aircraft (excluding Bristol Blenheim and Douglas Boston light bombers), of which fewer than 60 were four-engined bombers. However, the first examples of a new bomber had been delivered to No. 44 Squadron, this

Left: One of the first RAF squadrons to convert to the Lancaster Mk I in 1942 was No. 50 Squadron based at RAF Swinderby, Lincolnshire. No. 50 soon had its much improved bombers in action on heavy night-bombing raids.

Below: Against a backdrop of swirling clouds and fading evening light, a Lancaster Mk I of No. 83 Squadron, runs up its four Rolls-Royce Merlin engines before taxiing out for take-off and another night attack on Germany in 1942.

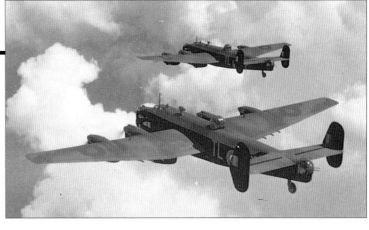

at the continuing inaccuracy of bombing attacks, not to mention the slow delivery of four-engined bombers, Harris at once ordered maximum priority for the introduction of new navigation and bombing aids (the rudimentary 'Gee' had been in limited service for about six months, and a short-range bombing aid, 'Trinity', had proved disappointing). He also gave orders for new tactics to be employed in an effort to increase bombing accuracy

Avro Lancaster being a four-engined development of the Manchester which, because of persistent engine problems, was soon discontinued and withdrawn.

1942 thus became the single most formative year for Bomber Command during the war. On 22 February Air Marshal Arthur Harris assumed the leadership of the command, a position he was to occupy with spectacular achievement for the remainder of the war. Disturbed

Early bombing twins

Limited by its bombload and service ceiling, the twin-engined Whitley's main impact was not in the bomber-offensive but was in 'nickelling' raids dropping propagandist leaflets over occupied Europe.

The Vickers Wellington Mk IC was the mainstay of Bomber Command through to late-1941, when it was progressively replaced by the bigger, four-engined Stirlings, Halifaxes and Lancasters.

Armstrong Whitworth Whitley Mk V
Whitleys helped carry the offensive into the heart of Germany, although nearly half of their bombs fell on open country. This Mk V flew with No. 77 Squadron in 1941.

Vickers Wellington Mk IC
The Wellington Mk IC with Pegasus XVIII engines and fitted with additional beam guns was the most successful bombing version built. This aircraft of No. 301 (Polish) Squadron flew from Swinderby and survived until 26 June 1942, when it was shot down on a raid over Bremen.

Right: A Boston Mk III of No. 226 Squadron returning to RAF Swanton Morley, on 7 May 1942. The first Boston Mk IIIs arrived during the summer of 1941, replacing Blenheims on daylight coastal raids and anti-shipping strikes.

Left: A formation of Short Stirling Mk Is of Mildenhall-based No. 149 Squadron. Stirling Mk Is flew long-range missions into Germany and Italy until replaced by the improved Mk III in 1943.

Above: A de Havilland Mosquito Mk IV of No. 139 Squadron operating from RAF Marham. The Mk IV was the first light-bomber version to go into service and could carry four 227-kg (500-lb) bombs and was powered by Merlin XXI engines.

Right: Crews from No. 106 Squadron at Coningsby celebrate with their CO, Wg Cdr Guy Gibson, the morning after the first 1,000-bomber raid on Cologne on 31 May 1942. Behind them is a Manchester IA (left) and a Mk I (right).

was awarded the Victoria Cross.

On the night of 30/31 May Harris launched his first '1,000-bomber' raid, undertaken as much as a propaganda coup as an attempt to swamp the German defences and thereby reduce the loss rate. A total of 1,046 bombers, culled from every Bomber Command squadron, as well as the operational training units, set out to attack Cologne in Operation 'Millennium'; 40

aircraft were lost out of the 898 that were believed to have bombed their target. At dawn the following day Bomber Command de Havilland Mosquito photo reconnaissance and bomber aircraft of No. 105 Squadron were over the city to observe the results of the raid in their first operational mission. Two nights later, on 1/2 June, 956 bombers attacked Essen for the loss of 31 aircraft, and on 25/26 June

and effect, and the first of these (the concentration of bombers in space and time over the target) was used with good results in a raid by 223 aircraft against the Renault factory near Paris on the night of 3/4 March.

ENTER THE LANCASTER

On the same night that the Renault works were being bombed, the great Lancaster bomber was making its operational debut, a mining sortie; its first bombing mission, a raid

by No. 44 Squadron on Essen, was flown on 10/11 March. Exactly one month later the RAF's first 3629-kg (8,000-lb) bomb was dropped by a No. 76 Squadron Halifax on the same target.

April saw the first of the Lancaster's spectacular 'set piece' attacks with a daylight low-level raid by 20 aircraft of Nos 44 and 97 Squadrons against the MAN plant at Augsburg on 17 April; seven aircraft were lost, but the leader, Squadron Leader John Nettleton,

Light bombers

Replacing Blenheims from May 1942, Mosquito Mk IVs of No. 2 Group proved very difficult for the Luftwaffe fighters to catch and enjoyed the lowest loss rate of any Bomber Command aircraft.

Also replacing Blenheims, the improved Boston Mk IIIs entered service in February 1942 and were used for low-level strikes against enemy shipping and coastal airfields and power stations.

de Havilland Mosquito Mk IV
Delivered in RAF Fighter Command markings (sky tailbands and yellow leading edges) this late Mosquito Mk IV light bomber was flown by No. 105 Squadron from RAF Marham in the summer of 1942. No. 105 made an epic Mosquito raid on the Gestapo HQ in Oslo on 25 September 1942.

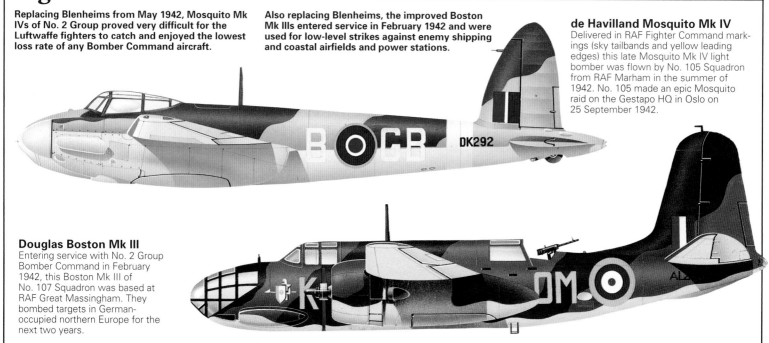

Douglas Boston Mk III
Entering service with No. 2 Group Bomber Command in February 1942, this Boston Mk III of No. 107 Squadron was based at RAF Great Massingham. They bombed targets in German-occupied northern Europe for the next two years.

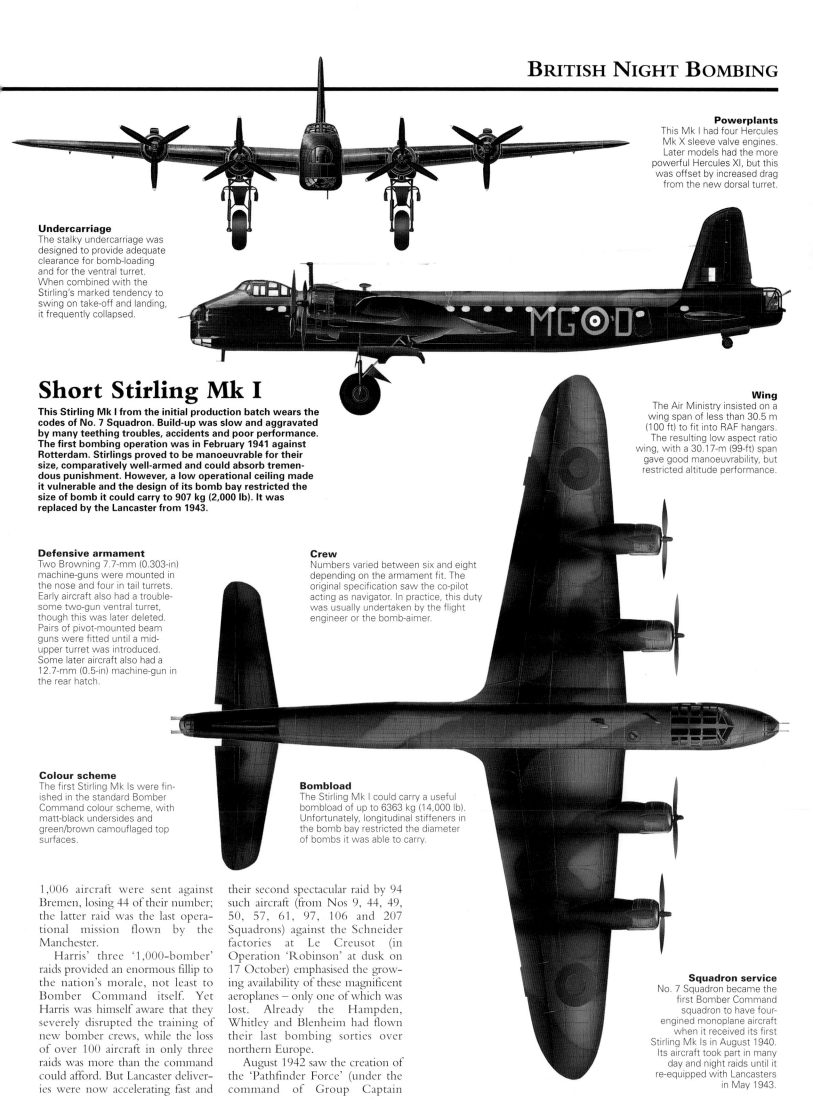

Powerplants
This Mk I had four Hercules Mk X sleeve valve engines. Later models had the more powerful Hercules XI, but this was offset by increased drag from the new dorsal turret.

Undercarriage
The stalky undercarriage was designed to provide adequate clearance for bomb-loading and for the ventral turret. When combined with the Stirling's marked tendency to swing on take-off and landing, it frequently collapsed.

Short Stirling Mk I

This Stirling Mk I from the initial production batch wears the codes of No. 7 Squadron. Build-up was slow and aggravated by many teething troubles, accidents and poor performance. The first bombing operation was in February 1941 against Rotterdam. Stirlings proved to be manoeuvrable for their size, comparatively well-armed and could absorb tremendous punishment. However, a low operational ceiling made it vulnerable and the design of its bomb bay restricted the size of bomb it could carry to 907 kg (2,000 lb). It was replaced by the Lancaster from 1943.

Wing
The Air Ministry insisted on a wing span of less than 30.5 m (100 ft) to fit into RAF hangars. The resulting low aspect ratio wing, with a 30.17-m (99-ft) span gave good manoeuvrability, but restricted altitude performance.

Defensive armament
Two Browning 7.7-mm (0.303-in) machine-guns were mounted in the nose and four in tail turrets. Early aircraft also had a troublesome two-gun ventral turret, though this was later deleted. Pairs of pivot-mounted beam guns were fitted until a mid-upper turret was introduced. Some later aircraft also had a 12.7-mm (0.5-in) machine-gun in the rear hatch.

Crew
Numbers varied between six and eight depending on the armament fit. The original specification saw the co-pilot acting as navigator. In practice, this duty was usually undertaken by the flight engineer or the bomb-aimer.

Colour scheme
The first Stirling Mk Is were finished in the standard Bomber Command colour scheme, with matt-black undersides and green/brown camouflaged top surfaces.

Bombload
The Stirling Mk I could carry a useful bombload of up to 6363 kg (14,000 lb). Unfortunately, longitudinal stiffeners in the bomb bay restricted the diameter of bombs it was able to carry.

1,006 aircraft were sent against Bremen, losing 44 of their number; the latter raid was the last operational mission flown by the Manchester.

Harris' three '1,000-bomber' raids provided an enormous fillip to the nation's morale, not least to Bomber Command itself. Yet Harris was himself aware that they severely disrupted the training of new bomber crews, while the loss of over 100 aircraft in only three raids was more than the command could afford. But Lancaster deliveries were now accelerating fast and

their second spectacular raid by 94 such aircraft (from Nos 9, 44, 49, 50, 57, 61, 97, 106 and 207 Squadrons) against the Schneider factories at Le Creusot (in Operation 'Robinson' at dusk on 17 October) emphasised the growing availability of these magnificent aeroplanes – only one of which was lost. Already the Hampden, Whitley and Blenheim had flown their last bombing sorties over northern Europe.

August 1942 saw the creation of the 'Pathfinder Force' (under the command of Group Captain

Squadron service
No. 7 Squadron became the first Bomber Command squadron to have four-engined monoplane aircraft when it received its first Stirling Mk Is in August 1940. Its aircraft took part in many day and night raids until it re-equipped with Lancasters in May 1943.

Left: Night bombing and bombing through overcast conditions were helped by the development of radar and radio navigation aids, using the experience of the first year of the bombing offensive, when many bombs missed their targets.

Below: Six Lancasters of No. 44 Squadron high over the North Sea. The Squadron flew its first operational mission with the Lancaster on 3 March 1942.

Left: The nose blister on the Lancaster gave the bomb aimer the best view of any wartime bomber. Here a bomb aimer presses the button on a Mark IX bomb sight to release his load over the target.

Below: Armourers attend to a 907-kg (2,000-lb) bomb about to be loaded aboard a Whitley Mk V in May 1941. The Armstrong Whitworth bomber continued to carry the night offensive to Germany until the end of April 1942.

D.C.T. Bennett), a number of squadrons tasked with leading major raids and marking the target with easily identifiable coloured bomb bursts. The PFF flew its first mission against Flensburg on the night of 18/19 August. Before the year was out a new navigation and bombing aid, 'Oboe', was first used in a raid by specially-equipped Mosquitoes of No. 109 Squadron on Lutterade on the night of 20/21 December. In the first 10 months of Harris' command the UK's bomber force had more than trebled its striking power, and could now begin to deliver its punches where they were intended to land.

Heavy bombers

The Avro Manchester was an operational failure, largely because of its unreliable Rolls-Royce Vulture engines. The more successful Handley Page Halifax was the first RAF four-engined bomber to drop bombs on Germany, on the night of 12/13 March 1941. The Avro Lancaster, powered by Rolls-Royce Merlin engines was the RAF's most famous and successful bomber of World War II.

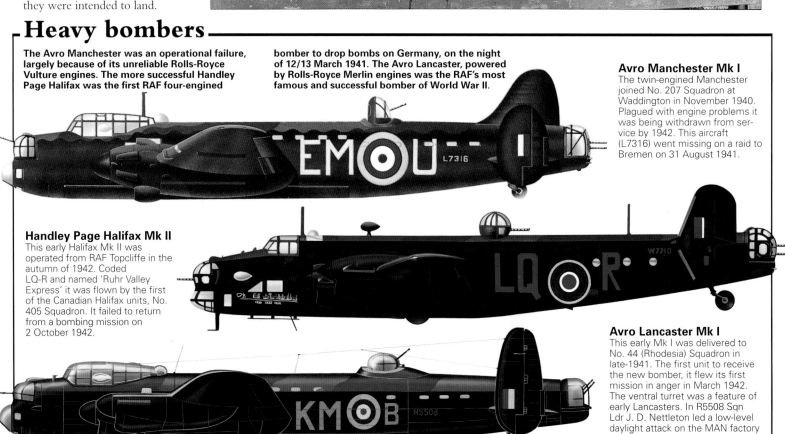

Avro Manchester Mk I
The twin-engined Manchester joined No. 207 Squadron at Waddington in November 1940. Plagued with engine problems it was being withdrawn from service by 1942. This aircraft (L7316) went missing on a raid to Bremen on 31 August 1941.

Handley Page Halifax Mk II
This early Halifax Mk II was operated from RAF Topcliffe in the autumn of 1942. Coded LQ-R and named 'Ruhr Valley Express' it was flown by the first of the Canadian Halifax units, No. 405 Squadron. It failed to return from a bombing mission on 2 October 1942.

Avro Lancaster Mk I
This early Mk I was delivered to No. 44 (Rhodesia) Squadron in late-1941. The first unit to receive the new bomber, it flew its first mission in anger in March 1942. The ventral turret was a feature of early Lancasters. In R5508 Sqn Ldr J. D. Nettleton led a low-level daylight attack on the MAN factory at Augsburg and was subsequently awarded the Victoria Cross.

Left: Another night, another sortie. Wellingtons bore the brunt of RAF Bomber Command's night campaign until the arrival of the four-engined 'heavies'. They then served with Operational Training Units, seeing further action on the 1,000-bomber raids over Germany.

Against the Odds

Bomber Command's operations in 1941 were marked by examples of human strength, mechanical weakness and by the courage of the young aircrew like 22-year-old New Zealander Sergeant James Ward of No. 75 (NZ) Squadron, whose battle against a fire in the air earned him the highest award for bravery.

"All of a sudden, over the middle of the Zuider Zee, I saw an enemy machine coming in from port," said a young New Zealand sergeant-pilot in an anonymous account broadcast by the BBC describing his adventures over Europe on the night of 7 July 1941. His name was James Ward, he came from Wanganui and he was 22. He would never see 23.

"There was a slamming alongside, and then chunks of red-hot shrapnel were flying all over the place. The squadron leader (R.P. Widdowson, though the listening public weren't allowed to know that) put the nose down, to try to dive clear.

"We'd been pretty badly damaged in the attack. The starboard engine was hit, and the hydraulics were out, which meant the landing gear was hanging half down and useless, and the bomb doors were open. The wireless was out, too, and the front gunner had been shot in the foot. Worst of all, fire was burning up through the upper surface of the starboard wing, where a fuel feed pipe had been split. We burst a hole in the side of the fuselage (for once the Wellington's fabric covering worked in its crew's favour) and some of us got going with the fire extinguisher, but the fire was too far out, and we couldn't reach it. Then we tried

throwing coffee from our flasks at it, but that didn't work either.

"I had a good look at the fire and I thought there was a sporting chance of reaching it by getting out through the astrodome, sliding down the fuselage, and out onto the wing. There was a short length of rope there, attached to the dinghy (stowed in a compartment at the rear of the starboard engine nacelle). We tied that around my chest and I climbed out. I still had my parachute on, and it was getting in the way. I wanted to take it off, but they wouldn't let me.

"I punched and kicked holes in the fabric so that I could get a hold of the structure members. Joe the navigator was holding on to the rope so that I wouldn't sort of drop straight off.

"I went out three or four feet along the wing. The fire was burning up through the wing like a big gas jet, and it was blowing back past my shoulder. I had the cockpit cover in one hand – I didn't realise how big and bulky it was – and the wind kept catching it and trying to blow it, and me, away. I kept bunching it under my arm, and

Right: Crews of Wellington Mk ICs of No. 149 Squadron at RAF Mildenhall walk to their aircraft prior to departure for a night mission. No. 149 Squadron started night operations in May 1940 and converted to Stirlings in November 1941.

then it would blow out again.

"I was lying flat on the wing, but I couldn't get very close because of the parachute on my chest. The wind kept lifting me, and once it slapped me right back against the fuselage, but I managed to hang on. I stuffed the cover down through the hole in the wing onto the pipe where the fire was, and it went out, but as soon as I took my hand away the terrific draught blew the cover out and away. I just couldn't hold on to it any longer.

"There was nothing to do then but to get back in. I pulled myself back along the wing, and up the side of the fuselage. Joe kept the rope taut, and that helped. I got back partly in to the astrohatch, but by that time I was completely done in. Joe pulled me in, and I just lay where I fell.

"Just when we were in reach of the English coast, the fire flared up again – some petrol had formed a pool inside, and that caught. I remember thinking to myself, 'This is pretty hard after having got as far as this', but after an initial flare-up it died right out,

much to our relief.

"The trouble was the undercart now. We pumped it down with the emergency gear, and then the pilot landed at another aerodrome, not our own, one that had a lot more space. He put it down beautifully, and though we ended up in a barbed wire entanglement, no-one was hurt."

For his heroism, Sergeant Ward was awarded the Victoria Cross, though he was to go missing later, on another sortie over Germany.

1941 can be characterised by human strength, mechanical weakness and by courage like Sergeant Ward showed on that July night. But to RAF Bomber Command, especially, that courage could never be enough. Britain, entirely alone apart from far-flung remnants of her Empire, was fighting a 'war of production' as much as a shooting war. When war depends on technology, he who can produce the most will win and Bomber Command was at the spearhead of technology.

Below: A German anti-aircraft defence battery opens up during an RAF night raid in November 1941. The British bombers needed cloud breaks to 'see' their targets, but this allowed the German searchlights to illuminate them for the waiting guns.

The Night Fighter War

1939-1945

Left: Despite official preference for Spitfire development, the Hurricane had a major advantage – its thicker wing sections could accommodate a variety of weapons including 20-mm cannon, as shown by this all-black Hurricane Mk IIC night-fighter.

Below: Designed from the outset as a night-fighter, the Heinkel He 219 was the best of this specialised breed of aircraft to see service during the war. Only small numbers reached the front line, but they were devastating against Allied bombers.

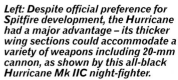

I n 1939 neither the RAF nor the Luftwaffe possessed in service a force of night-fighters capable of countering significantly the threat of the night bomber, both air forces depending almost exclusively upon *ad hoc* use of day fighters working in collaboration with searchlights and broadcast instructions from ground controllers. True, RAF Fighter Command was experimenting with a handful of Bristol Blenheims of No. 25 Squadron equipped with rudimentary airborne radar (AI.Mk III), but it was not until the night of 21/22 July 1940 that the first German bomber fell to the guns of a radar-equipped Blenheim.

In September 1940 the RAF began receiving its first purpose-designed night-fighter, the Bristol Beaufighter with AI.Mk IV and by early 1941 (during the latter stages of the German Blitz) the British night fighters were beginning to take a substantial toll of the night raiders. The Luftwaffe had recognised the threat posed by the RAF's night-bomber force in 1940 and had created the first of its

Below: A Boulton Paul Defiant Mk II night fighter, equipped with airborne interception radar and flown by No. 151 Squadron from RAF Wittering. These Defiants achieved the highest number of victories per interception of any British night fighter deployed during the winter of 1940-41. Defiants were the first RAF fighters in squadron service with a four-gun turret.

Left: The Ju 88G-6b was the first production night-fighter version of the Ju 88 with radial engines, all previous service variants having in-line engines with annular radiators. G-6bs also adopted the enlarged tail surfaces of the Ju 188.

night-fighter wings, Nacht-jagdgeschwader 1 (NJG 1), with Messerschmitt Bf 110s, in July of that year. For most of 1940 the German night-fighter crews attacked visually with the aid of searchlights, but by early the following year, under Oberst Josef Kammhuber, a chain of radar stations ('Giant Würzburg' sets) had been established from Denmark to the Swiss border to form the Himmelbett system. By June 1941 five night-fighter Gruppen were operational with Bf 110, Dornier Do 17 and Junkers Ju 88 night-fighters. After early trials with an infra-red-sensing device (Spanner Anlage) had been abandoned, early German airborne radar gave promising results and late in 1941 the Telefunken company was producing the Lichtenstein BC radar which had a range of about 4 kilometres (2.5 miles); by the following

Left: Home-based Mosquito night fighters first entered service in January 1942 and defended Britain for over three years. This NF. Mk II flew with No. 23 Squadron, the first to take the Mosquito to the Mediterranean when it moved to Malta in late-1942.

Luftwaffe night birds

The first German night fighter was the twin-engined Messerschmitt Bf 110 in July 1940. It had no aids other than a searchlight. It was not until 1942 that a successful airborne radar was adopted. The heavily-armed Fw 190A-6/R11 with its additional radar was effective in 1944. Fortunately for the Allies the He 219A Uhu did not enter mass production; it would have had a devastating effect on the bomber formations.

Messerschmitt Bf 110G

Messerschmitt Bf 110G-4b/R3 of 7.Staffel III/NJG 4, Luftflotte Reich based in north-west Germany in 1943-44. Equipped with FuG 220b Lichtenstein SN-2 radar, and FuG 16zY fighter director and flame dampers, this was the final G-series production model. Night-fighter colour schemes varied at this stage of the war.

Focke-Wulf Fw 190A

This pale-grey Fw 190A-6/R11 of I/NJG 10 was flown by Oberleutnant Hans Krause from Werneuchen in August 1944. The pilot's insignia comprised his nickname 'Illo' beneath the 'Wilde Sau' emblem. Krause was awarded the Knight's Cross. Note Neptun radar arrays and two-shade grey on upper wing surface.

Heinkel He 219A

An He 219A-2/R1 of I/NJG 1 operating from Westerland (Sylt) in the spring of 1945. The night-fighter camouflage included black undersurfaces applied during night ground-attack sorties against Allied ground forces crossing the North German Plain.

---

summer most Luftwaffe night-fighters were equipped with this or the simplified Lichtenstein C-1 version.

RADAR EQUIPPED

Meanwhile the RAF had standardised with the Beaufighter Mks IF and IIF, equipped with metric AI.Mk IV (with a range of about 6.4 kilometres/4 miles under ideal conditions) and by May 1941 some 200 aircraft were in service. At this time British ground control of night fighters was far superior to the German introduction in January 1941 of the plan position

Below: Unarmed Douglas Havoc 'Turbinlite' fighters carried AI radar and a large searchlight in the nose to illuminate a target for accompanying Hurricane fighters. The scheme achieved only limited success.

indicator (PPI) enabling a single controller to distinguish fighter and target on a single display, whereas the Germans employed two operators (one for each aircraft) at separate sets.

Early in 1942 the centimetric AI.Mk VII was introduced in the Beaufighter Mk VIF with Nos 68 and 604 Squadrons, followed by AI.Mk VIII, the new equipment providing better definition, although the pilot-display radar

Above: It was as a night fighter that the early Blenheims proved particularly successful. Some 200 Blenheim Mk IFs were converted with four under-fuselage machine-guns and airborne interception (AI) radar.

proved unpopular. Another night-fighting tactic, the use of airborne searchlights (Turbinlites) in Douglas Havoc aircraft to illuminate enemy bombers so that accompanying Hawker Hurricanes could close for the kill, was tried by 10 RAF

Black (k)nights

The Hurricane Mk IIC introduced four 20-mm Oerlikon/Hispano cannon. In mid-1941 it was the mainstay of Fighter Command's night intruder and home-defence squadrons. Beaufighter Mk IIFs entered service with eight night-fighter squadrons from April 1941. Undoubtedly the most successful of the RAF's black-painted night fighters was the fast, well-armed Mosquito.

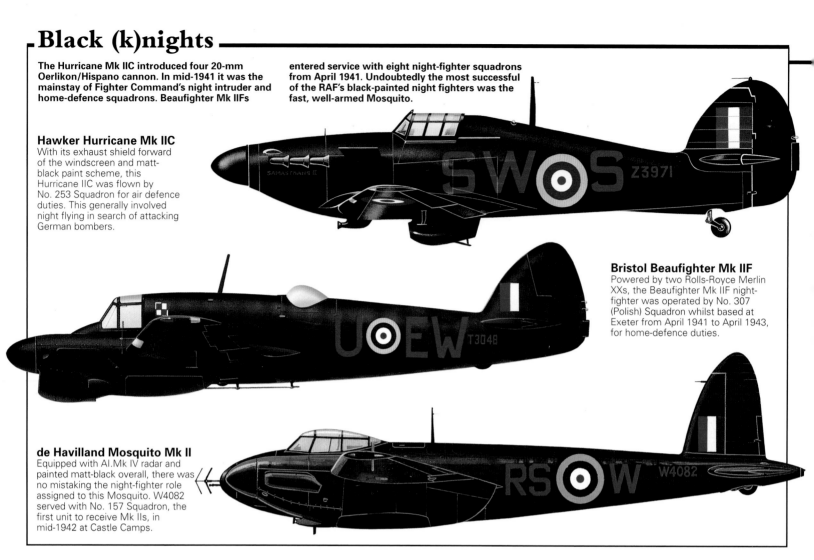

Hawker Hurricane Mk IIC
With its exhaust shield forward of the windscreen and matt-black paint scheme, this Hurricane IIC was flown by No. 253 Squadron for air defence duties. This generally involved night flying in search of attacking German bombers.

Bristol Beaufighter Mk IIF
Powered by two Rolls-Royce Merlin XXs, the Beaufighter Mk IIF night-fighter was operated by No. 307 (Polish) Squadron whilst based at Exeter from April 1941 to April 1943, for home-defence duties.

de Havilland Mosquito Mk II
Equipped with AI.Mk IV radar and painted matt-black overall, there was no mistaking the night-fighter role assigned to this Mosquito. W4082 served with No. 157 Squadron, the first unit to receive Mk IIs, in mid-1942 at Castle Camps.

squadrons during 1942-43, but met with little success and was abandoned. Havocs were also fitted with AI radar.

MOSQUITO

The finest of all British night fighters was unquestionably the de Havilland Mosquito, of which the Mosquito Mk II version entered service in May 1942. Fitted successively with AI.Mks IV, V, VIII, IX and the American Mk X, the Mosquito continued in service until the end of the war, gradually replacing the Beaufighter and ultimately serving with 24 squadrons of the RAF, performing night defence intruder and bomber support operations.

In the Luftwaffe, relatively little effort could be spared for offensive night-fighter operations, the pressing need being for night defence against the increasing attacks by RAF Bomber Command which, by 1943, were assuming a devastating scale. At the end of 1942 the German night-fighter force comprised a total of 389 operational aircraft, of which 300 were Bf 110s; Kammhuber's defences had destroyed a total of 1,291 British bombers during the year, about

Below: A pair of Messerschmitt Bf 110E-1/U1 night fighters of VII/NJG 4 over France. E-1/U1s carried the Spanner Anlage infra-red sighting sensor. As night fighters, Bf 110s were increasingly effective, serving in the role for nearly five years.

Left: The Heinkel He 219A-7/R1 carried SN-2 radar and armament of six 30-mm and two 20-mm cannon. The 'Roman' VI indicated fitment of FuG 220d with Streuwelle (dispersal waveband) No. VI.

Below: The last wartime night-fighter version of the Mosquito was the NF.Mk 30, introduced in 1944. From the summer, these aircraft provided protection for RAF bomber streams over Germany.

GERMANY'S NIGHT DEFENCE

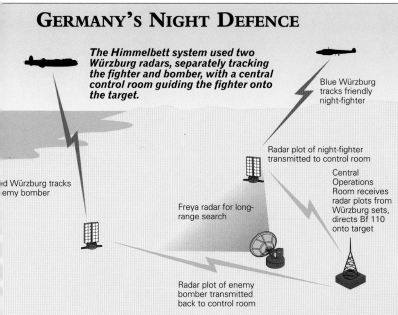

The Himmelbett system used two Würzburg radars, separately tracking the fighter and bomber, with a central control room guiding the fighter onto the target.

Blue Würzburg tracks friendly night-fighter

Radar plot of night-fighter transmitted to control room

Central Operations Room receives radar plots from Würzburg sets, directs Bf 110 onto target

Freya radar for long-range search

Red Würzburg tracks enemy bomber

Radar plot of enemy bomber transmitted back to control room

Above: The Junkers Ju 88G-6b carried an SN-2 radar array in the nose (often referred to as a 'toasting fork'), with a rear-warning aerial at the tail, though the latter was not always fitted. Schräge Musik (Jazz) upward-firing MG151 cannon were mounted amidships, allowing attacks on Allied bombers to be made from below.

Germany's night-fighter defences swiftly evolved from a system based on searchlights and visual reports of incoming enemy aircraft to a highly efficient layered defence, with a belt of coastal radar stations, a searchlight zone along the German border and with integrated defence zones around the most important targets.

By 1941 enemy bombers attacking the German heartland had to penetrate the Himmelbett zones on the Dutch coast, the illuminated night-fighter zones further inland, and then the combined night-fighter zones over the targets themselves. Fortunately for the Allied bomber crews each Himmelbett station could only deal with one aircraft at a time, so while one Lancaster was being dealt with, his comrades could usually slip through. British countermeasures, notably 'Window' (strips of aluminium foil deliberately dropped by aircraft in the formation to deceive the enemy radar), eventually rendered the system virtually unuseable.

This, combined with the limitations of the Himmelbett zones saw the new 'Wilde Sau' and 'Zamhe Sau' tactics introduced in mid-1943. 'Wilde Sau' met with early success and there was a rapid build-up of single-seat night-fighter units, but by October, RAF countermeasures began to bite. These included changes in tactics, the use of 'spoof' raids to confuse ground controllers and further radar jamming.

By the autumn of 1943 Himmelbett had been abandoned altogether. The new, more flexible system of night-fighter control now employed by the Luftwaffe was to be combined with new airborne equipment the following year. SN-2 radar, operating on frequencies as yet unjammed by the RAF, was used in concert with passive Naxos and Flensburg emissions detectors (which homed on Allied Monica tail-warning and H_2S radar emissions) and Schräge Musik cannon to put the Bf 110s and Ju 88s of the Nachtjagdgeschwaders in the ascendancy until the summer of 1944.

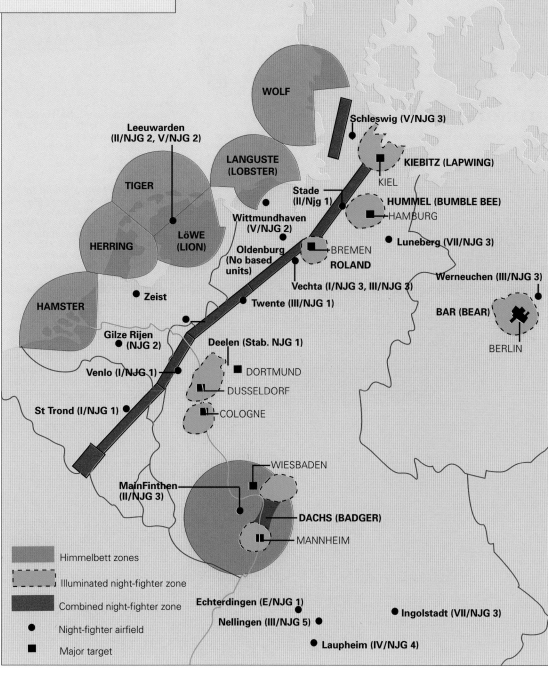

Radar
The Ju 88G-1 was fitted with FuG 220 Lichtenstein SN-2, with its distinctive Hirschgeweih aerial array. It also carried wing-mounted antennae for FuG 227 Flensburg, a passive device which homed on to the Monica tail-warning radars fitted to many British bombers.

Tail unit
The Ju 88G-1 was essentially similar to the Ju 88C-6c, but with revised armament and the more angular, increased-area tail surfaces of the Ju 188, to restore longitudinal stability and improve pitch control.

Powerplant
The Ju 88G-1 was fitted with BMW 801D air-cooled radials which produced 1267 kW (1,700 hp) each for take-off. The first radial-engined night-fighter versions were the Ju 88R-1, with BMW 801MAs, and the Ju 88R-2 with 801Ds.

Junkers Ju 88G-1

This most formidable night fighter was almost unknown until the crew of 4R+UR, a Ju 88G-1 of 7./NJG 2, became lost on the night of 12/13 July 1944 and landed in error at RAF Woodbridge, Suffolk, presenting the British with vital information about the SN-2 radar and FuG 227 Flensburg.

Crew
The crew of the Ju 88 was reduced to three in the night-fighter, by elimination of the bombardier/second pilot. A fourth crewman was later added to cope with the increased number of detection devices.

Fuel
Standard fuel tankage was provided in four wing tanks located either side of the engine nacelles, augmented by an auxiliary tank in the forward bomb bay.

two-thirds of them having fallen to his fighters. A serious setback, however, occurred on the night of 24/25 July 1943 when Harris' bombers first dropped large quantities of 'Window' jamming strips during their great raid on Hamburg. At a stroke the Würzburg and Lichtenstein screens of the Himmelbett system were rendered useless and this immediately prompted the introduction of new night-fighting tactics, codenamed 'Wilde Sau' and 'Zahme Sau' (respectively Wild and Tame Sow). The former involved the use of

freelancing day fighters which, being without radar, were unaffected by the 'Window' jamming. The latter tactic employed a master commentary from the ground.

It was also during the second half of 1943 that the Germans introduced upward-firing cannon (Schräge Musik) into their night fighters; stalking the British heavy bombers from astern, the German pilots positioned themselves below their target and opened fire. Being thus attacked from a blind spot, the British remained unaware of this new tactic and literally hundreds of bombers were thus shot down. By mid-1944 the best of all German night-fighters, the Heinkel He 219, had re-equipped I/NJG 1; some versions of this superb aircraft were

Left: The only Luftwaffe unit to operate the Messerschmitt Me 262B-1a/U1 night fighter was Kommando Welten (later 10./NJG 11). This interim two-seat night fighter is fitted with FuG 218 Neptun V air interception radar and FuG 350 ZC (Naxos) passive homer.

armed with as many as eight cannon (including Schräge Musik), its most successful exponent being Major Hein-Wolfgang Schnauffer (121 victories); on one occasion he shot down seven Avro Lancasters in the space of 17 minutes.

The night-fighter war was a constant battle of measures and countermeasures, of jamming, feints and deception. Although the Allies sustained technical superiority throughout the war, German ingenuity produced expedients that enabled the Luftwaffe to take an enormous toll of the night bombers over the Reich.

Below: The Focke-Wulf Ta 154 night fighter, constructed of wood, was Germany's equivalent to the DH Mosquito. Fitted with Hirschgeweih (Stag's Antlers) antennas for Lichtenstein SN-2 radar, it saw service with I/NJG 3 from January 1945.

Night Fighter

Even with help from radar, the Luftwaffe's night fighters found intercepting Allied bombers at night a risky business. Apart from their own anti-aircraft guns they had to beware the bomber's own fire power. Top-scoring Bf 110 night-fighter ace Leutnant Wilhelm Johnen describes his first mission in the role on 11 July 1941.

"I was on my feet in a flash when the warning came," he says, "and through the door and halfway to the aircraft before I knew what was going on. The ground controller told us to make for the Westerland sector, and I took off and climbed up through the cloud, the variometer showing a steady climb rate of nine feet per second and the airspeed indicator about 210 mph. The rain was lashing against the fuselage and running down the cockpit canopy in torrents.

"Right on top of them.

"My controller was very faint by now, and the headwinds had almost doubled our flying time to the interception point. Not only that, but the British had the benefit of a tail wind, and were moving very fast indeed. It felt just hopeless. The controller had vectored us onto a course of 130 degrees, and I suddenly had the feeling that we were right on top of them.

"Suddenly the aircraft was flung wildly to one side. We'd been right behind the Tommis without knowing it, and had got caught in their slipstream. 'There's one!' shouted Risop, my radio operator, 'Right ahead and level with us.' I let off the safety catch of the six cannon, and the red lights flashed up 'Ready', but in that instant the bomber broke away to starboard. We didn't see another thing all night, and eventually got home very late after making some mistakes with our navigation."

Even with effective ground control radar, intercepting bombers at night was a hit and miss affair. Up until 26 March 1942, the German night fighters had stayed out of the Ruhr valley itself for fear of becoming targets for their own anti-aircraft guns, but on that night the tactics changed. Johnen was one of the first crews to mix it with the bombers over their targets, taking them at their most vulnerable, flying straight and level on their bomb runs.

"The nearer I approached the target, the brighter it got around me. A sea of light from the searchlight batteries blinded me whenever I looked down. The flak was exploding all around, and I felt like I was flying through Hell itself. A shell burst about 50 yards ahead, and in the next moment the Bf 110 was shaken in an invisible giant's fist. Risop was firing off identification flares as fast as he could. 'Are those bloody idiots trying to shoot us down?' he roared, reloading the flare pistol yet again. I put the aircraft into a steep left-hand turn, and then suddenly the searchlights caught a British bomber ahead and below me. I dived on him, the aircraft shaking wildly as the airspeed indicator shot up to 330 mph. I fired bursts into the fuselage, tearing off huge chunks of fabric, and then the Tommi burst into flames and turned over on his back. There

were three, four, five others on fire too, falling like comets to the ground.

"By now, many of the bombers had lost their nerve, and were dropping their bombs wildly. Suddenly Risop shouted 'There's one above us.' I could just recognise the outline of an enemy aircraft, flying to the north, away from the conflagration on the ground. I forced myself to stay calm and pointed the nose up, toward the belly of the enemy aircraft. 'It's a four-engine,' stammered Risop. 'We haven't seen this type before!'" It was, in fact, one of the new Short Stirlings, biggest and slowest of the new breed of British heavy bombers. But, slow though it was, the Stirling had one thing going for it – a gun turret in its belly. This was to be Johnen's downfall that night.

"I was close now, and took a breather, thinking us safe in the bomber's blind spot. But I had made a big mistake. I throttled back to let him get a little way ahead. 'It's time to fire,' said Risop, 'otherwise his rear gunner will spot us. Put your trust in God, and wade in!' Those were Risop's last words.

"As I opened fire, so did he. The tracer came at us like water from a garden hose. He lashed my

cockpit and fuselage, and in a fraction of a second my aircraft had turned into a flaming torch. Risop slumped over his radio, killed by the machine-gun bullets. All around me was a sea of flame. I tried to get one leg over the side of the cockpit, but the centrifugal force held me in I gave up all hope of getting out, and sat, my hands up over my face. We must have fallen about 9,000 feet when suddenly the aircraft exploded, throwing me out. I was on fire myself by this time, and thought of my parachute, but the stout canvas had saved it from the flames. I landed in a flooded meadow, up to my neck in mud. Saved! Then I passed out."

Above: Normally Leutnant Johnen would have had no difficulty in climbing out of the Bf 110's cockpit, but after the fighter had been ripped apart by the unexpected fire from the underside of an RAF Stirling it was a very different matter.

Right: Messerschmitt Bf 110-4b/R3 with FuG 220 Lichtenstein SN-2 radar and earlier FuG 212 for close-in work. Severely outclassed in the day-fighter role, the Bf 110 was well suited to attacking bombers at night. Heavily armed, the type had good endurance and enough capacity to carry radar and other specialised electronic equipment.

THE TURNING POINT

Despite being a failure as an RAF interceptor, Sydney Camm's Typhoon proved its worth in 1943 and 1944 in the new role of close-support aircraft. Along with the American P-47 Thunderbolt, it proved devastating against German armour and infrastructure, with its four 20-mm cannon and eight rockets or two 227-kg (500-lb) bombs.

The beginning of the end of the war in Europe came with the failed German invasion of Russia, thwarted by the harsh winter of 1942-43. By then the US 8th Air Force had arrived in Britain and planning of an all-out invasion of occupied Europe was proceeding. Operation 'Overlord' came in June 1944. The Reich was to survive less than 12 months.

The 8th Air Force's contribution to the war effort was crucial. Their first raid on Germany from bases in England came in January 1943 and after two years daylight raids had helped deprive Germany of its ability to wage war. The human cost was huge for both sides.

From Demyansk to Stalingrad

DECEMBER 1941 – FEBRUARY 1943

Left: The Dornier Do 17Z-2 was capable of carrying a 1000-kg (2,205-lb) bombload. This example, one of the last in front-line service, fought on the Eastern Front in Autumn 1942 with 15.(Croat)/KG 53 'Condor Legion' Croatian Volunteer Staffel.

Throughout the first five months of Hitler's invasion of the Soviet Union the Germans enjoyed almost unrelenting success in their drive eastwards, only just (but disastrously) failing in their bid to capture Moscow before the onset of that first Russian winter. Having halted the German advance in front of their capital, the Soviet armies, better prepared for warfare in the savage cold, opened their counter offensives early in December 1941 on the Leningrad, Moscow and Kharkov fronts. Almost entirely paralysed by the weather conditions, the Luftwaffe decided to remove much of its strength from the East, redeploying V Fliegerkorps to Belgium, and five Gruppen of its latest Messerschmitt Bf 109F fighters to the Mediterranean, thereby reducing its strength from about 2,400 aircraft to 1,700 on the 3200-km (2,000-mile) Eastern Front. And despite a desperate lack of modern aircraft (as well as the loss of some 5,000 sustained since 'Barbarossa' opened the previous summer), the Soviets were able to force the German armies back as much as 320 km (200 miles) in some areas.

COUNTER OFFENSIVE

In the course of this violent reversal of fortunes for the German army, the Soviets pierced the German front line between the Army Groups 'Centre' and 'North' and, early in February 1942, succeeded in isolating the whole of X Corps at Demyansk. Realising that the loss of some 100,000 men in a crumbling front could mean disaster for the entire German army in the north, the Luftwaffe collected every available transport aircraft (the Ju 52/3m alone was scarcely affected by the winter conditions, having air-cooled engines) and started a massive supply operation to the Demyansk pocket. Between mid-February and mid-May, when the Germans were able to open up a land corridor to the trapped army, about 400 aircraft airlifted 24,000 tonnes of supplies and 15,500 troops into the pocket, and evacuated 20,000 casualties. Losses amounted to 262 aircraft, and the increasing toll being taken by the Soviet 20-mm and 37-mm AA guns brought realisation to the Germans of the impossibility of sustaining major air operations in more

Left: Ilyushin Il-2s depart from a forward base on a combat mission in 1942. These are early single-seaters. More Il-2 'Stormoviks' were built than any other type of aircraft in aviation history.

Above: 'Hero of the Soviet Union' – Russian fighter pilot I. Chubarev standing alongside a wrecked Luftwaffe aircraft that he had brought down by ramming it with his own fighter.

Over the Russian Front

The Henschel Hs 129 was designed to back-up the Ju 87 dive bomber. It carried more armour, with the pilot protected by a 7.62-cm (3-in) thick windscreen. It was operated in the close-support and ground-attack role. Built as a glider tug, troop transport, freighter and air ambulance, the Ju 52/3m remained in production throughout the war serving on every front, not least in Russia where it provided essential air supply.

Henschel Hs 129B
The German version of the 'Stormovik' was the Henschel Hs 129. This was heavily-armed and could absorb much battle damage in its role of destroying enemy tanks. Later versions appeared with massive anti-armour cannon carried under the central fuselage.

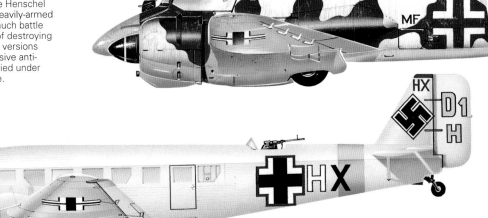

Junkers Ju 52/3m
During the last desperate days at Stalingrad, Junkers Ju 52s kept the ground troops supplied, as their landing strips were slowly wiped out by Soviet artillery. However, winter had set in with a vengeance and the Luftwaffe was unable to maintain its air operations.

THE GERMAN ADVANCE
JUNE 1941 – MAY 1944

FINLAND

Leningrad

ESTONIA

Demyansk

Cholm

Riga

Kalinin

Gori

LITHUANIA

Veliki Luki

Moscow

BELORUSSIA

Vyasma

LUFTFLOTTE I

Vilno

Smolensk

Tula

Mogilev

Minsk

Roslavl

Orel

Warsaw

Brest Litovsk

Gomel

FRONT LINE 18 NOVEMBER 1942

Saratov

LUFTFLOTTE II

FRONT LINE 22 JUNE 1941

Kursk

POLAND

Lublin

Rovne

Kiev

Konotop

Voronezyh

Przemysl

Belgorod

Kharkov

HUNGARY

Izyum

Stalingrad

Slavyansk

UKRAINE

LUFTFLOTTE IV

Zaporozhe

Stalino

Nikolaev

Astrakhan

RUMANIA

Odessa

Taganrog

Rostov

Perekop

Elista

Ploesti

Novorossisk

Mozdok

Bucharest

Sevastopol

BLACK SEA

Illustrating the areas of conflict between the Soviet and Wehrmacht forces, this map covers the period June 1941 to May 1944. The front-line as at 18 November 1942 was the extent of the German advance prior to the Stalingrad counter-offensive.

The extent of the front line in the USSR by December 1941 was awe-inspiring in its length: from Pechenga on the White Sea, the front stretched for some 2,380 km (1,480 miles) through tundra, forest, marshland, woods and steppes, via Lake Lagoda and the beseiged city of Leningrad, the salients in Belorussia at Bryansk and to the east of Smolensk and Vyasma and the grain fields of the Ukraine, to the Sea of Asov east of Rostov.

The Soviet winter counter-offensive started in the snows before Moscow on 5 December, with other offensives taking place in the north in an attempt to relieve Leningrad, and in the south against Kharkov. At several points the German armies, hamstrung by frozen guns and tanks in temperatures approaching minus 35 degrees Celsius, faced crisis: Germany's troops were at first totally unprepared for the severity of the Russian winter. In the savage fighting of the that winter, the Soviet armies made good ground.

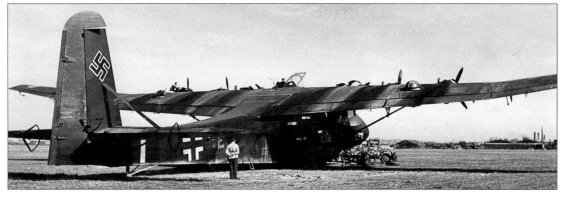

two-seat Il-2m3 'Stormovik' close-support aircraft.

While ferocious fighting raged around Demyansk to the north, the Germans went over to the offensive in the south, and in April 1942 Army Group 'South' attacked in the southern Ukraine and the Crimean peninsula, supported by VIII Fliegerkorps and the newly-formed 1.Fliegerdivision. Sevastopol fell on 4 July after a prodigious air assault in which VIII Fliegerkorps had flown 23,750 sorties and its He 111s, Ju 87s and 88s

than one theatre simultaneously; indeed, the losses at Demyansk was never completely made good and many of the Luftwaffe's most experienced transport pilots were lost. Moreover, after a disastrous period of reduced Soviet aircraft production during the latter half of 1941, while aircraft plants had been moved out of danger east of the Urals, production began to make

Above: Messerschmitt Me 323E-2 Gigant heavy transport of I/TG 5 in the southern sector of the Eastern Front in the summer of 1943. The I-III Gruppe of Transportgeschwaden 5 was formed in May 1943 and served in the USSR and Mediterranean.

spectacular recovery in 1942, particularly with improved aircraft such as the Yak-1 and LaGG-3 fighters and, soon after, the

Left: A Henschel Hs 129B-2 of 4(PZ) Sch.G1 on the Russian Front in 1942. The most novel armament, used against Russian armour, was a battery of six smooth-bore 75-mm tubes (seen here being loaded) firing recoilless shells down and to the rear with automatic triggering as the aircraft flew over metal objects.

Above: A Junkers Ju 87D of 9/St.G.77, with temporary winter camouflage, on the Eastern Front in the winter of 1942. Soon, the vulnerability of the Ju 87 would see its wholesale replacement by the Focke Wulf Fw 190A, the Stukas being reassigned to Nachtschlacht (night attack) units.

Above: An eighth 'kill' on the Russian Front being painted on the tail of a Messerschmitt Bf 109F by its pilot during the initial phase of the conflict on the Eastern Front. Several German pilots racked up large scores against the Russians.

had dropped 20,530 tonnes of bombs on the fortress town. With the reduction of the Barvenko pocket, the Soviet armies lost half a million men killed and as prisoners in just over three weeks and the way was now clear for Hitler's major summer offensive eastwards towards Voronezh and into the Caucasus to capture the Maikop oilfields.

Considerable efforts had strengthened the Luftwaffe in the east to 2,750 aircraft, and new types (the Ju 87D-1 and Henschel Hs 129B1/R2 anti-tank aircraft and Fw 190A fighters) were now entering service. The advance stormed forward and achieved considerable success until, after intervention by Hitler who, in this moment of assumed victory, assumed personal command, the 11th Army was switched from the Caucasus to the Leningrad front, and the 6th Army, under General von Paulus, was ordered against Stalingrad.

To the Soviets the city of Stalingrad was a patriotic symbol and the Soviet armies were ordered to stand firm, if necessary defending it to the last man. As von Paulus split his 6th Army to create two fronts, the Soviets hastily assembled a new army group and set about the destruction of the Axis forces piecemeal. On 23 November the Soviets closed their pincers to the west of the city just as the dreaded winter set in.

WINTER DEFEAT

The Soviet air strength in the area was not particularly great, with no more than about 600 Pe-2s, Yak-1s, LaGG-3s, Il-4s and a few of the new

Right: Although rugged, the Lavochkin LaGG-3 was under-powered and lacked manoeuvrability, but it performed well as a fighter and fighter-bomber to the end of the war and was used as an escort fighter for Il-2 ground-attack aircraft.

La-5s. When ultimately the Luftwaffe attempted once more to sustain an encircled army from the air, by assembling transport aircraft from every corner of Europe, they failed to repeat their earlier successes, for the Soviet armies quickly dominated with artillery every available landing ground round Stalingrad. By the end of November heavy snow was falling and temperatures plummeting. One by one the landing grounds were over-run, until by mid-January 1943 only

Above: The Gotha 242 tactical transport was a simple steel-tubed machine with fabric-covered fuselage and wooden wings and tail. Towed behind He 111s and Ju 52s, they were easy prey for the Soviets and were relegated to duties behind the front.

Gumrak remained available. When that also fell, only the dropping of supplies by parachute was possible. The last supply sortie was flown on 3 February, but the German 6th Army was already finished, shot, frozen to death or captured.

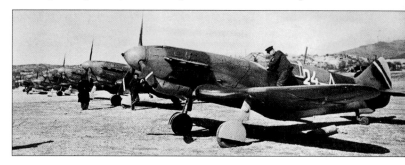

Red air force resistance

The Ilyushin Il-4 was derived from the mid-1930s TsKB-26 low-wing transport and its range, speed and reasonable offensive capability ensured widespread service against the invading Germans.

The series of fighter aircraft developed from the Yak-1 design ranks alongside leading contemporary fighter aircraft of the Allies and Axis, like the P-51 Mustang, Spitfire and Bf 109.

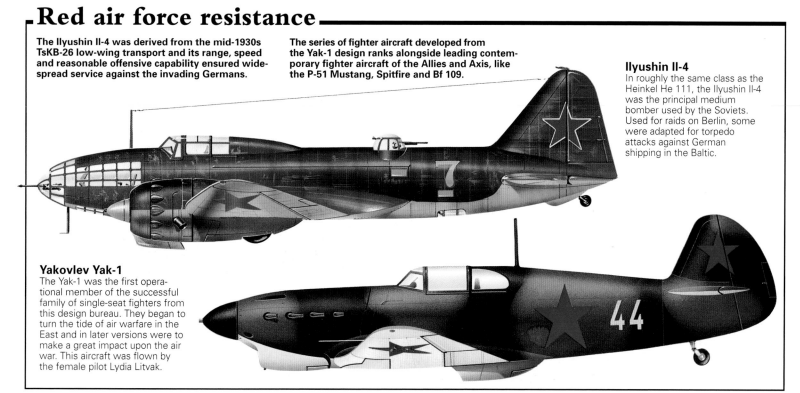

Ilyushin Il-4
In roughly the same class as the Heinkel He 111, the Ilyushin Il-4 was the principal medium bomber used by the Soviets. Used for raids on Berlin, some were adapted for torpedo attacks against German shipping in the Baltic.

Yakovlev Yak-1
The Yak-1 was the first operational member of the successful family of single-seat fighters from this design bureau. They began to turn the tide of air warfare in the East and in later versions were to make a great impact upon the air war. This aircraft was flown by the female pilot Lydia Litvak.

Alamein and 'Torch'

JANUARY 1942 – MAY 1943

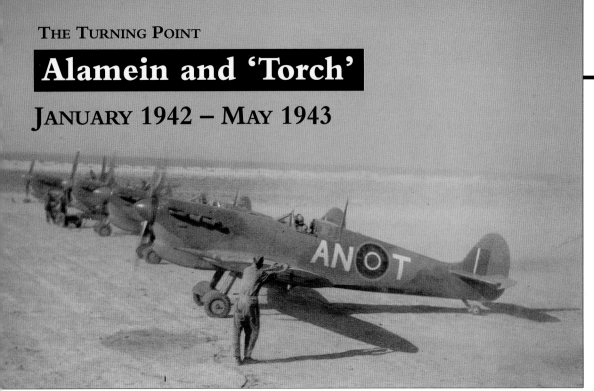

Left: These four Spitfires Mk Vs, with under-nose Vokes air filters, are from No. 417 Squadron, RCAF that flew in the Middle East from April 1942. By the eve of the Battle of El Alamein on 24 October 1942, the Western Desert Air Force had increased to two full groups.

airfields, maintaining a marginal but vital degree of air superiority over the less numerous aircraft of the Luftwaffe and Régia Aéronautica.

Auchinleck made a fatal error, however, preferring to concentrate on mopping up enemy resistance and strengthening his positions rather than striking forward at El Agheila before the enemy could counter-attack. It was Rommel who, with shorter supply lines, struck first and quickly forced the 8th Army back once more, this time beyond the Egyptian border. However, as a result of gallant delaying actions, notably by the South Africans at Tobruk and the Free French at Bir Hakim in May 1942, vital time was gained in which to establish a 'last defence line' before Cairo at El Alamein. It was at Bir Hakim on 6 June that the new Hurricane Mk IID 'tank

The redeployment of important elements of the RAF from North Africa to the Balkans in 1941 had left the British fatally exposed following Wavell's brilliant advance into Libya and with the arrival of the Afrika Korps, supported by Luftwaffe fighters and dive-bombers, the British army in the Western Desert was forced back almost to the Egyptian frontier once more. This was in turn followed by an offensive, Operation 'Crusader', commanded by General Auchinleck which relieved Tobruk and carried the 8th Army west once more to beyond Benghazi. Throughout this advance Hurricanes, Tomahawks and Blenheims of the RAF, RCAF, RAAF and SAAF were constantly in action, as were Wellingtons and Baltimores against enemy ports and

Left: Blenheims were replaced by Martin Baltimores with the Desert Air Force, entering service with No. 223 Squadron in January 1942. This Baltimore Mk III is leaving a trail of bombs across a line of vehicles.

Right: Hawker Hurricane Mk IIDs of No. 6 Squadron over the Western Desert searching for Afrika Korps tanks. Known as 'Tank Busters' these Hurricanes carried two 40-mm Vickers S cannon, used effectively against tanks, armoured vehicles and transports. The squadron adopted the name 'Flying Can Openers' after their exploits.

Desert fighter support

Used extensively against the Afrika Korps the Hurricane Mk IIB 'Hurribomber' could carry 227 kg (500 lb) of bombs under its 12-gun wings. This reduced its speed and made it vulnerable to

Luftwaffe Bf 109s. Even with reduced armour and less fuel, the P-39N Airacobra lacked the agility for air-to-air combat, but served the French well as a close-support fighter and fighter-bomber.

Hawker Hurricane Mk IIB
This tropicalised Hurricane Mk IIB was flown by No. 73 Squadron in the Western Desert in 1942. It carries its pre-war squadron flash on the fuselage sides. The Hurricane Mk IIB introduced the new 12 machine-gun wing and retained the bomb-tank shackles introduced on the Mk IIA series 2 'universal' wing.

Bell P-39N Airacobra
One of 165 Airacobras supplied by the US to the Forces Aeriennes Francaises Libres (Free French Air Force) in 1943, this P-39 was flown by Groupe de Chasse II/6 'Travail'. The unit was formed early in April 1943 and effectively contributed to the NW African Air Forces.

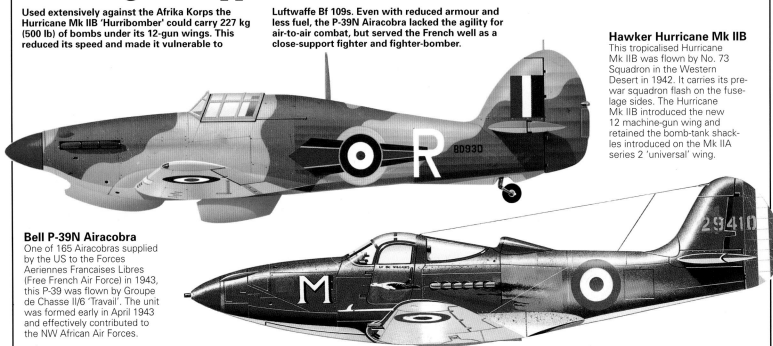

Attack bombers

Although it had tricky low-speed handling qualities and high critical speed, the Beaufighter Mk I gave good service in the hot and dusty conditions of the desert, well suited to its robust airframe.

The B-25C, operated by the USAAF and the RAF as the Mitchell Mk II, had increased range and could carry up to 2359 kg (5,200 lb) of bombs, for its attack missions in the Western Desert.

Bristol Beaufighter Mk IC

In the markings of No. 252 Squadron, RAF Coastal Command, this Beaufighter was based in the Mediterranean area from 1941, playing a decisive part in the Allied air effort. Operating from Egypt in mid-1942 it took part in wide-ranging attacks on enemy shipping and coastal targets. Improved Mk VIs were delivered in November 1942.

North American B-25C Mitchell

This B-25C Mitchell II was operated by the 488th Bomb Squadron, 340th Bomb Group, USAAF, based at Sfax, Tunisia in April 1943. The group of three Mitchell squadrons became operational with the US 12th Air Force in April 1943.

Left: Grumman F4F-4 Wildcats of the US Navy prepare to take-off from the USS Ranger in November 1942 as part of the Operation 'Torch' landings in North Africa. The Wildcats struck at French airfields in Morocco on this, their first mission in the Mediterranean.

Below: Halifax B.Mk Is of No. 462 Squadron were the only four-engined RAF bombers in the Middle East, arriving in July 1942. Though originally formed in Palestine from detachments of Nos 10 and 76 Squadrons, their sorties were flown against the Afrika Korps from Egypt.

buster' was first used to good effect against enemy armour. No. 6 Squadron, later known as the 'Flying Can-Openers', was the first to use the twin 40-mm Vickers 'S' gun-equipped Mk IID. This armament brought the Hurricane's top speed down to just 460 km/h (286 mph), but its anti-armour capability was devastating; during one day No. 6 Squadron destroyed 16 Axis tanks and their success continued into the following year.

LAST STAND

And so it was that after two years of advance and retreat in North Africa the famous 8th Army found itself with its back to the Suez Canal while the victorious Afrika Korps seemed poised for the final thrust. However, by prodigious efforts the Allied forces had accomplished a massive build-up by the time the Axis forces were brought to a halt at Alamein. In the 18 months since Tedder had assumed command in the Middle East his air force had undergone transformation, now comprising 96 squadrons, of which 60 were British, 13 American, 13 South African, five Australian, two Greek, and one each of Rhodesian, French and Yugoslav, for a total of 1,500 first-line aircraft, of which 1,200 were deployed in the Western Desert. Among his modern aircraft were Spitfire Mk Vs, Kittyhawks, Beaufighters, Beauforts, Marauders and Halifaxes, as well as 10 squadrons of Wellingtons and five Liberator squadrons. Against them were deployed some 3,000 Axis aircraft, of which only about 700 were based in North Africa, and only half of these were serviceable.

On the ground General Bernard Montgomery concentrated a vastly superior army, outnumbering the Axis forces by almost two to one in men, tanks and guns. On 23 October 1942 he was ready to strike at El Alamein, preparing his attack with a massive artillery bombardment of German and Italian positions as six squadrons of Wellingtons bombed them from the air. The next day the fighter-bombers joined in and the RAF and SAAF Hurricane Mk IID tankbusters went for the enemy armoured vehicles. For a week the great battle raged as German Ju 87s joined in attempts to halt the British armoured thrusts, but were almost

Left: A Messerschmitt Bf 110E of 8/ZG 26 based at Berca under Fliegerfuhrer Afrika in 1942. The support fighter saw action during the Alam Halfa and El Alamein conflicts. It continued to serve in North Africa in small numbers.

Above: A Junkers Ju 88D reconnaissance aircraft from 1(F)/121 that was shot down over North Africa after being intercepted by USAAF fighters. For desert operations it was fitted with engine sand filters, sun blinds and survival equipment.

invariably caught by covering British and American Kittyhawks. On 4 November the 1st Armoured Division broke through the enemy line and at once the Axis began a long westward retreat. At sea Axis supply ships, desperately trying to bring supplies to the Cyrenaican ports, were subjected to incessant air attack, no fewer than 18 vessels heavily laden with guns, fuel and food being either sunk or forced to return to Italy or Greece on account of damage.

MARSEILLE: FIGHTER ACE

Almost symbolic of the Luftwaffe's misfortunes at this time was the loss in an accident of Hauptmann Hans-Joachim Marseille, the widely-respected fighter pilot and highest-scoring pilot in the West;

'SWIFT IN DESTRUCTION'
This was the motto of No. 112 Squadron RAF, which flew Curtiss Tomahawks from July 1941, followed by Kittyhawks from December until mid-1944. Throughout the campaign in the Western Desert, No. 112 carried out support fighter-bomber missions for the 8th Army and after the rout of Axis forces at El Alamein, moved westwards into Tunisia.

Desert Hurricane

Hawker Hurricane Mk IIC of No. 94 Squadron, Egypt 1942. No. 94 was formed at Aden in March 1939 and disbanded at Sedes, Greece in April 1945. After being heavily involved in offensive sweeps and bomber escort over the Western Desert, including a period on Kittyhawks, by late-1942 the unit was based in the Nile Delta on defence duties and convoy patrols, tangling with the odd lone raider but generally being out of the action.

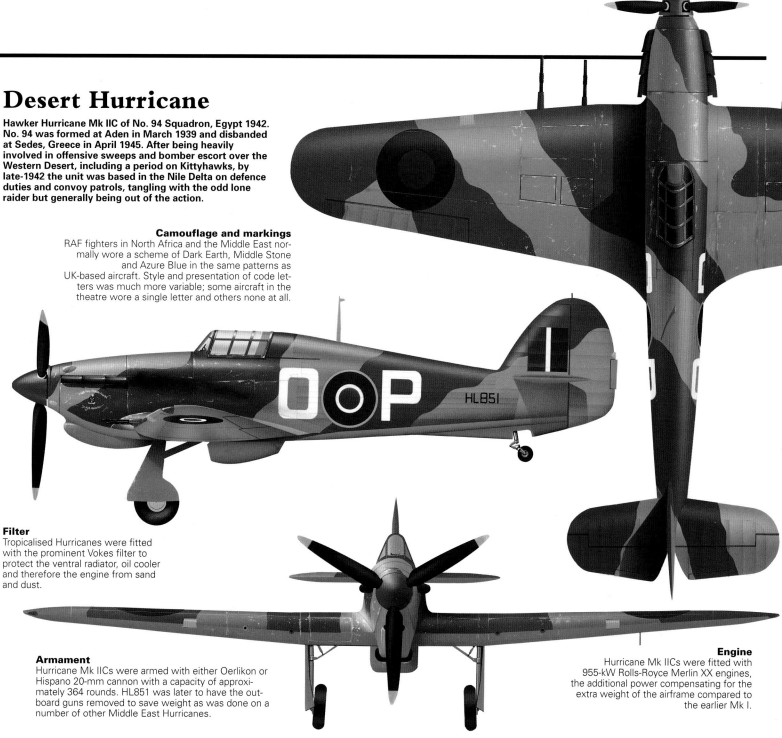

Camouflage and markings
RAF fighters in North Africa and the Middle East normally wore a scheme of Dark Earth, Middle Stone and Azure Blue in the same patterns as UK-based aircraft. Style and presentation of code letters was much more variable; some aircraft in the theatre wore a single letter and others none at all.

Filter
Tropicalised Hurricanes were fitted with the prominent Vokes filter to protect the ventral radiator, oil cooler and therefore the engine from sand and dust.

Armament
Hurricane Mk IICs were armed with either Oerlikon or Hispano 20-mm cannon with a capacity of approximately 364 rounds. HL851 was later to have the outboard guns removed to save weight as was done on a number of other Middle East Hurricanes.

Engine
Hurricane Mk IICs were fitted with 955-kW Rolls-Royce Merlin XX engines, the additional power compensating for the extra weight of the airframe compared to the earlier Mk I.

Left: Hawker Hurricane Mk Is of No. 237 Squadron taxi out for a mission in May 1942. Together with No. 208 Squadron, this unit was mainly responsible for tactical reconnaissance for the 8th Army.

Below: Luftwaffe groundcrew working under difficult conditions in the desert. Junkers Ju 87D-1/Trop aircraft like this one, suffered heavy losses in the air and on the ground, largely due to their lack of speed.

after attaining the extraordinary total of 158 victories he was killed while baling out of his Bf 109 after engine failure.

JG 27's Marseille was a 22-year-old Berliner who had already claimed seven Spitfires shot down while flying Bf 109Es over the English Channel. When Luftwaffe high command deployed two Gruppen of JG 27 to Libya from the Eastern Front, it had re-equipped with the 'F'-model and by the beginning of 1942 his score was around 50 and increasing rapidly. For example, on 3 June, while escorting Ju 87s, his Staffel was attacked by RAF P-40s: Marseille destroyed six in 11 minutes, using the bare minimum of ammunition. A fortnight later he downed six more aircraft, this time in six minutes. The following day his score stood at 101 and he was

Junkers bombers

The Ju 87D had a redesigned airframe with lower drag, increased bombload, armour and better, faster-firing defensive weapons and was used for army support rather than dive-bombing.

A tropicalised version of the lower-powered Ju 88A-5, the A-10 did not perform well in the high temperatures of North Africa and was withdrawn to bases north of the Mediterranean during 1942.

Junkers Ju 87D
Carrying a 1000-kg (2,205-lb) SC1000 bomb under its fuselage, this Ju 87D-1/Trop shows the much improved aerodynamic shape of the 'D' in comparison with the preceding 'B' model. 'S7+KS' was flown by 8 Stuka-geschwader 3 at Derna, Libya, in June 1942. It had an unusual brown/sand colour scheme.

Junkers Ju 88A
Flown by Lehrgeschwader 1 in support of Rommel's Afrika Korps, this Ju 88A-10 was withdrawn to Crete for anti-shipping strikes against the Royal Navy by October 1942. Here it was flown by II/LG 1 from Heraklion.

awarded Swords to his Knight's Cross.

The first day of September 1942 saw JG 27 at the zenith of their achievement. As Rommel advanced towards El Alamein, daily Ju 87 attacks on the Tobruk garrison were escorted by JG 27 fighters. Tedder's Middle East Command flew a total of 674 sorties to protect the British 8th Army; Marseille flew three times in the course of that day. By the late evening JG 27 had claimed 26 aircraft (20 Kittyhawks, four Hurricanes and two Spitfires) for the loss of one pilot killed, one taken prisoner and one posted missing. Marseille had destroyed no less than 17 himself.

SEVENTEEN IN A DAY

All 17 were identified in Allied records. Congratulations came at once from Generalfeldmarschall Kesselring and brought the award of the Diamonds to the Knight's Cross the following day. By 15

September Marseille had reached a score of 150 victories; that day he had shot down seven aircraft in 11 minutes. By dusk on the 30th, by which time he was flying a Bf 109G-2, he was dead – the victim of engine failure and bad luck as his parachute became entangled with his aircraft's tailplane.

As the victorious 8th Army swept eastwards for the last time, British fighters landed at Gazala, 160 kilometres (100 miles) inside Cyrenaica on 17 November; two days later they were at Matruba, 80 kilometres (50 miles) farther on. Two Hurricane squadrons even landed behind the enemy forces, so

Above: A Messerschmitt Bf 109F 'White 11' of 1/JG 27 behind Allied lines near to El Adem early in 1942. It had been hit in the radiator and the Luftwaffe pilot had made a successful crash landing in the desert, before being captured by British troops, here collecting souvenirs.

swiftly were the Allied fighters accompanying the advance.

It was at this moment that, as the Axis forces were desperately preparing to stand firm in Tripolitania, the Allies launched their master stroke when, on 8 November, American and British forces, sailed from the west, put ashore in considerable strength in

Above: A six-engined Messerschmitt Me 323D-2 transport landing at a desert airfield in North Africa, arriving from Trapani with ammunition and fuel. Serving with KGzbV 323 (later TG 5) the Me 323s suffered severely at the hands of Allied fighters and bombers.

Right: In the dust and sand of the Western Desert, that not only reduced visibility but caused severe wear to aircraft engines, these Hurricane Mk IID 'tank-busters' of No. 6 Squadron taxi out for take-off at Sidi bu Amid in January 1943, during the rout of the Afrika Korps.

Left: North African conditions were very harsh both for machines and men. If dust and sand were not blowing everywhere, then heavy rain turned airfields into quagmires. A flight of Luftwaffe Bf 109s leave an unmistakable take-off signature across their desert base.

Below: Curtiss Kittyhawk Mk IIs from No. 260 Squadron lined up on a desert landing ground (LG) in 1942, ready to escort a bomber formation on a raid against German bases in Libya.

Morocco and Algeria under cover of carrier-borne aircraft and others operating from Gibraltar.

These landings, Operation 'Torch', immediately threatened the whole Axis position in North Africa. Straightaway Tunisia was occupied by the Germans as air reinforcements from Italy and Sicily

Below: A pair of N. American B-25C Mitchells of the USAAF's 9th Air Force come in to land at a desert airfield captured from the Germans early in 1943 as the Allied forces moved relentlessly westwards. The wrecked aircraft, a Messerschmitt Me 210A, belonged to III/ZG 1.

landed at airfields in the north. RAF and USAAF fighters and bombers (Spitfires, Mosquitoes, Beaufighters, P-38s, P-39s, P-40s, B-17s, B-24s, B-25s and B-26s), as well as troop-carrying C-47s, poured ashore at Algerian airfields.

SURRENDER

The Luftwaffe made numerous raids but Allied air superiority was such that little vital damage was suffered. In the south the 8th Army, after being held at Mareth, broke through the enemy lines in March 1943 with constant air support from RAF and USAAF

fighters and fighter-bombers. By 1 May only a small perimeter in the north-east of Tunisia held out and, despite considerable efforts to sustain this by air from Sicily, the Axis forces in North Africa finally surrendered to the Allies under General Alexander on 12 May.

Below: On 8 November 1942, Operation 'Torch', the Allied invasion of French North West Africa, converted the El Alamein defeat into a crisis for the Axis in the whole Mediterranean theatre. Some difficulties in Anglo-American co-operation allowed some early German countermeasures.

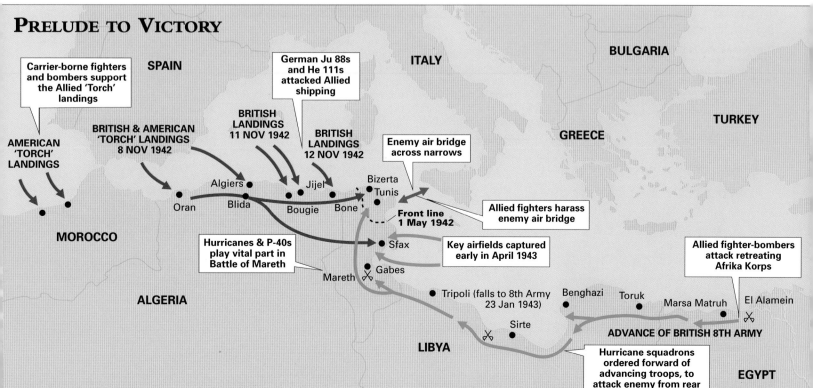

PRELUDE TO VICTORY

Carrier-borne fighters and bombers support the Allied 'Torch' landings

SPAIN

German Ju 88s and He 111s attacked Allied shipping

ITALY

BULGARIA

AMERICAN 'TORCH' LANDINGS

BRITISH & AMERICAN 'TORCH' LANDINGS 8 NOV 1942

BRITISH LANDINGS 11 NOV 1942

BRITISH LANDINGS 12 NOV 1942

TURKEY

GREECE

Enemy air bridge across narrows

Algiers
Oran
Blida
Bougie
Jijel
Bone
Bizerta
Tunis

Allied fighters harass enemy air bridge

MOROCCO

Front line 1 May 1942

Hurricanes & P-40s play vital part in Battle of Mareth

Sfax

Key airfields captured early in April 1943

Gabes

Allied fighter-bombers attack retreating Afrika Korps

Mareth

ALGERIA

Tripoli (falls to 8th Army 23 Jan 1943)

Benghazi
Toruk
Marsa Matruh
El Alamein

Sirte

ADVANCE OF BRITISH 8TH ARMY

LIBYA

Hurricane squadrons ordered forward of advancing troops, to attack enemy from rear

EGYPT

The Condor Threat

WORLD WAR II IN EUROPE

1940-1943

From the moment German forces reached the Atlantic coast of France, the threat to the UK's vital lifelines in the Atlantic (from surface raiders, submarines and aircraft) took on an infinitely more menacing character. The Luftwaffe had not envisaged long-range maritime air operations to the same extent as the RAF, its flying-boats and seaplanes (the Dornier Do 18 and Heinkel He 59) were more suited to short-range coastal work in the

The Heinkel He 115 was an outstandingly tough aircraft. In 1941, Fl. Fü Atlanik had a complement of 24 He 115B-2 torpedo-bombers with KüFlGr 906 and the reconnaissance 3.(F)/123. This example is seen circling two German warships.

North Sea).

Instead, work was hurriedly undertaken to adapt the one proven long-range aircraft possessed by Germany, the commercial Focke-Wulf Fw 200 Condor, to embark on land-based maritime operations over the Atlantic now that suitable bases existed in Norway and western France. The four-engined Fw 200 had originated in 1936 and in the two years immediately before the war had flown a number of spectacular long-distance flights. Stemming from a Japanese order for a maritime reconnaissance version

One of the first batch of American-built CVE escort carriers – HMS Biter – has six Hurricanes securely lashed down on the pitching deck in heavy Atlantic weather. Biter was launched on 18 December 1940 and undertook convoy escort duties for most of its service with the Royal Navy.

(which was not completed), the manufacturers continued the adaptation to meet Luftwaffe requirements, and six development aircraft were delivered to I/KG 40 in Denmark in April 1940. Two months later, equipped with Fw 200Cs, this unit moved to Bordeaux-Merignac to start opera-

From both ship and shore the Arado Ar 196 performed uncomplainingly on patrol duties. The type served in coastal waters around France, in the Aegean, the Baltic and Norwegian coasts.

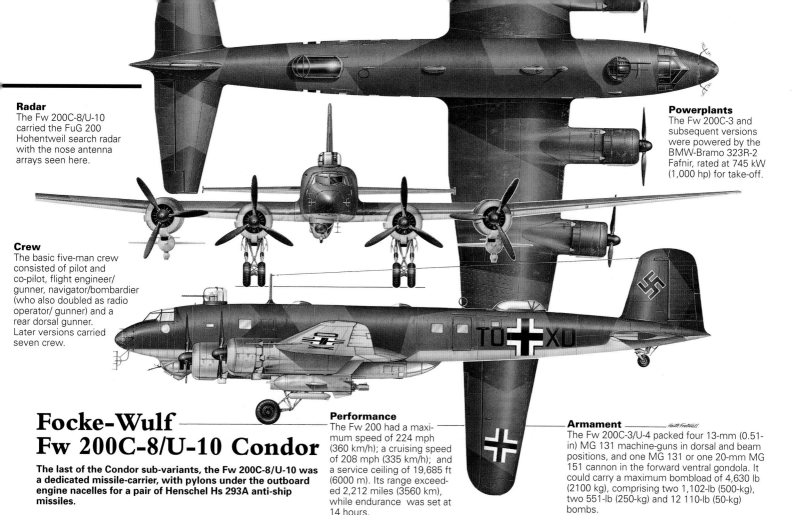

Focke-Wulf Fw 200C-8/U-10 Condor

The last of the Condor sub-variants, the Fw 200C-8/U-10 was a dedicated missile-carrier, with pylons under the outboard engine nacelles for a pair of Henschel Hs 293A anti-ship missiles.

Fw 200C-3 Condor F8+GH was photographed while serving with I/KG 40 in Greece in 1942. It does not carry the white Mediterranean theatre band and was probably on temporary detachment.

tions against British shipping, flying patrols from France over the Western Approaches and landing at Trondheim or Stavanger in Norway.

ALLIED SHIPPING SUNK

Under the command of Oberstleutnant Geisse, I/KG 40's 15 Fw 200Cs sank 90,000 tons of Allied shipping in August and September. On 26 October, an aircraft flown by Hauptmann Bernhard Jope attacked and crippled the 44,348-ton liner *Empress of Britain* off the Irish coast; the ship was later sunk by a U-boat while under tow.

Two Blohm und Voss BV 138s, widely known as 'Flying Clogs', and a Dornier Do 24 rest at their moorings, next to a slipway. Most BV 138s operated in the harsh environment of the northern oceans, seeing a lot of service around the Norwegian coast. They proved easy meat for Allied fighters.

By the end of 1940 a total of 26 Fw 200s had been completed, and such was the threat they posed to British convoys beyond the protection of land-based fighters that drastic steps were being taken by the British to protect their ships. The first of these involved the erection of catapults on merchant ships from which Sea Hurricane fighters could be launched on the appearance of a Condor. There was no possibility of providing aircraft-carriers for convoy escort at that stage of the war, so the Hurricane pilots, once launched against a raider, had either to ditch in the path of the convoy in the hope of being rescued or try to reach land. The first CAM-ship, SS *Michael E,*

Luftwaffe flying-boats and floatplanes

While the Condor won much of the glory as a result of its early successes and huge range, a variety of other aircraft played their part in the Luftwaffe's war against Allied shipping. Among the most important of these were the flying-boats and floatplanes, which performed patrol, minelaying and anti-shipping duties. They were augmented by land-based Ju 88s, He 111s and He 177s.

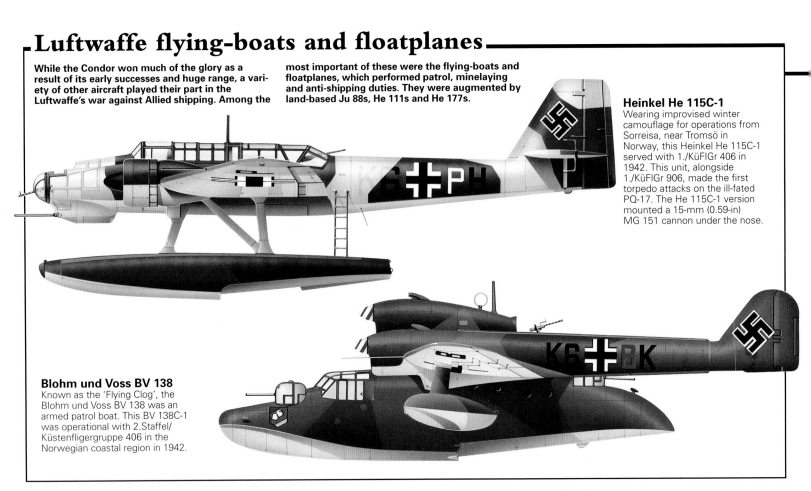

Heinkel He 115C-1
Wearing improvised winter camouflage for operations from Sorreisa, near Tromsö in Norway, this Heinkel He 115C-1 served with 1./KüFlGr 406 in 1942. This unit, alongside 1./KüFlGr 906, made the first torpedo attacks on the ill-fated PQ-17. The He 115C-1 version mounted a 15-mm (0.59-in) MG 151 cannon under the nose.

Blohm und Voss BV 138
Known as the 'Flying Clog', the Blohm und Voss BV 138 was an armed patrol boat. This BV 138C-1 was operational with 2.Staffel/ Küstenfliegergruppe 406 in the Norwegian coastal region in 1942.

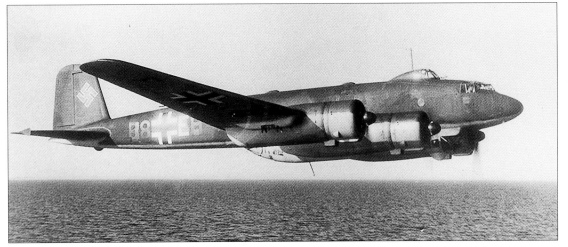

Above: The kill tally on a successful Condor, with the estimated tonnages of each victim. As well as attacking ships, the Condors shadowed Allied convoys, reporting their position to the waiting U-boat Wolf Packs, which could inflict even greater carnage.

Above: The first military version of the Focke-Wulf Condor was the Fw 200C-1. This Condor served with 3 Staffel of Kampfgeschwader 40, which operated from Bordeaux-Merignac. The Condor was regarded by the Allies as a real danger to convoys.

Left: A Sea Hurricane on the catapult of a CAM ship. Before escort carriers became available, they afforded one-shot protection to merchant ships and convoys, with only a minimal loss of cargo capacity. The cost was high, however.

set sail on 27 May 1941 but was torpedoed before launching her Hurricane. On 3 August, however, a Condor was shot down by a Sea Hurricane Mk IA flown by Lieutenant R.W.H. Everett, RNVR, after launching from the *Maplin*, a converted naval escort.

The next expedient was to provide merchantmen with flight decks (MAC-ships, or merchant aircraft carriers) and a substantial conversion programme began to prepare large numbers of Sea Hurricanes to enable them to operate from catapults and flight decks.

With the appearance of fighters over the Atlantic convoys the tactics of the Condors changed, the raiders preferring to retire, only returning once the Hurricane had ditched. Occasionally, the big aircraft stayed to fight it out. Their defensive armament underwent progressive increase until by the end of 1941 they carried three heavy machine-guns, two light machine-guns and a 20-mm cannon. Airframe strengthening and increased engine power allowed progressively heavier bombloads, but early in 1942 the employment of Fw 200s changed again, the aircraft being used to shadow and report the position of convoys to allow U-boats to close in for their

Left: The Fw 200C-3/U-2 featured a distinctive bulge in the gondola for the Lofte 7D bombsight. This necessitated a reorganisation of the ventral armament. The Condor proved vulnerable to Allied fighters, and even to prowling Sunderlands.

Above: The crew of an Fw 200 briefs prior to a mission. The Fw 200C-3/U-2 version of this maritime reconnaissance and anti-shipping aircraft had an increased crew of six, subsequently increased to seven in later versions.

attacks. Also in 1942 the Fw 200C-4 appeared with FuG 200 Hohentweil and Rostock shipping search radar.

The sailing of the first North Cape convoys to the USSR resulted in about half the in-service Condors being moved to Norway early in 1942, others later being transferred to southern Italy to operate against the Malta convoys. This dilution of the German raiders in the West was further exacerbated by the removal of 18 aircraft to assist in transport operations at Stalingrad at the beginning of 1943, and it was not until the middle of

that year that KG 40 was able to reassemble about 40 Fw 200Cs in western France.

By then a new weapon had appeared in the German anti-shipping arsenal; the radio-controlled, rocket-powered Hs 293A missile, two of which could be carried under the outboard engine nacelles of the Fw 200C-6 and Fw 200C-8 versions. On the first occasion the new weapons were flown operationally by III/KG 40, on 28 December 1943, the missile-carrying Condor was forced down by a patrolling Sunderland before the Hs 293s could be launched.

Any account of German maritime air operations should include mention of the Heinkel He 177 four-engined bomber. This aircraft also engaged in anti-shipping work, both as a carrier of the Hs 293A missiles, LT 50 torpedoes and FX 1400 Fritz X guided bomb and as a maritime reconnaissance aircraft serving with KG 40. In 1944, however, the relentless pressure by the Allies and loss by the Germans of their air bases in the Mediterranean and western France led to the with-

The weapon most associated with the Heinkel He 177A-5/R2 in the anti-shipping role was the Henschel Hs 293A missile. These were carried under the wings or, as here, on a special pylon fitted to the covered forward bomb bay.

drawal of the maritime units to Germany. There, they joined in the crucial work of transportation as the Allies closed the ring on the Reich, and maritime warfare by aircraft over the Atlantic drew to a conclusion.

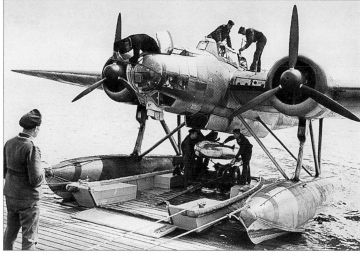

Left: The Heinkel He 115 was a hardy addition to the coastal fleet. It was used for all coastal duties, including patrol, anti-shipping and minelaying. This view shows the typical Heinkel planform, derived from the pre-war He 70 mailplane.

Above: A close-up of an He 115B shows the extensive glazing around the nose. There were flat-pane windows in the bottom of the nose for accurate aiming by the bombardier, whose duty it also was to fire the nose-mounted MG 15.

The Mighty Eighth Arrives

MAY 1942 – JUNE 1943

The Pearl Harbor debacle of December 1941 not only found the United States ill-prepared for war against Japan but ill-equipped to undertake participation in a war in Europe and it was to be many months before a sizeable air force could be assembled for an assault on Germany, an

Above: In mid-1942 the newly arrived B-17s quickly went into action on daylight raids against targets in France and Holland. They flew from bases in East Anglia with fighter cover provided by RAF Spitfires and suffered no losses until September.

assembly that would be diluted by attempts to create an expeditionary air force to support the Allied landings in North Africa which would materialise in November 1942.

The first administration elements of the US VIII Bomber Command under Major General Carl A. Spaatz arrived in the UK on 22 February 1942 (the same day that Harris took over the leadership of RAF

Bomber Command); it was not until May that year, however, that combat units began arriving with Boeing B-17s and Consolidated B-24s (of the 44th, 91st, 92nd, 93rd, 97th and 301st Heavy Bomb Groups) at Shipdham, Kimbolton, Bovingdon, Alconbury and Polebrook. Their first operation, by a token force of a dozen 97th Group B-17Es, was flown against Rouen under heavy RAF Spitfire

protection on 17 August; two days later a similar raid by 24 aircraft against Abbeville was flown in support of the Dieppe landings.

The provision of fighter escorts for these raids ran counter to American bomber tactics advocated at this time and was intended to allow the bomber crews to achieve a measure of operational experience before being called on to fly unescorted raids. The whole

Left: In the nose of a B-17 the bombardier sights his target through the telescopic eye-piece of the Norden bombsight. He takes over control of the aircraft using the Automatic Flight Control Equipment connected to the autopilot on the final bomb run.

Left: The port waist gunner, with a 12.7-mm (0.5-in) machine-gun on a B-24 Liberator. The advantage of this gun position was that the gunner could move around and was not cramped up like the turret gunners, but he had to stand over the gun for hours in the freezing cold.

Above: The crew of B-24 Liberator 'Jenny' from the 93rd Bomb Group happily celebrate their safe return from a bombing raid on Wilhelmshaven. The aircraft was on the first USAAF daylight operation against mainland Germany on 29 January 1943.

Left: A flight of Lockheed P-38H Lightnings operating over Europe. Although introduced as an interceptor fighter, the P-38 quickly proved its value as a long-range bomber escort, helping protect B-17s and B-24s as they flew missions deeper into Germany.

Below: B-24D Liberators lined up on the Consolidated Vultee Aircraft Corporation flight-line at San Diego, California ready for despatch to USAAF bomb wings in Europe. The B-24D was the first mass-produced version of the Liberator and featured turbocharged engines to improve performance at altitude.

Left: 'Lil', a B-17F of the 359th Bomb Squadron, 303rd Bomb Group, being bombed-up at Molesworth, Cambridgeshire, before setting off on a long-range mission against a German factory.

philosophy of the US Army Air Corps and US Army Air Force had, for a decade, centred on daylight bombing by formations of heavily-armed bombers capable of defending themselves by mutual gun protection. With the arrival in service of the high-flying B-17, altitude

had added a further element to their supposed immunity from fighter interception.

DAYLIGHT RAIDS

Already a number of B-17Cs (without tail guns) had been supplied to the RAF in 1941, but British experience on operations with these aircraft in unescorted daylight raids had not been satisfactory, as a result principally of tactical misuse. Undeterred, the Americans continued to fly more and more B-17Es

to the UK and for the remainder of 1942 contented themselves with relatively short-range operations against such targets as Amiens, Rotterdam and Wevelghem, all with heavy Spitfire escort and all without combat loss. The Luftwaffe drew first blood when, on 6 September during a raid by the 92nd, 97th and 301st Groups on St Omer, Messerschmitt Bf 109Gs of JG 2 and JG 26 shot down two B-17s. The following day a raid on Rotterdam escaped without loss

Bombers of the 8th

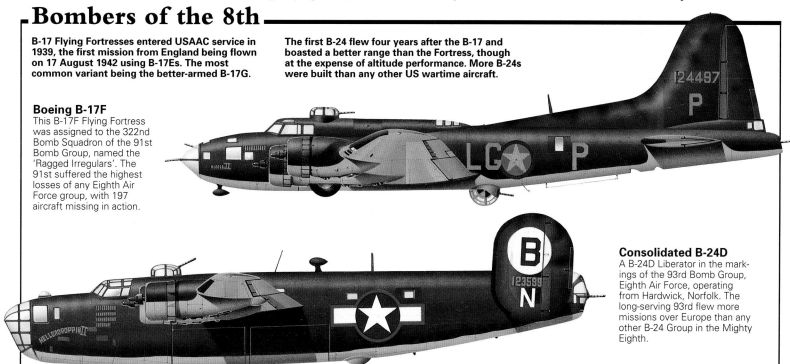

B-17 Flying Fortresses entered USAAC service in 1939, the first mission from England being flown on 17 August 1942 using B-17Es. The most common variant being the better-armed B-17G.

The first B-24 flew four years after the B-17 and boasted a better range than the Fortress, though at the expense of altitude performance. More B-24s were built than any other US wartime aircraft.

Boeing B-17F
This B-17F Flying Fortress was assigned to the 322nd Bomb Squadron of the 91st Bomb Group, named the 'Ragged Irregulars'. The 91st suffered the highest losses of any Eighth Air Force group, with 197 aircraft missing in action.

Consolidated B-24D
A B-24D Liberator in the markings of the 93rd Bomb Group, Eighth Air Force, operating from Hardwick, Norfolk. The long-serving 93rd flew more missions over Europe than any other B-24 Group in the Mighty Eighth.

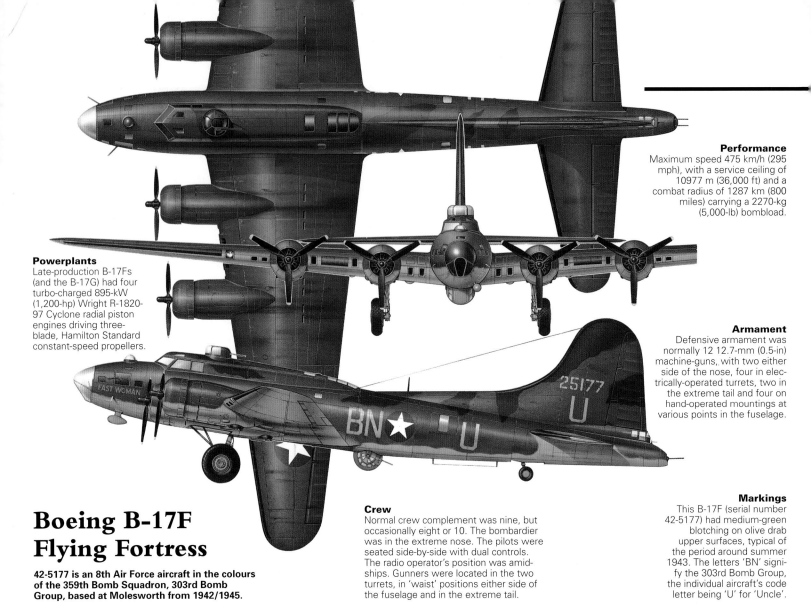

Performance
Maximum speed 475 km/h (295 mph), with a service ceiling of 10977 m (36,000 ft) and a combat radius of 1287 km (800 miles) carrying a 2270-kg (5,000-lb) bombload.

Powerplants
Late-production B-17Fs (and the B-17G) had four turbo-charged 895-kW (1,200-hp) Wright R-1820-97 Cyclone radial piston engines driving three-blade, Hamilton Standard constant-speed propellers.

Armament
Defensive armament was normally 12 12.7-mm (0.5-in) machine-guns, with two either side of the nose, four in electrically-operated turrets, two in the extreme tail and four on hand-operated mountings at various points in the fuselage.

Markings
This B-17F (serial number 42-5177) had medium-green blotching on olive drab upper surfaces, typical of the period around summer 1943. The letters 'BN' signify the 303rd Bomb Group, the individual aircraft's code letter being 'U' for 'Uncle'.

Crew
Normal crew complement was nine, but occasionally eight or 10. The bombardier was in the extreme nose. The pilots were seated side-by-side with dual controls. The radio operator's position was amidships. Gunners were located in the two turrets, in 'waist' positions either side of the fuselage and in the extreme tail.

Boeing B-17F Flying Fortress

42-5177 is an 8th Air Force aircraft in the colours of the 359th Bomb Squadron, 303rd Bomb Group, based at Molesworth from 1942/1945.

despite a vicious fight with Focke-Wulf Fw 190s of JG 1.

Gradually, as the B-17s began raiding further afield; the British fighters had to turn back part-way to the target leaving the bomber crews to prove their ability to defend themselves. On 9 October 108 B-17Es and B-24Ds raided Lille and on their return flight were attacked by the fighters of JG 2 and

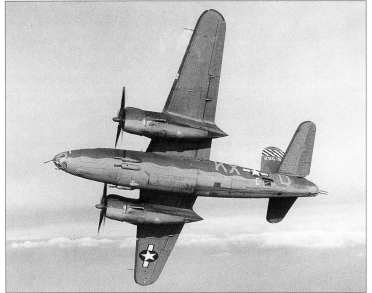

Left: Although rammed by a following B-17 when their aircraft slowed down with an engine failure, the crew managed to nurse this Fortress back to its base in England. The B-17's fin and rudder, together with the rear gunner's hatch were all smashed by the propellers of the second bomber.

JG 26. A measure of the savage battle that followed may be judged by the fact that the American gunners claimed to have destroyed 56 enemy fighters when in fact only

one, an Fw 190A-4 of JG 26, was shot down.

Already the German fighter pilots were evolving tactics to combat the big American bombers; they had learned that closing from astern and abeam subjected them to withering and prolonged crossfire from the massed 12.7-mm (0.5-inch) heavy machine-guns of the bombers. They discovered that the frontal attack was the most deadly (as had been demonstrated by RAF

Left: B-26 Marauders served only briefly with the 8th Air Force, their first mission taking place on 14 May 1943. On 17 May this low-level raid on a power station near Ijmuiden, was repeated with 11 aircraft – none returned. The B-26 was more suited to a tactical role; the few Bomb Groups operating the type (like the 387th) transferred to the 9th Air Force in November.

Below: Flying in close formation for defensive protection also had its perils. The port tailplane of this B-17 has been struck by bombs dropped by another Fortress higher up in the formation. Though very strong, stricken bombers such as this seldom recovered. Miraculously this crew survived.

Right: B-17Fs of the 390th Bomb Group, 13th Bomb Wing taking advantage of the bombers' ability to climb to high altitude, with their faster escorts, P-47 Thunderbolts, weaving a defensive pattern and making condensation trails above.

Below: These P-47D Thunderbolts of the 62nd Fighter Squadron, 56th Fighter Group escorting a B-24 Liberator, have distinctive nose and tail bands to help Allied aircrew identify them. The P-47 looked similar to the Luftwaffe's Focke-Wulf Fw 190 when seen from a distance.

Below: An Eighth Air Force Flying Fortress departing the French coast after a daylight raid on the submarine pens at St Nazaire. The bombers remained vulnerable to attack from Luftwaffe fighters all the way back to their East Anglian bases.

Fighter Command during the Battle of Britain), both the B-17E and B-24D being armed with only single hand-held guns in the nose. The head-on attack demanded great skill and nerve, allowing no more than a snap burst; however, it usually required no more than one or two cannon shells in the pilots' cockpit of a B-17 to bring about the bomber's end. In a raid by five groups on St Nazaire ('Ramrod' No. 38) on 23 November, four B-17s were shot down in frontal attacks. The biggest air battle to date, on 20 December, involved 101 B-17s and B-24s and nearly 200 Fw 190s during a raid on an aircraft park near Paris, too far from British bases for the Spitfires to

Fighters of the 8th

Entering service in January 1943 with the 4th FG the P-47C was thought heavy and unresponsive. It proved to be tough, have enormous firepower and performed well in combat.

After early difficulties the improved P-38J entered combat service in Europe during August 1943. With shortcomings as an interceptor it was used mainly for long-range ground-attack missions.

Republic P-47C
In the markings of the 334th Fighter Squadron, that became part of the Eighth Air Force's 4th Fighter Group in September 1942, this new P-47C Thunderbolt entered service at Debden, Essex in March 1943.

Lockheed P-38J
This Eighth Air Force P-38J Lightning carries the markings of the 338th Fighter Squadron of the 55th Fighter Group that was based at Nuthampstead, Hertfordshire. It was used for long-range bomber escort duties in the spring of 1944.

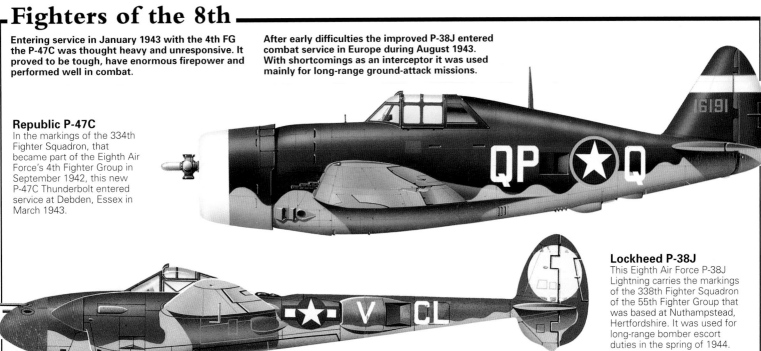

Left: Nine of the crew from B-17F 'Tinker Toy' pause for a photograph after returning from a bombing mission. They are carrying their parachutes and life-rafts. Some crew members have boots and fleece-lined leather jackets to combat the cold temperatures at high altitude .

Right: Eighth Air Force bombers and fighters were frequently adorned with nose art by their crews. These were often 'pin-ups' in various states of undress copied from such magazines as Esquire. This B-17F carries the colourful 'Miss Ouachita' on its nose.

provide continuous escort. Six B-17s were lost (each with a 10-man crew), and six Fw 190s were shot down by the American gunners.

The New Year brought the Americans' first raid on German territory when 91 heavy bombers attacked Wilhelmshaven on 27 January 1943, the raiders now flying more compact box formations to give increased mutual gun protection. Poor weather then restricted the VIII Bomber Command's attacks to relatively short-range targets until the late spring that year, by which time its strength had risen to 10 groups (despite the move by some units to North Africa to bolster the creation

Above: Eighth Air Force B-17s release their sticks of bombs on a daylight raid over Germany. Bombers were at greatest risk from anti-aircraft fire as they maintained a straight and level bomb run over a target below.

Below: A pair of 4th Fighter Group P-47Cs on their dispersal at Debden, Essex in April 1943. This big fighter was able to escort high-flying B-17s into Germany and proved a match for the Luftwaffe's Fw 190s above 4572 m (15,000 ft).

Above: The Scottish-born pilot of this Eighth Air Force B-17F, Lieutenant Bob McCallum, surveys the extensive damage to his bomber after its return from a mission over Germany in August 1943. On only his second mission the Fortress was hit by flak and caught fire. The ball-turret gunner, Sgt Maynard Smith climbed up into the aircraft and managed to extinguish the fuselage fire. He was awarded the Congressional Medal of Honor – America's highest award for bravery.

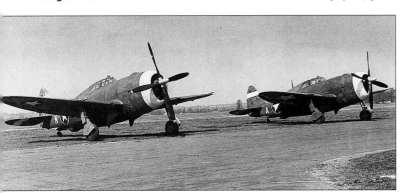

of the US 12th Air Force).

May 1943 marked a turning point for the American heavy bomber offensive. A raid on 1 May by 79 B-17s on St Nazaire found the bombers flying the last few miles to the target with their escorting Spitfires, losing seven of their number to the fighters of III/JG 2. On 4 May a raid by the newly-introduced B-17Fs, some with increased nose armament, attacked Antwerp, their escort of RAF Spitfires being joined by US VIII Fighter Command Republic P-47Ds for the first time; despite interception by upwards of 70 enemy fighters no bombers were lost. The philosophy of unescorted daylight raids by the Americans (like those by the RAF three years earlier) had been shown to be fallacious.

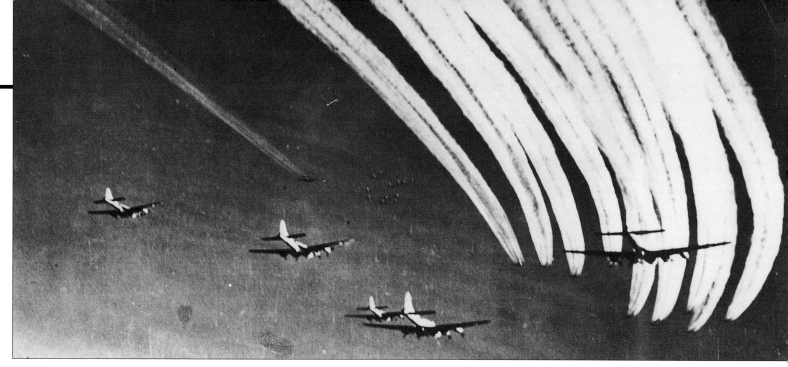

Left: North American P-51B-5-NA Mustang (43-6885) 'Texas Terrier III' of the 354th Fighter Squadron wearing battle claims on its nose. Four swastikas represent Luftwaffe 'kills' and eight bombs signify successful ground-attack missions. The P-51B, carrying two underwing fuel tanks and fitted with six 12.7-mm (0.5-in) guns in its wings, was the USAAF's first effective long-range escort fighter.

Above: One of the hallmarks of the Eighth Air Force daylight bombing raids over Europe were the vapour trail patterns produced by the bombers at high altitude. The crews did not like this signature across the skies as it pinpointed their position for the gunners below and the waiting Luftwaffe. The B-17s maintained close formation so as to offer maximum fire protection against the fighters.

IN ACTION

American bombers flew their first combat missions against occupied Europe in the summer of 1942, when a dozen bombers attacked railway yards at Rouen. At that time, the Eighth Air Force had just begun to establish its administrative echelons in England, and was in no position to play a major part in the air campaign against Germany – as yet. Though employed in small numbers at first, the US Army Air Force began to build its strength on the 'unsinkable aircraft carrier' which was the British Isles. By the spring of 1943, VIII Bomber Command of the Eighth Air Force was sending more than 100 bombers at a time on missions and numbers were climbing rapidly.

BUILDING BASES

The huge build-up of bombers, fighters and supporting aircraft required an equally large build-up of infrastructure and support facilities. Fortunately, the eastern counties of England are wide and flat. In some cases, the Americans simply took over older RAF stations, building and extending runways and putting in hangars, workshops, accommodation and all of the other facilities needed to keep bomber and fighter squadrons flying against the enemy. But there were only so many fields that could be taken over and a massive building programme saw the development of many new sites.

FLAT FIELDS

American bomber and fighter bases were concentrated in a broad strip of fertile flatlands stretching from the coast of East Anglia through the Fen country to the East Midlands. The RAF's night bombers were mostly based in Lincolnshire to the north.

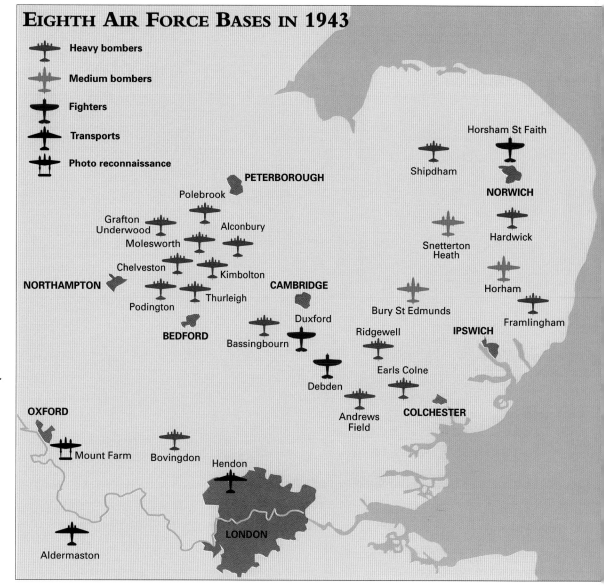

EIGHTH AIR FORCE BASES IN 1943

- Heavy bombers
- Medium bombers
- Fighters
- Transports
- Photo reconnaissance

Horsham St Faith
Shipdham
PETERBOROUGH
NORWICH
Polebrook
Grafton Underwood
Alconbury
Hardwick
Molesworth
Snetterton Heath
Chelveston
Kimbolton
NORTHAMPTON
Horham
CAMBRIDGE
Thurleigh
Bury St Edmunds
Podington
Framlingham
Duxford
BEDFORD
Ridgewell
IPSWICH
Bassingbourn
Earls Colne
Debden
COLCHESTER
OXFORD
Andrews Field
Mount Farm
Bovingdon
Hendon
LONDON
Aldermaston

The U-boat War

1942 – 1943

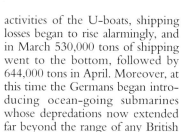

Above: When war was declared, the Avro Anson formed the mainstay of RAF Coastal Command. This Anson I of No. 48 Squadron, based at Hooton Park, is seen over a convoy leaving Liverpool. A few Ansons remained until late 1942.

Below: A Sunderland Mk I of No 10 Squadron RAAF on patrol from Mount Batten, in 1942, shows the two dorsal gunners' cockpits provided early in the war. By February 1943, Coastal Command had nine squadrons of Sunderlands.

The Battle of the Atlantic was essentially a campaign against the German U-boat, a struggle that lasted from the first day of the war to the last. There were other facets such as the German surface raiders, which could be and were dealt with by the Royal Navy on the high seas, and by RAF Bomber Command while in port; and the Luftwaffe's maritime aircraft which, by and large, were the eyes of the U-boats themselves. It was at the moment in 1940 when the German army occupied the French Atlantic ports

Above: The most important long-range type in RAF service was the Liberator, here exemplified by a Mk III. The Liberator allowed Coastal Command to considerably close the mid-Atlantic gap where convoys were unprotected by patrol aircraft.

(Brest, St Nazaire and Lorient) that the Battle of the Atlantic took an ominous turn for the UK. As soon as the U-boats could find haven in those western ports (and those in northern Norway), the Western Approaches to British ports became the hunting grounds for German submarines. RAF Coastal

Command, with its limited numbers of long-range aircraft, the Sunderlands and Hudsons, had its work cut out to escort the inbound convoys, let alone perform long and systematic sea patrols.

By February 1941, after a winter which not only restricted flying by the British aircraft but also the

activities of the U-boats, shipping losses began to rise alarmingly, and in March 530,000 tons of shipping went to the bottom, followed by 644,000 tons in April. Moreover, at this time the Germans began introducing ocean-going submarines whose depredations now extended far beyond the range of any British flying-boat.

RADAR-EQUIPPED

By mid-1941 more than half of Coastal Command's aircraft, which now included ex-Bomber Command aircraft such as the Whitley, had been equipped with ASV (air-to-surface vessel) radar which was capable of locating a surfaced U-boat in the dark or bad weather. Although this equipment had not yet produced many successful submarine 'kills', the threat of unheralded attack from the air certainly

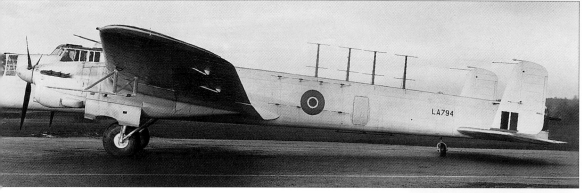

Above: A Whitley Mk VII, one of a number built for maritime reconnaissance duties that joined Coastal Command in 1942. It was the first operational aircraft to carry the new ASV Mk II air-to-surface radar, and the basic crew was increased to include a radar operator.

Right: A successful attack by a Whitley on a German U-boat 'somewhere' in the Bay of Biscay resulted in the destruction of the U-boat. The depth charges have exploded on their target, throwing up a column of water.

Above: The majority of RAF B-17Fs went to Nos 206 and 220 Squadrons operating from the Azores. They filled the important role of covering the mid-Atlantic, until replaced by the more effective Liberator. Radar aerials can be seen on the nose and under the wings.

Left: Wellington GR.Mk XIII JA412/S of No. 221 Sqn surveys the seas off the North African coast while on a sortie from Gibraltar in 1943. The aircraft carries the white low-visibility colours for maritime work and ASV Mk II search radar.

Below: Boeing Fortress IIA FK186 was one of many B-17Es alloted to Coastal Command. Arriving in the UK in March 1942, it joined No. 220 Squadron. Together with the Liberator, the B-17s were able to close off part of the 'Atlantic Gap'.

discouraged U-boat captains from passing through the Bay of Biscay on the surface, and thereby reduced by a small margin the submarine's cruising range. Other expedients were attempted to reduce the U-boat threat, in particular attacks by Bomber Command on factories engaged in submarine production, but these were regarded by that command as superfluous to the bomber's main tasks, and in any case had little lasting effect on account of poor navigation and bombing efficiency. Another task, undertaken jointly by Bomber and Coastal Commands, was the widespread mining of waters outside German ports in the North Sea and Baltic in attempts to prevent U-boats from being sailed from the naval yards into the Atlantic.

Though all these efforts collectively produced some results, it soon became all too clear that Admiral Karl Donitz was fast acquiring a very large fleet of submarines. When the United States entered the war against Germany he was able to order a sizable force of U-boats to operate off the American coast where, within six months, they sank an enormous number of unescorted ships.

By then, however, many improvements in tactics, weapons and aircraft were being introduced, not least the magnificent American Catalina flying-boat. Depth charges had been considerably improved, and the range of ASV (now fitted throughout Coastal Command) increased. And the Leigh Light, an

Early sub-hunters

The emphasis placed on Bomber Command operations meant that Coastal Command was initially limited to using the short-ranged aircraft with which it had begun the war, augmented by

Bomber Command's rejects. The Command never received Lancasters, and, apart from its relative handful of Sunderlands, had to rely on Lend-Lease for longer-range multi-engined types.

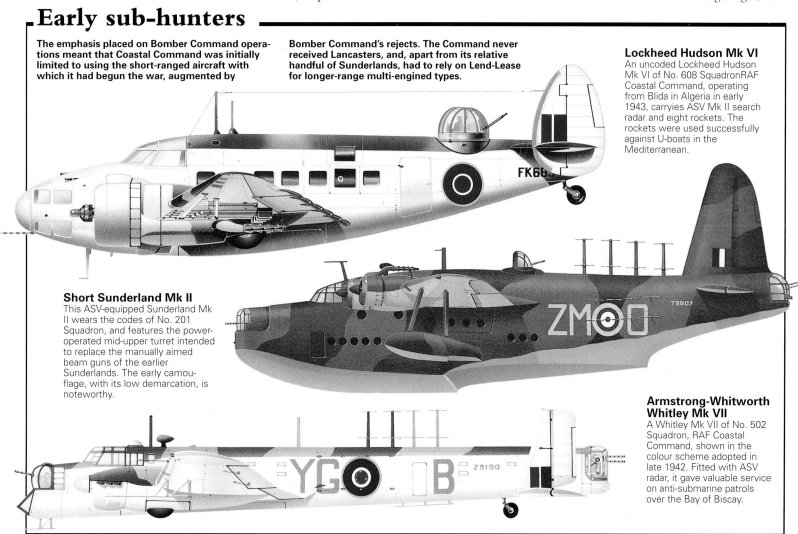

Lockheed Hudson Mk VI
An uncoded Lockheed Hudson Mk VI of No. 608 SquadronRAF Coastal Command, operating from Blida in Algeria in early 1943, carryies ASV Mk II search radar and eight rockets. The rockets were used successfully against U-boats in the Mediterranean.

Short Sunderland Mk II
This ASV-equipped Sunderland Mk II wears the codes of No. 201 Squadron, and features the power-operated mid-upper turret intended to replace the manually aimed beam guns of the earlier Sunderlands. The early camouflage, with its low demarcation, is noteworthy.

Armstrong-Whitworth Whitley Mk VII
A Whitley Mk VII of No. 502 Squadron, RAF Coastal Command, shown in the colour scheme adopted in late 1942. Fitted with ASV radar, it gave valuable service on anti-submarine patrols over the Bay of Biscay.

The Consolidated Catalina was operated by Coastal Command on long-range, extended-endurance patrols in the Atlantic and Bay of Biscay. Here a Catalina releases a depth charge close to the diving U-boat.

Greenland Gap, Donitz introduced 'wolf pack' tactics in August 1942 which, until the creation of hunter-killer groups of corvettes and frigates, decimated the convoys. When Coastal Command made greater efforts to attack U-boats in transit through the Bay of Biscay, the Luftwaffe responded by operating increased patrols by Junkers Ju 88s and Focke-Wulf Fw 190 fighters, and the numbers of air combats with RAF Sunderlands, Wellingtons and Beaufighters increased sharply before the end of 1942.

Gradually the number of VLR Liberators increased, and with the securing of the West African seaboard following the Torch land-

airborne searchlight, was in use, causing submerged travel by U-boats in transit to be further increased. There remained, however, a large gap in mid-Atlantic which could be covered neither by Catalinas from the UK nor by those in the USA, Canada and Iceland, and only a handful of the very-long-range (VLR) Liberator Mk Is were in service. The answer therefore lay in the use of

escort-carriers, small converted merchantmen capable of carrying half a dozen Swordfish aircraft equipped with ASV and depth charges.

To exploit the existence of the

Depth charges from a Sunderland straddle a U-boat, already partly disabled by another aircraft and unable to dive to escape further attack. The wake demonstrates the U-boat's attempts at evasion.

One of the most important jobs for Coastal Command was protecting the convoys sailing regularly to and from Britain. The transatlantic inbound convoys were the principal target for the U-boats.

Long range from Lend-Lease

The Catalina was actually evaluated by the RAF before the war, and was soon ordered in large numbers. The RAF's first Fortresses were delivered to Bomber Command, but proved unreliable, under-armed and lacking in payload. They were transferred to Coastal Command, which then received all of the later Fortress IIs. The very long range of the Liberator made it a natural for Coastal Command, which took the bulk of the 1,889 delivered.

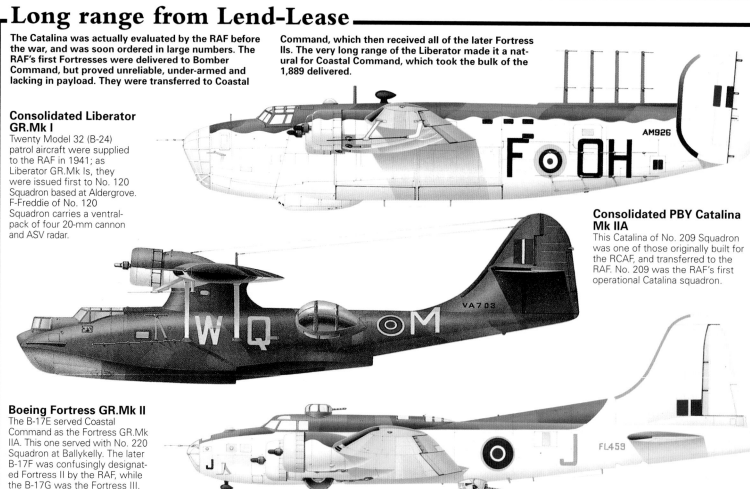

Consolidated Liberator GR.Mk I
Twenty Model 32 (B-24) patrol aircraft were supplied to the RAF in 1941; as Liberator GR.Mk Is, they were issued first to No. 120 Squadron based at Aldergrove. F-Freddie of No. 120 Squadron carries a ventral-pack of four 20-mm cannon and ASV radar.

Consolidated PBY Catalina Mk IIA
This Catalina of No. 209 Squadron was one of those originally built for the RCAF, and transferred to the RAF. No. 209 was the RAF's first operational Catalina squadron.

Boeing Fortress GR.Mk II
The B-17E served Coastal Command as the Fortress GR.Mk IIA. This one served with No. 220 Squadron at Ballykelly. The later B-17F was confusingly designated Fortress II by the RAF, while the B-17G was the Fortress III.

Guarding the Convoys

It was once calculated that a single four-engined aircraft operated by Coastal Command made a contribution to Britain's war effort 200 times greater than that of a similar aircraft serving with Bomber Command. Such a statement is highly controversial and Coastal Command's contribution is hard to quantify. Certainly it helped enforce the blockade which virtually cut off Germany's ports from merchant shipping, and played a crucial role in ensuring that Allied convoys 'got through' without suffering unacceptably high losses. The Command's aircraft also inflicted grievous losses on German shipping, and above all on the German navy's U-boat arm. But the war against the U-boat was never decisively won. As the war ended advanced new U-boats were entering service. They were capable of spending longer time submerged, and were pre-fabricated to escape the effects of bombing.

At first glance, the map opposite paints a reassuring picture, with convoy routes enjoying land-based air cover for much of their length. Even the gaps in the mid-Atlantic could be partly covered, using British and American aircraft-carriers. But in large areas of their radii of action, RAF VLR patrol aircraft were operating in enemy airspace, and outside the range of friendly fighters. Over the North Sea and off the Norwegian coast, for example, the RAF's lumbering Liberators, overloaded with fuel and weapons, had to contend with flak ships and enemy fighters. Many were shot down, and many simply disappeared, falling victim to weather, errors by exhausted crews, or even to the Liberator's fuel-burning heaters, blamed by many for unexplained losses. Even where they could operate unmolested, there were never enough patrol aircraft, and the wily U-boat skipper could often slip through the net.

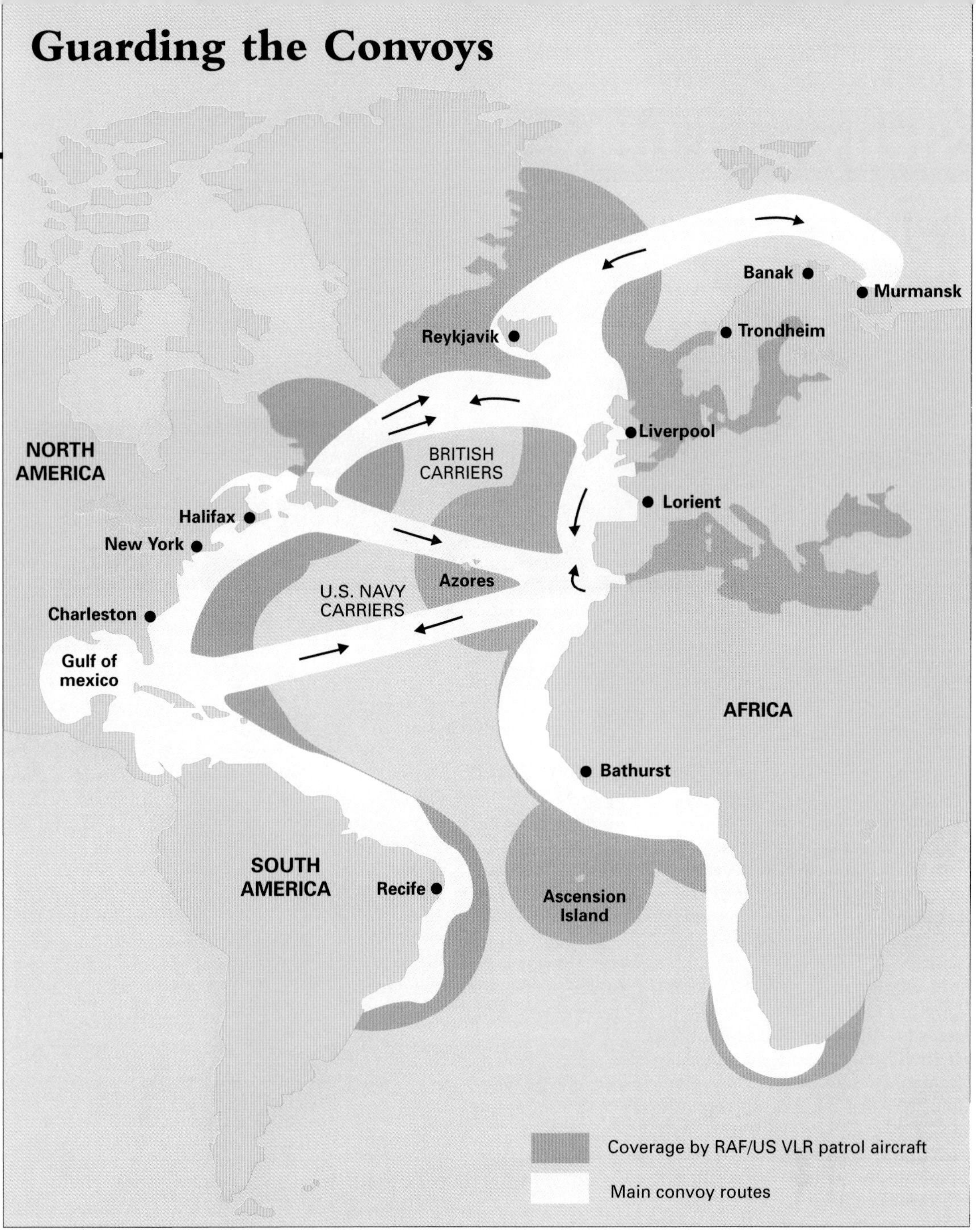

Map labels: NORTH AMERICA · SOUTH AMERICA · AFRICA · BRITISH CARRIERS · U.S. NAVY CARRIERS · Banak · Murmansk · Trondheim · Reykjavik · Liverpool · Lorient · Halifax · New York · Charleston · Gulf of mexico · Azores · Bathurst · Recife · Ascension Island

Coverage by RAF/US VLR patrol aircraft

Main convoy routes

ings (which were themselves achieved with very little interference from U-boats), the sinkings by enemy submarines were slowly reduced from the peak monthly total of 814,000 tons in November 1942 to an average of 130,000 tons a month during the last six months of 1943. The greater figures had been largely accounted for by the Americans' reluctance to adopt the convoy system in the western areas of the Atlantic, particularly off the Brazilian coast and in the Caribbean. This decision was reversed during the second half of 1943, by which time the Greenland Gap had been closed. With Catalinas, Sunderlands, Wellingtons and Liberators operating from Iceland in the north to Ascension Island in the south, the U-boat was reduced from a predatory wolf to a hunted dog.

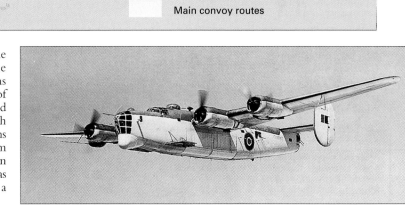

Above: Consolidated Liberator FL927/G was delivered as a Liberator Mk III, but was subsequently converted to GR.Mk V standard (shown here) as a Very Long Range (VLR) aircraft with a Leigh Light under the starboard wing for night anti-submarine duties.

A Catalina Mk IB of No. 202 Squadron, based at Gibraltar from April 1941, was one of a batch of 225 Catalinas delivered to Scottish Aviation at Prestwick and Saunders-Roe at Beaumaris for processing before delivery. The Catalina had a longer endurance than the Sunderland, but could not carry such a heavy warload.

Sicily and Italy

10 JULY – 11 SEPTEMBER 1943

Left: The A-36A Apache (as it was officially, though not commonly known) dive-bomber was armed with up to six 12.7-mm (0.5-in) guns and could carry two 227-kg (500-lb) bombs. A-36As created havoc in Sicily and southern Italy in 1943.

Throughout the final campaign which led to the destruction of Axis forces in northern Tunisia, the Allies had been assembling considerable strength at sea, on land and in the air with which to assault continental Europe from the south. It remained essential to keep the enemy guessing where that assault would be made: Sicily, Sardinia, the south of France or the Italian mainland.

In the event the blow fell on Sicily on 10 July 1943, by which date the Allied air forces in the Mediterranean (Mediterranean Air Command, commanded by Air Chief Marshal Sir Arthur Tedder) had grown to huge proportions, with 104 squadrons of fighters (Spitfires, Hurricanes, Beaufighters, Mosquitoes, P-38s, P-39s and P-51s), 95 squadrons of bombers (Mosquitoes, Bostons, Baltimores, Mitchells, Wellingtons, Marauders, Blenheims, Halifaxes, B-17s and B-24s) and 29 squadrons of transport aircraft (Halifaxes, Albemarles and Dakotas), as well as 43 other squadrons (reconnaissance, maritime patrol, torpedo bombers, meteorological, air-sea rescue and so on).

SICILY INVADED

Supported by fighters and bombers flying from Tunisia, Algeria and Malta, the main landings were carried out in southern Sicily the British 8th Army being put ashore from landing craft in the Gulf of Noto and the US 7th Army in the Gulf of Geta. A major feature of the operation was to be the landing of airborne forces near the Ponte Grande bridge in the British sector and at Gela in the American. Unfortunately owing to bad weather and inexperience among the American transport crews these airborne forces became widely scattered and 69 out of 137 Horsa and Hadrian gliders released fell in the sea. Nevertheless the scattering of the forces did serve to panic the Italian defenders, and by the 12th a bridgehead 32-km (20-miles) deep and about 80-km (50-miles) wide had been secured. Already a number of airfields had been over-run and airstrips constructed, and by the 15th more than a dozen fighter squadrons of the RAF, SAAF and USAAF were operating from Sicilian territory. From the outset the Allies possessed mastery of the air, although in the early stages of the invasion the Luftwaffe (notably Luftflotte II under Generalfeldmarschall Wolfram von Richthofen) and to a much lesser extent the Régia Aéronautica, attempted to mount air attacks against the invaders, using bombers based in Italy and Focke-Wulf Fw 190 fighter-bombers at makeshift airfields at Palermo, Castelvetrano and near Catania. Intruder Beaufighters and Mosquitoes operated with considerable success by night as British and American fighters sought out

Below: A Lockheed F-5E Lightning (unarmed, camera-equipped P-38J) of the 23rd Photo Squadron, 3rd Photo Group, taking off from an airfield in North Africa on a reconnaissance mission over Sicily in 1943.

Allied attackers

After the successful invasion of Italy efforts were made to change the name of the A-36 Apache to Invader. Both names were used, but it was Mustang that stuck. The A-36 differed principally from early P-51s in having dive brakes fitted above and below the wing. USAAF and RAF Marauders served over the skies of southern Italy, from bases in North Africa.

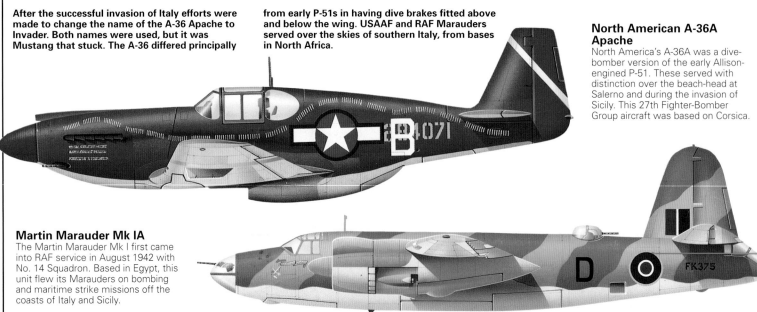

North American A-36A Apache
North America's A-36A was a dive-bomber version of the early Allison-engined P-51. These served with distinction over the beach-head at Salerno and during the invasion of Sicily. This 27th Fighter-Bomber Group aircraft was based on Corsica.

Martin Marauder Mk IA
The Martin Marauder Mk I first came into RAF service in August 1942 with No. 14 Squadron. Based in Egypt, this unit flew its Marauders on bombing and maritime strike missions off the coasts of Italy and Sicily.

Axis defenders

'Gustav', the Messerschmitt Bf 109G, was introduced in the late-summer of 1942 and was built in larger numbers than any other version. However, despite performance improvements, it was becoming Germany's second fighter, after the Fw 190. The three-engined Cant Z.1007 Alcione (kingfisher) first flew in 1937, the Z.1007bis variant having a 1000-kg (2,205-lb) internal bombload capacity.

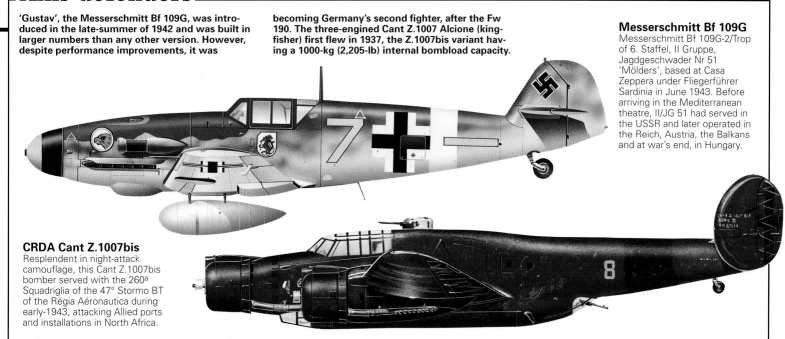

Messerschmitt Bf 109G
Messerschmitt Bf 109G-2/Trop of 6. Staffel, II Gruppe, Jagdgeschwader Nr 51 'Mölders', based at Casa Zeppera under Fliegerführer Sardinia in June 1943. Before arriving in the Mediterranean theatre, II/JG 51 had served in the USSR and later operated in the Reich, Austria, the Balkans and at war's end, in Hungary.

CRDA Cant Z.1007bis
Resplendent in night-attack camouflage, this Cant Z.1007bis bomber served with the 260ª Squadriglia of the 47° Stormo BT of the Régia Aéronautica during early-1943, attacking Allied ports and installations in North Africa.

Left: RAF groundcrew about to service a 'tropicalised' Spitfire Mk Vb of No. 43 Squadron at Pachino, Sicily in August 1943. The airfield was captured just days before the unit's arrival on 30 July. No. 43 spent the rest of the war in Italy.

Above: An unfortunate example of the Reggiane Re.2001s active in the defence of Italy in 1943.

and destroyed enemy aircraft in the air and on the ground by day. Within a week the German and Italian air forces were scarcely able to put up any worthwhile resistance in the air. When B-17s and B-24s appeared over the Strait of Messina such enemy fighters that attempted to intercept them had had to fly from Sardinia and central Italy.

By 5 August the entire western part of Sicily had been over-run and the Axis forces had been squeezed into an area in the north-east of the

Below: A Focke-Wulf Fw 190A Jabo (fighter-bomber) of I/SG 4 in central Italy in the summer of 1943.

island, with desperate efforts being made to protect the likely escape route through Messina. And all the time, as the Axis tried to send supplies and fresh forces south to bolster the defences in the 'toe' of Italy, RAF Wellingtons and Mitchells joined the American heavy bombers in attacks on communications centres at Battipaglia, Foggia and Salerno, as well as the airfields at Crotone, Grottaglie, Leverano and Vibo Valentia.

Yet for all the efforts by the Allied air forces the Axis commanders with great skill extricated the bulk of their land forces out of Sicily. But in the five weeks of fighting the German and Italian air forces had lost some 1,850 aircraft, compared with the loss of fewer than 400 British and American aircraft.

The stepping stone to Europe had been secured, yet the Allies paused less than three weeks before moving against the Italian mainland. Haste was essential as many of the enemy airfields in southern Italy had not been destroyed in recent attacks by Tedder's bombers, and delay would simply allow their repair. The Allied plan was to land the British 8th Army on the toe of

Italy, assault the Taranto naval base in the 'heel' with the 1st Airborne Division and then put ashore the US 5th Army in the Gulf of Salerno, some 320 km (200 miles) to the north.

ITALY SURRENDERS

The first landings across the Strait of Messina by the 8th Army were carried out on 3 September (Operation 'Baytown') and continued for five days, meeting relatively little resistance thanks to an unrelenting air offensive against the enemy supply route down the full length of Italy by medium and heavy bombers of the RAF and

USAAF. On 11 September the 8th Army reached a line from Belvedere to Crotone.

Two days earlier the US 5th Army had gone ashore at Salerno. On the eve of those landings, however, the Italian government had announced the nation's surrender.

Below: An Italian armourer adds some personal messages to bombs intended for Allied targets in southern Italy. The significance of the umbrella painted on the bomb in the foreground is unknown.

Adventures in Italy

SEPTEMBER 1943 – JUNE 1944

Left: A pair of Spitfire Mk IXs of No. 241 Squadron on patrol over the Naples area in 1943. The Mk IX was a stop-gap development to get the more powerful, two-speed, two-stage Rolls-Royce Merlin 60 engine into a basic Mk V airframe.

Below: B-17 Flying Fortresses of the USAAF's 15th Air Force flying over the Mediterranean en route from their bases in Italy in mid-1944, to military targets in France. Attacks were mounted on a shuttle basis from both England and Italy.

The surrender by the Italian government effectively deprived Germany of significant participation by the Regia Aéronautica in the defence of Italy against the Allies, and although some elements elected to fight on alongside the Luftwaffe, the majority either melted away to their homes or joined the Allies. The defection by their ally, as the Germans saw it, only served to stiffen their resolve to fight every yard of the way back through the Italian peninsula.

In attempts to leapfrog northwards and hasten their advance, the Allies planned two major seaborne landings behind the enemy lines, the first at Salerno on 9 September 1943 and another, rather later, at Anzio, which eventually took place in the following January.

As already stated, the landing by the US 5th Army at Salerno was in effect part of the planned invasion of Italy and, by diverting enemy forces from the 8th Army in the extreme south was intended to ease the establishment of a substantial

beach-head. In this it was singularly successful, but resistance by the Germans at Salerno was unexpectedly stiff. Against the troops that landed on the beaches the Luftwaffe used about four Staffeln of Fw 190 fighter-bombers, whose pilots had to contend not only with patrolling Spitfires and Lightnings but also barrage balloons brought ashore by RAF parties. The Luftwaffe was, however, able to score one significant success when a Do 217-launched Hs 293 guided missile scored a direct hit on the British battleship *Warspite*, which had been supporting the landings, and put her out of commission for six months.

SUCCESS IN THE BALANCE

The success of the landings remained in the balance for three days as the Germans counter-attacked strongly on the ground, and although the airfield at Monte Corvino had been captured at the outset it was unusable so long as it was dominated by German guns. By 15 September four landing strips constructed by Allied airfield engineers were in operation, one of them having been in use by Lightnings since 11 September. Within a week of the landings

Above: Attack on German transports in Italy by a P-47D Thunderbolt of the 79th Fighter Group, 15th Air Force. One of the three outstanding USAAF fighters of World War II, the big, radial-engined P-47 had eight 12.7-mm (0.50-in) guns in its wings, making it one of the heaviest-armed fighters.

Above: The Luftwaffe had some success with their advanced 'Fritz X' glide bomb, sinking the battleship Roma after Italy surrendered. 'Fritz X' and the equally sophisticated Hs 293 guided missile were launched from Dornier Do 217K-2s like this one. The latter was effectively used against the Warspite.

Right: A Messerschmitt Bf 109G-2/Trop on an airfield in Italy – an Italian Air Force three-engined Cant Z.1007bis heavy bomber is in the background. The Bf 109 was built in greater numbers (30,500) than any other fighter in World War II. It was flown by the Luftwaffe very effectively in all theatres.

Fighters over Italy

First flown on 19 April 1942, the Macchi MC.205V Veltro was a well-armed fighter-bomber powered by a licence-built Daimler-Benz DB.605 engine. It saw brief service before the Italian surrender.

Messerschmitt's Me 410 Hornisse was the last and most successful in the line of heavy fighters that commenced with the Me 210 in 1939. Over 1,000 Me 410s entered Luftwaffe service in 1943/44.

Macchi MC.205V Veltro
This aircraft was flown by 351° Squadriglia, 155° Gruppo, 51° Stormo from Monserrato in June 1943. It is an early example with two 7.7-mm (0.303-in) guns in the wings. Later aircraft had two 20-mm (0.78-in) cannon and two 12.7-mm (0.5-in) machine-guns, plus bombs if they were needed.

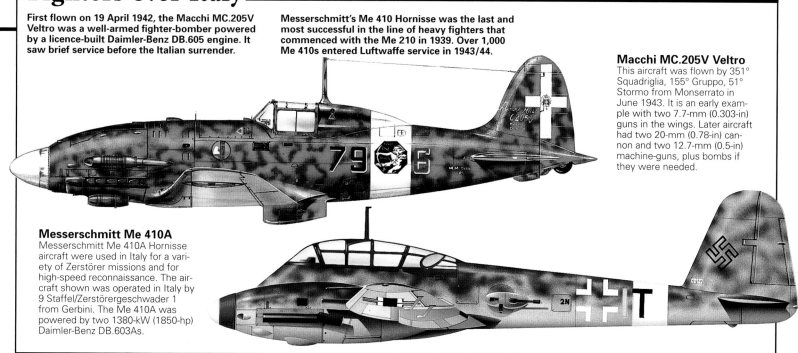

Messerschmitt Me 410A
Messerschmitt Me 410A Hornisse aircraft were used in Italy for a variety of Zerstörer missions and for high-speed reconnaissance. The aircraft shown was operated in Italy by 9 Staffel/Zerstörergeschwader 1 from Gerbini. The Me 410A was powered by two 1380-kW (1850-hp) Daimler-Benz DB.603As.

Left: De Havilland Mosquito NF.Mk IIs of No. 23 Squadron operating from RAF Luqa, Malta flew intruder missions over Southern Italy in the Autumn of 1943, the first 'Mossies' to serve in the Mediterranean. The squadron detached to Sigonella, Sicily later in the year and flew 'roving commissions' over enemy positions attacking trains, transport columns and airfields.

Below: Early autumn, 1943 was an eventful time for the Allied forces as they made slow progress northwards through Italy. Despite the Allied air forces superior numbers Generalfeldmarschall Kesselring displayed brilliant improvisatory skills and conducted his holding campaign as directed by Hitler to sap the Allies' strength and delay an invasion of NW Europe.

several squadrons of Seafires and Spitfires were ashore, and these joined the battle to blunt the enemy counter attacks; while the Royal Navy put ashore reinforcements of armour, the American 505th and 509th Airborne Regiments were dropped on 14 and 15 September in areas where the front line was most threatened. By the evening of 15 September enemy efforts to contain the beach-head were spent, thanks to the combined efforts of the British and American land, sea and air forces. On the following day units of the US VI Corps broke out

Above: This Italian-based Focke Wulf Fw 190 fighter-bomber operated from Viterbo with I/SG 4 in late-1943. It has been temporarily resprayed and has a partially obliterated balkenkreuz and swastika. The dorsal bulge houses MG 131s.

ADVANCES IN ITALY

ITALY
FRANCE
Turin • Milan • Brescia • Vicenza • Treviso • Llubljana • Zagreb
Verona • Padua
Parma • Farrara
• Genoa • Bologna • Ravenna
Nice • Bihac
Cannes • Rimini
St Tropez • Pesaro
22.8.44 • Pisa • Ancona
YUGOSLAVIA
CORSICA
6.6.44 — 1.1.44
Adriatic Sea
Mediterranean Sea
Rome • Nettuno • Cassino
Anzio
Naples • Salerno • Brindisi
Taranto
SARDINIA
Messina • Reggio
SICILY

Operation SHINGLE 21.1.44
The Allied air forces mustered over 2,600 aircraft to oppose over 450 Luftwaffe aircraft.

Operation AVALANCHE 9.9.43
Air cover was provided by land-based Spitfires, P-38s and A-36s, the Royal Navy providing Seafires and Martlets.

Operation SLAPSTICK 9.9.43
Little opposition here meant that several Allied air force units could become quickly established.

Operation HUSKY 10.7.43
The Allied invasion of Sicily was opposed by Luftwaffe Bf 109G fighters, Fw 190A fighter-bombers and Ju 88A bombers from first light. Allied fighter cover initially came from Spitfire and P-40 units.

Operation BAYTOWN 3.9.43
RAF fighters encountering only light opposition, thanks to Allied bombing of German supply routes.

KEY TO MAP
• localities
• air bases
← Allied invasion forces
— Allied advance northward

TUNISIA

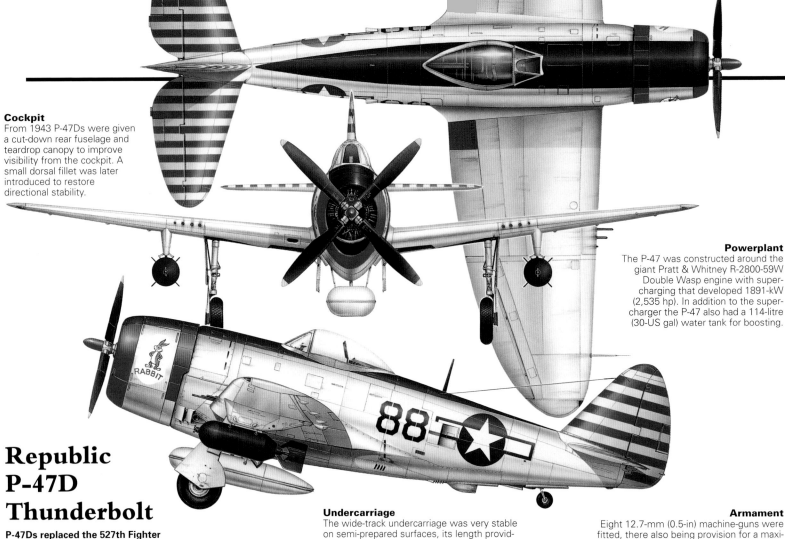

Cockpit
From 1943 P-47Ds were given a cut-down rear fuselage and teardrop canopy to improve visibility from the cockpit. A small dorsal fillet was later introduced to restore directional stability.

Powerplant
The P-47 was constructed around the giant Pratt & Whitney R-2800-59W Double Wasp engine with supercharging that developed 1891-kW (2,535 hp). In addition to the supercharger the P-47 also had a 114-litre (30-US gal) water tank for boosting.

Republic P-47D Thunderbolt

P-47Ds replaced the 527th Fighter Squadron's A-26 Invaders during 1944 in the fighter-bomber role.

Undercarriage
The wide-track undercarriage was very stable on semi-prepared surfaces, its length providing clearance for the big four-blade propeller. To save space inside the wing, the struts were telescopic when retracted.

Armament
Eight 12.7-mm (0.5-in) machine-guns were fitted, there also being provision for a maximum external load of 1134 kg (2,500 lb) including bombs, napalm or eight rockets.

from the perimeter in the south to link up with the advancing 8th Army at Vallo di Lucania.

ANZIO LANDING
Thereafter, the Allied advance northwards in Italy continued apace until by 1 January 1944 it was being

held by the Germans on a line running from the mouth of the River Garigliano in the south-west to Ortona on the Adriatic coast. When it became clear that the Germans were standing on a prepared line, and would be difficult to dislodge, the Allies once more launched a seaborne landing further north at Anzio, in the hope of turning the German right flank; at the same time it was hoped to draw the enemy air force into the air to

Below: A flight of Junkers Ju 52/3mg5ᵉ seaplanes of 1 Seetransportstaffel, based at Skaramanga (Piraeus) under X Fliegerkorps, on a supply mission over the Aegean during German operations against Kos and Leros.

protect that flank where it could be destroyed by the vastly superior numbers of Allied aircraft. A prelude to the landing which took place on 22 January, was an all-out air attack on the Italian airfields in central Italy, carried out to such good effect that not one enemy reconnaissance sortie was successful in detecting the landing force, and 50,000 British and American troops arrived unscathed on the enemy beaches. Here the Allied commander, Major General Lucas, made an error of judgement, preferring to consolidate his beach-head rather than to strike hard inland, a move that would unquestionably have severed the enemy supply routes to the south. As it was, the Germans

Above: With a total of 9,816 aircraft built, the North American B-25 Mitchell was by a short head the most important of the AAF's medium bombers, and certainly the most versatile and widely used. This aircraft is from the 414th BS.

Above: Bombs dropping over Rome in the first air-attack on the capital by B-17 Flying Fortresses of the North-west African Air Forces. The Allies entered Rome on 4 June 1944.

Above: A formation of Lockheed P-38s buzz their base in Italy as they return from escorting heavy bombers on a raid over Austria. These 15th Air Force fighters were dubbed 'fork-tailed devil' by the Luftwaffe.

had time to mount heavy-armoured counter-attacks which, though only just failing to break through to the beaches, succeeded in containing the landing areas and forcing the

invaders on to the defensive. In the air the Luftwaffe switched two Gruppen of Junkers Ju 88s to Italy from Greece and Crete, and one of Dornier Do 217s equipped with Hs 293 missiles to the south of France; these air reinforcements proved unsuitable for support of the land battle at Anzio and many of the Ju 88s were destroyed by air attacks on their airfields. In the event the enemy air force was unable to support the powerful German ground forces in the area; but equally the Allied ground forces were unable to break out of their beach-head, despite the overwhelming air superiority of the RAF and USAAF.

Above: From 1943 Martin B-26 Marauders appeared in Italy with the 17th, 319th and 320th Bomb Groups of the USAAF. Here, Marauders attack an ammunition dump at La Spezia, 40 miles south-east of Genoa in 1944.

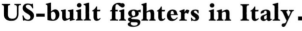

Left: The Allied bombers met less resistance from German night fighters, as their number was reduced to just over 400 by September 1943. This Italian searchlight battery is trying to illuminate bombers for the defending anti-aircraft guns.

BREAKTHROUGH

On 15 March the Allied air forces attempted to breach the main line in the south by destroying the great monastery at Monte Cassino. In

four hours wave after wave of medium bombers dropped over 1000 tonnes of bombs, pounding the ancient building to rubble. Yet still the line held, and it was not until May that the Allies were finally able to pierce the defences and resume their advance northwards. The Anzio pocket was reached and relieved, and on 4 June the Allies at last entered Rome.

US-built fighters in Italy

During April 1944 Merlin-engined P-51B/C Mustangs re-equipped the 31st and 52nd Fighter Groups, providing long-range escort for the bombers and ground-attack support for the armies.

The first major production version of the Airacobra, the P-39N was an effective ground-attack aircraft, being rugged and able to absorb and remain airborne with severe battle damage.

North American P-51C Mustang
This red-tailed P-51C was flown by the 332nd Fighter Group, the only black fighter unit in the USAAF. The 'razorback' Mustang did not have the good all-round visibility that the British-devised Malcolm hood gave to the RAF's aircraft.

Bell P-39N Airacobra
In Italian Co-Belligerent Air Force markings, this P-39N was based at Canne, Italy with 4° Stormo (Caccia Terrestre). This unit operated flew reconnaissance and air-support missions over the Adriatic Sea.

Hamburg, Ruhr and Berlin

1943–1945

Top: Rolls-Royce Merlin-engined Avro Lancaster – mainstay of the night bombing offensive.

Below: Mosquito B.Mk XVI with a pressurised cockpit could fly at 12200 m (40,000 ft). This aircraft was flown by No. 571 Squadron with No. 8 (Pathfinder) Group.

Shortly after the 'Torch' landings in North Africa, the British and American leaders conferred at Casablanca to determine the future course of the war. One result was a directive, put before Air Marshal Harris, setting out his bombing priorities, which were "The progressive destruction... of the German military, industrial and economic system, and the undermining of the morale of the German people to a point where their capacity for armed resistance is fatally weakened." To begin to achieve this objective RAF Bomber Command was now fairly well-equipped, possessing on 4 March 1943 a total of 18 Lancaster squadrons, 11 of Halifaxes, six of Stirlings and 15 of Wellingtons, all operational at night, for a total of 321 Lancasters, 220 Halifaxes, 141 Stirlings and 268 Wellingtons.

GREAT OFFENSIVE

The first manifestation of the great night bombing offensive that now broke over Germany, and lasted until the end of the war, was what came to be known as the Battle of the Ruhr. This started on the night of 5/6 March 1943 with a raid by 442 aircraft against Essen – the first full-scale operation in which the

Above: A Lancaster photographed at 5486 m (18,000 ft) over Hamburg on the night of 30/31 January 1943, the night that pathfinder Stirlings and Halifaxes used H_2S radar for the first time operationally over Germany.

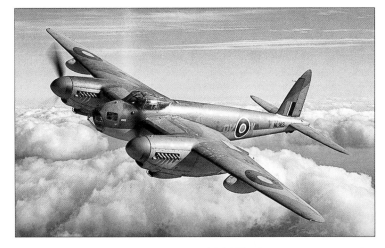

Below: A line-up of 12 Vickers Wellington Mk IIIs and Mk Xs. When the offensive began, RAF Bomber Command had 15 squadrons of Wellingtons with a total of 268 aircraft on strength.

Right: The seven-man crew boarding Lancaster Mk I ED810 (VN-Z) of No. 50 Squadron at RAF Skellingthorpe on 15 April 1943. They took part in a heavy night-bombing raid on the German city of Stuttgart. The crew are wearing Mae Wests and carrying their parachutes and soft leather helmets. Fur-lined boots are necessary to combat the low night-time temperatures.

navigation and bombing aid 'Oboe' was successfully used.

Six weeks later Bomber Command carried out one of its most famous raids of all time, the attack (Operation 'Chastise') on 16/17 May by 19 Lancasters of No. 617 Squadron, led by Wing Commander Guy Gibson, against the Möhne, Eder, Sorpe and Schwelme dams whose hydro-electric stations supplied power to the industrial Ruhr. Dropping special 4196-kg (9,250-lb) 'bouncing' mines, the Lancasters breached the Möhne and Eder dams for the loss of eight aircraft; Gibson survived to be awarded the Victoria Cross for

Performance
Maximum speed of 411 km/h (255 mph) with a service ceiling of 5486 m (18,000 ft) and a combat radius of 1537 km (955 miles) carrying a 5909-kg (13,000-lb) bombload.

Crew
Early Halifax Mk Is had a crew of either six or seven men. The navigator manned the nose turret as well as aim the bombs and a flight engineer was also included.

Powerplants
This early production HP.57 Halifax Mk I has four 842.6-kW (1,130-hp) Rolls-Royce Merlin-X in-line engines driving three-blade Rotol propellers. Later marks used Bristol Hercules radial engines.

Armament
Defensive armament consisted of six 7-mm (0.303-in) Browning machine-guns in the nose and tail; and four 7-mm (0.303-in) Vickers GO machine-guns – two on each side, midships.

Markings
L9530 has camouflaged upper surfaces and black undersides. The large code letters (MP) denote No. 76(B) Squadron, part of No. 4 Group, Bomber Command.

Handley Page Halifax Mk I

Based at RAF Middleton St George, L9530 was flown by No. 76 Squadron. It carries the unofficial crest of Pilot Officer Christopher Cheshire.

his leadership on the raid.

The Battle of the Ruhr continued until June, and was considered highly successful for the widespread damage caused, being made possible principally on account of the radio aids available which were efficient at the relatively short ranges involved in flights to the Ruhr.

OPERATION 'GOMORRAH'
As new Lancaster and Halifax squadrons continued to join Bomber Command, Harris was now determined on the destruction of a single vital city in Germany, and on the night of 24/25 July launched 791 heavy bombers against Hamburg, the first of four massive raids on the city in 10 days (Operation 'Gomorrah'), carried out in concert with the heavy bombers of the USAAF which attacked the city during daylight hours. Hamburg was chosen not only on account of its importance as an industrial city but for the manner in which the great port could be distinguished on H$_2$S radar, a blind bombing and navigation aid that had been in use by Bomber Command for some six months.

Above: Bombs about to be loaded onto a Short Stirling Mk I of No. 218 Squadron at RAF Marham. A design feature that limited the Stirling's usefulness was its divided bomb bay, which restricted the heaviest bomb that could be carried to 1814 kg (4,000 lb).

Right: Ground staff manoeuvre a bomb trolley conveying a 1814-kg (4000-lb) 'blockbuster' bomb under the bomb bay of a Mosquito. From February 1944 some B.Mk IVs and all B.Mk IXs were modified to carry this large bomb that had hitherto been confined to the heavy bomber force.

('Oboe' could not be used because of Hamburg's distance from the UK.) A vital ingredient in the raids on Hamburg was the first significant use of 'Window'; vast clouds of tin-foil strips dropped by the bombers to saturate enemy radar screens with spurious signals. In the four Bomber Command raids 2,630 bombers attacked Hamburg, dropping 8759 tonnes of bombs which destroyed more than 6,000 acres of the port, killed more than 41,800 inhabitants and injured over 37,000. The loss of 87 aircraft represented less than three per cent of the aircraft despatched and was well within sustainable limits.

The devastating Battle of Hamburg encouraged Harris to open his last great setpiece assault, this time on Berlin itself (although numerous other targets continued to be attacked before, during and after the attacks on the German capital). On the night of 18/19 November 1943, Bomber Command sent 444 bombers, of which 402 attacked the city, losing nine aircraft, while a simultaneous attack was carried out by 325 bombers on Mannheim, the first occasion on which two heavy raids were launched on a single night.

Top: A Halifax bomber silhouetted during an attack on a flying bomb site on the night of 5/6 July 1944.

Above: Flying from RAF Linton-on-Ouse, this Halifax was from No. 35 Squadron, a pathfinder unit.

Top right: A Lancaster of No. 101 Squadron drops a cloud of reflective 'Window' to jam German radar.

Right: The 5443-kg (12,000-lb) 'Tallboy' bomb could only be carried by modified Lancasters.

RAF bombers of 1942

The Short Stirling was the RAF's first four-engined monoplane heavy bomber. Entering service in August 1940, its load limitations saw it being replaced by the Halifax and Lancaster in 1943.

Entering service in May 1942, bomber versions of the Mosquito were Bomber Command's fastest aircraft, equipping 38 squadrons. Their greatest successes were as Pathfinders for the night offensive.

Short Stirling Mk I
This aircraft (W7455) is in the colours of No. 149 Squadron, based at RAF Mildenhall Suffolk, in the early part of 1942. Most Stirling Mk Is were operated by No. 3 Group, Bomber Command from 1940 to 1943.

de Havilland Mosquito B.Mk IX
As built, the B.Mk IX carried 'Oboe' Mk I, a 907-kg (2,000-lb) bombload and had an operational ceiling of about 10975 m (36,000 ft). Virtual immunity from Luftwaffe night fighters meant exhaust flame dampers were not fitted. LR508 was a pathfinder with No. 105 Squadron.

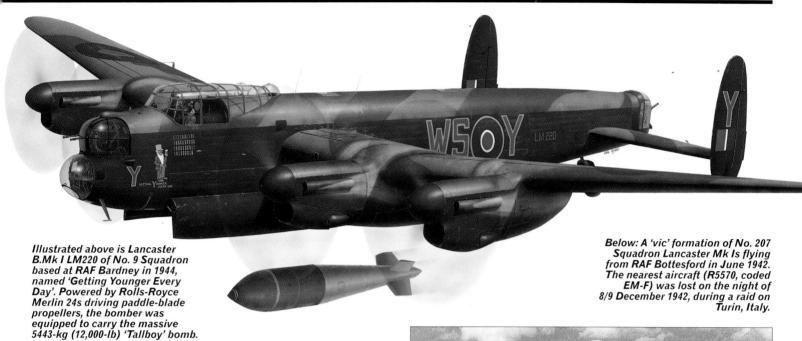

Illustrated above is Lancaster B.Mk I LM220 of No. 9 Squadron based at RAF Bardney in 1944, named 'Getting Younger Every Day'. Powered by Rolls-Royce Merlin 24s driving paddle-blade propellers, the bomber was equipped to carry the massive 5443-kg (12,000-lb) 'Tallboy' bomb.

Below: A 'vic' formation of No. 207 Squadron Lancaster Mk Is flying from RAF Bottesford in June 1942. The nearest aircraft (R5570, coded EM-F) was lost on the night of 8/9 December 1942, during a raid on Turin, Italy.

Left: The crew of Halifax HR837 from No. 158 Squadron based at RAF Lisset, amidst the damage caused by a 'friendly' bomb dropped by another Halifax flying above it while over Cologne on 28/29 June 1943. HR837 completed 11 more operations before being transferred to No. 1656 Heavy Conversion Unit on 12 April 1944.

The offensive against Berlin continued through the winter of 1943/44, almost invariably in bad weather but, despite the employment of Bomber Command's specialist Pathfinder Group, No. 8, commanded by Air Commodore D.C.T. Bennett, and the use of sophisticated marking and radio countermeasures techniques, the concentration of damage and accuracy of bombing fell far short of expectations. A total of 16 major raids was launched before the 'battle' ended on 24/25 March 1944, involving 9,111 bomber sorties. The raids cost the command a total of 587 aircraft and more than 3,500 aircrew killed or missing – an unsustainable loss rate of 6.4 per cent. The damage and casualties inflicted were considerably less than at Hamburg, and the Battle of Berlin failed in its purpose of breaking the spirit of the German people.

One other major raid was launched by Bomber Command at this time (before it was switched to attacks in support of the coming Normandy landings); 795 four-engine bombers being sent to Nuremberg on 30/31 March 1944. On account of inaccurate weather forecasting, inefficient pathfinding and poor raid planning, the bomber stream disintegrated and suffered heavily from German night-fighter attacks; more than 100 bombers were lost. Worse, Nuremberg was scarcely hit by the bombers.

During the final eight months of the war, Bomber Command returned to Germany in greater strength than ever. It was to end the war with 56 Lancaster squadrons, 17 of Halifaxes and 18 of Mosquitoes, for a total of 2,370 aircraft. New navigational and radar jamming equipment and new types of bomb were also available. The 5443-kg (12,000-lb) 'Tallboy' had proved its worth in the sinking of the battleship Tirpitz in 1944 and the even larger 9979-kg (22,000-lb) 'Grand Slam' was to be employed against strategically important bridges at Bielefeld and Arnsberg the following year.

The RAF's priority target, however, was the German oil industry, an industry that was so completely devastated that it was to be the chronic lack of aviation fuel that finally grounded the once-formidable Luftwaffe.

Left: Bomb trolleys carry their deadly load to the waiting aircraft at RAF Marham. The armourers are making final adjustments before loading four of the 227-kg (500-lb) bombs on to this de Havilland Mosquito B.Mk IV (DZ360) of No. 105 Squadron.

The Dambusters Raid

Known as Operation 'Chastise', the breaching of the Möhne and Eder dams in Germany's Ruhr Valley was one of World War II's most daring bomber raids. Carried out by the cream of the RAF, the 'Dambusting' mission took a heavy toll on the young pilots that flew them.

By the dead of night, a select group of RAF bombers mounts a precision attack on the Ruhr dams, spearheading one of World War II's most spectacular missions. The power stations served by the huge dams fed Germany's greatest industrial complex, but the dams were immensely strong structures. A bomb capable of breaching one would have been far too heavy for even the sturdy Avro Lancaster to carry. Barnes Wallis, one of Britain's greatest aircraft designers, proposed a less conventional weapon. He showed that, if an explosive could be detonated against the underwater portion of the dam, the shock waves would weaken and, eventually, collapse the structure. Wallis designed a spinning cylindrical mine which, when dropped from low level, would ricochet along the water surface

before sinking against the dam wall and detonating by means of hydrostatic fuses. Tests with half-size weapons proved that the idea could be successful. Britain's Air Ministry identified the most important targets as the Möhne, Eder, Sorpe, Lister, Schwelme and Ennepe dams. Wing Commander Guy Gibson was chosen to head an elite new unit, No. 617 Squadron. Gibson, a veteran of three tours of operations, was allowed to hand-pick his aircrews.

Over the next two months, Gibson trained his men in extreme

Right: One of No. 617 Squadron's Lancaster Mk IIIs specially modified for the 'Dams Raid' in May 1943. The dorsal durret was removed and the lower fuselage rebuilt to take the trapeze from which the bomb was released.

Above: Photographic reconnaissance of the Möhne Dam after the raid by Lancasters of No. 617 Squadron led by Wg Cdr Guy Gibson, reveals a breach in the top of the dam, the water from the lake having flooded the land below. The damage to the wall was not as extensive as had been hoped for.

precision flying skills, but he could not reveal their targets for security reasons. A night attack was planned for the 16 May 1943, to take advantage of both maximum moonlight and high water behind the dams. The crews were given no mission details until the day before the raid. By then, 20 modified Lancaster B.Mk IIIs had been delivered to RAF Scampton in Lincolnshire. The bomb had to be

Left: A modified Lancaster Mk III taxies in at RAF Scampton after a training flight by No. 617 Squadron. This unit was specially formed in great secrecy on 23 March 1943 as part of No. 5 Group with the early destruction of the Möhne and Eder Dams as its primary objective.

'DAMBUSTERS' MAY 1943
An Avro Lancaster Mk III of No. 617 Squadron runs in at high speed and very low level, trying to avoid the German flak. It had to precisely release its Barnes Wallis-designed 'bouncing bomb' for it to be effective against the wall of the dam.

massive target in the moonlight. He flew a perfect attack as the gun defences burst into life. Flight Lieutenant J.V. Hopgood's Lancaster was hit by flak as it approached. As Squadron Leader H.B. Martin's Lancaster bored in, Gibson flew over the dam to draw off enemy fire. Martin's mine dropped accurately. 'Dinghy' Young, accompanied by Gibson and Martin to distract the enemy gunners, dropped a third mine on target. It was the next attack, by Flight Lieutenant D.J.H. Maltby, that caused the great concrete structure to collapse. The circling pilots watched in awe as a 100-m (110-yard) breach opened up, and 134 million tonnes of water burst into the valley below. Ordering Martin and Maltby to return home, Gibson set course for the Eder. Located in a deeper valley than the Möhne, the Eder dam proved a far more difficult target to attack. Flight Lieutenant D.J. Shannon had to make six abortive runs before successfully delivering his mine. Maudslay's mine struck the Parapet and blew up on impact, destroying the Lancaster. It was the last remaining weapon, dropped by Pilot Officer L.G. Knight, that finally breached the Eder, causing an even greater spectacle than at the Möhne, as 200 million tonnes of water burst down the narrow valley.

Farther afield, McCarthy made his way alone to the Sorpe, where he dropped his mine accurately, but only succeeded in crumbling a stretch of the dam's parapet. Gibson ordered three of the mobile

released at exactly 18.3 m (60 ft) above the water, at a speed of 402 km/h (250 mph), and at a distance of between 366 m (400 yards) and 411 m (450 yards) from the target. Precision was vital to avoid the bomb disintegrating on impact, or bouncing over the target. The height was measured by two spotlights under the nose and tail, whose beams formed a figure '8' on the surface of the water at precisely 18.3 m (60 ft).

Gibson led nine aircraft against the Möhne dam. A second group of five Lancasters, led by Flight Lieutenant Joseph C. McCarthy, an American, was to attack the Sorpe dam. The remaining five Lancasters, under Flight Lieutenant W.C. Townsend, were to serve as a 'mobile reserve'. The Sorpe formation took off just before 21.00, but ran into flak over the Netherlands. Two Lancasters were destroyed, and two forced to turn back. Only McCarthy himself was left, flying 100-km behind the others after a delayed take-off. Gibson's force, operating in three flights of three aircraft, flew further to the south. Gibson led the first flight, followed at 10-minute intervals by Squadron Leader Henry Maudslay and Squadron Leader 'Dinghy' Young. The reserve group took off at about midnight.

Skirting the main Ruhr defences, Gibson easily sighted his

reserve aircraft to back up this attack, but only one managed to do so, and the damaged dam survived. The last two reserve Lancasters were ordered to make for the Lister and Schwelme dams. The latter dam was attacked, but without success. The aircraft detailed for the Lister dam was apparently shot down – its crew failed to return to base. Wing Commander Guy Gibson was awarded the Victoria Cross for his unsurpassed bravery and determined leadership.

GALLANT HEROES

Gibson became synonymous with the generation of men who, night after night, braved enemy flak and fighters to take the war to the

Above: Wg Cdr Guy Gibson, Commanding Officer of No. 617 Squadron, with his crew about to board Lancaster Mk III ED932, in which he led the 'Dams Raid' from RAF Scampton on 16/17 May 1943. He was awarded the Victoria Cross for gallantry.

German homeland. Although he was to lose his life over enemy territory a year later, his squadron – proudly adopting the nickname 'Dambusters' – survived as an elite unit. Charged with mounting especially hazardous attacks, No. 617 successfully accounted for a long list of vital targets, from helping to sink the German battleship *Tirpitz* to destroying the Bielefeld viaduct in western Germany.

Right: The full extent of the damage inflicted on the areas below the breached Möhne and Eder Dams only became apparent some days later as the flood water spread through the valleys downstream. The effect on German morale was at least as important as the actual interruption to the war effort.

'Dams Raid' Lancaster

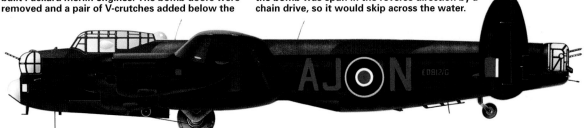

The bombers used in the raid were specially modified Lancaster B.Mk IIIs, powered by four American-built Packard Merlin engines. The bomb doors were removed and a pair of V-crutches added below the aircraft's centre of gravity from which the 4196-kg (9250-lb) weapon was suspended. Before launch, the bomb was spun in the reverse direction by a chain drive, so it would skip across the water.

Lancaster B.Mk III
Lancaster B.Mk III (Mod) ED912/G of No. 617 Squadron, based at RAF Scampton in May 1943. This was a specially modified aircraft to drop the oil drum-shaped 'Upkeep' dam-busting mine, shown on its special trapeze under the cutaway fuselage. The 'G' suffix to the serial number indicates a top secret aircraft for which an armed guard was to be provided.

Kursk and the Ukraine

JUNE 1943 – MAY 1944

Above: A Schwarm of Junkers Ju 87Ds breaks formation before landing after a mission in the winter of 1942-43. Winter conditions on frontline airfields were extremely harsh, with engine starting a recurrent problem.

Below: A winter-camouflaged Ju 88A-4 of AufKlGr. 122 over the Eastern Front in 1943. This view illustrates well the extensive glazing which afforded the Ju 88's crew excellent visibility.

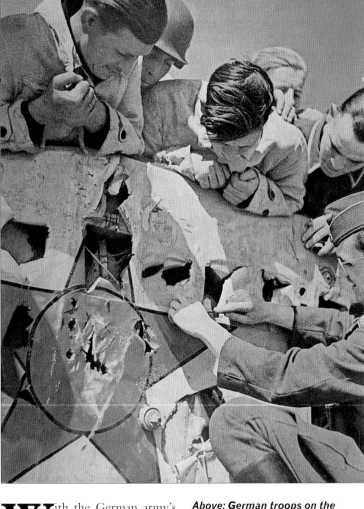

Above: German troops on the Eastern Front gather around the wreckage of a downed Soviet bomber to inspect the damage.

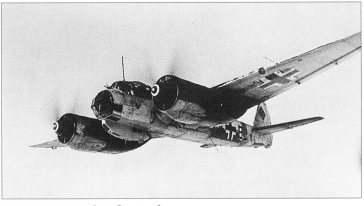

With the German army's surge eastwards thwarted at Stalingrad during the winter of 1942-43, the German high command decided on a major offensive on the central sector of the Eastern Front in June 1943 to eliminate the large Soviet salient around Kursk. Because of German fears of an Allied invasion of Europe in the Mediterranean, the great attack, Operation Zitadelle, was delayed until 5 July.

Both sides desperately needed a major victory, the Germans to break a deteriorating stalemate south of Moscow, and the Soviets to convince themselves that they were capable of defeating the German army in the summer, and not merely in the mud and snow of winter. Deployed on the central front were 4,600 aircraft of the 1st, 2nd, 15th and 16th Air Armies of

Soviet defenders

After its virtual destruction during the initial German invasion, the Red Air Force was rebuilt using aircraft produced in factories east of the Urals. By mid-1943 the Soviet air forces had large numbers of highly effective combat aircraft, most dedicated to support of the ground forces. The Lavochkin La-5FN was a superb tactical fighter, while the Ilyushin Il-2 was arguably the best ground attack aircraft of the war. Types like these allowed the USSR to challenge German air superiority.

Lavochkin La-5FN

This Lavochkin La-5FN was flown by the 1 Czechoslovak IAP in the Ukraine in 1944. Several Czech units were formed within the Red Air Force. The La-5FN was among the aircraft which turned the tables on the Luftwaffe, proving fast enough and manoeuvrable enough at low level to outfight the Bf 109 and Fw 190. The Soviets also managed to produce a steady flow of well-trained pilots, while the Luftwaffe suffered as the war progressed from a woeful lack of skill and experience in all but the few remaining *Experten*.

Ilyushin Il-2

The Il-2 was conceived as a specialised armoured ground-attack aircraft. The Russian national insignia assumed many forms, including stars with circles in the centre, with dark/light shades in each of the five arms or with a yellow (or white) border when on a dark background. This Il-2m3 on the Eastern Front in 1943 had stars with borders.

Above: By far the most important variant of the basic Il-2 design was the Type 3, which incorporated 15° of sweepback on the outer wings in an attempt to eradicate the stability problem of the Il-2M.

Below: Il-2s depart from a forward base on a combat mission, probably in 1943. These are quite early single-seaters, though the nearest aircraft has a VYa cannon whose barrels were longer than those of the ShVAK.

the Soviet air force, plus 2,750 of the 5th and 17th Air Armies held in reserve. They comprised huge numbers of Ilyushin Il-2 and Il-2m3 Sturmovik close-support aircraft armed with improved guns and other anti-tank weapons, together with like numbers of Lavochkin La-5FNs, Yakovlev Yak-9s and American-supplied Bell P-39Q Airacobras. Against them the Luftwaffe could muster some 2,100 first line aircraft, out of a total of about 2,500 deployed on the entire Eastern Front. Principal German aircraft included the Focke-Wulf Fw 190A, Junkers Ju 87D, Messerschmitt Bf 109G, Heinkel He 111, Junkers Ju 88 and Henschel Hs 129. The Luftwaffe, however, was to suffer acute fuel shortages during that desperate summer, largely as the result of the activities of Soviet partisans who

destroyed large numbers of supply trains and severely damaged the German communications network, particularly in the key Minsk-Smolensk sector.

BLITZKREIG

Operation Zitadelle opened during the afternoon of 5 July. Crack Panzer divisions equipped with the new Panther and Tiger tanks were hurled into a typical Blitzkreig wedge assault against superior numbers of Soviet tanks in the greatest, most ferocious armoured battle in history. In support, the German armies flew formations of Hs 129 anti-tank aircraft armed with 37-mm guns and hollow-charge armour-piercing bombs, as well as large numbers of Ju 87D bombers. The Luftwaffe's support aircraft did enormous damage among the massed Soviet tanks and, after a

Left: A Soviet armourer prepares a VYa 23-mm cannon on an Il-2M3. In 1942, the ShVAK guns were replaced by the much harder-hitting VYa. The rear gunner of this two-seater had a 12.7-mm (0.5-in) UB machine-gun with 150 rounds of ammunition.

Below: As the war in the east progressed, both VVS and Luftwaffe used night harassment techniques against opposing infantry, small aircraft dropping light bombs. Among the wide range of types used by the Luftwaffe was the Heinkel He 50.

153

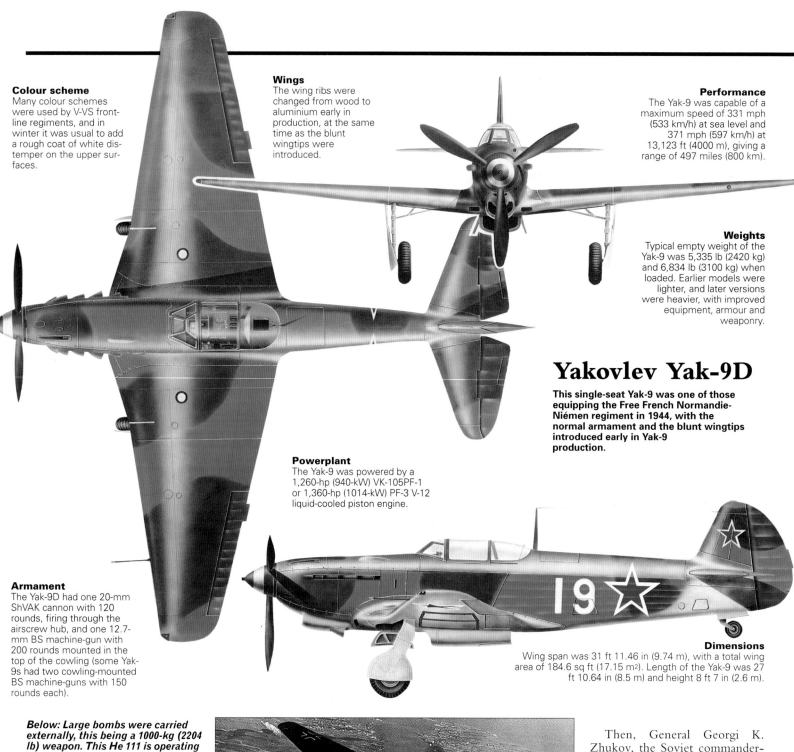

Colour scheme
Many colour schemes were used by V-VS front-line regiments, and in winter it was usual to add a rough coat of white distemper on the upper surfaces.

Wings
The wing ribs were changed from wood to aluminium early in production, at the same time as the blunt wingtips were introduced.

Performance
The Yak-9 was capable of a maximum speed of 331 mph (533 km/h) at sea level and 371 mph (597 km/h) at 13,123 ft (4000 m), giving a range of 497 miles (800 km).

Weights
Typical empty weight of the Yak-9 was 5,335 lb (2420 kg) and 6,834 lb (3100 kg) when loaded. Earlier models were lighter, and later versions were heavier, with improved equipment, armour and weaponry.

Yakovlev Yak-9D

This single-seat Yak-9 was one of those equipping the Free French Normandie-Niémen regiment in 1944, with the normal armament and the blunt wingtips introduced early in Yak-9 production.

Powerplant
The Yak-9 was powered by a 1,260-hp (940-kW) VK-105PF-1 or 1,360-hp (1014-kW) PF-3 V-12 liquid-cooled piston engine.

Armament
The Yak-9D had one 20-mm ShVAK cannon with 120 rounds, firing through the airscrew hub, and one 12.7-mm BS machine-gun with 200 rounds mounted in the top of the cowling (some Yak-9s had two cowling-mounted BS machine-guns with 150 rounds each).

Dimensions
Wing span was 31 ft 11.46 in (9.74 m), with a total wing area of 184.6 sq ft (17.15 m2). Length of the Yak-9 was 27 ft 10.64 in (8.5 m) and height 8 ft 7 in (2.6 m).

Below: Large bombs were carried externally, this being a 1000-kg (2204 lb) weapon. This He 111 is operating on the Eastern Front in January 1943 and has a washable white distemper applied over the standard camouflage for winter operations.

Above: A Ju 88A-4 of III LG.1 over the Russian Front in 1943. From 1940, all Ju 88s were based on the long-span A-4 version which had better handling, no structural limitations and the more powerful Jumo 211J engines.

week's desperate fighting on the flat grasslands, involving more than 3,000 tanks not to mention the Soviets' 20,000 artillery pieces, it seemed that the Germans were on the point of breakthrough.

Then, General Georgi K. Zhukov, the Soviet commander-in-chief, ordered into action a completely fresh tank army supported by swarms of Il-2s. Generalfeldmarschall von Manstein, the German commander, feared the annihilation of his exposed armoured thrust. He urged the supreme command to allow a withdrawal of German forces to the heavily defended line on the Dniepr river, but was peremptorily overruled by Hitler who ordered a fighting stand to be made, during which the Soviet air force took a heavy toll of the vital German transport vehicles. The Soviets went on to widen the Kursk salient, and then launched a sustained attack northwards toward Orel.

Much of the blame for the defeat at Kursk was laid at the door of the Luftwaffe. In spite of the policy of absolute priority of aircraft and

resources on the Eastern Front, which were to be protected by the maintenance of fighter superiority, the Germans lost more than 900 aircraft during the week-long battle over Kursk compared with some 600 Soviet aircraft lost. German air superiority, unquestioned in the first two years of the war, now rapidly evaporated. The tide had indeed turned in the air war. Coming close on the heels of the destruction of the Luftwaffe in Sicily, the priority in the East was now abolished, many fighters and all Zerstörer units being withdrawn for 'defence of the Reich'. The ground attack (Schlacht) units of

the Luftwaffe underwent fundamental reorganisation, the Fw 190F and Fw 190G gradually replacing the aged Ju 87D; at the same time, the Nachtschlachtgruppen (night strike groups) were upgraded in importance, their largely nuisance operations being widened to embrace a concerted campaign against the Soviet railway network.

Right: Luftwaffe personnel examine a crashed Il-2 Sturmovik on the Russian Front. One of the most famous of the Soviet Union's wartime aircraft, total production of the Il-2 totalled 36,000, built between 1941 and 1944.

Luftwaffe Schlachtflieger

To take part in the huge land battles on the Eastern Front, the Luftwaffe developed its ground attack units enormously. The Ju 87D remained a stalwart of the campaign, as did the specialised Henschel

Hs 129. Perhaps the most capable aircraft were the Fw 190F and G, used in numbers by SchG 1 and 2. These could carry heavy bombloads and introduced dedicated anti-personnel weapons.

Focke-Wulf Fw 190F
This Fw 190F-2 was flown by Leutnant Fritz Seyffardt of 6./SchG 1, based in the Ukraine in May 1943. Seyffardt was one of several ground attack pilots to achieve respectable kill totals, ending the war with 30 kills, mostly over Ilyushin Il-2s. The speed and bomb-carrying ability of the Fw 190F made it a capable attacker, but there were never enough to radically affect the outcome of the fighting.

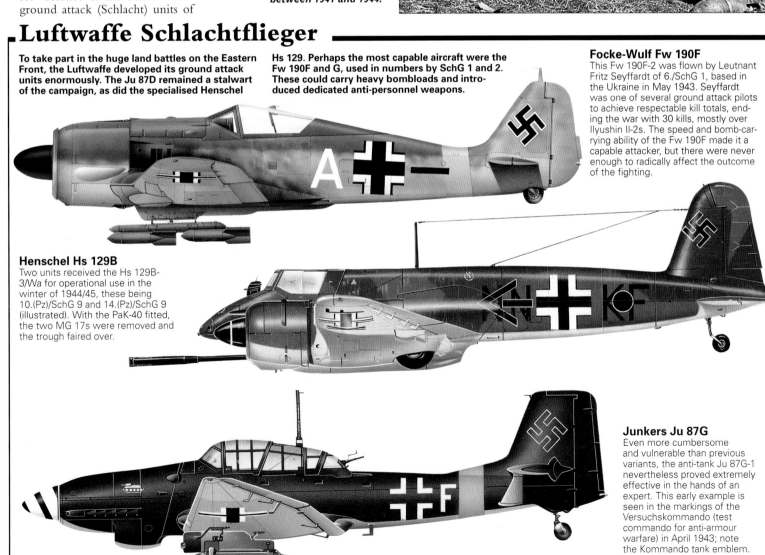

Henschel Hs 129B
Two units received the Hs 129B-3/Wa for operational use in the winter of 1944/45, these being 10.(Pz)/SchG 9 and 14.(Pz)/SchG 9 (illustrated). With the PaK-40 fitted, the two MG 17s were removed and the trough faired over.

Junkers Ju 87G
Even more cumbersome and vulnerable than previous variants, the anti-tank Ju 87G-1 nevertheless proved extremely effective in the hands of an expert. This early example is seen in the markings of the Versuchskommando (test commando for anti-armour warfare) in April 1943; note the Kommando tank emblem.

The widespread withdrawal of German fighters from the East gave the Soviets the opportunity to exploit their growing strength in the air. Their own fighters were now more of a match for the Germans, and thanks to numerical superiority could at least provide powerful protection for the Soviet bombers and Il-2s if they could not dominate the front.

SOVIETS FIGHT BACK

In January 1944, with the support of 1,200 aircraft including those of

Above: The Petlyakov Pe-2 first proved its versatility as a light bomber during the battles for the Kursk Salient in 1943. Although later overshadowed by the Tupolev Tu-2, the Pe-2 performed well until the end of the war.

the Red Banner Baltic Fleet, the 2nd Soviet Shock Army secured the relief of Leningrad. By that time the Yak-9 and La-5FN were able to overwhelm the German fighters, and many of the Luftwaffe's most experienced pilots, men like Heinz Schmidt with 173 victories and Max Stotz with 189, were killed.

Above: Indications that the Luftwaffe might not be invulnerable came early. Here smiling Soviet pilots celebrate with their leader Gussarov (centre), who shot down 15 German aircraft between 11-17 May 1942.

Meanwhile in the south, following a Soviet offensive at the end of 1943 in the Kiev region, the Soviets opened their crushing winter campaign in the Ukraine. In January 1944, as the 1st Guards Army and 1st Tank Army smashed their way west towards Zhitomir, supported by General Krasovsky's 2nd Air Army, they trapped some 60,000 Axis troops in the Cherkassy pocket. Roughly half of that number managed to escape during the following month, thanks to air supplies dropped to them by Luftwaffe transport aircraft. In May the last

German aircraft left the isolated Crimea, where 300 Luftwaffe machines were lost as 26,000 Germans fell into Soviet hands.

Nose detail of a crashed Soviet Il-2 Sturmovik in summer 1944. The engine is a large 1007-kW (1,350-hp) liquid-cooled AM-35. The cockpit seated the pilot and radio operator/rear gunner/observer in tandem.

Above: Leutnant Fritz Seyffardt jumps from his Schlacht Fw 190, coded green A. Seyffardt flew the type with 6./SchG 1 and then with 5./SG 2 'Immelmann', trying to stop the advance of the Red Army.

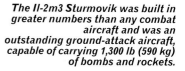

Shturmovik!

Many Soviet veterans remember the Il-2 as the aircraft which won the Great Patriotic War. Here a young Soviet pilot describes his first combat mission, flying as a gunner in the Il-2 Shturmovik of his new flight commander.

"The C.O. had ordered that I should fly in the aircraft of the flight (zveno) commander. This is Senior Lieutenant Leonid Yefremov, a young, thick-set, rectangular lad of about 23 years old. His snub-nosed face, a boyish aggressiveness on it, is comic.

"Have you ever flown in a Sturmovik? No! Well then, take as many newspapers as you can, you'll need them, for I expect you'll leave your dinner in the cabin." He said to his air gunner, "Vanya, show the battalion commissar how to play your instrument. I don't want to be vulnerable if I meet up with the Messerschmitts". I climb into the cabin and soon the engine is roaring.

Then suddenly...My body is dragged towards the tail. I have to brace myself against the sides of the cabin so as not to hit my forehead against the machine-gun. A few moments later the earth is dropping, falling away beneath us. I can just make out the voice of the pilot somewhere behind the crackling in the earphones, "Well, battalion, still alive?"

"Yes I am."

"Well then, as you're alive, keep both eyes skinned, for heaven's sake."

I report to the pilot, that our two companions are joining up.

"Thank you, they'll form up close to us now."

Suddenly we spot a column of tanks.

"Are you going to attack ?" I ask.

"Don't be in such a hurry,

they're ours, but in five minutes time any that we see will be enemy ones. Keep your eyes open, especially towards the sky."

Then we experience explosions of A.A. shells. The pilot weaves the aircraft from side to side as he starts evasive action. The no. 2 and no. 3 are doing the same. It's a most unpleasant sensation, but the AA fire at last breaks off.

"Well, battalion, have you still got your dinner or have you given it up to God ?"

"I've still got it, still got it. All in order." I make my report as boldly as possible.

"Their firing was pretty poor. If they don't get me the first time, they've had it. I don't let the second salvo get near the aircraft."

"Battalion, attention, in a moment we'll be making our attack." At once his voice loses its boyish intonation and becomes very commanding.

"Prepare to attack" Almost at once, "Attack!" For a fraction of a second I am lifted up and feel weightlessness. The tail of the aircraft rises in the air. The others are diving with us. I see a flash and black cigars belching flames race towards the earth, overtaking our aircraft. These must be the rocket projectiles. Then my whole body shakes as the great aircraft shudders all over. I guess that the cannons are being fired. So this is what a Sturmovik attack means. The aircraft shuddering with the fever of the cannon fire.

"Look out, the swine have got their Oerlikons on to us." The earphones give this warning.

Oerlikons ? What are Oerlikons?" The aircraft again goes into evasive action. In the very thick of the enemy equipment fires are raging and several bright red balls seem to hang over this crushed press of vehicles. They seem to hang for a moment and then apparently breaking their bonds they race up and flash past the cabin to rise up into the sky. Oerlikon. This unknown word is now clear to me.

At this moment out of the very bellies of our fellow Shturmoviks a stick of bombs falls away. Not looking away I follow their path down until the whole stick has dived into the melee of vehicles and tanks. The explosions throw out fiery sparks. Now the aircraft is again climbing up into the sky.

"Well battalion, are you still alive?"

"I'm alive."

"Why didn't you open fire?"

"I didn't manage to, I was so pressed down I would not have been able to swing the gun."

Fair enough. Don't try to fire when we're coming out of the dive or you'll hit our tail. But now we'll be making the second run, then you fire some bursts. I'll go lower. O.K.?"

"O.K. I'll try."

The aircraft makes a steep turn at height. The other two aircraft are close beside us. "Stand by, battalion, I'm going in again."

Once more the tail rises and I'm lifted out of my seat against the gun. The fuselage shudders and I already know that this means that the cannon are firing. The earth is now close. The vehicles, tanks,

The Il-2m3 Sturmovik was built in greater numbers than any combat aircraft and was an outstanding ground-attack aircraft, capable of carrying 1,300 lb (590 kg) of bombs and rockets.

Germans in green uniform race past us. Suddenly the heaviness leaves my shoulders.

"Battalion, it's now your turn to speak, fire!"

With a feeling of relief I put my eye to the sight. In the cross-wires there are the running soldiers, the rearing horses, the vehicles and trailers.

I press the trigger with my thumbs. A long line of tracer goes across the mass of enemy equipment. The gun almost jumps from my hands. I hold it tighter and again press on the trigger.

"That's the stuff, carve them up".

"I'm going in on the column again. Stand by, only short bursts or you'll melt the barrel," says the pilot. "Going right down to the deck," warn the earphones, "Fire, Fire! Look, they're running like spiders !" I hear a warrior's laugh of triumph.

The cross wires of the sight slip over the very centre of the enemy column. I press strongly on the trigger. The line of tracer draws a punctured line along the column. The tracer bullets pour out, stinging and I don't as much see this as feel it. I see how one of the lorries bursts into flames.

"Enough. You'll melt the gun." This said jokingly to me and then, in the commander's tone, "hunchbacks, join up, join up."

"We'll return to the chicken house," says the pilot and at once adds "congratulations on your first operational sortie, comrade battalion commissar."

The Il-2 was originally built as a single-seater, but combat experience rapidly showed the need for rear defensive armament. A second cockpit with rear-facing gunner was added in the Il-2M, reducing the numbers lost to Luftwaffe fighters. The greatest assets of the Il-2 were its simplicity and strength, which allowed it to operate in all conditions and with low-skilled and often brutal maintenance. The semi-retracting undercarriage allowed it to make wheels-up landings with only minor damage.

Daylight Heavies Triumph

1943–1945

During mid-1942, the USAAF's 8th Air Force arrived in England and embarked on a massive daylight 'precision' bombing campaign which lasted until the end of the war, complementing the RAF's night offensive. Boeing B-17s were augmented by Consolidated B-24 Liberators, seen here bombing a target near Tours in France.

been conceived as an escort fighter and, until long-range drop tanks could be produced for it, its radius of action remained much the same as that of the Spitfire Mks V and IX, at about 150 miles (240 km).

VULNERABLE BOMBERS

This was an uncomfortable period for Major General Ira C. Eaker, commanding the US 8th Air Force. The Americans were under political pressure to extend their bombing operations further afield, but their early Boeing B-17E, B-17Fs and Consolidated B-24Ds were demonstrably unable to fend for themselves in the face of fast-increasing fighter opposition over France and the Low Countries. VIII Fighter Command was transferred from British to American control in an effort to co-ordinate better escort tactics by the P-47s as the first efficient drop tanks were issued to the fighter groups; these still enabled the P-47s to fly only 50 miles (80 km) farther,

Below: Serving with the 379th Fighter Squadron, 362nd Fighter Group, 9th Air Force, this is a P-47D-II-RE equipped to carry a bomb on the fuselage centreline. Two 150-US gal (568-litre) wing drop tanks could be carried in place of the centreline tank when a bomb was carried.

Just as the Casablanca Directive was issued by the Allied Chiefs of Staff on 21 January 1943, setting out the objectives of the British and American bomber offensive, the first American Republic P-47 unit (the 56th Fighter Group) was reaching operational status in England. Two months later the 4th Fighter Group (formed out of volunteer-manned squadrons of the RAF) converted from Supermarine Spitfires to P-47s. These groups, together with the 78th, joined the RAF's Spitfires in escorting the American daylight raids over Europe in May. Unfortunately, the P-47 had not

Left: P-47B Thunderbolts of the 56th Fighter Group in formation during training in the US. Aircraft '1' is flown by the CO, with pilots of the 61st Fighter Squadron flying the other aircraft. Using P-47Cs, this group was the first to fly Thunderbolts in the European theatre of operations.

Right: The North American P-51 Mustang was the most effective escort fighter of the war, with sufficient range to escort the bombers all the way to the target, and agile enough to be able to fight Bf 109s and Fw 190s on even terms when it got there. Here Don Gentile, one of the Mustang's greatest exponents, walks away from 'his' P-51B.

however. On 26 June some 250 B-17s attacked Villacoublay, and only the P-47s remained with the bombers all the way. As soon as the Spitfires turned back, the Americans were attacked by the Messerschmitt Bf 109Gs and Focke-Wulf Fw 190As of JG 2 which quickly shot down five B-17s, while JG 26 destroyed four P-47s.

Gradually, the American fighter pilots worked out their own tactics, mastered the tricky fuel handling of the P-47 and, by the late summer of 1943, were beginning to take an increasing toll of German fighters. Thus encouraged, the 8th Air Force launched its first long-distance raid against Schweinfurt and Regensburg deep inside Germany on 17 August, it being intended that fighters would cover the bombers as far as the

German border, return for fuel and then meet the raiders on their way home. Unfortunately, the presence of fog at some of the bomber bases caused the timing of the two raids to go wrong, thereby enabling the enemy fighters to make two interception attacks after the escort had turned for home. Of the 376 aircraft despatched, some 60 were shot down. A second mission to

Flames and debris spew backwards from an 8th Air Force B-17 hit moments before bomb release in April 1944. The USAAF suffered far greater losses than the RAF during bombing raids, mainly due to their insistence on daylight attacks.

the ball-bearing plant at Schweinfurt was flown by 291 B-17s on 14 October but, still without fighter protection for

Above: The elimination of paint from the B-17 gave a measurable gain in speed on reduced fuel consumption (because cruising speed was pre-set at a figure all aircraft could easily maintain at full load). These B-17Gs, built by Douglas, served with the 711th Bomb Squadron, 447th Bomb Group, based at Rattlesden.

Right: Boeing B-17s bore the brunt of the American offensive, and gained the appreciation of many of its crews for its ability to withstand terrible punishment and still make it back to base. Here a tight formation release their bombloads over the target at Marienburg in Germany.

Daylight heavies

The Boeing B-17 and Consolidated B-24 conducted the USAAF's strategic offensive against Germany. With its aircrafts' sophisticated Norden bombsights and daylight tactics, the USAAF presented itself as practitioners of pinpoint bombing of selective targets, aimed at devastating key industries, as compared to the RAF's crude bludgeoning of area targets by night, which aimed to disrupt German industry and morale as a whole. In fact, RAF night bombing (using Pathfinders and navaids like H2S) was more accurate than the USAAF's day bombing, taken as a whole.

Consolidated B-24D Liberator
The Little Gramper was a Consolidated B-24D flown by the 491st Bomb Group as a lead-ship. These war-weary aircraft were used to assemble the huge formations over England, ensure everyone was in position and then send them on their way. The colours were deliberately bright for high visibility.

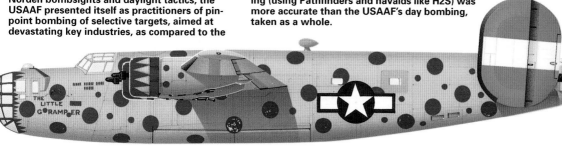

Boeing B-17G Flying Fortress
This famed B-17G *A Bit o' Lace* of the 711th BS, 447th BG based at Rattlesden, had nose art painted and signed by Milton Caniff (nose art, often featuring the female form, was invariably well executed). The 447th did not use squadron code letters but ended the war with this colourful yellow scheme.

more than half the flight, 60 more bombers were shot down; five others crashed in England and 133 were badly damaged.

FIGHTERS ARRIVE

The remedy for these catastrophic losses was already at hand, however, with the arrival in England during that autumn of the 354th Fighter Group, the first to fly the superb North American P-51 Mustang, a long-range fighter that was to remain unrivalled for the remainder of the war. When a third attack by 238 B-17s of the USAAF's 1st Bombardment Division returned to Schweinfurt on 24 February 1944, the fighter escort accompanied the

entire raid and bomber losses were held to 11 aircraft.

Throughout 1944 the Americans continued to build up their bomber strength, the B-17G, the B-24G and the B-24H being introduced with twin-gun nose turrets to counter the deadly head-on attacks by German fighters. In the latter half of February a concerted day and night assault by RAF and US bombers (Operation Argument, otherwise known as 'Big Week') was launched, in which a total of 16,500 tons of bombs was dropped in five days and nights, the Germans losing more than 150 fighters. On 4 March the Americans carried out their first daylight raid on Berlin

(complementing RAF Bomber Command's night Battle of Berlin, then at its height): 609 B-17s and B-24s with P-47, Lockheed P-38 and P-51 escort achieving considerable damage for the loss of 68 bombers and 13 fighters.

Like those of RAF Bomber

Command, the heavy bombers of the US 8th Air Force were largely withdrawn from strategic operations in preparation for the coming Normandy invasion, switching to attacks on German airfields and transportation targets in France and the Low Countries.

Above: Easter egg and pin-up girl. This special 'egg' has been prepared by members of the 8th Air Force Ordnance Unit to be dropped over Germany in Easter 1944. A hoist is being used to move the bomb.

Right: Colonel Tom Christian, Group Commander of the 361st Fighter Group, leads three aircraft of the 375th Fighter Squadron. The P-51D marked an improvement over the earlier P-51B in many respects.

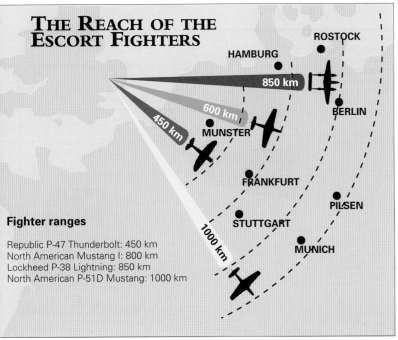

THE REACH OF THE ESCORT FIGHTERS

ROSTOCK

HAMBURG

850 km

600 km

450 km

MUNSTER

BERLIN

FRANKFURT

PILSEN

1000 km

STUTTGART

MUNICH

Fighter ranges

Republic P-47 Thunderbolt: 450 km
North American Mustang I: 800 km
Lockheed P-38 Lightning: 850 km
North American P-51D Mustang: 1000 km

Left: The Eighth Air Force always planned on operating with a fighter escort. This was originally provided by short-ranged RAF Spitfires, which could range little further than Paris. There were never enough P-38s to escort the 8th Air Force bombers, and the aircraft were, in any case, to prove unreliable and ineffective. The Republic P-47 entered 8th Air Force service in March 1943, and this proved more reliable, and more effective, though it could reach little further than the German border. In RAF service the Allison-engined Mustang I had proved capable of attacking targets in Germany, but the aircraft's performance was poor at high altitude, and it was not suitable for bomber escort duties. The Merlin-engined Mustang offered even greater range, with superior altitude performance, and promised to be able to escort the bombers all the way to any target, even Berlin. This was of crucial importance, promising to make the difference between success and failure of the daylight bomber offensive.

In August the American bombers began heavy attacks on the German oil industry, synthetic oil plants at Gelsenkirchen and Ludwigshafen being attacked by British-based bombers on 16, 24 and 26 August, and the Ploesti oil plants by Italian-based B-24s of the 15th Air Force on 17 and 18 August. In September the B-17s and B-24s raided Bremen, Koblenz, Frankfurt, Hamm, Karlsruhe, Kassel, Magdeburg, Mainz, Munster, Osnabruck and Stuttgart. The toll of German cities and industries devastated by bomb and fire continued to rise.

HITLER POUNDED

As the German army was forced back within the boundaries of the Reich, so the ferocity of air fighting increased as the German fighter pilots struggled to defend their homeland. The Messerschmitt Me

Liberators of the 458th Bombardment Group, based at RAF Horsham St Faith, en route to a target, with a P-51 escort. Bombers began to lose their drab camouflage soon after it was removed from the fighters of the Eighth Air Force. In clear, cloudless weather, towards the end of the war, USAAF bombers proved more accurate than the RAF's night bombers, but as soon as there was cloud, heavy flak or fighter opposition, accuracy figures declined dramatically.

163 rocket interceptor and Me 262 jet fighter appeared and began to take a serious toll of the bombers but – the perimeter contracted from the west, east and south, as Allied bombers 'shuttled' to bases in the Soviet Union, as the Allied long-range fighters maintained constant attacks on the German airfields, and as enemy oil stocks dwindled – the British and American heavy bombers continued to pound Hitler's Germany into rubble. By late April 1945 the 8th Air Force bombers had little left to attack but targets in southern German, Austria and Czechoslovakia. Their last major raid was on the Skoda works at Pilsen on 25 April 1945.

Above: Waist gunners inside a B-17. Two 0.5-in (12.7-mm) machine-guns on hand-operated mountings were fitted just aft of the trailing edge of the wing, firing through opening side ports.

Above: By mid-1944, most USAAF fighters operating in Europe had shed their camouflage in favour of natural metal, a step instigated primarily to gain extra speed in combat. This P-38L Lightning is escorting B-17Gs over Germany.

Right: Flight crew and ground crew discuss the successful 50th mission of B-17 Idiot's Delight on a base in East Anglia in March 1944. Mascot Flak Jr is being held by one of the crew. The pilot is signing the release for the aircraft.

'Little Friends'

Flying in daylight over the enemy homeland in a lumbering B-17 or B-24 was a dangerous business, even with the protection of escort fighters, which were soon referred to by the grateful bomber crews as 'Little Friends'. The P-51 and P-47 formed the backbone of the Eighth Air Force's escort fighter force, but also undertook independent fighter sweeps and ground attack missions.

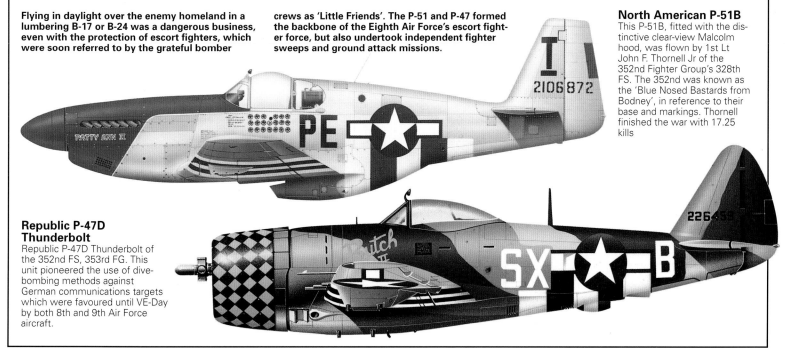

North American P-51B
This P-51B, fitted with the distinctive clear-view Malcolm hood, was flown by 1st Lt John F. Thornell Jr of the 352nd Fighter Group's 328th FS. The 352nd was known as the 'Blue Nosed Bastards from Bodney', in reference to their base and markings. Thornell finished the war with 17.25 kills

Republic P-47D Thunderbolt
Republic P-47D Thunderbolt of the 352nd FS, 353rd FG. This unit pioneered the use of dive-bombing methods against German communications targets which were favoured until VE-Day by both 8th and 9th Air Force aircraft.

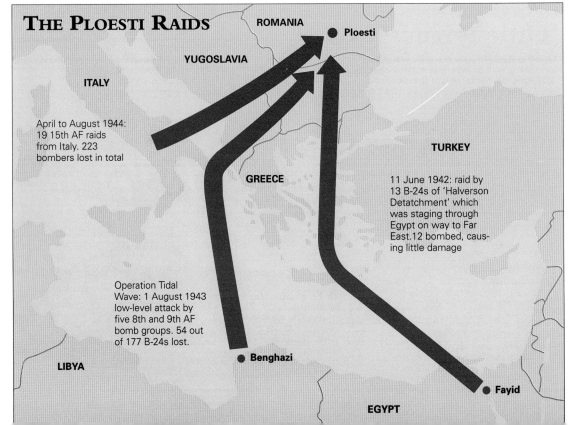

B-24 bombardier over Ploesti

Leroy Newby was the bombardier of a B-24 of the 460th Bombardment Group, and he flew on the nightmare mission to Ploesti, during which he and his crew had to face heavy flak and enemy fighters.

"There was a chorus of groans when the curtains were drawn back and the crews in the briefing room could see where the blue yarn stretched out to indicate our target for the day. Sherm and me, though, we weren't surprised. We'd been to the special briefing for lead bombardiers and navigators half an hour earlier. We already knew the 460th was going to Ploesti."

Leroy Newby - Ted to friends - was a young lieutenant whose job was as simple and straightforward as could be: all he had to do was wait until he had the target located in his bombsight and then press the release toggle. Of course, the Germans and Bulgarians defending Ploesti would have other ideas, and something of the order of a thousand anti-aircraft guns to put them into practice....

"Our *Hangar Queen* was

Left: B-24s fly over the burning refineries at Ploesti on 1 August 1943. Of the 177 Liberators (some borrowed from the 8th Air Force) that took off from bases in North Africa, 54 were destroyed and 532 aircrew were killed or captured.

assigned as deputy lead in the first attack unit. If the mission lead plane aborted or was forced out of formation en route, all the responsibility for navigation and target pick-up would fall on us. Gulp.

"They had passed out pictures taken by P-38s just a few days before. Our specific target was the Xenia refinery, complete with its 'tank farm' storage complex, on the northwest edge of the city.

"We departed base and were soon leaving a thick contrail along with 500 other bombers. Sherm was hard at it, updating his weather information.

"'Newb, the weather data looks okay to me,' Sherm finally said. I sighed with relief. No changes. All I had to do was find the target.

"'Lead bomb doors are opening,' called out Bob Kaiser. I immediately opened ours, and flipped the switch that armed the bombs. Then I looked around me.

"There wasn't a single cloud at our altitude, though it was cloudy higher up. Small, dense clouds that dispersed and reformed . . . not over the city itself, but forming a ring: black clouds below, white clouds above...."

The black clouds were Flak 37 guns, 88-mm pieces that fired shells weighing over 20 pounds. Above were the heavier Flak 39s that fired 34-lb 105-mm shells at

The big oil refineries at Ploesti in Romania were the source of the majority of oil supplies for the Nazi war machine. The target was considered so vital that the commander of the 9th Air Force (then based in North Africa) expected to lose 50 per cent of his force in an all-out attack, but considered it would be "well worth it" if the target was hard hit with total losses. For Operation Tidal Wave, the famous low-level attack on Ploesti, two Libyan-based B-24 groups were joined by three more from the 8th Air Force based in England. The 1 August 1943 raid is a legend in USAF history: the Liberators flew so low that their gunners fought duels with anti-aircraft gunners on the ground, at least one B-24 was set alight by flames from burning oil tanks, and a total of four Medals of Honor was won by aircrew participating in the raid. With the capture of bases in Italy in 1944, more frequent, high-level raids could be mounted on the Romanian oilfields. The raids on Ploesti finally halted production in August 1944, as the Russian armies approached. The attacks on German oil targets generally, more than any other factor, kept much of the Luftwaffe grounded in the last months of the war.

THE PLOESTI RAIDS

ROMANIA

Ploesti

YUGOSLAVIA

ITALY

April to August 1944: 19 15th AF raids from Italy. 223 bombers lost in total

GREECE

TURKEY

11 June 1942: raid by 13 B-24s of 'Halverson Detatchment' which was staging through Egypt on way to Far East.12 bombed, causing little damage

Operation Tidal Wave: 1 August 1943 low-level attack by five 8th and 9th AF bomb groups. 54 out of 177 B-24s lost.

LIBYA

Benghazi

Fayid

EGYPT

TARGET PLOESTI
B-24J **Hangar Queen** *of the 460th BS was assigned as deputy lead in a later attack on Ploesti. Leroy Newby was the bombardier.*

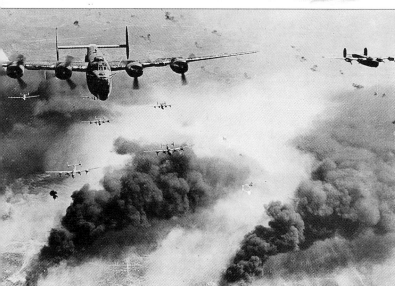

Left: Among the most memorable missions flown by Liberators during the course of the war was the attack on the Concordi Vega oil refinery at Ploesti, Romania, in June 1944. 15th Air Force B-24Js are seen under heavy anti-aircraft fire on a later Ploesti mission.

Right: On 23 June 1944, 761 heavy bombers hit the Ploesti refineries, the largest force to be sent against the Romanian target, followed by another 377 on 24 June. On 9 and 15 July, both raids were directed by pathfinder aircraft.

the B-17s, 4,000ft above.

"The black and white clouds came in different sizes and shapes. Small, sharp, jagged clouds were the fresh ones, and they were harmful if they were close. If you saw the red flash of the explosion itself, then there was a good chance that you were near enough for it to damage your aircraft. The larger, rounded puffs were old explosions.

"What they were doing was setting up a box barrage, bigger by far than the size of the bomber formation, and surrounding the bomb release point. The gunners, each firing a round every three or four seconds, tried to keep the box filled with exploding shells. They knew they couldn't stop the formation, but by hitting a 'plane or two, causing the formation to split open to avoid the careening aircraft, they could affect our accuracy.

"As for us, our instructions were very clear. Fly into, and through, the box of flak. No evasive action, just get in and get out. A straight line is the shortest distance....

"Being deputy lead, I had to

run checks of my own to compare with the computations going on in the lead aircraft. I worked away at it for a while, and then, before things got too serious, I tried to locate the actual aiming point. I got a shock. I'd been expecting a two-abreast tank farm that ran generally east-west in a rectangular strip. The picture in my bombsight was a square tank farm. Nothing like our target. I checked with the pictures: nothing like it.

"'Sherm,' I shouted, 'did we turn early?'

"'Yeah,' he answered, 'about a minute. Why?'

"'This is the wrong target!'

"'Right or wrong,' came the pilot's voice, 'this is the one we're going to bomb.' Because the target was such a different shape, all the data I'd entered about bomb drop

A 15th Air Force Liberator just after making a high-level bomb run over Ploesti. Note the vapour trails and open bomb bay. Almost 7,500 bomber sorties were flown against Ploesti, totalling some 13,469 tons of explosives and incendiaries.

intervals and such was meaningless, and there was no time to apply more than a hasty correction.

"Luckily, we were going to attack the tank farm on the diagonal, so there was still a chance that we'd get our stick of eight bombs inside it and do some real damage. Then I realised that the area over the target was actually blanketed by dense cloud, and I wasn't going to be able to see the aiming point for the last 20 or 30 seconds of my bomb run.

"I was now fully alert, I could see that we were about eight seconds away from bomb release. The cloud covered the aiming point itself, and all I could do was rely on offsets, guessing at where our target lay from things that I could see. I watched the sight tick off the last seconds of angle, then heard the bomb releases let go. 'Bombs away!' I tried to play it cool but I couldn't. I knew I'd done well

under difficult conditions.

"'Bomb doors closed,' I reported next, more matter-of-factly this time. Despite it being minus 60 outside, and not much warmer inside, I was soaked from the waist up. Even my feet felt warm, and that was really rare.

"As we banked away from the target, Major James's voice came over the intercom. 'We've been working for the government up to now,' he said, 'but from here on in, we're in business for ourselves.' He was right. Our sole job now was to get home in one piece.

"The return trip was fairly uneventful and the coffee and doughnuts served by the Salvation Army sure tasted good after that mission, and the shot of old Overholt whiskey that we were allowed after every mission hit the spot, too. And it was our turn to stand down tomorrow. The world didn't seem so bad a place after all."

Back into France

JUNE – SEPTEMBER 1944

Above: As the Allies advanced inland after D-Day, the fighter-bomber units of the US 9th Air Force moved from bases in southern England to semi-prepared strips near the front line. Here, examples of 'bubble-top' and 'razor-back' P-47Ds await the take-off signal at a forward base.

Below: a Marauder crosses a Normandy beach scattered with landing craft as it returns from a mission over France. The medium-bombers of the 9th AF and the RAF were tasked with disrupting communications to prevent German forces massing for counter-attacks.

Almost exactly four years after the British Expeditionary Force had staged its near-miraculous evacuation from Dunkirk, the Allies once more set foot in strength on French soil when on 6 June 1944, under the supreme command of General Eisenhower, British, American and Canadian forces landed in Normandy. They did so with complete mastery of the air.

For some months past the RAF and USAAF had been preparing the way for the invasion, British and American heavy bombers striking at key points in the French road and rail system to prevent the movement of reinforcements once the invading forces had landed. To this task was added the offensive against the flying-bomb sites in the Pas de Calais, while the fighter-bombers and light bombers of the 2nd

Above: Wearing partially-removed 'invasion stripes' and an impressive bomb tally, 'DeeFeater', a Martin B-26B Marauder of the 596th Bomb Squadron, 397th Bomb Group flies over England after the invasion. The 596th BS moved to Dreux in France during the campaign to keep close to the front line.

Left: A P-51D Mustang displays a full set of the 'invasion stripes' applied on the eve of D-Day to all aircraft directly involved in supporting the landings to distinguish them as friendly. Unusually here, the white stripes are edged in black. In July stripes began to be removed from upper surfaces to restore some camouflage effect.

Tactical Air Force struck at coastal targets (the E-boat bases, radar stations, airfields and coastal gun batteries) along the French coast. On the eve of the landings themselves the Allied Expeditionary Air Force comprised 173 squadrons of fighters and fighter-bombers, 59 squadrons of light and medium bombers and 70 squadrons of transport aircraft; in addition to some 50 other support

Left: Airspeed Horsa and General Aircraft Hamilcar gliders line up on RAF Tarrant Rushton's runway, just prior to D-Day. The Halifax glider tugs belong to No. 298 Squadron. The Horsa carried 20-25 troops, while the latter could hold a seven-tonne light tank into battle.

squadrons, there was also the might of RAF Bomber Command and the US 8th Air Force. In all, the Allies could count on close to 12,000 aircraft with which to support the invasion.

6 JUNE 1944

The assault on the French coast was indeed a highly co-ordinated effort by the land, sea and air forces. As 145,000 men went ashore from the sea on the first day, considerable use was made of airborne forces, the US IX Troop Carrier Command's C-47s dropping large numbers of paratroops behind the American beachhead area, their task being to consolidate an area from which an advance could be made up the Cotentin peninsula to capture the port of Cherbourg. In the event the American airborne operations were not wholly successful, the 81st and 101st Airborne Divisions being scattered over too wide an area to be fully effective. In the eastern sector, behind the British and Canadian beaches, the Stirlings, Albemarles, Halifaxes and Dakotas of the RAF's Nos 38 and 46

Groups dropped 4,310 paratroops and towed about 100 gliders to secure vital objectives such as coastal batteries, river bridges and road junctions.

As part of the elaborate deception plans undertaken to conceal the true location of the assault area during the night of 5/6 June a squadron of Lancasters (No. 617)

had flooded the skies over the Channel far to the north-east with 'Window' in a slow-moving cloud designed to suggest on enemy radar an approaching invasion fleet; a similar operation was carried out by Halifaxes and Stirlings off Boulogne. These feints certainly played their part in discouraging the Germans from committing their reinforcements until the real landings had gained a powerful foothold in Normandy.

ALLIED AIR UMBRELLA

Throughout that first day, as more and more men and vehicles

Above: In a textbook example of a precision strike, Allied bombers sever a rail viaduct in France during the Normandy campaign. Just visible at the top of the picture (and on the shadow of the bridge) is a train, which reportedly managed to come to a stop before the breach.

Left: One of the better Allied tanks in Normandy was the British Sherman Firefly with the 17-pdr gun, though it was available only in limited numbers. Allied tactical air-power did much to reduce the threat of the generally-superior German tanks.

Allied support aircraft

Douglas Boston Mk IIIs entered service in late-1941 as an anti-shipping and daylight medium-bomber. Their primary role on D-Day was smoke-laying, to shield the invading flotilla.

de Havilland's 'Wooden Wonder', the Mosquito was unmatched by anything in the USAAF inventory in the high-speed reconnaissance role. Almost 200 were delivered to the Americans.

Douglas Boston Mk IIIA

The USAAF's Douglas A-20C became the Boston Mk IIIA in RAF service. No. 342 ('Lorraine') Squadron was employed on smoke-laying missions on D-Day. No. 2 Group, Bomber Command's medium-bombers were transferred to the AEAF in the lead-up to the landings.

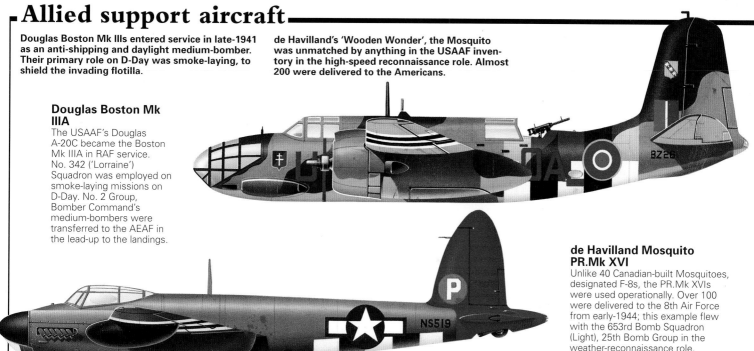

de Havilland Mosquito PR.Mk XVI

Unlike 40 Canadian-built Mosquitoes, designated F-8s, the PR.Mk XVIs were used operationally. Over 100 were delivered to the 8th Air Force from early-1944; this example flew with the 653rd Bomb Squadron (Light), 25th Bomb Group in the weather-reconnaissance role.

Unit
'Buzz Buggy' served with the 81st Troop Carrier Squadron, 436th Troop Carrier Squadron based at Membury, Berkshire. It took part in parachute dropping missions throughout the rest of the war, including the Arnhem operation.

Capacity
The C-47 could carry up to 28 fully-equipped paratroops, or 18 stretchers in the casualty evacuation role. Small vehicles such as jeeps could also be carried.

Crew
The Dakota normally had two pilots and a radio operator as flight crew, and a jumpmaster or loadmaster for paratroop or freight missions respectively. Three medical staff were usually carried on casualty evacuation missions.

Powerplant
C-47s and C-53s were powered by two Pratt & Whitney R-1830 air-cooled 14-cylinder radial engines, each of which gave up to 895 kW (1,200 hp) at take-off.

Douglas C-47A Skytrain

The Douglas C-47 and its derivative, the C-53 Skytrooper, bore the brunt of the Allied airlift effort on D-Day and afterwards. Cargo-lifting, parachute dropping and glider-towing missions were amongst the vital roles carried out by the ubiquitous C-47, known in the RAF as the 'Dakota'.

Other designations
The C-47A was the version of the basic DC-3 airframe produced in the largest numbers, but more than 20 different designations were applied to variants impressed from airline service alone. These included; C-48,-49,-50,-51,-52, -68 and -84 with a variety of subtypes. For example, a C-48C was a DC-3A originally built for Pan Am.

Above: The first tasks of the Allied engineers following the invasion were to build artificial harbours ('Mulberrys', one of which can be seen in the background) and to build emergency landing strips for aircraft out of fuel or too badly damaged to make it across the Channel. This P-38J Lightning has been saved by one such strip, built virtually on the water's edge within a week of D-Day.

Below: Coastal Command's strike forces were employed in keeping the German naval forces in France (by this time no longer comprising large surface warships) away from the invasion fleet. This is a Beaufighter TF.Mk X of No. 455 (RAAF) Squadron.

Left: With smoke-laying tubes visible below the aircraft, these No. 88 Squadron Boston Mk IIIAs are seen during Operation 'Starkey'. During this September 1943 exercise tactics to be used in June 1944 were tested by tempting an enemy response to a Channel convoy.

stormed ashore, the Allied air forces put up an enormous umbrella of protective fighters to keep watch for the Luftwaffe. Indeed the German air force reacted slowly and sluggishly with the relatively small number of aircraft available (a total of around 500 serviceable aircraft in the whole of Luftflotte III's assigned area). Only a small number of enemy air attacks developed and the damage caused by them was negligible. The Allies, on the other hand, recorded a total of 14,674 operational sorties on that first day, for the loss (mainly to flak) of 113 aircraft.

The initial assault phase ended with the delivery of 256 gliders to the inland dropping zones, carrying reinforcements to the men of the British 6th Airborne Division. Heavy tank-carrying Hamilcar gliders were now used for the first time to bring the Tetrarch tank into action.

For four days after D-Day the Allies were content to consolidate their beachhead as the tactical support Typhoons, Spitfires, Mustangs, Lightnings and Thunderbolts ranged over northern France, attacking road convoys and trains struggling to deliver German reinforcements to the battle area. Within 10 days more than half a million men had been landed on the Normandy beaches, scarcely troubled on their voyage from the

Above: A vital part was played by Allied photo-reconnaissance aircraft in plotting the movements of enemy supplies and reinforcements so that they could be targeted by the tactical air units. In addition to Spitfires, both the RAF and USAAF used Mosquitoes in this role. This is an RAF PR.Mk XVI – note the camera windows under the fuselage and the 'invasion stripes'.

Below: The Spitfire was widely used as a fighter-bomber in Normandy, a role for which the type was not entirely suited. Battle of Britain ace Squadron Leader Geoffrey Page is seen with fingers crossed in his 'bombed-up' No. 132 Squadron Spitfire Mk IX in France. He was severely wounded in September. No. 132 was back in Britain by September and in December had left for the Far East.

UK by the Luftwaffe, thanks to the continuing efforts of the 2nd Tactical Air Force to pin the German aircraft to their bases. By 10 June (after only three days' work by the airfield engineers) the first landing strip on French soil had been completed and thereafter RAF Spitfires and Typhoons were able to operate close-up behind the land battle, the Typhoons in particular proving deadly with their rocket armament.

BREAKOUT

The Americans were the first to break out of the beachhead, striking north towards Cherbourg before the end of June, and west and south during July. By the middle of August the British 2nd Army and the Canadian 1st Army had advanced south from Caen so that some 16 German divisions

Above: The British equivalent of the 9th Air Force was the 2nd TAF (Tactical Air Force). 2nd TAF struck at German communications, headquarters, supply depots and armour concentrations. The main bomber type used was the B-25, such as these Mitchell Mk IIs of No. 226 Squadron seen just after D-Day. Mosquitoes were also widely used.

faced encirclement and annihilation at Falaise. After a week of pounding from the air and ground the bulk of the German 7th Army was decimated and the remainder in flight across France, all the while harried by the rocket-firing Typhoons, the Thunderbolts and Lightnings by day, and the Mosquitoes of the RAF's No. 2 Group by night. On 25 August Paris was liberated by its own citizenry and on 3 September the Welsh Guards swept into Brussels.

AEAF fighter-bombers

It was during the Normandy campaign that Allied fighter-bombers came into their own as a close-support weapon against targets directed by commanders on the ground. For this role the RAF had the superb (if imperfect) Typhoon, designed as a fighter but more successful in ground attack. The Americans detailed quantities of their air superiority fighters, the P-47 Thunderbolt and P-51 Mustang, to close air support, the latter, with its liquid-cooled engine, proving vulnerable to ground fire.

Hawker Typhoon Mk IB
Built by Gloster Aircraft, this aircraft wears the markings carried by No. 198 Squadron between mid-1943 and D-Day. On 10 April 1943 No. 198 flew its first 'Rhubarb' fighter-bomber sortie against targets of opportunity across the Channel. It moved to France in July 1944.

North American P-51B Mustang
At least two pilots of the 353rd Fighter Squadron, 354th Fighter Group scored kills in the 'Beantown Banshee'. The 354th was the first Group in Europe (of either the 8th or 9th air forces) to receive Mustangs, and was still operating P-51Bs at D-Day, when many groups had converted to the P-51D.

Typhoon Attack

The Typhoon proved a devastating weapon against enemy ground forces when called into action from an airborne 'cab rank' position. Forward air controllers were stationed with Allied armoured units and could call in enormous firepower at very short notice. Ground fire of all calibres could be murderous, however, and many pilots never pulled out of their attack runs.

"I was a little afraid of the brute as I stood in front of it. I felt it was something mysterious and dangerous and I longed to master the monster, to break it in, like a thoroughbred," writes Belgian ace Charles Démoulin of his first encounter with the Typhoon. Decorated with the Croix de Guerre and the DFC, Squadron Leader Demoulin was to fly over 500 sorties in the legendary 'Tiffy' during the last three years of World War II.

"The long-awaited Typhoon had been planned to replace the Spitfire but was in fact a cruel disappointment to the RAF. Far faster from ground level to 10,000 ft, the Typhoon lost most of its power at the altitude where much of the combat took place. This was an insurmountable setback, for even with its supercharger the huge 2,200-hp engine could not compensate for the seven tons it had to move through the sky – against a mere 3.5 tons for the Spitfire."

The early Typhoon also had a bad habit of losing its ailerons in a steep turn, and the tail rivets wouldn't stand the stress of a steep dive. And as if that weren't enough, the Napier 24-cylinder sleeve-valve engine had an average life of about five flying hours before it packed up without warning. The cylinder sleeves causing the trouble were changed more often, and even replaced with another kind of steel, but engine reliability was never up to the standard of the Rolls-Royce engine in the Spitfire.

"Added to these vices, the aircraft had to be held hard with full rudder on take-off to counteract the torque, and oxygen had to be on at all times because the cockpit filled with exhaust fumes!" No wonder young pilots were nervous

Below: With Allied air superiority over the battlefield, the German Panzer armies had little protection from air attack. If they remained in depots, they would be destroyed by medium and heavy bombers, if they moved into the open, they were easy meat for the rocket-armed Typhoons. This knocked-out Panther V shows the foolishness of breaking cover on a clear day.

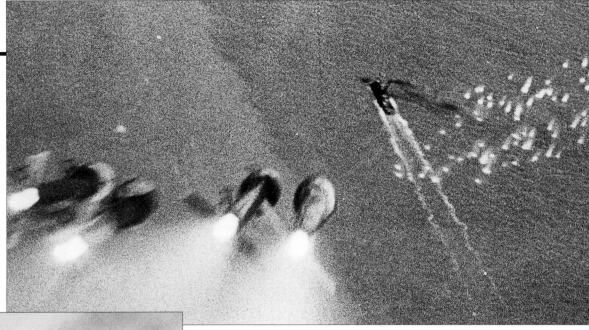

Right: A battery of rockets from a Typhoon streak towards a Dutch barge. Typhoons were also tasked with attacking targets of opportunity, and coastal shipping came under that ambit as well as motor transport and tanks. The splashes are caused by sighting rounds from the Typhoon's cannon.

Below: The standard 27.2-kg (60-lb) RP (rocket projectile) as fitted to the Typhoon was guaranteed to destroy soft-skinned and lightly-armoured vehicles with one hit, which was usually sufficient to disable a main battle tank. The Typhoon crews worked hard to support the frantic pace of operations in Normandy.

as they prepared for take-off on their first flights.

But many – and not just in the RAF – became great supporters of the Typhoon as a fighting machine, crediting the aircraft with playing a decisive role in the destruction of the German army.

"The Typhoon was a wonderful war machine, with its formidable armament of four 20-mm cannon firing more than 600 rounds per minute and its level top speed of about 410 mph. A new kind of warfare was found for this monster: low-level fighter sweeps, low-level attack, dive-bombing and, later, equipped with eight 60-lb rockets, as an assault aircraft specialising in ground attack. As such it was the most successful tank and armour buster ever produced.

"Working the 'Cab Rank' system, the Typhoons were able to respond in minutes to any call from the forward troops. 'Cab Rank' consisted of direct radio liaison between a controller pilot advancing with the attacking ground troops, and the airborne Typhoons, the ground-based controller calling down one or more aircraft from the 'Cab Rank'. The guidance became so accurate and the description so precise that a low-level aircraft could pinpoint targets as small as a sniper or a Panzer hidden in a thicket.

"Short of the atomic bomb, the war still had to be won by classic means – by beating the enemy on the ground and by occupation of his territory. It was by destroying most of the German armoured forces that the 2nd Allied Tactical Air Forces made the balance tip in our favour during and after the Normandy battle."

From June to September 1944, an average of 380 Typhoons made some 35,000 sorties, launching 265,000 rockets and firing 13,000,000 20-mm shells. This was at the cost of 243 Typhoons lost, 173 severely damaged and 75 less badly hit by flak. During the same period over 1,000 German tanks out of 3,000 (reinforcements included) were put out of action by Typhoons. They destroyed 12,000 to 15,000 vehicles, over 50 trains, about 30 barge-bridges and a great many gun positions. Thousands of German soldiers fell to their fire.

Left: From 11 July, No. 257 Squadron was fully engaged in the Normandy battles with its Typhoon Mk IBs. Apart from a brief interlude with rockets, the squadron operated in the bombing role until disbanded in March 1945. Ground-attack sorties were punishing on aircraft and pilots alike and the replacement rate for both was very high.

British Flat Tops

1940-1945

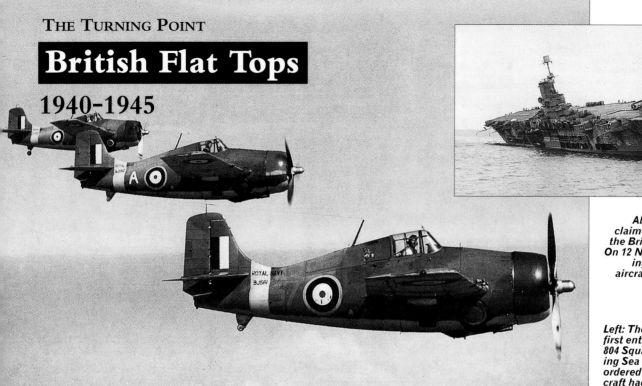

Above: German wartime radio claimed many times to have sunk the British carrier HMS Ark Royal. On 12 November 1941, while returning to Gibraltar after flying off aircraft reinforcements for Malta, she was torpedoed by U-boat U-81 and sank some 14 hours later.

Left: The Grumman Martlet Mk I first entered FAA service with No. 804 Squadron in July 1940, replacing Sea Gladiators. Originally ordered by the French, these aircraft had fixed wings, a Wright Cyclone engine and four guns.

The British, American and Japanese navies made considerable use of aircraft-carriers throughout World War II, indeed the survival of the three US fleet carriers of the Pacific Fleet at the time of the attack on Pearl Harbor was counted as of major importance in America's ability to countenance a successful war against Japan. And it was the US Navy and that of Japan which fought the great set-piece naval battles involving the aircraft-carrier in the role of capital ship.

The UK, on the other hand, after desultory and generally costly use of carriers in isolation on anti-submarine work and in support of land operations, lost both the old *Glorious* and *Courageous* in the first nine months of the war, neither as a direct result of air action. In due course the Royal Navy came to employ the much smaller escort carriers and the

hybrid merchant aircraft carriers in the role of anti-submarine convoy escort, their complements of but a dozen or so aircraft being deemed adequate for the strictly limited-range patrols. By the end of 1940 the Royal Navy possessed a total of seven fleet carriers, comprising the veteran *Argus, Furious, Eagle* and *Hermes,* and the modern *Ark Royal, Illustrious* and *Formidable;* to these were to be added the *Victorious* and *Indomitable* in 1941, and the *Implacable* and *Indefatigable* (all of 23369 tonnes/23,000 tons) in 1944.

MALTA SUPPLIED

One of the first vital tasks undertaken by the British carriers was the reinforcement of Malta and the Middle East with the transporting of crated aircraft to Takoradi in West Africa after Italy's entry into the war in 1940; the frequent sailing of carriers with fighters for Malta involved no fewer than 25 operations before the end of 1942, the *Argus* making five voyages, the *Ark Royal* 12, the *Furious* seven, the *Victorious* one and the *Eagle* nine (as well as two by the American *Wasp*), delivering a total of 718 aircraft.

The first outstanding action by

Below: Equipping eight operational squadrons by mid-1941, the Fairey Fulmar was to play a vital and successful role in the shadowing of the German battleship Bismarck. Here a Fulmar lands on HMS Victorious after a patrol of the shipping lanes.

Above: Fairey designed the Albacore as a replacement for the Swordfish, though the 'Stringbag' was to outlive its intended successor, FAA pilots preferring the older machine.

Right: Designed as a torpedo-bomber, the Grumman Avenger was, in FAA service, also used to drop mines and depth bombs.

Fighters of the Fleet

The first seaborne Sea Hurricanes were the CAM-ship-based 'Catafighters'. Arrester hook fitted Mk IBs for the carriers followed, though these were soon replaced by Seafires. The FAA formed its first Corsair squadron in 1943; eight units were so equipped by the end of the year. The first examples of the Grumman Wildcat in FAA service had been ordered by France and were known as Martlets.

Hawker Sea Hurricane Mk IB

The Sea Hurricane brought true fighter capability to the fleet's carriers. A conversion of the land-based fighter, it suffered the penalties of not being designed for carrier operations. This example was built in Canada as a Hurricane Mk X.

Vought Corsair Mk IV

The excellent Vought Corsair had been adopted by both the US Navy and the Royal Navy as their standard fighter. This example served with No. 1850 Squadron on HMS *Vengeance* off Japan in the summer of 1945. The US Navy's high-gloss midnight-blue finish was retained, along with US-style national markings.

Grumman Martlet Mk II

This Grumman Martlet Mk II served with No. 888 Squadron aboard HMS *Formidable*. US-style markings were adopted for participation in the 'Torch' landings in 1942. The Martlet Mk IIs had folding wings; the Mk Is were delivered with fixed wings.

Left: A Fleet Air Arm Grumman Martlet II being 'waved down' on the deck of a Royal Navy carrier. The Martlet had a distinguished service record, gaining immense respect from pilots for its manoeuvrability, reliability and potent firepower.

and destroying her steering, thereby allowing the British heavy ships to close their quarry. On 13 November that year *Ark Royal* was torpedoed by a U-boat in the Mediterranean and sank on the following day while under tow.

The air war in the Mediterranean involved British carriers in their most hazardous and spectacular fighting, particularly while protecting the Malta convoys. A total of 13 such convoys was sailed either from Gibraltar or Alexandria between

Below: In the heat of the Mediterranean circa 1942, Martlets, Albacores and Sea Hurricane Mk IBs are seen aboard an unidentified RN carrier. Sea Hurricane Mk IBs were converted from Hurricane Mks I, IIA and IIB as well as a few Canadian-built Mk Xs and XIIs.

carrier-borne aircraft of the Royal Navy was the brilliantly executed night attack by 21 Swordfish led by Lieutenant Commander Kenneth Williamson from the *Illustrious* on 11/12 November 1940 against the Italian fleet at Taranto harbour. Three of Italy's six battleships were sunk or crippled for a cost of two aircraft, an action that restored the balance of naval power in the Mediterranean following the elimination of the French fleet at Dakar.

In the famous naval action in the North Atlantic which finally brought about destruction of the German battleship *Bismarck*, Swordfish from the *Ark Royal* on 26 May 1941 scored two vital torpedo hits on the enemy ship, slowing her

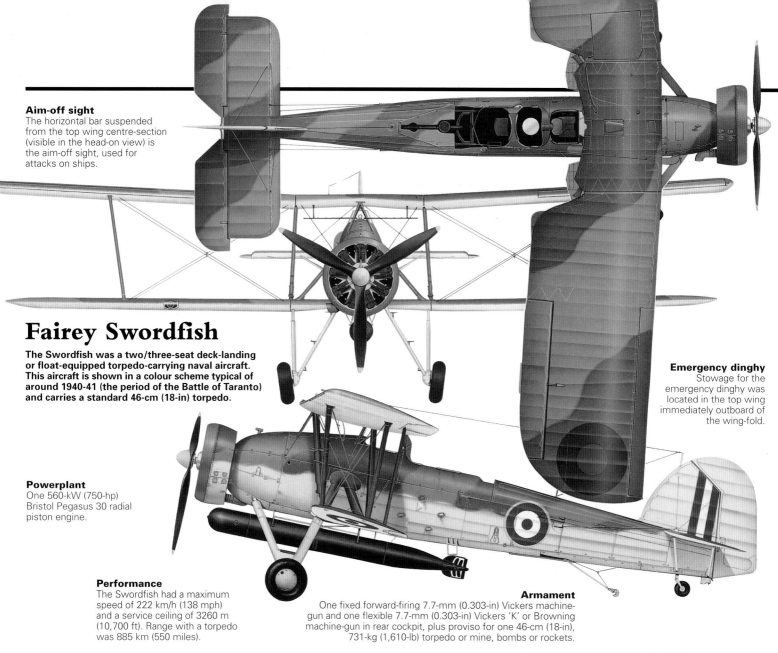

Aim-off sight
The horizontal bar suspended from the top wing centre-section (visible in the head-on view) is the aim-off sight, used for attacks on ships.

Fairey Swordfish

The Swordfish was a two/three-seat deck-landing or float-equipped torpedo-carrying naval aircraft. This aircraft is shown in a colour scheme typical of around 1940-41 (the period of the Battle of Taranto) and carries a standard 46-cm (18-in) torpedo.

Emergency dinghy
Stowage for the emergency dinghy was located in the top wing immediately outboard of the wing-fold.

Powerplant
One 560-kW (750-hp) Bristol Pegasus 30 radial piston engine.

Performance
The Swordfish had a maximum speed of 222 km/h (138 mph) and a service ceiling of 3260 m (10,700 ft). Range with a torpedo was 885 km (550 miles).

Armament
One fixed forward-firing 7.7-mm (0.303-in) Vickers machine-gun and one flexible 7.7-mm (0.303-in) Vickers 'K' or Browning machine-gun in rear cockpit, plus proviso for one 46-cm (18-in), 731-kg (1,610-lb) torpedo or mine, bombs or rockets.

August 1940 and January 1943, eight of them including carriers in their escort. Most of their sailings provoked enemy air action, and of the 80 merchant ships which set out 24 were sunk. The bitterest convoy action involving carriers was that of August 1942 when, in Operation 'Pedestal', 14 merchantmen were accompanied by no fewer than four carriers, two battleships, seven

cruisers and 24 destroyers. The convoy had to run the gauntlet of mines, E-boats and U-boats, as well as more than 200 German and Italian bombers and torpedo bombers and, despite all the efforts of the pilots of the carrier-borne Sea Hurricanes and Wildcats (as well as up to 200 aircraft based on Malta itself), casualties were heavy, the carrier *Eagle* being sunk by a

Above: Seafire Mk IBs on the flight deck of a Royal Navy fleet carrier in 1943 – part of a batch of 48 conversions from Spitfire Mk VBs. Apart from the introduction of a retractable 'V' frame arrester hook, they were almost identical to their land-based counterparts.

Left: No less than 19 FAA squadrons received Corsairs, with a total of 1,977 being built for the Royal Navy. The long-range fuel tank on this Corsair Mk II has burst after coming adrift in a heavy landing, its contents catching fire.

U-boat and the *Indomitable* and *Victorious* being damaged; two cruisers, a destroyer and nine merchantmen were also sunk, and two cruisers and five merchantmen damaged.

For the most part the convoys that sailed to the Soviet Union past the North Cape from Iceland were protected by the small escort carriers, as were the merchant convoys which sailed into British ports from the Atlantic, their aircraft being mainly tasked with anti-submarine duties, although on some occasions they were launched to intercept shadowing enemy aircraft. Use of fleet carriers in the Atlantic was confined to covering the passage of important troop convoys, fleet carriers only occasionally being deployed against U-boats.

HERMES LOST

In the Far East the UK suffered an early loss when the *Hermes*, one of the oldest carriers afloat and the first to be designed as such from the outset, was sunk by Japanese carrier-borne dive bombers off Ceylon on 9 April 1942 without having taken any significant part in the war in the Far East. In the last year of the war the *Illustrious*, *Indefatigable*, *Indomitable* and *Victorious* formed the carrier element of Task Force 57,

Right: The Fairey Barracuda acquitted itself well in its exacting range of duties, more often used as a dive-bomber than a torpedo-bomber. The type saw service in the Atlantic and Pacific theatres.

Left: Prior to the raid of 3 April 1944 on the Tirpitz *in Alten fjord, crews are briefed with the aid of a relief map of the area. Forty-two Barracudas were flown from* Victorious *and* Furious *in two groups with heavy fighter escort, and the battleship received 15 direct hits, killing 300 of the crew.*

taking part in the operations off the Ryukus with strikes by Corsairs, Hellcats and Avengers. *Formidable* relieved *Illustrious,* and on 1 April 1945 *Indefatigable* was hit by a Japanese suicide aircraft, only her armoured deck preventing fatal damage. Both *Victorious* and *Formidable* were later hit by these weapons, and both were similarly saved from destruction.

Left: A No. 818 Squadron Fairey Swordfish Mk II, one of the main Blackburn-built production batch, aboard escort carrier HMS Tracker. *Swordfish were widely used from the relatively small escort carriers, particularly in the North Atlantic.*

Torpedo-bombers

An attempt to replace the venerable Swordfish, the Fairey Albacore was always overshadowed by its illustrious forebear. Despite its enclosed cockpit, it was never as popular with its crews.

Grumman's TBF, which served with distinction in US Navy service in the Pacific, was made available under Lend-Lease arrangements from 1943. Until January 1944 it was known as the 'Tarpon'.

Fairey Albacore
Though not as well-known as the Swordfish, Albacores performed usefully, especially in the Mediterranean. Mid-1942 saw the peak in Albacore operations, with no fewer than 15 squadrons equipped aboard carriers protecting convoys to Russia as well as in the Indian Ocean and Mediterranean.

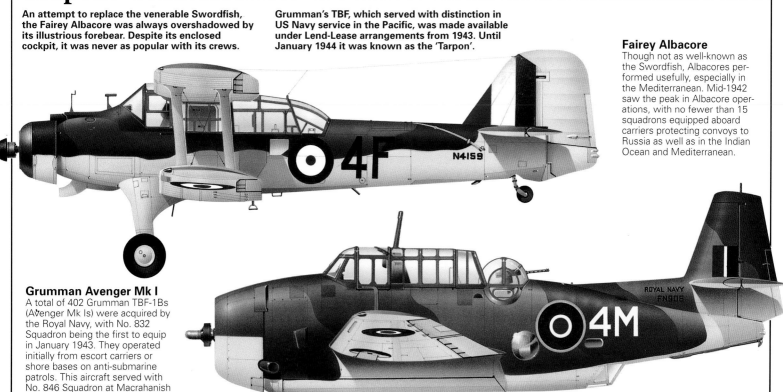

Grumman Avenger Mk I
A total of 402 Grumman TBF-1Bs (Avenger Mk Is) were acquired by the Royal Navy, with No. 832 Squadron being the first to equip in January 1943. They operated initially from escort carriers or shore bases on anti-submarine patrols. This aircraft served with No. 846 Squadron at Macrahanish in western Scotland.

Race to the Reich

AUGUST 1944 – MAY 1945

The destruction of German Forces south of Caen in mid-August 1944 was followed by the collapse of organised resistance throughout northern France as the Canadian 1st, British 2nd, and US 1st and 3rd Armies sped eastwards during the latter part of that month, Paris being liberated (from within) on 25 August. The British reached Brussels on 3 September and Antwerp on the following day. The US 3rd Army reached Verdun on 1 September, sweeping on to Metz and linking up with the US 7th Army as it advanced northwards having landed in the south of France on 15 August.

During this great onrush the Allied air forces were constantly in action, as their ground echelons strove to establish and re-establish fresh bases close-up behind the advancing armies. Before the crossing of the Seine, Mosquitoes, Mitchells, Mustangs, Bostons,

Above: The Thunderbolts of the 9th Air Force undertook the bulk of US fighter-bomber missions in Europe in the last months of the war, but the type was still a worthy dogfighter as the 18½ kill markings on this P-47D show. This was the mount of No. 353 Fighter Squadron's commanding officer Glenn Eagleston, who is receiving guidance from an airman as he taxies across his French base in late-1944.

Right: After the devastation wreaked on the French railway system in the build-up to D-Day, the Allied air force turned their attention to the German system. This marshalling yard near Limburg was flattened by 9th Air Force medium and light bombers. Some degree of service could often be resumed in a few days with emergency repairs.

Spitfires and Wellingtons of No. 2 Group attacked the ferries and barges at Rouen and elsewhere as German fighters attempted to interfere; these were engaged by No. 83 Group's Spitfires and the US 9th Air Force's P-47s and P-51s, which

together claimed more than 100 of the enemy destroyed during the last week in August.

As RAF Bomber Command joined in attacks on German coastal garrisons from St Nazaire to Dunkirk, which had been bypassed

by the advancing armies, the Dakotas, Stirlings and Halifaxes of RAF Transport Command were called on to mount the British airborne assault at Arnhem, while the C47s of the US IX Troop Carrier Command delivered the 82nd and 101st Airborne Division against targets on the Maas and Waal rivers. Unfortunately there were insufficient RAF aircraft available to carry the entire British 1st Airborne Division (and the Polish Parachute Brigade) in one journey and, while

Left: As with the other main US fighters, the P-51 and P-47, the Lockheed P-38 Lightning was employed as a fighter-bomber. In addition to conventional dive-bombing, the P-38 was used for formation level bombing guided by a modified aircraft with a bomb-aimer housed in the nose. There were several such variants, such as this P-38L with AN/APS-15 BTO (Bombing Through Overcast) radar.

Left: When Allied troops began to capture German airfields they made a number of surprising discoveries, including French Dewoitine D.520 fighters, used as operational trainers by the Luftwaffe. Captured US and British aircraft in airworthy condition were also found.

Below: The Messerschmitt 262 was potentially the best fighter of the war, but was not available in sufficient numbers when needed. By the time they entered service, even fuel for towing tractors was scarce.

Walcheren at the entrance to the Scheldt, thereby opening up the great sea port of Antwerp. In attacks which lasted from 3 October to 8 November Bomber Command attacked gun batteries and dykes, dropping almost 9000 tonnes of bombs as the 2nd Tactical Air Force flew some 10,000 sorties, dropped 1500 tonnes of bombs and fired 11,600 rockets.

On 16 December the 5th and 6th Panzer Armies, assisted by bad weather and the element of surprise, attacked in the Ardennes between the US 9th and 7th Armies, and within a week had penetrated some 96 km (60 miles). The poor weather prevented large-scale air action and it was without significant air support that the Americans were eventually able to counter-attack and crush the German attack. Among the enemy

the American forces duly secured their targets, the British attack at Arnhem failed despite the constant delivery by air of supplies. Unfortunately, as a result of recurring administrative problems, the 2nd Tactical Air Force was not brought fully into action to support the Arnhem action, and Nos 38 and 46 Groups lost 55 transport aircraft shot down and 320 others damaged by flak.

OVER THE RHINE

Elsewhere the Germans kept up attacks on the vital Nijmegen bridge over the Waal, now in British hands, sending among other aircraft the Mistel weapon; this comprised an unmanned Ju 88 bomber packed with explosives with a piloted fighter mounted on top, the pilot at the last minute releasing the bomber and guiding it towards its target. These attacks failed to hit the bridge and during the last week in September the Spitfires of No. 83 Group claimed the destruction of 46 German aircraft.

The airborne attacks in the north had been part of an Allied plan to cross the lower Rhine in force, liberate the Netherlands and outflank the Ruhr. Farther south, however,

the Americans were meeting with stiff resistance and by 18 November had reached a line running roughly along the German borders with Belgium, Luxembourg and France. Meanwhile the RAF had been engaged in supporting a major operation to clear the island of

Right: Although designed to replace the Bf 110 in the long-range fighter role, the high speed and heavy firepower of the Me 410B made it an effective interceptor. Unfortunately, it was not manoeuvrable enough to shake-off Allied escort fighters.

Reich defenders

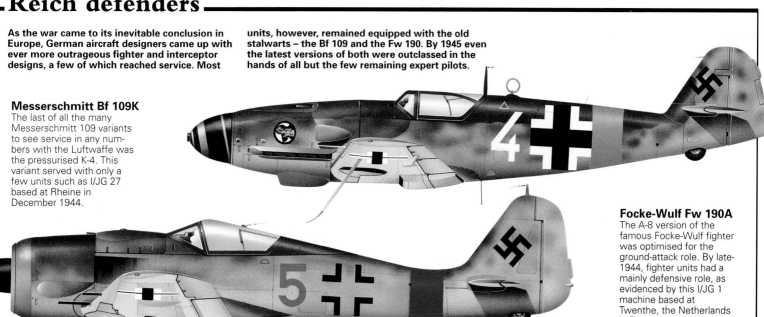

As the war came to its inevitable conclusion in Europe, German aircraft designers came up with ever more outrageous fighter and interceptor designs, a few of which reached service. Most units, however, remained equipped with the old stalwarts – the Bf 109 and the Fw 190. By 1945 even the latest versions of both were outclassed in the hands of all but the few remaining expert pilots.

Messerschmitt Bf 109K
The last of all the many Messerschmitt 109 variants to see service in any numbers with the Luftwaffe was the pressurised K-4. This variant served with only a few units such as I/JG 27 based at Rheine in December 1944.

Focke-Wulf Fw 190A
The A-8 version of the famous Focke-Wulf fighter was optimised for the ground-attack role. By late-1944, fighter units had a mainly defensive role, as evidenced by this I/JG 1 machine based at Twenthe, the Netherlands in December 1944.

Focke Wulf Fw 190D-9

The last major variant of the successful Fw 190 series, the D-9 had many features of the later Ta 152s, such as the Jumo engine, but retained the short wing of earlier models. Regarded as an 'emergency solution' until the Ta 152 could enter service, the D-9 was in fact superior to most fighters of its time and built in reasonable quantity.

Engine
Unlike previous Fw 190 models which were powered by the BMW 801 radial, the D series were fitted with the liquid-cooled Jumo 213, giving 1670 kW (2,242 hp) at sea level. The unusual annular radiator allowed a low-drag airframe with the same frontal area as the Fw 190A-G series.

Armament
Originally, the D-9s were armed with a pair of 20-mm MG 151 cannon in the wings and a pair of 7.9-mm (0.31-in) MG 17 machine guns above the engine, all guns firing through the propeller arc. Later, the wing cannon were removed and the fuselage guns replaced with 13-mm (0.51-in) MG-131 machine guns.

Undercarriage
The Fw 190 featured an outboard-mounted, inward-retracting main undercarriage layout. This design corrected one of the main faults of the Messerschmitt 109 (and the Spitfire), namely tricky ground-handling characteristics of the narrow-track outward-retracting landing gear.

Unit
This particular unit served with the Third Gruppe of Jagdgeschwader 6 (III/JG 6) at Welzow in March 1945, one of a number of units to receive the type before the end of the war. The coloured fuselage bands signified aircraft assigned to home defence.

Left: The Hawker Tempest supplanted the Typhoon (from which it was developed) in many squadrons from the Spring of 1944. Tempests were utilised mainly as fighters over Europe and on air defence (anti-V-1) duties in England.

Below: British paratroops await take-off in a Dakota for the ill-fated Arnhem landings, 17 September 1944. Operation 'Market Garden' was nearly a success but suffered from poor co-ordination and a lack of air support.

aircraft that did appear were some of the new bomber versions of the Me 262 jets.

The bad weather that had dogged Allied air operations during the Ardennes attack improved gradually during the last few days of 1944, and Allied offensive action by the 2nd Tactical Air Force was resumed. However, unsuspected by

British and American intelligence, the Luftwaffe had for some weeks been planning a great setpiece operation against the RAF and USAAF bases in northern Europe, the OKL believing that sufficient destruction could be caused to severely disrupt Allied operations to buy time to reorganise the defence of Germany. After assembling some 800 fighters

Above: The introduction of the longer-ranged bubble-canopy P-51D spelled the end for the Luftwaffe fighter force as serious opposition. The pilot of this P-51D, 2nd Lieutenant Urban Drew of the 361st Fighter Group shot down a pair of Me 262s on the same day in the last weeks of the war.

Left: The skies over Germany were no place for a lone Luftwaffe fighter in the Spring of 1945. This Fw 190 has been caught at low level by an American fighter, whose gun camera records the fatal hits (probably on the auxiliary fuel tank), and its destruction.

and 11 the bases at Asch, St Trond and Le Culot, and JG 53 the base at MetzFrescaty. Surprise was almost universal as the attacks came in soon after 09.00 hours. Considerable damage was caused and about 500 Allied aircraft were destroyed or later scrapped but, after the defences had recovered from the shock, about 300 German aircraft were shot down or crashed on the way home. But whereas the Allies were able to replace their losses within a few days (relatively few aircrew were killed), the German losses, which included some 230 airmen, were little short of disastrous. Indeed the folly of the operation was voiced by many senior German commanders, but they were confronting Nazi leaders fanatically blind to the realities of unquenchable Allied air supremacy and the inevitable grounding of the Luftwaffe through lack of fuel, just four months away.

and fighter-bombers of all types (including Me 262 and Ar 234 jets) from units all over the Reich the attack, Operation 'Bodenplatte' (Baseplate), was launched soon after first light on New Year's Day 1945, JG 1, 3, 6, 26, 27 and 77 attacking bases at Volkel, GilzeRijen, Eindhoven, Brussels, Ursel, Antwerp and Woensdrecht, JG 2, 4

Right: During the 'Battle of the Bulge' poor weather hampered the Allied air forces and US troops in Bastonge were besieged. On 27 December the weather lifted enough for supply drops, as watched here by the crew of a US mobile AA gun.

High-speed Tempest

The Typhoon, which had originally been designed as a Spitfire replacement, proved a deadly ground attacker but a disappointment as a fighter. Its main faults were addressed in the Tempest, which introduced a new wing, improved engine and enlarged fin. The Tempest was one of the fastest aircraft of the war at low level and proved particularly suitable for intercepting 'Divers', or V-1 flying bombs.

Hawker Tempest Mk V
No. 486 (NZ) Squadron moved from Matlaske to the Continent in September 1944 after a successful period intercepting V-1 flying bombs. In addition to the two V-1 kills marked here, NV706 also shot down a Bf 109 in February 1945 in the hands of Squadron Leader K. G. Taylor-Cannon who scored four kills with the squadron.

Havoc Pilot into Battle

Of the three types of medium bomber in service with the USAAF in Europe at war's end, the least well-known was the Douglas A-20 Havoc, though it had carried out the first missions of the 8th Air Force in 1942. A single-pilot aircraft, it lacked the glamour of its contemporaries, but could take a lot of punishment and still brought crews home. Here, an A-20 pilot describes a particularly harrowing mission.

"**D**on't worry about the aircraft overhead," General Eisenhower told his troops in the outline briefing for Operation 'Overlord', the D-Day landings on the north coast of France, "they'll be ours." He was right. However, that did not necessarily mean that missions over France were a picnic for the crew involved.

"The instant we got within range of the guns, they started firing. We were getting light and heavy flak in intense and accurate doses. The only evasive action we could take was a constant weaving which at least made the ground gunners move their guns, if nothing else. McEvilly was talking to me all the time, pointing out the landmarks, so I'd know we were on course. The two gunners were pretty calm and cool, considering the amount of flak being sent up. Every few seconds I'd look the 'plane over, along with those of my wingmen, and even at this point, I could see quite a few holes in fuselages and wings.

"Suddenly McEvilly called out. 'Here's our IP' (Initial Point for the bomb run.) At the same instant I saw what I thought was our first box ahead of us, and also the target. At this point I was quite excited, as our navigation was working out perfectly despite poor visibility. The A-20s in front of us were catching hell and it was as bad to watch them as it

was to be in it ourselves. They had already settled down on their target run when the proverbial hell broke loose. A box barrage of 1,500 – 2,000 bursts of heavy flak came up just as they dropped their bombs and three ships burst into flames from direct hits. We couldn't watch them any longer, as we were near enough to begin our target run, and we had to settle down to straight and level flying.

"We were pretty silent now, as we had all seen what happened ahead of us, and were tightening ourselves up, expecting the worst. McEvilly was busy on his sight and took a quick look around. All aircraft were still there and flying OK, but my own aircraft had a lot of holes in it. Even as I watched I saw two four-inch holes appear in the left wing as if by magic. Mike was saying 'Steady – left – left –,' and then the long-awaited 'Bombs away'.

"With bombs gone, I made a steep diving turn left and had a chance to look around again. What I saw didn't please me. There were

at least 2,000 bursts of heavy flak filling the sky around us and light flak tracers were coming from every direction. I had decided to head for the deck and come out fast, but as we were diving down, the flak increased and McEvilly hollered down the intercom, 'I don't think we'll ever get down in one piece.'

"After taking a quick look around I decided he was right. Looking ahead I saw a low-lying bank of clouds so we headed for them, still weaving and bobbing like a broken field runner. We were at about 2,500 ft and Meldrum was shooting at the flak positions. I helped keep his morale up, and he swears he killed 'hundreds of them'.

Right: A formation of A-20s of the 647th Bomb Squadron, 410th Bomb Group with full 'invasion stripes' crosses the channel on its way to bomb yet another marshalling yard. All the Havocs are 'gun-nosed' except that at the top of the picture which carries a bomb-aimer, upon whose signal the rest of the formation would release their load.

Left: The main medium bomber used by the US air forces in the European theatre was the Martin B-26 Marauder. Despite a poor early reputation, the B-26 went on to have the lowest loss-rate of any US bomber. Medium-level operations exposed aircraft to the heaviest concentrations of flak, however, and many Marauders fell like this.

heavy and light flak the enemy bade us farewell for the afternoon.

"Out over the Channel we took stock. No-one was hit, though a piece of flak broke the glass in the nose where Mike had bent over his sight. Our A-20 was a sieve, but still flying with both engines still running. The left engine sounded rough and as all the engine instruments were shot out I couldn't tell much about it.

"As we neared the English coast, we had a conference to determine whether to make for the base or land at an emergency field and chose the latter as the most sensible answer.

"After making a wide circle of the field we came in on the approach. I didn't want to make any steep turns without a rudder, so it took us four minutes to circle the field. As we settled down into the field, we could see people watching. It was an emergency field and they figured something was likely to happen. There was a strong crosswind and I knew we would hit crooked as the 'plane couldn't be straightened up at the last instant. Suddenly we hit and started to bump along. I knew without looking that we had a flat tyre and warned the boys to hold on. We were moving left towards a steep embankment, but we stopped right on the edge of it. I breathed a sigh of relief, got out and wanted to kiss the ground."

"It was at about this point that I felt my rudder pedals swing free and informed the boys that my rudder pedals were out. The A-20 was flying pretty well though and we were just going into the cloud bank when Hyroad told me that one of our 'planes appeared to be going down or at least had dropped out of formation.

"An important point I forgot to mention is that we got a good look at the target as we turned away and we had hit it squarely. At this time, however, we were too busy to be elated over that.

"The cloud cover was working swell, as it was thick enough to screen us but thin enough for us to keep our formation. Suddenly, however, we ran smack through some heavy clouds and got separated from all but one A-20. As I checked my aircraft over I noticed oil pressure was dropping and at the same time my fuel pressure was low. This spelled single engine operation to me, which on instruments, is rather difficult, and with no rudder is next to impossible. I

checked my trim tab and found it OK. I warned McEvilly and the gunners to be ready to jump at an instant's notice. If the trim tab didn't compensate for the rudder I'd have to cut the good engine and abandon ship.

"As if we didn't have enough trouble, we started getting ice. In less than a minute, we had an inch of it on the wings and the ship was feeling heavy. But by this time I decided the engine would be OK for if it were going to stop it should have stopped already.

"Now we were emerging from the clouds and could see water ahead, but we were still over land.

Right: The Douglas A-26 Invader began to reach English-based combat units in September 1944, and equipped several bombardment groups by the end of hostilities. A number of nose configurations appeared on the A-26, including a glazed bombardiers nose, and four, six and eight-gun solid noses. This is a six-gun A-26B, also armed with dorsal and ventral twin-gun turrets and pairs of single-gun packs under each wing.

We had about 90 seconds to fly for the coast and they started shooting again. We were all mad by now so we flew right out in the open but did take the precaution of a little weaving. With a parting flurry of

Final Year in the East

MARCH 1944 - MAY 1945

Above: Colonel M.V. Avdyeyev leads a formation of 6th Guards Fighter Aviation Regiment Yak-9s on patrol over the Crimea in 1944. Some 16,000 Yak-9s were delivered, and these did more than any other aircraft to help turn the tide against the Germans.

Below: German assistance and a force of 350 modern combat aircraft, including this Bf 109G-6, were not enough to help Finland halt the Soviet steamroller, and the campaign in Finland ended in September 1944.

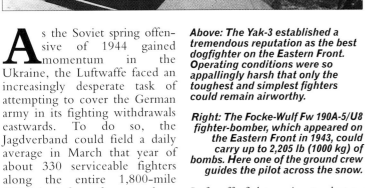

As the Soviet spring offensive of 1944 gained momentum in the Ukraine, the Luftwaffe faced an increasingly desperate task of attempting to cover the German army in its fighting withdrawals eastwards. To do so, the Jagdverband could field a daily average in March that year of about 330 serviceable fighters along the entire 1,800-mile (2897-km) front from northern Finland to the Black Sea. Opposing them were around 3,000 first-line Soviet aircraft, of which roughly half were modern fighters. The balance was to some extent redressed by the superlative quality and experience of many of the German pilots, but even among these the losses were very heavy. Nevertheless, on 23 March 1944 JG 54 was the second

Above: The Yak-3 established a tremendous reputation as the best dogfighter on the Eastern Front. Operating conditions were so appallingly harsh that only the toughest and simplest fighters could remain airworthy.

Right: The Focke-Wulf Fw 190A-5/U8 fighter-bomber, which appeared on the Eastern Front in 1943, could carry up to 2,205 lb (1000 kg) of bombs. Here one of the ground crew guides the pilot across the snow.

Luftwaffe fighter wing to destroy its 7,000th enemy aircraft (a milestone already reached by JG 51 'Mölders' in the previous September).

FINNS DEFEATED

By that month the Soviet armies had overrun all but the eastern quarter of the Ukraine and were attacking through a gap between the 1st and 4th Panzer Armies. In the north on 10 June, the Soviets attacked the Finns and invaded the Karalian isthmus with the 21st and 23rd Armies, supported by 750 aircraft of the 13th Air Army. Bolstered by a tiny detachment of Luftwaffe pilots and aircraft, the Ilmavoimat (Finnish air force) maintained a stout resistance with about 350 aircraft but, 10 days later, the key city-port of Viborg fell to the Soviets and on 4 September a ceasefire ended the campaign in Finland.

A measure of the scale of operations on the Eastern Front in mid-1944 may be gained by the fact that, compared with 54 divisions deployed against the Allies in France and Belgium, Germany had massed 164 divisions against the Soviets; yet compared with about 2,600 Luftwaffe aircraft in the East the Soviet air force now mustered a total of 13,000 first-line aircraft. Astonishingly, the Luftwaffe was able to display its traditional skill and when, in June 1944, the US 8th and 15th Air Forces began their shuttle bombing flights to Soviet bases, about 180 He 111s of KG 4,

Above: Luftwaffe pilot Captain Phillip achieved 213 victories on the Eastern Front. The emblems are II Group, I Group and III Group of JG 54 'Grunherz', Luftflotte 1.

Below: Supremely versatile and universally popular, the Focke-Wulf Fw 189 Uhu was essentially a low-altitude aircraft, befitting its tactical reconnaissance role.

Above: Taken in the latter part of 1944, this photo shows Il-2M3 two-seaters on the Eastern Front, which by this time had been pushed forward beyond the borders of the Soviet Union into Poland, Romania and other countries.

Below: Lavochkin's best wartime fighter was the La-7, distinguished by the smooth upper cowl lines. Like the Yak-3, the La-7 was exceptionally agile at low level, where most of the fighting on the Eastern Front took place.

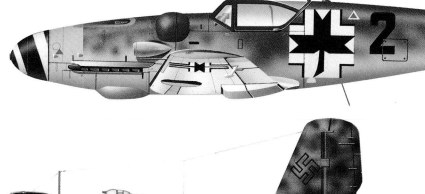

Last of the Luftwaffe

By late 1944 the Luftwaffe was a shadow of its former self, facing superior aircraft, and even some better trained pilots on every front. The rapid introduction of new types and the assistance of new allies could do little to change the course of the war, and catastrophe followed calamity as the once-mighty Luftwaffe covered the Wehrmacht's retreat.

Messerschmitt Bf 109G-10
Messerschmitt Bf 109s were used throughout the entire Russian campaign. By 1944, the Bf 109G-10 was in action and these proved a challenge to Soviet pilots if flown well. Three years of war had taken their toll on the *experten* and the Jagdgruppen, and many Bf 109s were flown by less experienced pilots and units. This G-10 was flown by Kroat Jagdstaffel at Eichwalde, as denoted by the fuselage cross and fin shield.

Heinkel He 177A-5/R6
A Heinkel He 177A-5/R6 Greif operated by 1 Gruppe, KG 1 'Hindenburg' in May 1944. Led by Oberstleutnant Horst von Riesen, KG 1 assembled some 90 He 177s for attacks on Allied communications and military concentrations.

Arado Ar 232B-0
The ugly Arado Ar 232B-0 was a four-engined development of the twin-engined Ar 232A (of which only two prototypes were built). Nicknamed *Tausendfussler* (millipede), a small number served on the Eastern Front in 1944.

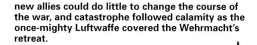

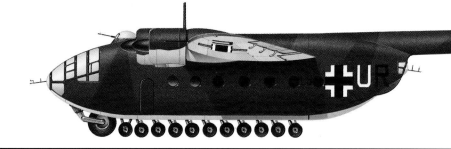

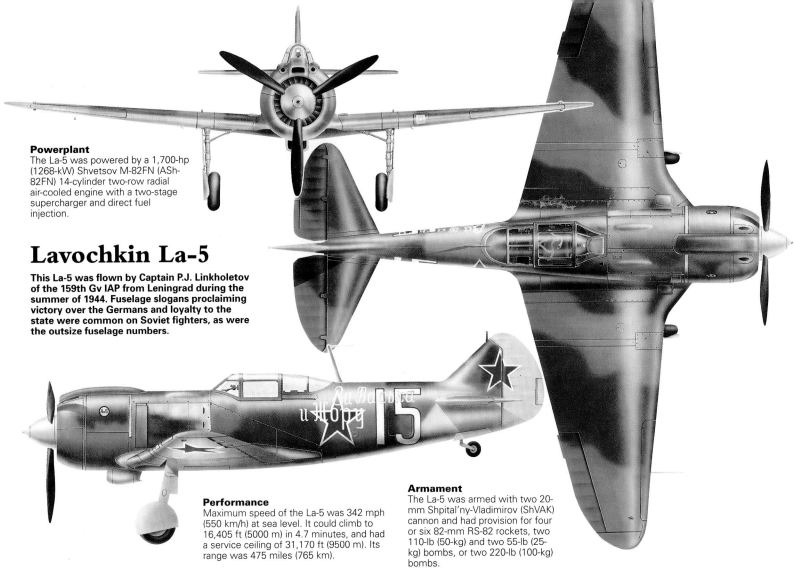

Powerplant
The La-5 was powered by a 1,700-hp (1268-kW) Shvetsov M-82FN (ASh-82FN) 14-cylinder two-row radial air-cooled engine with a two-stage supercharger and direct fuel injection.

Lavochkin La-5

This La-5 was flown by Captain P.J. Linkholetov of the 159th Gv IAP from Leningrad during the summer of 1944. Fuselage slogans proclaiming victory over the Germans and loyalty to the state were common on Soviet fighters, as were the outsize fuselage numbers.

Performance
Maximum speed of the La-5 was 342 mph (550 km/h) at sea level. It could climb to 16,405 ft (5000 m) in 4.7 minutes, and had a service ceiling of 31,170 ft (9500 m). Its range was 475 miles (765 km).

Armament
The La-5 was armed with two 20-mm Shpital'ny-Vladimirov (ShVAK) cannon and had provision for four or six 82-mm RS-82 rockets, two 110-lb (50-kg) and two 55-lb (25-kg) bombs, or two 220-lb (100-kg) bombs.

The long-nose Fw 190D-9 appeared on the Russian Front in early 1945 and restored some of the balance over the Yak-3 and La-7. Several were captured by the Soviet navy Baltic Fleet and used by them.

27 and 55 caught the American B-17s on the ground at Poltava on 22 June, destroying 47 of them as well as the base's fuel dump.

SOVIETS STORM THROUGH

The city of Vilna fell to the Soviet armies on 9 July, completing the recapture of Belorussia and opening the way for an advance into north-eastern Poland while, farther south, Marshal Konev's forces reached the Vistula 130 miles (210 km) south of Warsaw. At this point German resistance on the central front stiff-ened and the swift advance by the Soviet armies temporarily over-extended their supply lines. The Soviets therefore switched the focus of their great offensive to the Balkans, and on 20 August two Soviet army groups, supported by more than 1,700 aircraft of the 5th and 17th Air Armies, launched an offensive on the Odessa front against Romania, where the puppet Axis government was overthrown three days later. Bulgaria capitulated on 8 September, but despite the loss of almost 20 German divisions and the capture of the Ploesti oilfields, the surviving Axis air forces in the Balkans (largely comprising the Luftwaffe's Luftflotten II and IV – the former redeployed from France in August – and the small

Hungarian air force) continued to fight desperately against the huge Soviet air forces.

HEAVY LOSSES

By December 1944 the Eastern Front extended from the mouth of the Niemen river on the Baltic coast to Warsaw and on to Budapest. During the previous six months the German army had suf-fered the loss of more than 800,000 men in the east and almost 400,000 in the west and south. The Soviets now fielded 55 armies and six tank armies, while their first-line aircraft strength had increased to more than 15,500, against which Germany could muster fewer than 2,000.

Following requests by the Americans, who had suffered some 40,000 casualties during the

Ardennes offensive late in December 1944 and sought relief from German pressure, the Soviets started their final winter offensive earlier than originally planned. On 13 January 1945 the drive opened in East Prussia but met with stub-born resistance at the fortress town of Konigsberg, efforts by the Soviet air force to assist being hampered by bad weather. On 17 January Warsaw was finally captured, and a fortnight later the 5th Shock Army and 2nd Guards Army crossed the frozen Oder river at Kustrin, only

Towards the end of 1943, the first Petlyakov Pe-2FTs left the assembly lines with new VK-105PF engines, the same as used for the Yak-3 and Yak-9. This gave the Pe-2FT a welcome increase in performance of 40 km/h.

RUSSIAN ACES

The great Soviet drive in the centre was held in two stages. The second offensive, known as the Lvov-Sandemii campaign, started on 13 July 1944. Mention should be made of the work of the 2nd VA. Ten units were given Gvdaya (Guards) titles, while 17 pilots became Heroes of the Soviet Union. From 1944, the standard of combat fighting of Soviet fighter pilots had steadily improved, and by the end of the war many had gained large scores.

Below: Dimitri G. Glinka, seen here in 1943 and already an ace. By the end of the war he was credited with 50 'kills'.

Above: On the Second Belorussian Front in 1944, Soviet fighter pilot 1st Lt Kiselyov is pictured with the burnt out wreckage of his ninth downed enemy aircraft.

Right: Lt Colonel Ivan N. Kozhedub, the V-VS's leading ace, claimed the last of his 62 'kills' on 19 April 1945. Flying a Lavochkin La-7 with the 176 'Guards' IAP, Kozhedub destroyed 12 enemy aircraft, including an Me 262 jet fighter on 15 February 1945.

Below: Alexander Pokryshkin is congratulated after another successful aerial battle. By the end of the war he had been awarded the title 'Hero of the Soviet Union' three times.

Above: Alexander I. Pokryshkin was a leading ace in the Kuban campaign in 1943 flying P-39 Airacobras of N.V. Isayev's 16th GV IAP, then as a Captain. Promoted to Major, he became a full Colonel by 1945.

Left: Pictured on the Second Belorussian Front in 1945, Lt Natasha Meklin of the Tamansky (Women's) Air Regiment made some 1,000 combat sorties during World War II.

Left: Production of the Il-4 long-range bomber lasted from 1936 until 1944. This line-up of new aircraft of the final version awaits delivery in 1944. Powered by 1,000-hp M-88B engines, the Il-4 achieved a maximum speed of 410 km/h.

about 50 miles (80 km) east of Berlin; to the southeast Soviet armies reached and invested Breslau.

The final three months of the war were characterised by increased savagery in the air as the shrinking perimeter of Hitler's Reich eased the problems of defence. The Luftwaffe even switched a large proportion of its surviving fighter forces (including JG 1, JG 3, JG 6,

Right: The best-known Red Air Force fighter unit (at least in the West) was the French-mannd 'Normandie' regiment, given the honour title 'Niemen' in 1944. After flying Yak-9s, the unit changed to the excellent Yak-3 (illustrated).

Victory in the Air

By 1945 the Luftwaffe had been beaten on all fronts. Yak-9s roamed at will, picking off young inexperienced German pilots (and some of the exhausted *experten*) while Il-2s supported Zhukhov's headlong rush on Berlin. Though crude and lightweight, Russia's combat aircraft were establishing a well-earned reputation for combat effectiveness.

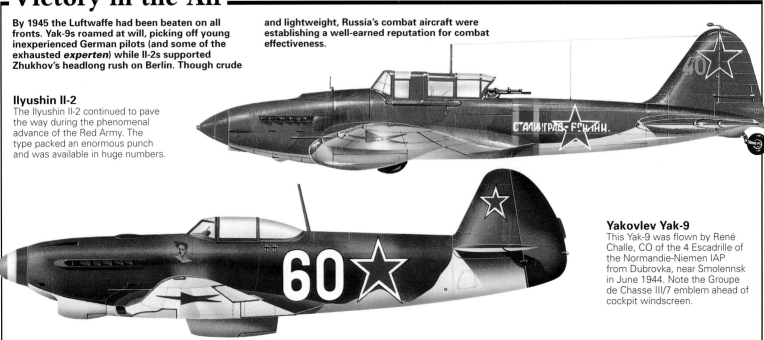

Ilyushin Il-2
The Ilyushin Il-2 continued to pave the way during the phenomenal advance of the Red Army. The type packed an enormous punch and was available in huge numbers.

Yakovlev Yak-9
This Yak-9 was flown by René Challe, CO of the 4 Escadrille of the Normandie-Niemen IAP from Dubrovka, near Smolennsk in June 1944. Note the Groupe de Chasse III/7 emblem ahead of cockpit windscreen.

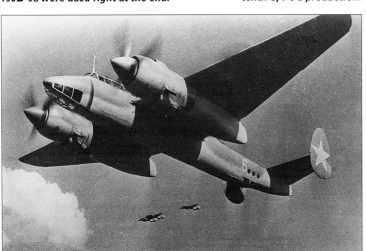

Above: Pilots of Schlachtgeschwader 2 'Immelmann' rest between missions. The Stab and II Gruppe used Fw 190As and Fs on the Russian Front. A few Fw 190D-9s were used right at the end.

Below: Throughout the war, the designation Tu-2S remained unchanged, despite modifications. Only 1,111 of this fast, popular aircraft were built – about one-tenth of Pe-2 production.

JG 11 and JG 77) from the west and south to the east, believing that their pilots would stand a better chance of countering the Soviet air force despite the overwhelming odds. The German air force resorted to desperate measures to halt the advancing Soviets, employing the extraordinary Mistel composite aircraft in widespread attacks on the Soviet bridges and bridgeheads over the Oder and Vistula, and achieving a considerable measure of success.

As the Soviet armies fought their way through Berlin's streets early in May, the once-vaunted Luftwaffe lay scattered on its few remaining airfields, finally grounded without fuel and at the mercy of Allied bombers.

Above: A line-up of 1st Czechoslovak Fighter Regiment Lavochkin La-5FN fighters at Proskurov in the Ukraine on 11 September 1944. The regiment was formed with a nucleus of ex-RAF Czech pilots.

Below: The twin-engined Ar 232 V2. Because of the demands of Fw 190 production for BMW engines, most Ar 232s had lower-powered engines. Ar 232s of Transportflierstaffel 5 flew missions into Soviet territory.

Sporadic attacks were made against bridges on the Eastern Front, but heavy losses were suffered by the Mistels. Development continued with the combination of Ju 88G-10s (Mistel C) and H-4s (Mistel B) with the Fw 190A-8. Here an Fw 190 releases its Ju 88 missile, closely followed by a second combination.

Mistel attack

Using surplus Ju 88 night-fighters or bombers as makeshift guided missiles was just one of the desperate schemes attempted by the Luftwaffe during the final year of the war. A pilot tells his story.

"The Mistels were diving now, their airspeed indicators hovering around 600 km/h. The leading Oberfeldwebel turned into his final approach from the south and went into an even steeper dive, sending his speed up still further. He had to retrim the aircraft to counteract the increased forces acting on his controls, but the target, the railway bridge at Steinau, remained steady in his reflex sight.

"This was the most important part of the whole procedure, to keep the composite aircraft rock steady on the final target approach flight. Even the slightest movement on the controls affected the delicate mechanism of the gyroscopes controlling the automatic pilot. 'Flying on your nerves,' the pilots called it, discussing such missions to well-defended targets, but now, in action, there wasn't the time to think about it. Altitude, airspeed and target were the important things.

"The ideal release point was around a thousand metres from the target. At that distance the flying bomb was unlikely to miss. But at that range, neither were the light anti-aircraft gunners.

"The airspeed indicator was up to 650 km/h now, the Mistel in a steady high-speed dive, correctly trimmed and free of any acceleration. The autopilot was working perfectly, and the whole contraption could have been flown hands-off if necessary. But where was the AA fire we dreaded, and where were the other aircraft?

"I could see the bridge clearly now, make out its every detail. An iron girder structure, resting on pillars of solid masonry. To be sure of destroying it, the Mistel would have to hit one of these pillars, and that would need pinpoint precision and a fair bit of luck as well.

"In the sight I could see, framed, the bridge section on the left bank. A final slight correction, and the illuminated graticule and the pillar coincided exactly. Now! A slight pressure on the release button, the muffled sound of light detonations as the explosive bolts

went, and then the controlling fighter was free again! A steep bank to the west, and then I could look around at the spot on the ground where I had aimed the flying bomb. An enormous fountain was climbing, climbing up into the sky. I couldn't decide whether it was water or mud, earth and more solid debris from the bridge structure itself.

"But there was little time for sightseeing, for now the Soviet anti-aircraft guns were firing like mad, and anyway a great cloud of smoke was billowing over the bridge, obscuring it from view. Suddenly, another Bf 109 appeared alongside. The initial cold shock, that it could have been an enemy fighter, gave way to joyous relief at having a comrade alongside for

company and mutual protection. We both stuck up our thumbs. No problems!

"Neither of us cared exactly where we were. Out of habit we'd both pressed our stopwatches over the target, and now relied on spotting a railway line, a town or, better still, an Autobahn, to help us locate ourselves. We were both 'old foxes', and navigating in daylight, in good weather, over our own homeland was certainly no problem. And we'd both successfully flown our first live Mistel operation!"

The Einsatz-Staffel of IV Gruppe of KG 101 flew its first operation with the Mistel 1 pilotless missile on 24 June 1944, with the pilot of the Bf 109F-4 fighter aiming the Ju 88A-4 missile.

The Jet Goes to War

MAY 1944 – MAY 1945

Among the closely guarded secrets of the early part of the war was the work being done both in the UK and Germany on the gas turbine as a powerplant for aircraft. In particular, British intelligence was unaware that Germany had successfully flown a small research jet aeroplane, the Heinkel He 178, as

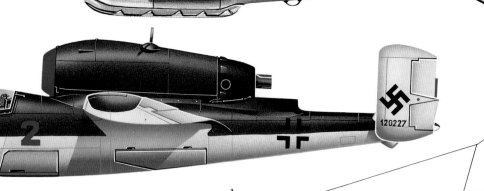

Left: The pilot climbs into a Messerschmitt Me 163B-1a at Bad Zwischenahn where it was flown by the trials and test unit Erprobungskommando 16 that accepted its first aircraft in May 1944 and pioneered the rocket plane's entry into service with the Luftwaffe.

early as 27 August 1939, five days before the outbreak of World War II. For years parallel work had been carried out by Frank Whittle in the UK but, because of lack of official interest, his work had been slow and underfinanced. It was not until May 1941 that the first British research jet, the Gloster E.28/39, powered by a Whittle

Above: A Rolls-Royce Welland-powered Gloster Meteor Mk I, the 11th production aircraft, that was delivered to No. 616 Squadron in July 1944. The Meteor was the only Allied jet to see action in the war.

engine, was first flown.

In the belief that the war would be short-lived, work on the development of an operational jet

Jet and rocket pioneers

German engineers made giant strides with turbojet and rocket propulsion. The Me 163 suffered many accidents resulting from its lethal fuel mixture but was mildly successful as an interceptor. The

He 162 was an abortive attempt to provide a mass-produced jet fighter and was too late for service. The Ar 234 was the world's first jet bomber. Its service entry was delayed by production problems.

Messerschmitt Me 163B

This Komet saw service with JG 400 at Brandis. It was one of 279 aircraft delivered to the Luftwaffe and had two 30-mm Rheinmetall MK 108 cannon fitted in the wing roots, each with 60 rounds of ammunition carried in the top of the fuselage.

Heinkel He 162A

Powered by the improved BMW 003E-1 turbojet, this He 162A-2 Salamander was flown by II/JG 1 at Leck in the spring of 1945. For operations, 50 aircraft were reorganised as part of the Einsatz Gruppe I/JG 1. No encounters with Allied aircraft were confirmed before the war ended.

Arado Ar 234B

Ar 234B Blitz reconnaissance bombers were powered by two Junkers Jumo 004B turbojets. This aircraft, carrying bombs under its engine nacelles, was flown by 9/KG 76 in February 1945. Ar 234s made high-level reconnaissance flights over England, beyond the reach of fighters.

Below: A Messerschmitt Me 262A-1a Schwalbe of EJG 2. In the interceptor role the twin-jet could carry 24 R4M rockets under its wings, in addition to the four built-in 30-mm MK 108 cannon. It had 100 rounds for the upper guns and 80 for the lower pair, giving formidable firepower.

METEOR VERSUS FLYING BOMB
Meteor Mk Is joined the battle against the 'Doodlebugs' on 27 July 1944, when an aircraft from No. 616 Squadron flew its first successful operational sortie from RAF Manston, Kent.

aircraft in Germany went ahead relatively slowly until 1940, the Heinkel company pushing on with development of its pioneer HeS 3b and HeS 6 turbojets. Discouraged by the problems with single-engine installation, however, the company ventured to produce a twin-jet fighter, the He 280, the first prototype of which, powered by two 500-kg (1,102-lb) thrust HeS 8 (109-006) turbojets, was flown on 2 April 1941. This design was not adopted by RLM for production and is of interest if only to illustrate

the weight of interest by the German aircraft industry in jet power, while the UK was still only taking its first faltering steps in the concept.

Meanwhile the Messerschmitt company had also opted for a twin-jet layout for a fighter. This turbojet fighter, the Me 262, was designed around a pair of Junkers 109-004A turbojets, of which the first example was bench-run in November 1940. Because flight engines were not available in time, the first Me 262 prototype was flown under piston

Below: For take-off the Arado Ar 234A, the first version of the Blitz, sat on a large trolley. This could be steered by the pilot using its nosewheel; brakes were fitted to the mainwheels. Once it reached flying speed the trolley was released. A retractable skid and outriggers were used for landing.

Right: A Messerschmitt Me 163B-1a receiving hydrogen peroxide (T-stoff) fuel for its Hellmuth Walter RII-211 rocket motor. It could carry only enough fuel for six minutes at full throttle after which it would have to glide back to its base – leaving no margin for error by the pilot.

Left: An Me 163B takes off, jettisoning its take-off dolly. If jettisoned too early this could bounce back up into the departing Komet; sometimes they refused to release at all. However, compared with the hazards of landing on the aircraft's retractable skid, take-offs were relatively safe.

Right: JG 400, based at Brandis in 1944, carried the famous badge depicting a 'rocket-powered flea' and the inscription 'Wie ein floh – aber Oho!' (Only a flea – but Oho!) on the noses of its Me 163B-1as. JG 400 recorded nine Allied bomber kills, including two probables.

engine power on 18 April 1941, and it was not until 15 March 1942 that a Messerschmitt Me 262 was flown under all-jet power, being fitted with a pair of 840-kg (1,852-lb) thrust Junkers 109-004A-0 turbojets. By October that year 60 Me 262s had been ordered for use as development aircraft. From the fifth aircraft onwards a nosewheel landing gear arrangement was adopted in place of the tailwheel type previously used.

It was not until November 1943 that any urgency was afforded to the Me 262 programme, and it was Hitler himself who, despite protests from the Luftwaffe, insisted that the aircraft should go ahead, but only as a bomber which he assumed to be

capable of carrying a 500-kg (1,102-lb) bomb to England. Nevertheless, Messerschmitt continued also to press ahead with a fighter version armed with four 30-mm cannon, and during the summer of 1944 the first pre-production Me 262A-0s were delivered to Erprobungsstelle Rechlin for service trials, the fighter version being named the Schwalbe (swallow) and the bomber the Sturmvogel (stormbird). The first operational fighter unit, Kommando Nowotny (led by the fighter ace Major Walter

Above: This Me 262A-1a was flown by III Gruppe of Ergänzungs-Jagdgeschwader 2. The conversion unit, formed on 2 November 1944 at Lechfeld, flew many sorties against Allied aircraft in the spring of 1945. Leutnant Bell downed a P-38 Lightning with this particular aircraft on 21 March 1945.

Nowotny), was formed at Achmer and Hesepe on 3 October 1944 with about 20 Me 262A fighters for defence against the American daylight heavy bombers. Although the appearance of the new jets caused consternation among the American crews, the early jets achieved poor

Above: Messerschmitt AG built no fewer than 70 pre-production Me 163Bs at Regensburg, all assigned to particular operational or mechanical problems. The most dangerous phase of flight was the landing, which had to be perfect every time. Here the 35th Me 163B, coded GH+IN, glides safely to a halt on its skid.

Right: Gloster Meteor F.Mk III EE274 operating with No. 616 Squadron at B.58 Melsbroek, Belgium early in 1945. Deliveries of these more reliable Welland-powered Meteors to the RAF commenced on 18 December 1944 and a No. 616 detachment joined the 2nd Tactical Air Force in Belgium in January.

Messerschmitt Me 262A

This Messerschmitt Me 262A-1a wears the markings of
9 Staffel of Jagdgeschwader 7 based at Parchim in early-1945
under 1 Jagddivision of I Jagdcorps, operating in defence of
the Reich in its dying weeks.

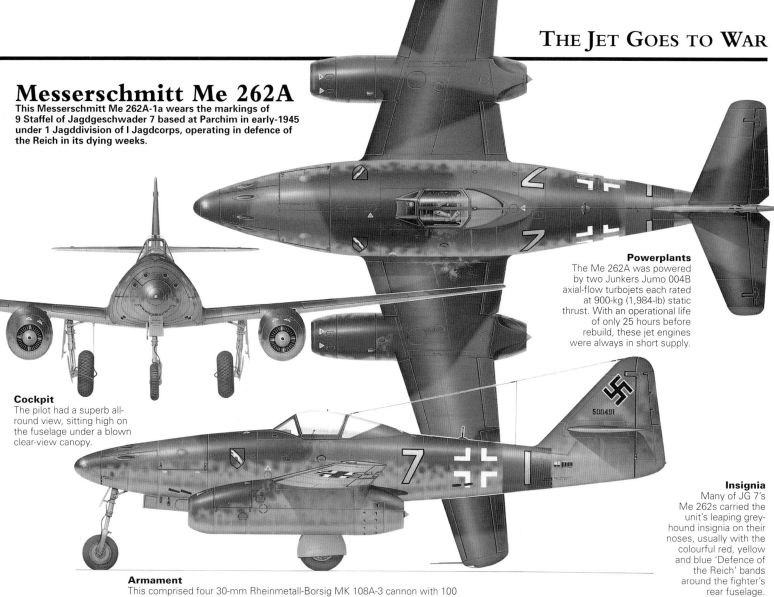

Powerplants
The Me 262A was powered
by two Junkers Jumo 004B
axial-flow turbojets each rated
at 900-kg (1,984-lb) static
thrust. With an operational life
of only 25 hours before
rebuild, these jet engines
were always in short supply.

Cockpit
The pilot had a superb all-
round view, sitting high on
the fuselage under a blown
clear-view canopy.

Insignia
Many of JG 7's
Me 262s carried the
unit's leaping grey-
hound insignia on their
noses, usually with the
colourful red, yellow
and blue 'Defence of
the Reich' bands
around the fighter's
rear fuselage.

Armament
This comprised four 30-mm Rheinmetall-Borsig MK 108A-3 cannon with 100
rounds per gun for the upper pair and 80 rounds for the lower guns, aimed with a
Revi 16B gunsight or Askania EZ42 gyro-stabilised sight. It also had provision for
12 R4M air-to-air rocket projectiles under each wing.

*Left: While an Me 262 gets close in
behind a USAAF P-51 Mustang,
another P-51 bears down on the
less manoeuvrable jet fighter, in
this gun-camera photograph. The
Mustangs were escorting heavy
bombers on a raid over Germany.*

*Below: Operated by the German
Aviation Experimental
Establishment (DVL) in April 1944
for high-speed testing and engine
trials, this Me 262 was in fact the
first prototype to fly on turbojet
power alone on 18 July 1942. It was
written off on 12 September 1944
following an Allied air raid.*

results because of their sluggish
acceleration after pilots had been
cruising slowly to increase patrol
time. When Nowotny was killed on
8 November a new unit, JG 7,
came into being, and early in 1945
another unit, Jagdverband 44 commanded by General Adolf Galland
and crewed by some of the
Luftwaffe's top fighter pilots
(including Barkhorn, Steinhoff,
Lützow and Späte) was formed.
Although lack of fuel and poor
serviceability reduced the average
airworthy strength of this unit to no

*Above: This Me 163B-1a, under tow
from a 'Scheuschlepper' tug,
carries the colour scheme adopted
by JG 400 Erganzungstaffel, the
Komet training squadron based at
Brandis. Operating the aircraft with
its highly volatile fuel caused many
problems for this training unit.*

more than about six aircraft, JV 44
destroyed more than 40 Allied
aircraft in about a month.

JET DEFENDERS

Before the end of the war Me 262
fighters equipped about half a

widespread use which could have threatened the continuation of the heavy American daylight bomber offensive in the last year of the war. They were not immune to attack from Allied fighters, particularly in the hands of experienced pilots, and there were occasions when Tempest and P-51 pilots succeeded in downing the enemy jets.

Despite its late start, the RAF introduced the Meteor Mk 1 twin-jet fighter into service (with No. 616 Squadron) in July 1944, before the first fully-operational Luftwaffe jet fighter unit was formed. Benefiting from British jet research, the Americans too had produced a jet fighter – the Lockheed P-80 Shooting Star. By VE-Day two examples were being readied for combat in Italy and two had reached England.

However, despite these developments there was no jet-versus-jet combat in World War II.

Above: A Heinkel He 162A at speed showing clearly the turned-down wingtips first introduced to overcome manoeuvrability problems. The aircraft had such difficult handling characteristics that even experienced fighter pilots found it an unforgiving handful to fly.

Below: This two-seat Me 262B-1a/U1 under test in the USA after the war. It had been captured after service with 10/NJG 11. Its armament was two 30-mm MK 108A-3s and two 20-mm MG 151/20 cannon. The air interception radar in the nose was a FuG 218 (Neptun V).

which had been equally protracted, but which also entered service on a limited scale) undoubtedly caused some concern to the Allies on account of their very high speed and heavy armament, Hitler's interference certainly prevented their

Below: An Me 262A 'Schwalbe' captured intact by advancing American troops on 18 April 1945. Except for a damaged undercarriage it was fairly intact. Partly hidden in a wood, it was fuelled and its guns were loaded. Over the period from March 1944 to 20 April 1945 the Luftwaffe received 1,433 Me 262s.

dozen Gruppen, including some night-fighter Staffeln whose two-seat radar-equipped Me 262B-1a/U1 aircraft were used in the night defence of Berlin in the last weeks of the war. Bomber versions of the Me 262 also entered service alongside another German jet bomber, the Arado Ar 234, an exceptionally 'clean' twin-jet aircraft which was also used to fly reconnaissance missions at up to 12250 m (40,200 ft) over the

UK and Italy without any fear of interception by Allied fighters.

Although the appearance of these German jet aircraft (as well as the rocket-powered Messerschmitt Me 163 Komet, development of

Right: The adoption of a tricycle undercarriage on the improved Arado Ar 234B enabled bombs to be carried under the fuselage centre-section. This aircraft has a 1000-kg (2,200-lb) SC1000 'Hermann' bomb used for the attacks on the Remagen bridges early in 1945.

Into Combat

Had it not been for Hitler's demand that the Messerschmitt Me 262 be developed as a bomber, the Allies would have faced a much more devastating adversary in a high-performance air defence fighter. Erprobungskommando 262 evaluated the new aircraft operationally in the fighter role from mid-1944. Leutnant 'Quax' Schnoerrer of EKdo 262 recounts his early experiences.

"When I took off with my mob on 21 March, I thought it was to go against a large American force attacking the Leipzig/Dresden area. The radio jamming was particularly heavy that day and as a result communication was just about impossible. At 24,000 ft and still south of Dresden, I came upon a lone B-17 Flying Fortress flying east at the same altitude as the main force but 16 miles off to the side and four behind. It had four P-51 Mustangs as its escort and it seemed to me that it must be on some special mission. I decided to have a go at it.

"I made a pass close beneath the Mustangs, who followed my lads away, trailing black smoke. That meant they were flying at full throttle. I looked down at the airspeed indicator. Plenty in reserve and no need to worry about them.

"The Boeing was ahead of me now, making a left-hand turn. At about 3,000 ft the rear gunner opened up to try to harass me into making a mistake, but that was all over in seconds. At about a third of that range my wingman and I both opened up with our cannon, giving it a short burst, allowing our guns to lead the bomber. We saw a dozen rounds or more strike the fuselage and between the engines, and then our superior speed took us past him.

"We curved round in a wide circle, the Mustangs still behind us but just dwindling dots now, and observed the bomber's end. It spun down through 6,500 ft, pieces breaking off the whole time and then exploded."

A scene perhaps more reminiscent of 1943 than of 1945. By that time the Luftwaffe wasn't shooting down too many Allied bombers on the raids that were taking them

daily ever deeper into Germany, in ever-increasing strength. Just one thing stood between the Allies and total air supremacy – the world's first jet fighter.

However, Hitler's insistence that the Me 262 be employed in the bombing role, plus the daily devastation of German industry caused by the Allies bombing campaign, prevented the large-scale introduction of Me 262 fighters. Consequently, providing pilots with enough experience in the radical new fighter to allow successful combat operations hampered their effectiveness further.

Leutnant Schnoerrer also encountered 'teething' difficulties during early operational flying. In fact, on one of his first jet missions he had a very lucky escape. After making an attack on American B-17s he entered a high-speed dive to escape pursuing fighters.

"I pulled back on the stick with all my strength, but the 262 just refused to come out of the dive. Finally, in desperation, I jettisoned my canopy to evacuate the aircraft: this caused a change of trim, and the aircraft came out of it by itself. When I landed I could see the ripples on the skin of the wings. The aircraft was a complete write-off."

Despite the brilliance of the design the Me 262 entered service too late to change the course of the war. By early-May 1945 the shortage of resources and pilots had rendered the Luftwaffe's jet aircraft force impotent.

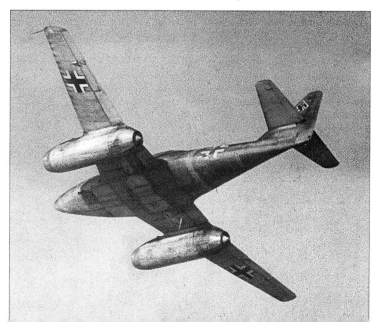

Right: The Me 262 was a remarkably responsive yet docile aircraft, with pleasantly harmonised controls and comfortable stick forces. A tendency to snake at high Mach numbers made it somewhat more difficult to get its guns onto a target at long range.

WORLD WAR II IN THE PACIFIC

The Imperial Japanese Navy's principal torpedo-bomber was to be known to the Allies as 'Kate'. The Nakajima B5N was, despite its vulnerability, able to score notable successes at Pearl Harbor and later in the Pacific theatre.

Japan made its intentions clear with the attack on Pearl Harbor that began the Pacific war on 7 December 1941. They gambled all on a war of short duration, but for almost four years battles were to rage on land, sea and in the air.

Capital ships of the Pacific Fleet ablaze at their moorings. USS West Virginia (BB-48), in the foreground, was hit by six or seven torpedoes and two bombs and lost 105 crew, including its captain. Behind is the USS Tennessee (BB-43).

The Japanese air attack on the American naval base at Pearl Harbor, Hawaii, was the manifestation of militarist expansionism that had gained expression in the Tokyo government as the result of a decade of successful adventures on the Chinese mainland, which had witnessed unremitting strengthening of Japan's army and navy. It was acknowledged that such territorial expansion in the Pacific would inevitably provoke war with the United States, and to have any chance of defeating the industrial might of that nation it was essential to open hostilities sooner rather than later, so as to take advantage of the USA's unpreparedness. The Roosevelt administration, on the other hand, after years of pre-occupation with events in Europe, began backing its traditional friends, the UK and France, against Germany, with the supply of war materials; it woke up to the Japanese threat in the Pacific during 1941, but could do little but make token efforts to strengthen American outposts on Wake and Midway islands.

DIPLOMACY FAILS

Even as Japanese and American diplomats met in Washington in attempts to reduce acrimony between the two nations and so to avert war, a large Japanese naval task force was at sea on course for Pearl Harbor. This force was not in fact the principal Japanese thrust, but was intended to prevent the US Pacific Fleet from interfering with their major assault in the south against the East Indies, whose oil and rubber resources were so vital to Japan's long-term strategic plans.

The strike force which made for Pearl Harbor comprised the six attack carriers, *Akagi, Hlryu, Kaga, Shokaku, Soryu* and *Zuikaku,* supported by two battleships, two

Above: On Ford Island, bewildered sailors look over the assembled PBY Catalina flying-boats and OS2U Kingfisher floatplanes, all with varying degrees of damage. A total of 188 American aircraft were destroyed. Only 30 of the 350 attacking aircraft were shot down.

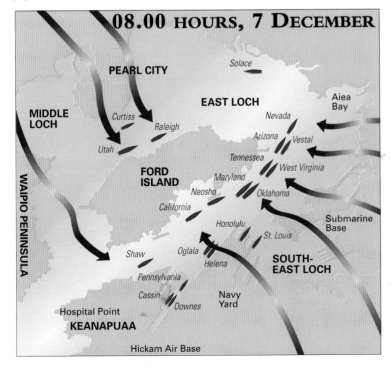

08.00 HOURS, 7 DECEMBER

PEARL CITY

Solace

MIDDLE LOCH

EAST LOCH

Aiea Bay

Curtiss

Raleigh

Nevada

Utah

Arizona Vestal

Tennessee

FORD ISLAND

Maryland

West Virginia

Neosho

Oklahoma

California

Honolulu

St. Louis

Submarine Base

WAIPIO PENINSULA

Shaw

Oglala

Helena

SOUTH-EAST LOCH

Pennsylvania

Cassin

Downes

Navy Yard

Hospital Point

KEANAPUAA

Hickam Air Base

Left: The first wave of more than 180 Japanese aircraft, led by Commander Fuchida, closed on Oahu from the north, with dive-bombers and fighters peeling off to deal with the various air bases while the torpedo bombers took Pearl Harbor from two sides.

Below: A still from a Japanese newsreel, this frame shows a Zero from the Hiryu departing on a sortie over Pearl. A6Ms provided fighter cover for the strike aircraft, but as their was little opposition to the attack, they resorted to strafing ground and waterborne targets.

Left: A Japanese photograph showing Pearl Harbor ablaze after the devastating attack. The most vital targets of all, however, had been missed. By chance, the three Pacific fleet carriers, Enterprise, Lexington *and* Saratoga *were at sea at the time of the attack.*

Above: Dawn, 7 December 1941, north-east of Hawaii. Aboard the carrier Shokaku, *a Mitsubishi A6M2 Zero fighter and several Nakajima B5N2 torpedo-bombers prepare to launch. In all, 94 of the latter took part in the Pearl raid; only six were lost.*

heavy cruisers, one light cruiser, nine destroyers and three submarines. Anchored in Pearl Harbor were eight battleships, eight cruisers, 29 destroyers, five submarines and 44 other naval vessels. Fortunately for the Americans the Pacific Fleet's three aircraft-carriers, *Enterprise*, *Lexington* and *Saratoga*, whose survival was to be crucial in the subsequent Pacific war, were at sea or on the west coast of the USA.

Led by Commander Mitsuo Fuchida, the first wave of the Japanese air strike, comprising 51 Aichi D3A1 dive-bombers, 49 Nakajima B5N2 level bombers, 40 B5N2 torpedo-bombers and 43 Mitsubishi A6M2 Zero fighters,

Left: Ford Island, Pearl Harbor, as seen from a Japanese aircraft in the first wave of the air attack. The torpedo burst alongside 'battleship row', which marks a hit on either the USS *West Virginia or* USS *Oklahoma, and places the time at about 08.00 hours.*

Fighters at Pearl

Mitsubishi's A6M came as a revelation to the US Navy, with its exceptional range and manoeuvrability. It was destined to take part in almost every major action involving the Imperial Japanese Navy.

The Wildcat was one of a new breed of aircraft to enter service with the US Navy and Marine Corp. Only a handful of Squadrons had re-equipped with the F4F at the time of Pearl Harbor

Mitsubishi A6M2 Zero
One of the Zeros making up the fighter complement aboard the *Hiryu*, this machine took part in the attack of 7 December 1941. The navy had taken delivery of 328 A6Ms by then; these equipping most front-line fighter units. This total comprised the initial production A6M2 Model 11 and (from the 65th aircraft) Model 21 with folding wingtips for easier stowage aboard carriers.

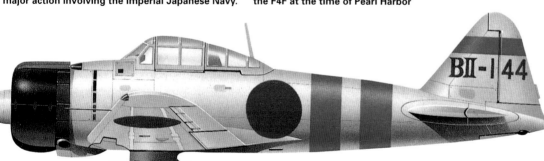

Grumman F4F-3A Wildcat
The Wildcat was one of the US Navy's state-off-the-art aircraft when they entered the war. This aircaft is from VF-6 aboard USS Enterprise and flown by Ensign James G Daniels on 7 December 1941. Enterprise was at Wake island when the Japanese attacked Pearl Harbour.

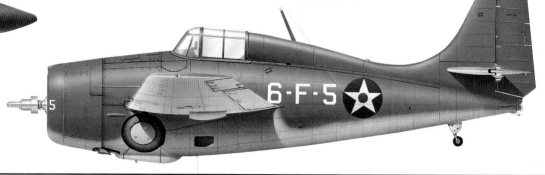

Above: An official Japanese photograph of B5N2s en route to Pearl Harbor. Only five of these torpedo bombers were shot down. Thirty aircraft were lost in total; a small number for the results gained.

Above: USAAF aircraft were lost at Hickham Field. This B-17C of the 19th Bombardment Group lies near Hangar No. 5 after the attack. Many Flying Fortresses were lost at Hickham; the following day more were destroyed at Clark Field in the Philippines.

Below: The destroyer USS Shaw was in Floating Dock No. 2 on 7 December. Bombs hitting the forward portion of the ship ruptured oil tanks and spread fire throughout the ship. Eventually the forward magazine exploded spectacularly, as seen here.

started launching from their carriers at 06.00 on 7 December 1941; 75 minutes later a second wave of 78 D3A1s, 54 B5N2s and 35 A6M2s, led by Lieutenant Commander Shigekazu Shimazaki, took off and set course for the American base.

The first bomb to strike home in the devastating attack fell at 07.55 on the naval air station on Ford Island, destroying six PBY flying-boats and putting out of action an entire patrol squadron. The attack achieved total surprise. Expecting to find five carriers anchored in Pearl Harbor, the Japanese pilots were quickly ordered to concentrate their attention on the battleships, neatly moored along Ford Island. The battleship *Nevada,* at the head of the row, was hit by a single torpedo

before her crew cast off and the ship took a couple of direct hits by bombs; as she made for the open sea she was again hit by bombs and had to be beached with 50 dead aboard. Next in line, the *Arizona* was hit by several torpedoes as well as eight bombs before her shattered hulk sank to the shallow bottom, taking 1,103 crewmen with her. The *West Virginia* received half a dozen torpedo hits and settled to the bottom with 105 dead. Next, the *Oklahoma* was hit by five torpedoes and capsized, trapping 415 men. The last ship in 'battleship row' was the *California,* struck by two torpedoes; with unsecured watertight compartments she eventually foundered three nights later having lost 98 of her crew.

AIRCRAFT DESTROYED

Elsewhere numerous other naval vessels were sunk or severely damaged as the Japanese pilots turned their attention to the airfields and naval air stations. At K'aneohe Field

27 of the 33 PBY flying-boats were destroyed and the remaining six damaged. At Ewa Field there were 49 US Marine Corps fighters and scout bombers; after the Japanese attacks 33 had been destroyed, and none of the remainder could be flown. The story was much the same at the US Army's Hickham Field, where the aircraft were lined up in neat rows; at Wheeler Field 42 US Army aircraft were also destroyed.

Total cost to the Japanese raiding formations amounted to nine A6M2 fighters, 15 D3A1 dive-bombers and five B5N2s, plus one of the latter which ditched near its carrier. Five midget submarines

were also lost without achieving any damage. The air attack had gained spectacular results, killing 2,335 American personnel, leaving four battleships sunk or sinking, damaging four others, sinking three destroyers and a minelayer, and severely damaging two cruisers and a repair ship. In all, 188 aircraft had been destroyed in the air and on the ground, and almost every other aircraft (including several which arrived over Pearl Harbor at the height of the raid having flown from *Enterprise* in ignorance of the attack) was damaged to some extent.

The last of the Japanese aircraft had been recovered aboard their carriers by 13.00 on 7 December. By then the United States was finally at war.

Left: The Japanese carrier Akagi, commissioned in 1927, led the task force of 7 December. Notable features included the small port side island, boiler gases exhausting via a massive downward-curved funnel on the starboard side. The ship was sunk in June 1942.

Malaya and Burma

DECEMBER 1941 – JUNE 1942

Left: A pair of Mitsubishi G3M2 Naval Type 96 attack-bombers (Allied codename 'Nell'). Some 200 G3M2s were serving with front-line Japanese units at the outbreak of war and 60 took part in the mission which led to the sinking of the Prince of Wales and Repulse.

Below: A formation of Brewster Buffaloes from No. 243 Squadron based at Kallang, Singapore. Rejected as a first-line fighter in Europe, Buffaloes diverted to the Far East for the defence of Singapore were hopelessly outclassed by the Japanese Zero.

If the Japanese gained total tactical surprise in their attack on Pearl Harbor, strategic surprise was no less complete against the British in Southeast Asia. Token forces had been spared for the defence of the Malayan peninsula for some years, particularly for the British naval base at Singapore. By December 1941 the British air forces in the whole of the Far East fielded 362 aircraft, of which 233 were serviceable. In Malaya there were four RAF squadrons of Blenheims (Nos 27, 34, 60 and 62), two squadrons (Nos 36 and 100) of antiquated Vildebeest torpedo biplanes, two RAAF squadrons of Hudsons (Nos 1 and 8) and three Catalina flying-boats of No. 230 Squadron. Fighter defence rested upon 52 Buffaloes of No. 243 Squadron, RAF, No. 488 Squadron, RNZAF, and Nos 21 and 453 Squadrons, RAAF. Ranged against this force was the Imperial Japanese Army's 3rd Hikoshidan comprising 11 Sentais and four independent Chutais. Powerful elements of the Japanese fleet were also available, although in the early stages of the Malayan campaign most of its aircraft were shore based, including at least two Sentais of the excellent Mitsubishi A6M fighter.

On 7 December 1941 Japanese forces moved against northern Malaya and were soon ashore at

Kota Bharu. The RAF's initial task was to locate and report the whereabouts of Japanese invasion convoys; the Blenheims, Hudsons and Vildebeests were soon in action but were able to do little to hinder the landings. On the following morning Singapore experienced the first of many air raids, and it soon became clear that the Buffaloes were quite inadequate to match the modern Japanese aircraft. Elsewhere at Alor Star a Japanese raid destroyed all but two of No. 62 Squadron's Blenheims. By the evening of 8 December only 50 RAF aircraft remained serviceable.

Meanwhile reinforcements had been ordered to Singapore, the battleship *Prince of Wales* and the battle cruiser *Repulse* having arrived on 2 December. On 8 December these ships set sail to find and attack the

Above: There had not been enough Hurricanes to defend Singapore in January 1942, but subsequently the type became the RAF's main fighter in action against the Japanese, remaining in Burma until the end of the war. Engine air filters were fitted for the tropical conditions.

Japanese invasion fleets in the north, but within 48 hours had been spotted by the Japanese who dispatched 60 Mitsubishi G3M2 and 26 G4M1 bombers to attack. Devoid of fighter protection, the British warships were quickly sunk, with heavy loss of life.

SINGAPORE FALLS

The other reinforcements (51 Hurricanes shipped by sea) took much longer to arrive and were not ready for action until 20 January 1942, by which time the Japanese army had advanced to within 160 km (100 miles) of Singapore. On that day 27 unescorted Japanese bombers were caught by the Hurricanes whose pilots destroyed eight of the raiders. The next day the bombers returned with an escort of A6M fighters which in turn shot down five Hurricanes without loss. Within a week only 21 Hurricanes were airworthy; by the time the Japanese opened their

direct assault on Singapore island only 10 Hurricanes and a handful of Buffaloes and Vildebeests were available at any one time, and these continued to fight as best they could throughout the two-week evacuation, despite their landing strip at Kallang being under constant Japanese fire. On 15 February the island fortress surrendered.

Long before the fall of Singapore the Japanese had embarked on the conquest of Burma to safeguard their right flank in Southeast Asia. Emulating the German pattern of terror raids, Japanese bombers attacked Rangoon on 23 December 1941, showering the densely-packed marketplaces with fragmentation bombs, killing 2,000 civilians

Below: When the A6M2 Zero was pitted against the Allies in December 1941, its speed, range and manoeuvrability took them by surprise. During the first six months of the war, Zeros of the Striking Force and the 11th Air Fleet proved more than a match for most Allied fighters.

Below: Unable to counter the threat from Japanese aircraft based in Thailand, the Buffaloes of No. 453 Squadron, RAAF fell back to Singapore on 24 December where they merged with No. 21 Squadron. However, the shortcomings of the Buffalo soon led to heavy losses.

Opposing forces

In the opening period of conflict the RAF and its Allies were outclassed by the superior Japanese front-line fighters and bombers. Many of the Far East-based aircraft were obsolete or unserviceable.

Bombers like the Blenheim were decimated by the well-armed Japanese fighters, while there was little defence for the Fleet against the torpedo bombers like the Mitsubishi G3M 'Nell'.

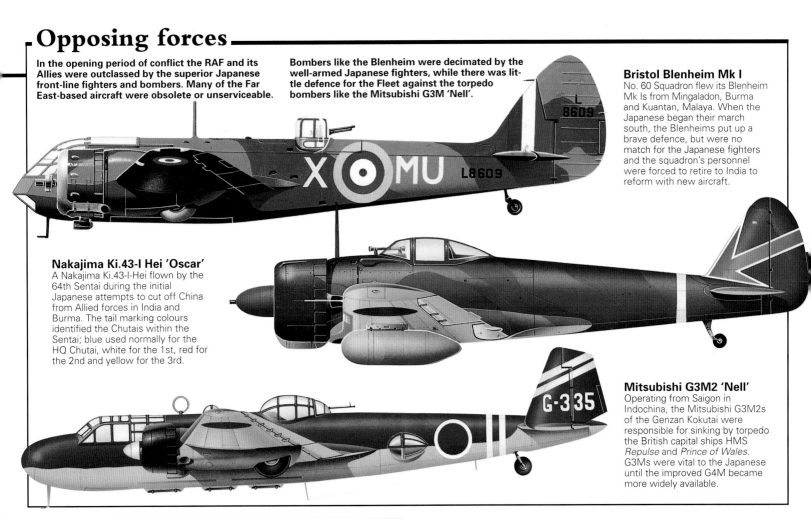

Bristol Blenheim Mk I
No. 60 Squadron flew its Blenheim Mk Is from Mingaladon, Burma and Kuantan, Malaya. When the Japanese began their march south, the Blenheims put up a brave defence, but were no match for the Japanese fighters and the squadron's personnel were forced to retire to India to reform with new aircraft.

Nakajima Ki.43-I Hei 'Oscar'
A Nakajima Ki.43-I-Hei flown by the 64th Sentai during the initial Japanese attempts to cut off China from Allied forces in India and Burma. The tail marking colours identified the Chutais within the Sentai; blue used normally for the HQ Chutai, white for the 1st, red for the 2nd and yellow for the 3rd.

Mitsubishi G3M2 'Nell'
Operating from Saigon in Indochina, the Mitsubishi G3M2s of the Genzan Kokutai were responsible for sinking by torpedo the British capital ships HMS *Repulse* and *Prince of Wales*. G3Ms were vital to the Japanese until the improved G4M became more widely available.

Above: The Mitsubishi Ki-21 'Sally' began to see major service during the autumn of 1938 over China. Initially successful against negligible Chinese air defences, the Ki-21 was terribly outclassed when faced with Allied fighter aircraft.

the Japanese brought up no fewer than 40 aircraft.

Despite the presence of Ki.27 and Ki.43 escort fighters, the Buffaloes and P-40s claimed the destruction of 36 of the Christmas Day raiders, and continued to dispute air superiority over Rangoon for more than a month; however, although reinforced by 30 Hurricanes and a squadron of Blenheims, they could not halt the Japanese advance in southern Burma and on 30 January 1941 the important British airfield at Moulmein was over-run. Threatened by an encircling thrust from the north-east, the great port of Rangoon was evacuated early in March and the surviving components of the RAF began the long retreat northwards. Using such makeshift airstrips that existed in the dense jungle, the squadrons of 'Burwing' (Blenheim Mk IVs of No. 45 Squadron, No. 67 Squadron with some aged Hurricanes and a few Hudsons of No. 139 Squadron) carried out sporadic attacks on the invaders; their last significant attack was made on Japanese aircraft at Mingaladon airfield on 21 March, the destruction of 27 enemy aircraft being claimed.

By mid-1941 the Japanese had

in this raid and 5,000 more in a Christmas Day attack. However, whereas most of the Far Eastern air force, such as it was, had been deployed for the defence of Singapore, Burma was of less obvious strategic value and accordingly merited much weaker air defences. In all, these comprised just 16 Buffaloes of No. 67 Squadron, RAF and 21 P-40s of the American Volunteer Group (AVG). For the attack on Burma

Left: Capable of over 563 km/h (350 mph), the Nakajima Ki-43 Hayabusa (Allied codename 'Oscar') was built in larger numbers than any other front-line aircraft used by the Japanese Army. Remaining in production throughout the war, a total of 5,900 of these fighters were built by war's end.

Below: Mitsubishi G3M 'Nell' bombers of the Japanese 22nd Air Flotilla, whose task was to supplement the support given by the 3rd Air Division to the 25th Army in Malaya and North Borneo. Its 90 G3M2s were augmented by 42 G4M1s from the 21st Air Flotilla.

over-run almost the whole of Burma. In the final stages of the campaign the Dakotas of No. 31 Squadron, RAF, and the C-47s of the 2nd Troop Carrier Squadron, USAAF, evacuated 8,616 men, women and children from Magwe, Myitkyina and Shwebo. It was only the onset of the monsoon season that brought the invaders to a halt at India's border, within bombing range of the vital port of Calcutta.

Loss of the East Indies

DECEMBER 1941 - APRIL 1942

Left: By the end of 1941, things were going so well for the Japanese in Malaya and the Philippines that a new offensive was begun early in 1942. By seizing Timor, the Japanese severed the air reinforcement route from Australia to the Netherlands East Indies.

Below: A Mitsubishi Ki-21 Army Type 97 Heavy Bomber (codename 'Sally') in flight. Much liked by Japanese airmen because of its good handling characteristics and easy maintenance, the Ki-21 gave good service during the early months of the war.

A s if to emphasise the vital importance to Japan of concluding a swift and successful war in the Pacific, the capture of the Philippines, Marianas, Carolinas, East Indies and New Guinea was virtually completed within the space of four months.

Just three days after the attack on Pearl Harbor, the Japanese overran the garrison on Guam in the Marianas on 10 December 1941. Five hundred US Marines on Wake Island, attacked the following day, held out until 23 December, blasted from the air and sea despite all the handful of F4F Wildcats could do against the raiding Japanese bombers, flying from Kwajalein in the Marshall Islands. In all, 21 Japanese aircraft were shot down.

By the time Wake Island fell the Japanese were already making rapid progress in their Philippine invasion where heavy raids on the fateful 7 December had destroyed 12 of the

---

TARGET TOKYO: THE DOOLITTLE RAID

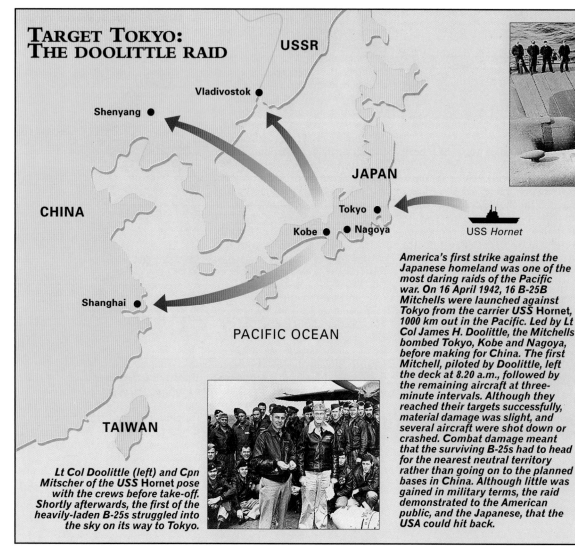

USSR
Vladivostok
Shenyang
JAPAN
CHINA
Tokyo
Kobe ● Nagoya
USS Hornet
Shanghai
PACIFIC OCEAN
TAIWAN

Above: On 14 April 1942, Lt Col Jimmy Doolittle led 16 B-25B Mitchells on an epic morale-boosting raid on Tokyo. They launched from the deck of the USS Hornet, despite the fact that the B-25 was never designed for such a take-off.

America's first strike against the Japanese homeland was one of the most daring raids of the Pacific war. On 16 April 1942, 16 B-25B Mitchells were launched against Tokyo from the carrier USS Hornet, 1000 km out in the Pacific. Led by Lt Col James H. Doolittle, the Mitchells bombed Tokyo, Kobe and Nagoya, before making for China. The first Mitchell, piloted by Doolittle, left the deck at 8.20 a.m., followed by the remaining aircraft at three-minute intervals. Although they reached their targets successfully, material damage was slight, and several aircraft were shot down or crashed. Combat damage meant that the surviving B-25s had to head for the nearest neutral territory rather than going on to the planned bases in China. Although little was gained in military terms, the raid demonstrated to the American public, and the Japanese, that the USA could hit back.

Lt Col Doolittle (left) and Cpn Mitscher of the USS Hornet pose with the crews before take-off. Shortly afterwards, the first of the heavily-laden B-25s struggled into the sky on its way to Tokyo.

One of Doolittle's B-25s takes off from the Hornet. The aircraft were modified to carry 1,141 US gal of fuel, almost double the normal capacity. They were probably the heaviest aircraft that had ever taken off from an American aircraft-carrier.

The attackers

The Japanese Imperial Navy's D3A divebomber came as an unpleasant shock to the Allies – during the early part of 1942, it wiped out most of the Allied surface vessels in the southwest Pacific. The

Mitsubishi Ki-30 Army Type 97 Light Bomber (code-named 'Ann') was used by the Japanese 5th Air Division to support the East Indies campaign. The type was afterwards relegated to training duties.

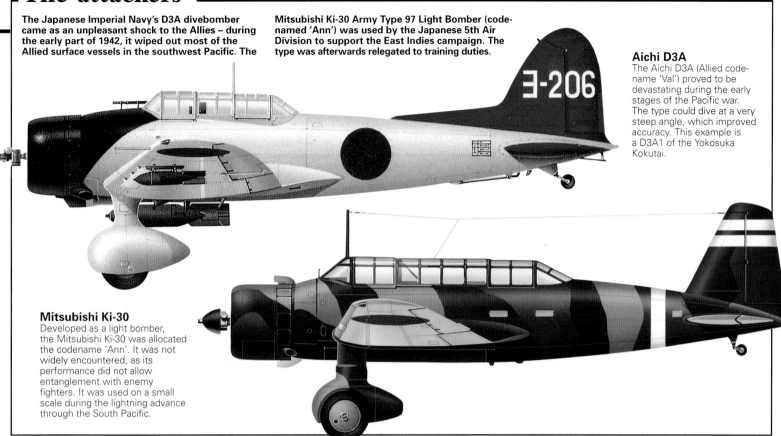

Aichi D3A
The Aichi D3A (Allied code-name 'Val') proved to be devastating during the early stages of the Pacific war. The type could dive at a very steep angle, which improved accuracy. This example is a D3A1 of the Yokosuka Kokutai.

Mitsubishi Ki-30
Developed as a light bomber, the Mitsubishi Ki-30 was allocated the codename 'Ann'. It was not widely encountered, as its performance did not allow entanglement with enemy fighters. It was used on a small scale during the lightning advance through the South Pacific.

Left: Nakajima B5N2 Naval Type 97 'Kate' carrier-borne torpedo bombers fly over Wake Island when the 2nd Carrier Division attacked the island on 21 December 1941. The B5N2 continued to be used in the offensive role until 1944.

Below: The Battle of the Java Sea, which settled the fate of the Netherlands East Indies, took place on 27 February 1942. A hastily assembled Allied land force was outfought and Java was occupied on 12 March. Here a B-17 burns after a raid on Bandung airfield.

Below: In the Pacific, the objective was to stop the Japanese drive and push it back to the home islands. Here Lt Edward H. 'Butch' O'Hare stands by his US Navy F4F-4 Wildcat, in which he downed five Japanese aircraft in combat.

Right: Douglas TBD Devastators were the main torpedo-bombers aboard US carriers for the first year of the war. Slow and vulnerable, they were savaged by Japanese fighters. Seen on deck is a mix of Devastators and SBD Dauntlesses.

35 B-17s in the theatre, and went on to knock out the others in the following days; this force had been regarded as second only in importance to the American Pacific Fleet. As the Americans retreated in Luzon towards the Bataan peninsula, General MacArthur attempted to save Manilla from needless damage and casualties by declaring it an 'open city'. He might have saved himself the trouble, for on 27 December the Japanese subjected it to a series of savage air attacks. As MacArthur prepared to make a stand on the Bataan peninsula following the Japanese capture of Cavite on 2 January 1942, other enemy forces were embarking in large convoys for landings in New Guinea and the Solomon Islands, where they duly arrived on 23 January.

Meanwhile, as the British and Commonwealth forces in Malaya failed to stem the Japanese advance towards Singapore, efforts were being made to rush RAF reinforce-ments of fighters to the Far East, and although some Hurricanes did arrive during January to assist in the defence of the great port, it was the same story everywhere: too little, too late. A regrouping of Japanese carriers in mid-February allowed four of them, the *Hiryu*, *Soryu*, *Akagi* and *Kaga*, to steam through the East Indies and launch nearly 200 aircraft for a very heavy raid on the Australian port of Darwin, sinking a dozen ships and causing immense damage in the town.

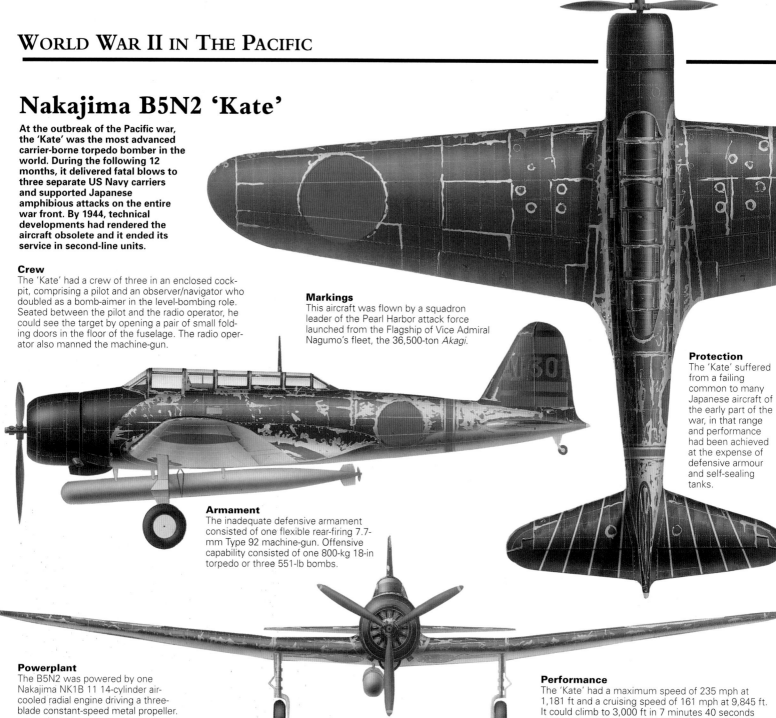

Nakajima B5N2 'Kate'

At the outbreak of the Pacific war, the 'Kate' was the most advanced carrier-borne torpedo bomber in the world. During the following 12 months, it delivered fatal blows to three separate US Navy carriers and supported Japanese amphibious attacks on the entire war front. By 1944, technical developments had rendered the aircraft obsolete and it ended its service in second-line units.

Crew
The 'Kate' had a crew of three in an enclosed cockpit, comprising a pilot and an observer/navigator who doubled as a bomb-aimer in the level-bombing role. Seated between the pilot and the radio operator, he could see the target by opening a pair of small folding doors in the floor of the fuselage. The radio operator also manned the machine-gun.

Markings
This aircraft was flown by a squadron leader of the Pearl Harbor attack force launched from the Flagship of Vice Admiral Nagumo's fleet, the 36,500-ton *Akagi*.

Protection
The 'Kate' suffered from a failing common to many Japanese aircraft of the early part of the war, in that range and performance had been achieved at the expense of defensive armour and self-sealing tanks.

Armament
The inadequate defensive armament consisted of one flexible rear-firing 7.7-mm Type 92 machine-gun. Offensive capability consisted of one 800-kg 18-in torpedo or three 551-lb bombs.

Powerplant
The B5N2 was powered by one Nakajima NK1B 11 14-cylinder air-cooled radial engine driving a three-blade constant-speed metal propeller.

Performance
The 'Kate' had a maximum speed of 235 mph at 1,181 ft and a cruising speed of 161 mph at 9,845 ft. It could climb to 3,000 ft in 7 minutes 40 seconds and had a maximum range of 1,075 nm.

February had begun with the first significant American offensive air action when, on 1 February, carrier aircraft attacked the Japanese base at Kwajalein. This was a minor triumph amid a chapter of disasters, and several ships (mostly troop transports) were either sunk or damaged. But nothing could deflect the Japanese from their next prize, the rich island of Java, defended by some 120,000 Allied troops with scarcely any air cover. Sumatra was effectively abandoned to the Japanese, for its few small airfields were capable only of supporting small numbers of fighters (some Hurricanes had arrived by sea, only

Left: The Aichi D3A1 'Val' was designed as a carrier-borne dive-bomber. It served with Admiral Nagumo's Strike Force and acquitted itself well, despite its approaching obsolescence and its vulnerability to even the least effective Allied fighters. With proper air cover, the Allies could have saved many of the ships which fell to the 'Val'. Over 470 of these aircraft were delivered to the Japanese navy.

Left: An Allied agreement in early 1942 defined the Indian Ocean west of the Malayan peninsula as a British zone of responsibility, but the Royal Navy could only muster a token force for its protection. Here, the heavy cruisers HMS Cornwall and HMS Dorsetshire are under air attack on 5 April 1942.

to be quickly overwhelmed). The Americans accordingly sailed the veteran carrier *Langley* from Freemantle in Australia, with 32 P-40Es aboard and orders to land them at Tjilatjap on the south coast of Java; also sailed at the same time

Below: An early production Douglas SBD-3 Dauntless, sporting an overall light grey colour scheme and small national insignia, flies over USS Enterprise (CV-6). The SBD was at the forefront of operations in the Pacific.

Right: The Curtiss P-36/Hawk 75 was an intermediate development between the Hawk biplane and the P-40 Warhawk. It was exported to the Netherlands – these aircraft are serving in the Netherlands East Indies in early 1942.

was the freighter *Seawitch* with 27 other fighters in crates. The carrier *Langley* was discovered by Japanese aircraft when only 70 miles (113 km) from its destination and sunk with the loss of all its aircraft; the *Seawitch* arrived a day or so later but was unable to unload its cargo, which was then dumped overboard. On that day, 28 February, a large Japanese fleet put ashore its invasion force on Java's north coast. Without any effective air cover the fate of the island and its defenders was sealed. With little cohesive action by ships of the British, Dutch, Australian and American

navies, the Japanese carrier aircraft were able to sink the Allied naval vessels piecemeal, while the Battle of the Java Sea cost them the loss of 14 out of 19 ships and delayed the invasion of Java by no more than a single day. On 9 March the defend-

ers of Java surrendered and 98,000 British, American and Dutch troops passed into captivity. Two days later General MacArthur was ordered to leave Corregidor island in Manila Bay to establish new headquarters in Australia, leaving an embattled garrison to slog it out until it was finally forced to surrender on 9 April. Of the 76,000 taken prisoner, 10,000 were to die in captivity.

CARRIERS SURVIVE

These shattering Allied losses had involved giving up virtually every island between continental Asia and Australia to the Japanese. The cost in men and materials had been prodigious, yet one factor alone perhaps saved American strategy in the Pacific: the survival of the three big carriers, *Enterprise, Saratoga* and

Lexington. When a fourth carrier, the *Yorktown,* was transferred from the Atlantic to the Pacific, the effective number of carriers remained at three when *Saratoga* was damaged by a submarine's torpedo and put out of action for five months.

It was to be the *Yorktown* that staged a morale-boosting operation on 18 April 1941 when, accompanied by the *Enterprise,* it steamed to within 620 miles (1000 km) of Japan and launched 16 US Army B-25 Mitchells, led by Lieutenant Colonel James Doolittle, in a raid on Tokyo. Little material damage was caused, and all the aircraft were lost after force landing in China (their crews were repatriated later), but the raid's effect on the morale of the American nation was enormous, coming as it did after four months of unremitting defeat and disaster.

Undoubtedly the finest Japanese aircraft of the early years of the war, the Mitsubishi A6M 'Zero' seemed untouchable in a dogfight. It remained a major threat until the stronger, faster Grumman F6F Hellcat was introduced in 1943.

Valiant defenders

The Japanese assembled an armada of some 2,950 aircraft for their push through the Pacific. They set a 100-day timetable for the invasion of Malaysia and Singapore, Guam, Wake Island, Luzon and Java.

Allied aircraft were outnumbered, and many were obsolete, and despite a brave and desperate defence the Allies endured a succession of defeats. Java fell on 9 March, within the Japanese timetable.

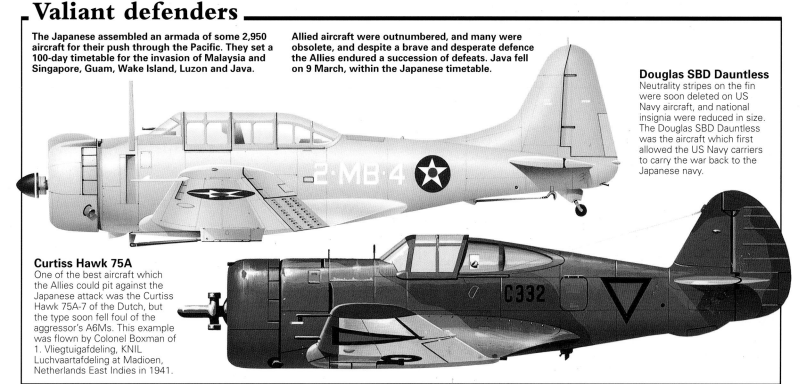

Douglas SBD Dauntless
Neutrality stripes on the fin were soon deleted on US Navy aircraft, and national insignia were reduced in size. The Douglas SBD Dauntless was the aircraft which first allowed the US Navy carriers to carry the war back to the Japanese navy.

Curtiss Hawk 75A
One of the best aircraft which the Allies could pit against the Japanese attack was the Curtiss Hawk 75A-7 of the Dutch, but the type soon fell foul of the aggressor's A6Ms. This example was flown by Colonel Boxman of 1. Vliegtuigafdeling, KNIL Luchvaartafdeling at Madioen, Netherlands East Indies in 1941.

Chennault's Flying Tigers

DECEMBER 1941 – JUNE 1944

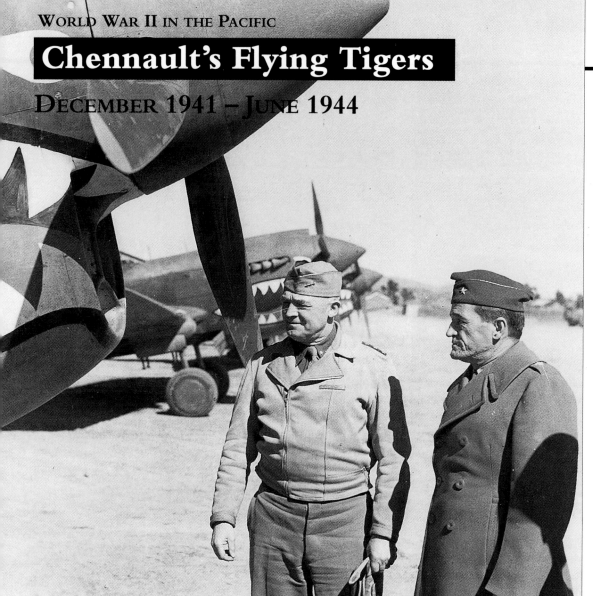

Left: Lt General Henry H. 'Hap' Arnold, Chief of the USAAF (left) with Brig. General Claire Lee Chennault of the 14th Air Force, at a meeting at the start of the 1943 limited offensive. Chennault and Brig. General Clayton L. Bissell were constantly at odds over supplying the China Air Task Force (then the 14th Air Force).

at Mingaladon to cover the Burmese port of Rangoon. This had all been achieved by the time the Japanese entered the war in December 1941.

The Americans were quickly in action against the Japanese, shooting down six of a formation of 10 enemy bombers which attacked Kunming on 20 December, but fared less well when the Japanese attacked Rangoon on 23 December, losing two pilots. Thereafter the American Volunteer Group (AVG), as it became known, contributed substantially to the defence of Burma but, despite extraordinary ingenuity to keep the

Below: The 23rd Fighter Group in China was originally the American Volunteer Group, famously known as the 'Flying Tigers'. This tiger wears Uncle Sam's hat to signify his entry into United States service in 1942 and grasps a shredded Japanese flag.

A s the call 'Remember Pearl Harbor' reverberated throughout the United States in 1942, a force of American airmen and aircraft was carrying the war to the Japanese in China and, despite virtual isolation by distance and relative inaccessibility, did much to slow their advance in Southeast Asia.

As long ago as 1936 a retired USAAC major, Claire Lee Chennault, had been invited by the Chinese to create a fighter defence system against the Japanese by instructing young pilots in modern fighting tactics and improvising with the few aircraft available. In due course the Chinese government negotiated to obtain 100 P-40Bs from the USA under Lend-Lease terms (of these 90 arrived at Kyedaw in 1941), Chennault having in 1940 recruited 80 ex-USAAC, US Navy and US Marine Corps volunteer pilots and 150 groundcrew members. With scarcely any official backing from Washington, Chennault organised this force into two squadrons operating out of Kunming to protect the vital Burma Road (which carried supplies to the Chinese) and a third

Left: The American Volunteer Group in China blossomed into the 23rd Fighter Group – this group of officers and enlisted men of one of the constituent squadrons, the 74th Fighter Squadron, pose on one of their P-40 aircraft at Kunming, China on 1 February 1943.

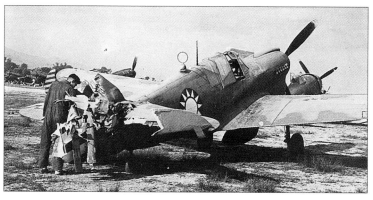

Above: During the last two years of the war 377 Curtiss P-40 Warhawks were supplied to China. Most were P-40Ns, as seen here. The damage to the fin and rudder of this example was possibly caused by a ground collision. Note the P-47 Thunderbolt in the background.

Adversaries over China

Though Curtiss lost a USAAC competition for a new fighter to Seversky, the company persevered and won export orders for their radial-engined Model 75 Hawk. The USAAC eventually placed an order, the type serving as the basis for the later inline-engined P-40. 'Dinah' was the Allied code-name for the Ki-46, originally built as a high-speed reconnaissance and destined to serve until 1945.

Curtiss 75 Hawk
The predecessor of the Curtiss P-40 was the P-36, known to Curtiss as the Hawk 75. Flown alongside the P-40 in the colours of the Chinese Nationalist Air Force from Kunming, these fighters were not as capable as the P-40 and gave the Japanese little trouble.

Curtiss 81-A2 Hawk
Flown by Charles Older of the 3rd Squadron 'Hell's Angels' of the American Volunteer Group commanded by Brig. General Claire L. Chennault, this Curtiss Hawk (P-8268) was based at Kunming, China, in the spring of 1942. Among its distinctive markings are 10 victory symbols below the windscreen.

Mitsubishi Ki-46-II
The Mitsubishi Ki-46-II 'Dinah' was allowed almost free reign over the skies of China in late-1941 and early-1942. The opposing Curtiss fighters did not have the performance to catch it at its operating height. This example served with the 51st Dokuritsu Dai Shijugo Chutai (Independent Squadron).

Below: A P-40 undergoing maintenance under armed guard at the Chinese Air Service Command facility at Kunming, where both Chinese and American servicemen worked on the AVG's aircraft. 'Tiger's teeth' on the nose of the aircraft were an AVG trademark.

Right: Curtiss Model 75Ms Hawk (export version of the P-36) were delivered to China from August 1938. This version was supplied with non-retractable undercarriage. Only 30 were built by Curtiss, with 82 reputedly built by the Central Aircraft Manufacturing Company.

aircraft serviceable (as spares were available only by cannibalisation) the American losses mounted rapidly. The American pilots were credited with 286 victories over Burma and southern China within four months (the true figure was probably nearer 150) and by March, when Rangoon fell to the Japanese, only six P-40s and six Hurricanes (which had been provided by the RAF as reinforcements) remained airworthy in the squadron in the south; 14 others were still flying from Kunming.

As the Japanese army advanced inexorably north through Burma the AVG continued to retain its identity under its indefatigable con-dottiere, fighting alongside the Buffaloes (and later Hurricanes) of No. 67 (Fighter) Squadron RAF, and striving to operate in appalling conditions from hastily prepared strips hacked out of the Burmese jungle. By May 1942 the beaten Allied army in Burma had retreated as far as Imphal, capital of the Indian state of Manipur, as the survivors of the AVG made their way back into China.

AVG RECOGNISED
Despite constant opposition to the existence of the AVG by the American ground commander in

THE 'FLYING TIGERS'

During only 30 weeks of combat, the American Volunteer Group (AVG) in China claimed 297 enemy aircraft confirmed destroyed, and 40 destroyed on the ground. Twenty-six aces emerged from the ranks of the 'Flying Tigers' – two later earned the Medal of Honor ('Pappy' Boyington and Jim Howard). Four pilots were lost in air combat, six died from ground fire whilst strafing, three died in accidents and three more were killed by enemy bombs. Three became POWs.

Major J.R. Alison

John Alison (left) was a frustrated instructor pilot in England and Russia until he managed to wrangle an assignment with the AVG. On 30 July 1942, he found three Japanese 'Betty' bombers at 4572 metres (15,000 ft) and proceeded to shoot them all down. He became one of the legendary aces in the theatre with 10 aerial victories. His decorations included the Distinguished Service Cross, Distinguished Flying Cross, Silver Star, Legion of Merit, Purple Heart – and a British Distinguished Service Order.

Brig. General C. L. Chennault

Retired USAAC Captain Claire Lee Chennault worked at building an air force for the Nationalist Chinese. He believed that a well-led force of fighters could stop a large force of bombers – not a popular school of thought in the Air Corps of the 1930s. He left in the spring of 1937 at the age of 47, suffering slight deafness. By early-1941, he was planning to obtain American aircraft to be flown by volunteers against Japan. On the AVG's absorption into the USAAF, he was promised higher priority in obtaining supplies and equipment. Promoted to Colonel on 9 April 1942, he became a Brig. General six days later as the AVG formed the nucleus of the new CATF.

Capt. A. Baumler

Captain Albert 'Ajax' Baumler (right) was a top-notch pilot who emerged from the Stateside arrivals. His P-40 carries the insignia of the 23rd Fighter Group in China. The 23rd was, at first, the only fighter group to oppose the Japanese in China and followed what became a consistent course of air operations – bombing and strafing enemy airfields, troop and supply installations and preventing effective bombing by the Japanese Air Force.

Col R. L. Scott

The first commander of the 23rd Fighter Group was Colonel Robert L. Scott, an adventurer at heart. Arriving in China in April 1942, he managed to obtain a P-40 from Chennault and flew combat missions with the AVG. He is seen sitting in the cockpit of his P-40K-I with kills recorded on the fuselage. Before he left for the States, he assumed the leadership of Fighter Command, CATF in February 1943 and was able to pass on his experience of P-40 operations in China.

Lt L. H. Couch

The 16th Fighter Squadron of the 51st Fighter Group was also attached to the 23rd. One of the 16th's notable pilots was 1st Lieutenant Llewellyn H. Couch, from North Carolina. He is seen here with his personal Curtiss P-40E 'Lillian I' at Peishihwa, China on 22 October 1942. A fortnight later, Couch scored his only confirmed kill, over a Mitsubishi A6M Zero. His final tally stood at one kill, one probable, and one enemy aircraft damaged, all of which were Zeros.

China, Lieutenant General J.W. ('Vinegar Joe') Stilwell, who saw the 'Flying Tigers' only as a bunch of barely disciplined mercenaries intent on diverting supplies from his own troops (rather than a vital protection of his own supplies), the American government came to accept the importance of the AVG in China, and forthwith dispatched a number of the improved, six-gun P-40E, of which 30 reached Chennault's command. Chennault himself was reinstated in the active list of the USAAF and promoted to major general, while the AVG was renamed the China Air Task Force as President Roosevelt personally directed Stilwell to ensure it received all possible assistance and supplies.

KUNMING HELD

Largely through the continuing efforts of Chennault's pilots, the

Left: Sergeant Elmer J. Pence, with the help of his pet monkey, adds another Rising Sun symbol to a Curtiss P-40E of the 26th Fighter Squadron, 51st Fighter Group, which was operating in China in 1944 as part of the 14th Air Force. The 197-litre (43-US gallon) centreline drop tank was a standard fitting on many P-40s to improve range.

Above: The American Volunteer Group was divided into three squadrons of 18 aircraft each. The 1st Pursuit Squadron, whose emblem is shown, was the 'Adam and Eve' (commemorating the first pursuit in history), led by Robert Sandell. The 2nd was known as the 'Panda Bears' and the 3rd, the 'Hell's Angels'.

Madam Chiang Kai-shek, the National Secretary of Aviation (regarded by many as the real power in Nationalist China) had given Chennault nearly $9m via the China Defense Supplies Corporation to obtain the fighters he wanted. One hundred Hawk 81-A2s were assigned to China, these being replaced later with versions of the P-40 Warhawk, shown here. Note the 'Hold'n my own' tail art.

Above: An early P-40B (Hawk Model 75-A2) of the 23rd Fighter Group landing at Kunming, China, after a mission on 15 September 1942. Some of these aircraft had seen action with the RAF in the Western Desert, with others coming from Panama.

concentrations and railways; they also flew escort for American bombers attacking Canton, Shanghai and Hong Kong. They operated against the Japanese during the enemy offensives towards Changsha and Chungking, and in the Tungting Hu region. They remained at Kunming until September 1943 when they moved to Kweilin in the north to provide air defence of the Chinese terminus of the 'Hump' air route for supplies from India to China. In due course

the Flying Tigers gave up their P-40s in favour of the P-51D, and it was with these aircraft that they were in action against the Japanese forces which advanced down the Hsiang Valley in June 1944, earning a Distinguished Unit Citation. The following spring they helped to rout the enemy and then harassed the Japanese during their final retreat in China. Chennault himself was appointed to command the US 14th Air Force from its inception until the end of the Pacific War.

Japanese failed to reach and capture Kunming, although the Burma Road ceased to be of use with the Japanese in possession of almost all Burma. On 4 July 1942 the China

Air Task Force was formally integrated into the USAAF (later as a component of the 14th Air Force) as the 23rd Pursuit Group, its three component squadrons becoming the 74th, 75th and 76th Pursuit Squadrons.

During the following year these were in constant action against the Japanese, intercepting raids on Allied airfields and strafing enemy airfields, river craft, troop

Above: A formation of Kawasaki Ki-48s (Allied codename 'Lily') over China. The Ki-48 was a fast bomber, broadly comparable to the Bristol Blenheim and the Russian Tupolev SB-2. Designed originally as a day bomber, being fast enough to escape interception, it was manufactured in large numbers from the summer of 1940 to the autumn of 1944. Those in China were among the first in service.

Left: Pilots run to their P-40s on a base in China after hearing the air-raid warning. Chennault was continually amazed that the Japanese did not try to destroy the 'Flying Tigers' on the ground, since there was no protection or dispersal system in operation. Lines of P-40s at Pearl Harbor had suffered terribly in similar circumstances.

The Battle of the Coral Sea

1942

On the same day that the British fortress of Singapore fell to the Japanese, Admiral Halsey took the Enterprise group out of Pearl Harbor to hit Wake Island.

Pursuing their drive south-wards towards Australia early in 1942, the Japanese mounted what they termed Operation MO to capture Port Moresby in New Guinea, thereby eliminating Allied air attacks on their bases at Kavieng and Rabaul in the Solomons, and laying open the coast of Australia for attacks by their own land-based bombers. To do this a number of naval groups and invasion fleets were assembled, totalling 70 ships of which two were large carriers (the *Shokaku* and *Zuikaku*), and one a small carrier (the *Shoho*); between them these ships embarked 51 B5N

The Grumman F4F Wildcat was the principal fighter available to the US Navy until 1943. At Coral Sea, in 1942, the F4Fs found it difficult to contain the superior Mitsubishi A6M Reisen. These Wildcats are lined-up on the deck of the Lexington on 18 May 1942 during the ship's last days.

'Kate' torpedo bombers, 42 D3A 'Val' dive-bombers and 54 A6M 'Zero' fighters. In addition, the Japanese could call on about 120 aircraft land-based at Rabaul. The US task force in the area (Task Force 17 under Rear Admiral Frank Fletcher) included the carriers *Lexington* and *Yorktown*, whose air strength comprised 25 TBD Devastator torpedo-bombers, 74 SBD Dauntless dive-bombers and 44 F4F Wildcat fighters.

As the result of code-breaking, American intelligence learned that a Japanese fleet would enter the Coral Sea early in May, so that Admiral Fletcher, guessing that Port Moresby was its destination, was able to scout the area around Guadalcanal. Finding a small Japanese force off Tulagi on 4 May, Fletcher launched three strikes from the *Yorktown*, dropping 76 bombs and 22 torpedoes and sinking a destroyer and three minesweepers

for the loss of one TBD and two F4Fs. The *Lexington* meanwhile was still far to the south.

FLAT-TOPS FOUND

On the night of 5/6 May the two large Japanese carriers entered the Coral Sea but, despite land- and carrier-based patrols by both sides, neither fleet was detected for many hours, although the Japanese aircraft found and sank the detached American destroyer *Sims* and the

Aichi D3A1 Naval Type 99 Carrier-Bomber Model 11 – Allied codename 'Val'. The 'Val' had a fixed spatted undercarriage, and in its heyday was a highly effective aircraft although it could carry only one 250-kg bomb under the fuselage and two 60-kg bombs underwing.

oiler *Neosho*. Early in the morning of 7 May a *Yorktown* aircraft apparently reported two Japanese carriers and four heavy cruisers 225 miles (360 km) northwest of the American task force (now joined

Airbrakes extended, this Dauntless is caught in classic dive-bomber pose. Early SBDs could carry a 1,200-lb (545-kg) bombload, but this increased with the later SBD-5 model. This SBD-3 was aboard USS Enterprise (CV-6) in March 1942.

The Japanese carrier Shokaku is seen ablaze and badly damaged, although still afloat, on 8 May 1942 following an attack by US Navy aircraft during the Battle of the Coral Sea.

up), and within two hours 93 aircraft had been launched to the attack; unfortunately, the sighting report had been decoded incorrectly and the force detected was of no importance and comprised no carriers. The American strike did, however, come up with the Japanese covering group consisting of the light carrier *Shoho* and its escorting ships. Despite the presence of a few enemy fighters, the 53 SBDs and 22 TBDs went into the attack, sinking the *Shoho* with 13 bombs and seven torpedoes; it was after this attack that Lieutenant Commander Robert Dixon radioed back to *Lexington* his famous signal 'Scratch one flat-top'. That evening the Japanese commander, Admiral Takagi, launched a search/strike by 27 aircraft, these being intercepted by American Wildcats whose pilots claimed nine aircraft shot down. The survivors had a difficult flight back to the Japanese carriers and only seven succeeded in landing on.

LEXINGTON LOST

Early on 8 May Japanese air patrols found the American carriers and, just as a strike by 69 D3As and B5Ns was approaching the *Lexington* and *Yorktown*, a force of 82 American aircraft was making for the Japanese carriers, whose position had just been reported 175 miles (280 km) to the northwest. At 11.15 the Japanese attack started, and five minutes later two torpe-does and five bombs struck the *Lexington*, and one bomb hit the *Yorktown*. The former was badly damaged but, as the Japanese aircraft made off, the crew of the big carrier appeared to be controlling the raging fires. An hour later, however, its aviation fuel tanks exploded and at about 20.00 in that evening the *Lexington* was abandoned to be sunk by American torpedoes, the first American carrier to be lost in World War II.

The American strike aircraft had meanwhile spotted the Japanese carriers, aircraft from the *Yorktown* attacking the *Shokaku* an hour before noon; all their torpedoes missed or failed to explode, and only two bombs found their mark. Although damaged and unable to launch or recover aircraft, the *Shokaku* remained afloat, while the *Zuikaku* recovered all the surviving strike aircraft.

Both sides now withdrew, the Japanese having one small carrier sunk and a large carrier badly damaged. Admiral Takagi had lost more than 100 of his aircraft and, with no more than 39 survivors able to fly, decided to postpone the invasion of Port Moresby for two months. More important was the loss of many of the best and most experienced Japanese naval airmen, a loss that would be keenly felt in the great battles to come.

US VICTORY

The sinking of the *Lexington* was a considerable blow to the Americans who, now that the *Yorktown* was also damaged, had only the *Enterprise* and *Hornet* operational in the Pacific. Despite the adverse ship loss tally, and the fact that Japan could still count five large carriers operational in the Pacific, the Battle of the Coral Sea (the first in history to be fought by opposing warships that never saw nor fired on each other, and the first fought entirely by aircraft) was generally regarded as an American victory. Admiral Fletcher had succeeded in his purpose of frustrating a Japanese invasion of Port Moresby. It was the first sign that the lightning Japanese advance was slowing.

Coral Sea should have been a major Allied victory – Port Moresby had been saved, the Shoho sunk, the large carrier Shokaku damaged and most of its aircraft destroyed. However, while the damaged US carriers Yorktown and Lexington, with the Hornet and Enterprise on the way to relieve them, headed for Pearl Harbor for repairs, a series of internal explosions on the Lexington led to its abandonment and subsequent total loss.

The Tide Turns at Midway

3/5 JUNE 1942

The Japanese strategic plan in the Pacific was to establish by conquest an outer defence perimeter from Kiska in the Aleutians to Port Moresby, passing through Midway, Wake, the Marshalls and the Gilberts. Key bastion of this line of defence would lie at Midway, whose capture would extend the homeland warning network and serve as a base for the future capture of Pearl Harbor. Moreover the Japanese naval commander-in-chief, Admiral Yamamoto, believed that any battle to defeat the US Pacific Fleet must be fought and won in 1942 before the vast American naval building programme bore fruit, and correctly assumed that an attack on Midway would bring about such a battle.

For the assault on Midway Yamamoto assembled four fleets, of which one was an invasion force

Above: PBY-5 Catalinas operated by the US Navy played a vital part leading up to the battle, providing warning of the approaching Japanese fleet. Their prodigious 4500-km (2796-mile) range was useful when flying from Midway.

Below: The shattered Japanese carrier force retreated westward from Midway, leaving the crippled 'Mogami'-class cruisers Mogami and Mikuma, part of the 7th Cruiser Squadron, to make for the safety of Wake Island.

and three were heavy support forces; in all, these forces included five large carriers (the *Akagi*, *Kaga*, *Hiryu*, *Soryu* and *Junyo*), three light carriers, 11 battleships and 100 other naval vessels. Of the large carriers, the first four embarked a force of 81 B5N 'Kate' torpedo bombers, 72 D3A 'Val' dive-bombers and 72 A6M Zero fighters. The American fleet covering Midway was divided between two task forces under Rear Admiral Fletcher and included the carriers *Enterprise*, *Hornet* and *Yorktown* (the latter having completed speedy repairs since sustaining damage in the Battle of Coral Sea a month earlier); the American ships carried 42 TBD Devastator torpedo-bombers, 82 SBD Dauntless dive-bombers and 79 F4F Wildcat fighters. There were also valuable American PBY patrol flying-boats and some of the new TBF Avenger torpedo aircraft based at Midway, as well as some older aircraft.

As yet the Japanese were not aware that any American task force was in the area of Midway, and only after a number of incomplete sighting reports had been received did suspicion dawn that American carriers were nearby. All through 3 June the American aircraft based on Midway carried out attacks on the Japanese fleet, inflicting little damage but forcing the carriers to keep launching their fighters for defence.

Right: The USS Yorktown at Midway, turning hard to port in an attempt to avoid a torpedo attack by 'Kate' aircraft from the Japanese carrier Hiryu. The Hiryu was found some miles to the north-east and sunk by American aircraft that day.

Above: Airbrakes extended, this Douglas SBD Dauntless is caught in classic dive-bomber pose at Midway. Early SBDs carried a 545-kg (1,200-lb) bombload, but by the end of the war this had increased with the introduction of the SBD-5.

This in turn prevented the Japanese from launching strikes against the American naval force, now known to include at least one carrier.

HEAVY LOSSES

Early on 4 June a PBY reported the positions of two Japanese carriers but, suspecting that at least two other carriers were also in the area, Admiral Fletcher launched only two limited strikes, one of which (from the *Hornet*) failed to locate its target, some of its aircraft running out of fuel and landing in the sea, the remainder having to land on Midway. The other strike, composed of 15 TBDs of Torpedo Squadron Eight (VT-8), found and attacked the *Kaga*; every one was shot down. This was followed by 14 TBDs of VT-6 from the

Mighty Avenger

Grumman's TBF Avenger was a strongly-built, mid-wing monoplane with a weapons-bay large enough for a torpedo or 908 kg (2,000 lb) of other ordnance. Making its operational debut at Midway in June 1942, well over half the Avengers constructed were to be built by General Motors' Eastern Aircraft division, as the TBM.

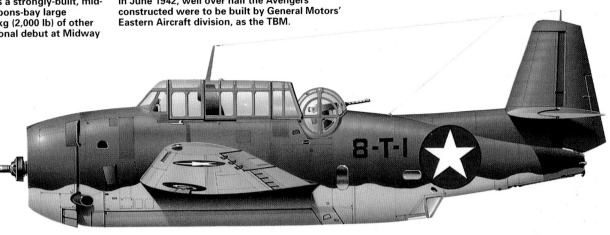

Grumman TBF-1 Avenger

This TBF-1 was one of those that went into action with Navy Squadron VT-8 on 4 June 1942 and failed to return. The aircraft had only just arrived to replace the unit's TBDs. Fortunately the navy already had no doubt that in this aircraft they had the world's best carrier-based attack aircraft.

Above: When darkness fell on 4 June in mid-Pacific, the smoking hulls of four Japanese aircraft carriers signified the turning fortunes of war. Their aircraft also suffered. Here a 'Kate' from one of the carriers plummets towards the sea after a direct hit.

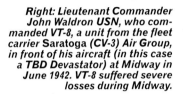

Right: Lieutenant Commander John Waldron USN, who commanded VT-8, a unit from the fleet carrier Saratoga (CV-3) Air Group, in front of his aircraft (in this case a TBD Devastator) at Midway in June 1942. VT-8 suffered severe losses during Midway.

Enterprise; only four survived. Last came 12 TBDs of VT-3 from the *Yorktown*; all of which were shot down. And not a single torpedo found its mark.

By now the *Akagi*, *Kaga*, *Soryu* and *Hiryu* were fairly close together, and their position was known. At 09.55 the first SBDs came in to the attack and within 30 minutes the first three of these carriers had been heavily damaged by direct bomb hits. Thus far the American losses among the carrier aircraft amounted to 37 TBDs, 16 SBDs and 14 F4Fs. At 10.40 on 4 June the surviving Japanese carrier *Hiryu* launched a strike by 18 dive-bombers whose pilots discreetly followed the departing SBDs back to their carrier, the *Yorktown*, and carried out a highly courageous attack. All but five of the Japanese aircraft were shot down, but the heavy damage inflicted caused the carrier to sink three days later. Ironically, just as the attack on the *Yorktown* started, 10 of her SBDs attacked the *Hiryu*, scoring four direct hits.

The final stages of the Battle of Midway involved isolated attacks by American shore-based aircraft against the Japanese fleet, but little further damage was done. The *Soryu* eventually sank during the evening of 4 June with 718 men; five minutes later the *Kaga* blew up and sank with 800 of her crew. The *Akagi* and *Hiryu* both remained afloat until 5 June, both being abandoned to be torpedoed by Japanese destroyers, the *Hiryu* taking 416 of her crew to the bottom. As the Japanese fleet withdrew, now without air cover, a strike by 57 SBDs from *Enterprise* and *Hornet* found the Japanese cruisers *Mikuma* and *Mogami*, sinking the former and badly damaging the latter.

Midway may be regarded as one of history's decisive battles. It ended Japan's carrier domination of the Pacific, without which the American fleet could at last begin to contain the forward momentum of the Japanese advance. That advance would continue for many months, but with the cumulative losses among her best naval airmen at Coral Sea and Midway the Imperial Japanese Navy would no longer operate in safety from the air. Midway confirmed the carrier as the major warship in the Pacific; within a month the USA would have a further 131 carriers in construction or on order.

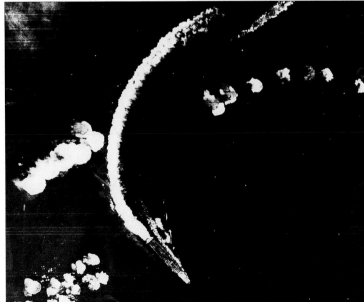

Above: The Japanese carrier Hiryu under attack by Midway-based B-17 bombers early in the battle that was to mark the turning point against the Japanese sweep across the Pacific. No bombs found the target on this occasion, but the carrier was sunk later by navy SBD Dauntlesses.

After Midway: The Solomons

AUGUST 1942 – FEBRUARY 1943

Operation 'Cactus' was the Allied invasion of the island of Guadalcanal in the Solomons chain. Japanese forces had built up on the island with the intention of cutting communications between the US and its bases in Australia. On 7 August 1942, a massive assault was launched, with many strikes by carrier-based Douglas SBD Dauntless dive bombers.

Left: Grumman had built fighters for the US Navy since 1931, but their first monoplane was the F4F Wildcat, which entered USN service in late-1940. Generally inferior to the Zero in performance, the Wildcat was more durable and more heavily armed, and with better-trained pilots, achieved a kill ratio of nearly six-to-one in air combat during 1942.

The loss of four Japanese carriers at Midway gave the Americans the chance of seizing the initiative, if only for a short time, before the Japanese reorganised their fleets. It was therefore decided to mount a series of operations whose ultimate object was to recapture Rabaul in the north of New Britain. To do this it was necessary to secure the Solomon Islands which stretched away to the south east for 960 km (600 miles) and particularly the large jungle-clad island of Guadalcanal with its half-completed airfield (later named Henderson Field), as well as the island of Tulagi where the Japanese had established a seaplane base.

On 6 August 1942 Task Force 61, under Vice-Admiral Fletcher, with the carriers *Enterprise*, *Saratoga* and *Wasp*, a battleship, 14 cruisers, 31 destroyers and 23 transports, entered the Solomon Sea. Aboard these ships were 99 F4F Wildcat fighters, 103 SBD Dauntless dive-bombers and 41 TBF Avenger torpedo bombers, plus 19,000 US Marines. Early the following day the US Marines went ashore on Tulagi and Guadalcanal, and within 24 hours the Japanese local defences had been overwhelmed, prompting immediate reaction by the Japanese commander at Rabaul who sent a raid by 27 G4M bombers, escorted by 18 A6M Zero fighters against the invasion force. Among the

Japanese fighter pilots was Saburo Sakae, a veteran who had already amassed a score of 57 victories; after claiming his 58th victim (an SBD) he was hit by crossfire from a formation of TBFs. His aircraft was badly damaged but, despite injuries to both eyes and being paralysed down his left side, he managed to fly his aircraft the 1030 km (640 miles) back to Rabaul after a flight of more than six hours. (He later rejoined combat operations to gain a total victory tally of 64, including an aircraft shot down on the last day of the war).

JAPANESE RETALIATION

After a second air strike, which cost the Japanese 15 aircraft, a night attack by enemy surface forces caught part of the American invasion force unawares between Tulagi and Guadalcanal, sinking four heavy cruisers with the loss of 1,000

Left: Ordnancemen aboard Enterprise load a 227-kg (500-lb) bomb onto a Dauntless of Scouting Squadron 6 (VS-6). The date was 7 August 1942, the first day of air attacks on Guadalcanal. For the next five months, the Solomon Islands were the centre of furious naval and air activity, the Allies controlling the skies by day and the Japanese the sea at night.

Right: All major powers made use of large flying-boats in the war. These are Kawanishi H6K2, Naval Type 97s – known to the Allies as 'Mavis'. A total of 176 of this parasol-winged boat was built. Designed for maritime reconnaissance, in 1942 they were also used as long-range bombers.

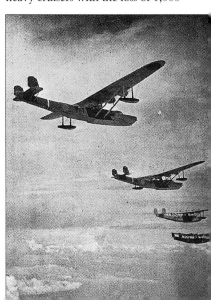

Defenders of Guadalcanal

In the Spring of 1942, the A6M Zero had met modern Wildcat fighters for the first time at the Battles of the Coral Sea and Midway, but it was another year before an example was captured, evaluated and weaknesses identified. The D4Y Suisei (Comet) was a high-speed light bomber first operated in the reconnaissance role. G4Ms were built in larger numbers than any Japanese bomber.

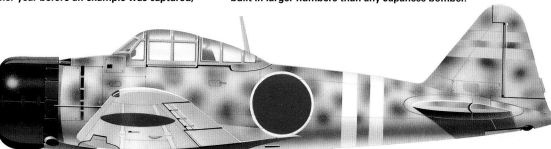

Mitsubishi A6M2 Zero
The A6M2 was the first version of the Navy Type 0 Naval Fighter to enter service and was the fighter that swept all before it from Pearl Harbor to the Dutch East Indies. This Zero ('Zeke' to the Allies) flew with the 6th Kokutai at Rabaul.

Yokosuka D4Y3 Suisei
'Judy', as it was known to the Allies, has been compared to the de Havilland Mosquito as a high-speed bomber, used for reconnaissance and as a night fighter. It was the fastest carrier-borne dive-bomber of World War II, the type seeing service in the Solomons. This is a late-production, radial-engined D4Y3 Model 33.

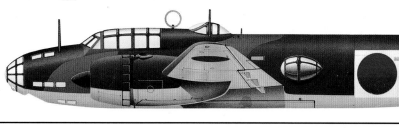

Mitsubishi G4M1
G4Ms served from Australia to the Aleutians in large numbers, despite having unprotected fuel tanks and a lack of armour that earned it the nickname 'Flying Lighter'. This aircraft of the 705th Kokutai was part of the large build-up of Japanese aircraft on Rabaul.

Below: Featuring in the Solomons, 'Judy' gained a reputation as one of the better dive-bombers of the war; it had a reasonable turn of speed, at least when compared to other aircraft of this type. However, the D4Y carried little protection against enemy gun fire – a problem not addressed by the Japanese – thus its full potential was never realised.

Right: The Consolidated PBY Catalina was the main US patrol aircraft of the war and the first US aircraft to carry sea-search radar. The 'Cat' was also used for anti-submarine, transport and air-sea rescue missions. In the Solomons, specially-camouflaged 'black cats' attacked Japanese surface ships at night with torpedoes.

lives in the Battle of Savo Island. Worried by the presence of a large land-based air force, and with his cruiser escort seriously depleted, Fletcher obtained sanction to withdraw his carriers from the area. Throughout the following week the US Marines toiled to complete the airstrip on Guadalcanal and, despite constant attacks by Japanese aircraft, 19 US Marine Wildcats and 12 SBDs landed on the new airfield from the escort carrier *Long Island*.

JAPANESE COUNTERATTACK

Events now followed rapidly. The Japanese dispatched a carrier-escorted invasion force with the carriers *Ryujo*, *Shokaku* and *Zuikaku* (with 168 aircraft) to land 1,500 troops for the recapture of Guadalcanal. On 24 August, after the Japanese force had been sighted by PBYs, the American carriers hastily returned, their SBDs and

Left: The Battle of Santa Cruz was the last major sea action of the Solomons campaign. The Japanese had two carriers badly damaged, but the loss of Hornet *and damage to* Enterprise *reduced the available US carrier force to one. Here, a bomb misses* Enterprise, *the bomber itself crashed on the far side of the ship.*

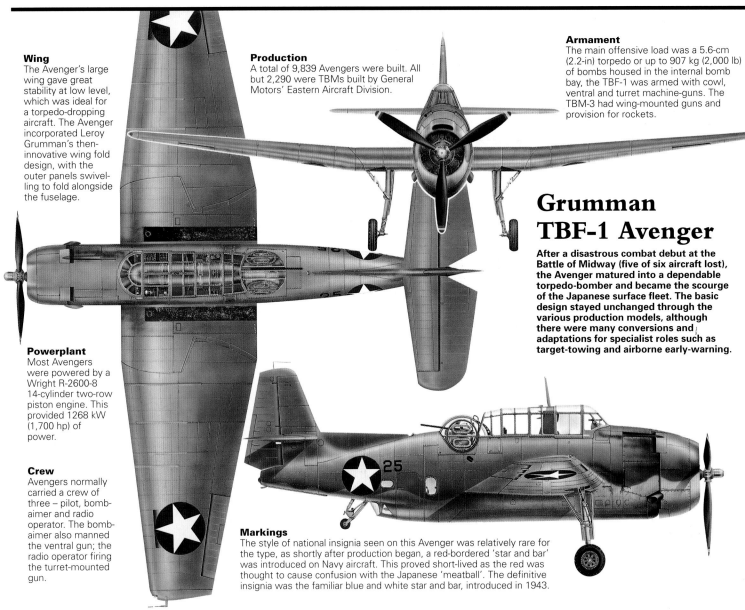

Wing
The Avenger's large wing gave great stability at low level, which was ideal for a torpedo-dropping aircraft. The Avenger incorporated Leroy Grumman's then-innovative wing fold design, with the outer panels swivelling to fold alongside the fuselage.

Production
A total of 9,839 Avengers were built. All but 2,290 were TBMs built by General Motors' Eastern Aircraft Division.

Armament
The main offensive load was a 5.6-cm (2.2-in) torpedo or up to 907 kg (2,000 lb) of bombs housed in the internal bomb bay, the TBF-1 was armed with cowl, ventral and turret machine-guns. The TBM-3 had wing-mounted guns and provision for rockets.

Grumman
TBF-1 Avenger

After a disastrous combat debut at the Battle of Midway (five of six aircraft lost), the Avenger matured into a dependable torpedo-bomber and became the scourge of the Japanese surface fleet. The basic design stayed unchanged through the various production models, although there were many conversions and adaptations for specialist roles such as target-towing and airborne early-warning.

Powerplant
Most Avengers were powered by a Wright R-2600-8 14-cylinder two-row piston engine. This provided 1268 kW (1,700 hp) of power.

Crew
Avengers normally carried a crew of three – pilot, bomb-aimer and radio operator. The bomb-aimer also manned the ventral gun; the radio operator firing the turret-mounted gun.

Markings
The style of national insignia seen on this Avenger was relatively rare for the type, as shortly after production began, a red-bordered 'star and bar' was introduced on Navy aircraft. This proved short-lived as the red was thought to cause confusion with the Japanese 'meatball'. The definitive insignia was the familiar blue and white star and bar, introduced in 1943.

Below: May 1942 saw the Japanese consolidating their hold on the Solomons, from which they could threaten Australia. On 7 August 1942 a Marine force went ashore on Tulagi and Guadalcanal. This photograph was taken from an SBD that day after a raid on Tenambogo.

Right: The A6M3 Navy Type 0 Model 32 reached the Solomons theatre before the US invasion. This latest model of the ubiquitous Zero featured folding wingtips for carrier operations and was known to the Allies at first as 'Hap', then 'Hamp', and later 'Zeke 32'.

Below: SBD Dauntlesses take-off from an airstrip on Russell Island in November 1942. The landings on Guadalcanal were to be the first of a long series of actions aimed at isolating Japan's key position in the south-west Pacific. The 'island-hopping' up the island chain was bitterly contested.

Above: Most Japanese heavy bomber units operated the Mitsubishi Ki-21-II 'Sally'. Very successful in the early part of the war, and remaining in service until the surrender, it was outclassed by modern Allied fighters. This Ki-21 operated with the 14th Bomber Sentai, 3rd Chutai.

Above: The Mitsubishi Ki-46 'Dinah' was the principal Japanese reconnaissance aircraft of the war. With a top speed of 600 km/h (375 mph) and a ceiling of 10830 m (35,530 ft) the Dinah was almost immune from interception until the last part of the war.

Below: Following the capture of the Solomons, the islands became a major base for US and New Zealand aircraft. Land-based naval aircraft such as SBD Dauntlesses, F4F Wildcats and Marine Corps TBF Avengers like these carried out patrols and anti-shipping strikes.

TBFs sinking the *Ryujo* that afternoon. But shortly afterwards, as both sides launched strikes against the opposing carriers, a big air battle developed. The *Enterprise* was hit by three bombs, but despite severe damage, remained in action. By the end of the day the Battle of the East Solomons had cost the Japanese the loss of a light carrier and 61 aircraft, and the Americans withdrew the *Enterprise* for repairs, her SBDs landing on Guadalcanal to help the US Marines. Following an attack by land-based B-17s which sank a Japanese destroyer and damaged another, the Japanese temporarily abandoned their attack on the island.

Japanese submarines then took up the hunt, torpedoing the *Saratoga* on 31 August (the carrier being withdrawn once more for repairs), and sinking the *Wasp* on 15 September.

One further major battle was fought in the Solomon Islands campaign, the Battle of Santa Cruz Islands, fought at the end of October. By then the Americans could deploy but two carriers, the *Enterprise* and *Hornet* with a total of 70 Wildcats, 72 SBDs and 29 TBFs. Against them Yamamoto sent a force which included the *Shokaku*

and *Zuikaku* once more, and the *Junyo* and *Zuiho* with a total of 222 aircraft. On 26 October the *Enterprise* launched a search/strike by 16 SBDs which found and scored two hits on the *Zuiho*. On the same day a 62-aircraft strike attacked the American carriers, hitting the *Hornet* (which sank later), while at the same moment American SBDs attacked the Japanese carriers, hitting the *Shokaku* with at least three bombs. The Japanese launched a further strike whose pilots were able to concentrate on the *Enterprise* which was hit by three more bombs but which, by skillful manoeuvring, avoided nine torpedoes.

TACTICAL VICTORY

The Battle of Santa Cruz Islands ended the Solomon campaign at sea; it was a tactical victory for the Japanese despite damage to two

carriers and the loss of 90 aircraft. The Americans, who lost 74 aircraft, were now down to one operational carrier in the Pacific, the *Enterprise* returning to sea after hasty repairs. Desperate fighting went on in Guadalcanal itself for seven months until in February 1943 the Japanese evacuated 11,000 survivors, leaving

21,000 dead on the island; by that time the battle had cost them 900 aircraft, two battleships and the *Ryujo* sunk, as well as 21 other naval vessels. Not until the Battle for the Marianas in June 1944 would major units of the Japanese navy again engage their counterparts in the US Pacific Fleet.

Right: USS Wasp had 29 serviceable Grumman F4F Wildcat fighters aboard on 7 August 1942. To protect slower attack aircraft increasing numbers of escort fighters were needed. A number of Marine Corps F4F units were committed to the front line during the fight for control of the Solomons.

Island Hopping

OCTOBER 1943 – JULY 1944

Left: Sweeping across Karas harbour in Dutch New Guinea, one of these Douglas A-20Gs is caught by flak and plunges out of control. This scene was to be repeated many times throughout the rest of the Pacific war as American bombers pounded Japanese defences.

Below: By early-December 1943, the 45th Fighter Squadron, 15th Fighter Group, 7th Air Force, had moved to Nanumea Island, east of the Solomons. Here mechanics are servicing 'Geronimo', a Curtiss P-40 Warhawk.

Fortified and garrisoned by the Japanese during the 1930s, the Marshalls, Carolines and Marianas formed a defence perimeter across the Pacific which interrupted the direct routes from the USA and Pearl Harbor to Southeast Asia, the East Indies and Australia. Following Japan's attack on Pearl Harbor the British colonies in the area, the Gilbert and Ellice islands, were captured and incorporated into the Japanese defence perimeter. And it was the tiny atolls of Tarawa and Makin that were to be recaptured first by the Americans, their airfields providing the key bases from which further island-hopping operations would be covered.

Operation 'Galvanic', the assault on the Gilberts, involved the newly-organised Task Force 50 under Rear Admiral Charles A. Pownall, the largest assembly of

carriers hitherto concentrated: six fleet and five light carriers supported by six fast battleships, six cruisers and 21 destroyers. Split into four task groups, these carriers opened their attacks on 19 November 1943 with raids on Jaluit and Mili in the Marshalls to prevent Japanese aircraft based there from interfering

Right: The continuing need to differentiate between the US national insignia and those of the Axis powers brought major changes in 1943, with white rectangles added to the star, as here on a formation of Grumman F4F Wildcats.

over the Gilberts, keeping up their attacks for five days as the US Army went ashore on Makin on 20 November, supported by aircraft from the *Essex*, *Enterprise* and *Bunker Hill* fleet carriers and the *Belleau Wood*, *Monterey* and *Independence* light carriers. Meanwhile another carrier task group with the *Saratoga* and *Princeton* under Rear Admiral

Left: A B-24 Liberator being loaded with fragmentation bomb clusters prior to a raid on Tarawa on 18 November 1943. Each bomb bay could carry 1814 kg (4,000 lb) of bombs, and the bomb doors rolled up the outside of the fuselage in a similar way to a roll-top desk.

Frederick Sherman had been hitting airfields on Bougainville in the Solomons, where the carrier aircraft destroyed 33 Japanese aircraft and sank nine supply ships and 11 lesser vessels for the loss of three aircraft. And in a major air strike on Rabaul, American carrier aircraft damaged four Japanese cruisers, while the crews of 97 Hellcats, Dauntlesses and Avengers claimed the destruction of about 25 enemy aircraft.

US CARRIER LOST

In yet another task group of Task Force 50, the escort carrier *Liscome Bay*, which was about to launch a strike over the Gilberts on the morning of 23 November, was struck by a torpedo from the Japanese submarine *I-175*. On board were almost 200 bombs of weights up to 907 kg (2,000 lb), and the torpedo evidently struck the bomb store. There was a colossal explosion which blasted the vessel apart and killed 643 crew members including Rear Admiral Henry M. Mullinnix, the task group commander. This was the only US warship lost during this phase of the American drive across the central Pacific.

Right: Douglas SBD-5 Dauntless aircraft returning from a bombing run on an airfield on Param Island in the Truk Atoll, with other SBDs bearing down to strafe the remains. The SBD-5 was powered by the improved R-1820-60 engine.

Left: The most widely employed Japanese land bomber was the Mitsubishi G4M, codenamed 'Betty'. This had paved the way for the lightning advance through the Pacific in 1942, although it proved no match for Allied fighters.

The successful assault on Tarawa was accomplished in three days. It also marked a new air fighting tactic by naval aircraft, that of radar-guided night-fighting. A radar-equipped TBF Avenger, accompanied by a pair of F6F Hellcats, would be launched, and the TBF would vector the F6Fs into visual range of the target. In the first operational sortie, on 26/27 November, the F6Fs were slow in closing up to the TBF and it was left to the latter's pilot, Commander John Phillips, to shoot down the first target, a G4M 'Betty', with his two wing machine-guns; later in the same sortie, as the F6Fs closed up, the

Below: Only the immense industrial capacity of the United States could have sustained the vast effort required to conduct a war on the scale of the Pacific campaign, with forces committed to huge strategic drives through the theatre.
The two main axes in the Pacific were from Australia and along the Solomon Islands, and a fleet-borne push from atoll to atoll through the central Pacific – island hopping.
In the central Pacific, Admiral C. Nimitz was the Allied forces commander; the south Pacific forces were under the command of Admiral W. Halsey, while the south-west Pacific forces were the responsibilty of General D. MacArthur.

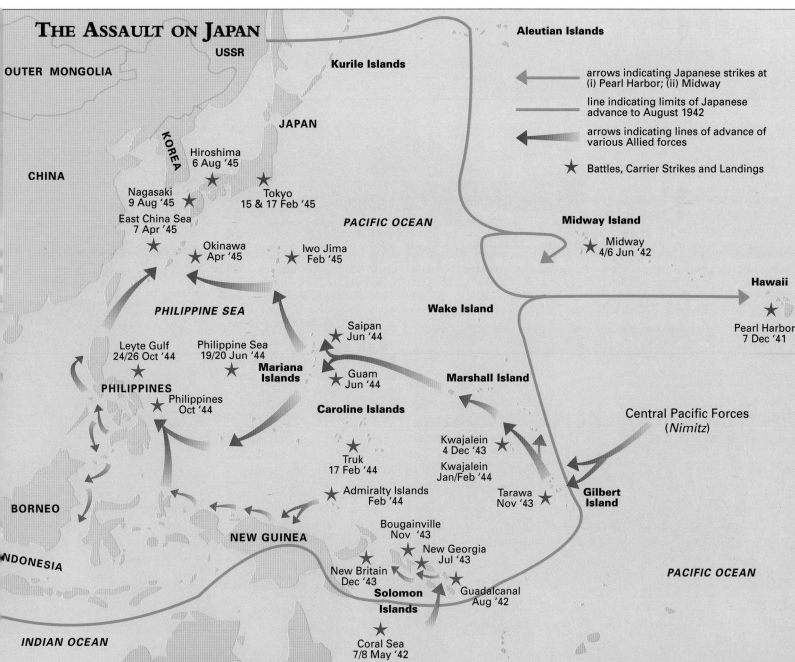

THE ASSAULT ON JAPAN

Aleutian Islands

OUTER MONGOLIA

USSR

Kurile Islands

arrows indicating Japanese strikes at (i) Pearl Harbor; (ii) Midway

line indicating limits of Japanese advance to August 1942

arrows indicating lines of advance of various Allied forces

★ Battles, Carrier Strikes and Landings

JAPAN

KOREA

CHINA

Hiroshima 6 Aug '45

Nagasaki 9 Aug '45

Tokyo 15 & 17 Feb '45

East China Sea 7 Apr '45

PACIFIC OCEAN

Midway Island

Midway 4/6 Jun '42

Okinawa Apr '45

Iwo Jima Feb '45

Hawaii

Pearl Harbor 7 Dec '41

PHILIPPINE SEA

Wake Island

Leyte Gulf 24/26 Oct '44

Philippine Sea 19/20 Jun '44

Saipan Jun '44

PHILIPPINES

Mariana Islands

Guam Jun '44

Marshall Island

Central Pacific Forces (*Nimitz*)

Philippines Oct '44

Caroline Islands

Kwajalein 4 Dec '43

Kwajalein Jan/Feb '44

Truk 17 Feb '44

Tarawa Nov '43

Gilbert Island

BORNEO

Admiralty Islands Feb '44

Bougainville Nov '43

New Georgia Jul '43

NEW GUINEA

PACIFIC OCEAN

INDONESIA

New Britain Dec '43

Solomon Islands

Guadalcanal Aug '42

INDIAN OCEAN

Coral Sea 7/8 May '42

Land-based air power

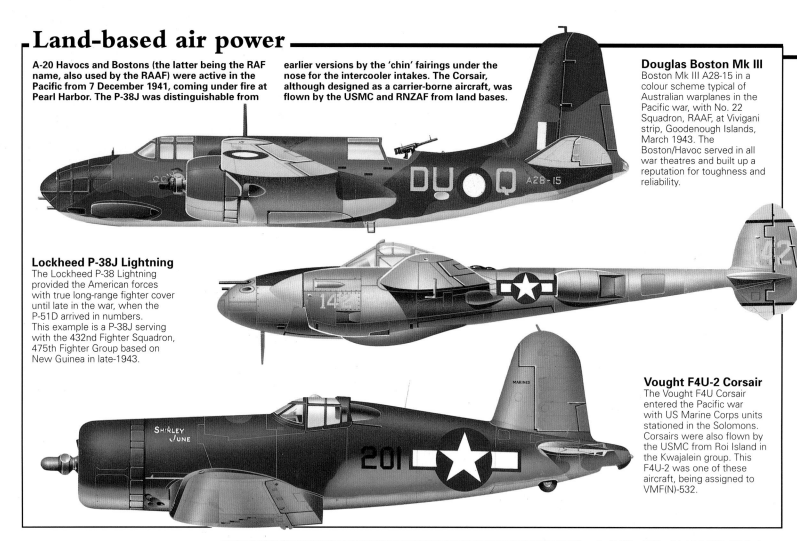

A-20 Havocs and Bostons (the latter being the RAF name, also used by the RAAF) were active in the Pacific from 7 December 1941, coming under fire at Pearl Harbor. The P-38J was distinguishable from earlier versions by the 'chin' fairings under the nose for the intercooler intakes. The Corsair, although designed as a carrier-borne aircraft, was flown by the USMC and RNZAF from land bases.

Douglas Boston Mk III
Boston Mk III A28-15 in a colour scheme typical of Australian warplanes in the Pacific war, with No. 22 Squadron, RAAF, at Vivigani strip, Goodenough Islands, March 1943. The Boston/Havoc served in all war theatres and built up a reputation for toughness and reliability.

Lockheed P-38J Lightning
The Lockheed P-38 Lightning provided the American forces with true long-range fighter cover until late in the war, when the P-51D arrived in numbers. This example is a P-38J serving with the 432nd Fighter Squadron, 475th Fighter Group based on New Guinea in late-1943.

Vought F4U-2 Corsair
The Vought F4U Corsair entered the Pacific war with US Marine Corps units stationed in the Solomons. Corsairs were also flown by the USMC from Roi Island in the Kwajalein group. This F4U-2 was one of these aircraft, being assigned to VMF(N)-532.

TBF's turret gunner opened fire at what he assumed to be a Japanese bomber but was in fact the fighter flown by Commander Butch O'Hare, the US Navy's first fighter ace and holder of the Medal of Honor. He was never seen again.

The next phase of the American offensive involved the assault of Kwajalein and Namur islands in the Marshalls; Operation 'Flintlock', on 31 January 1944. In support was Task Force 58, reconstituted under Rear Admiral Mark A. Mitscher from TF 50, now with six fleet and six light carriers. Among their aircraft were the first F4U-2 Corsair and F6F-3N Hellcat radar night-fighters. During the six-day operations to capture the key Marshall islands, American carrier aircraft destroyed some 150 Japanese aircraft (mostly on the ground), for the cost of 49 of their own number.

ON TO ENIWETOK

Following the capture of Kwajalein, Sherman's carrier task group descended upon Eniwetok atoll, 480 km (300 miles) to the west and almost mid-way between the Marshalls and the next archipelago, the Carolines. Eleven days after the fall of Kwajalein the amphibious forces of the US 5th Fleet went ashore and eliminated the Japanese garrison at Eniwetok.

The climax of the American destruction of Japan's central Pacific defence perimeter arrived with the

Left: The Mitsubishi A6M3 ('Zeke' 22) was the version without folding wingtips that was used in the south-west Pacific from the spring of 1942. These Zeros are with 204 Flying Group at Rabaul in New Britain in 1943.

Below: On 21 August 1943 a formation of Liberators on a bombing mission came across a Naval Type O Transport, Aircraft Model 11 or L2D (a Douglas DC-3 licence-built in Japan) which was promptly shot down by the dorsal gunner from one of the B-24s.

Left: Smoke plumes rise from installations on Dublon Island in September 1944 as B-24 Liberators of the 7th Air Force continue the neutralisation of the Japanese Truk bastion. Battered Eten Island lies to the right of Dublon.

assault on Truk atoll, capital of the Carolines, 1050 km (650 miles) north of Rabaul in New Britain. The first air strikes on Truk (apart from pre-emptive attacks launched during previous assaults elsewhere) were flown at dawn on D-Day, 17 February 1944. On the airstrips the US Navy pilots found 365 Japanese aircraft parked nose to tail, destroyed at least 125 of them and sank 30 merchant vessels, a cruiser, three destroyers and a sub-chaser.

Right: US paratroopers dropped from USAAF C-47 Skytrain transports float down on to the beach-head at Noemfoor in July 1944. This advance brought the Allies to New Guinea's western end.

Below: 'El Diablo IV', a B-25D-10-NC, flies over New Britain Island while operating with the 5th Air Force to attack Cape Gloucester. More than 2359 kg (5,200 lb) of bombs could be carried by the Mitchell; 2,290 B-25Ds were built.

Curtiss SB2C-3 Helldiver

Despite its great accomplishments in the Pacific theatre, the Helldiver was never popular with aircrew – the designation was said to mean 'Son of a Bitch, 2nd Class'. This aircraft flew with CV-19 aboard the USS *Hancock*, 1943-44.

Powerplant
The SB2C-3, which began to appear in 1944, had an uprated Wright Cyclone R-2600-20 14-cylinder, air-cooled radial piston engine.

Armament
After the first 200 SB2C-1s, fitted with four 12.7-mm (0.50-in) machine-guns, fixed armament was changed to two 20-mm (0.79-in) cannon. In addition, the Helldiver had two 7.6-mm (0.30-in) guns in the rear cockpit and an internal bombload of 454 kg (1,000 lb). The SB2C-4 had wing fittings for eight 12.7-cm (0.5-in) rockets or up to 454 kg (1,000 lb) of additional bombs.

Dive brakes
The SB2C-3 illustrated shows the plain (unperforated) flaps originally fitted, which caused a severe buffet when used as dive brakes.

Undercarriage
For carrier landings, a substantial undercarriage was a necessity. The retractable mainwheels comprised two Curtiss oleo-pneumatic shock-absorber struts raised inwards into the undersides of the wings.

WORLD WAR II IN THE PACIFIC

The success of the devastating air strikes deprived the Japanese of effective air cover when the amphibious forces assaulted the islands, and in contrast to the 2,677 Japanese defenders who died the US casualties totalled 399.

Reduction of the Japanese garrisons in the large archipelagoes, successfully accomplished between November 1943 and February 1944, was followed by a temporary withdrawl of the American carrier forces to regroup for the next phase, the great thrust into the south-west Pacific.

Above: A B-24 Liberator makes an emergency landing on one mainwheel after an attack against the Marshall Islands. By the end of 1943, the B-24 was by far the most important long-range bomber in the Pacific area.

Left: A B-25 Mitchell of the 5th Air Force low over the harbour at Rabaul, New Britain, in an attack which sank or damaged 26 Japanese ships on 2 November 1943.

Below: On 16 June 1943, Lieutenant Murray J. Shubin (below with his P-38 Lightning named 'Oriole') of the 339th Fighter Squadron destroyed five enemy fighters and claimed a sixth as a probable during a 45-minute air battle.

Imperial Japanese warriors

The Imperial Japanese Navy had been operating flying-boats since the 1930s and the 'Mavis' (its Allied codename) gained a reputation as one of the best flying-boats of the war. 'Dinah' was the name given to the Ki-46, a high-speed reconnaissance type and bomber that was initially immune from fighter attack. The Ki-49 bomber first flew in 1939 and later filled transport and ASW roles.

Kawanishi H6K
A fine flying-boat from the Kawanishi stable was the H6K 'Mavis', that was widely employed on maritime reconnaissance, anti-shipping and transport duties. However, the vulnerability of the flying-boat soon drove the H6K to areas away from US fighter opposition.

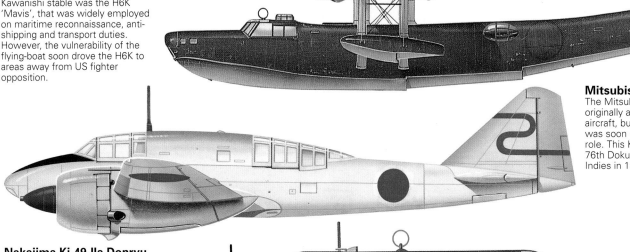

Mitsubishi Ki-46-II
The Mitsubishi Ki-46 was used originally as a fast reconnaissance aircraft, but this effective aircraft was soon employed in an offensive role. This Ki-46-II flew with the 76th Dokuritsu Hikochutai, East Indies in 1943.

Nakajima Ki-49-IIa Donryu
The 'Storm Dragon' ('Helen' to the Allies) was found to be underpowered, and more powerful engines came with the Ki-49-II. Shown here is a Ki-49-IIa of the 3rd Chutai, 61st Sentai. Its lack of speed was to remain a problem.

Corsair versus Zero

Captain R. Bruce Porter, USMC, recounts his experience flying Corsairs in the summer of 1943, as he downs a Zero during an early-morning patrol while flying from near Guadalcanal.

"We were at 18,000 ft and heading north-west... the remainder of the squadron, and three other alert squadrons, were dispersed nearby or right behind us. Thus we had 32 Corsairs and Wildcats flying as a leading wedge and nearly an identical number coming on as a follow-up force. The New Zealanders managed to launch another 30 P-40 fighters...

"I do not think I was ever so exhilarated as I was during that flight... I was just commenting to myself what a beautiful day it was when my earphones suddenly crackled with an incoming all-squadrons message: 'Tally ho! Zeros at 11 O'clock. Angels 25.' I charged my guns and turned on my reflector sight, which cast an image of a gunsight, complete with distance calibrations, on the windscreen in front of my face.

"Within seconds, I saw silvery glints against the bright-blue background of the sky. The enemy

Left: Pictured in the cockpit of his A6M2 Zero in 1943, this cheerful pilot is believed to be WO Yoshira Hashiguchi of the 3rd Flying Group in 1943. The Zero's gun sighting system is visible behind the windscreen.

fighter formations were coming in from all directions... all the best training in the world could not abate the instant of surprise when my eyes locked on to a target of their own.

"I never consciously pressed my gun-button knob... I seemed to know enough to allow my instincts to prevail over my mind. My guns were bore-sighted to converge in a cone about 300-yards ahead. Anything within that cone would be hit by a stream of half-inch steel-jacketed bullets. My Corsair shuddered slightly as all the guns fired, and I saw my tracer passing just over the Zero's long birdcage canopy...

"My turn was easy. I did not pull too many Gs, so my head was absolutely clear. I came up with a far deflection shot and decided to go for it. It gave the Zero a good lead and fired all my guns again. As planned, my tracers went ahead of him, but at just the right level. I kicked my left rudder to pull my round in towards his nose.

"If that Japanese pilot had flown straight ahead, he would have been a dead man. Instead, that superb pilot presented me with a demonstration of the Zero's best flight characteristic... as soon as my quarry saw my tracer pass in front, he simply pulled straight up and literally disappeared from within my reflector sight... I was so in awe of the manoeuvre that I was literally shaking with envy... then I pulled my joystick into my belly and banked as hard to the left as I dared.

"There he was! He was just beyond my reach. If I were to get a clear shot, I would have to pull up in an even steeper climb... I held my breath and sucked in my gut to counteract the pressure, but I felt the forces of gravity steadily mount up and press me into my seat...

He had me in a tight loop by then. All the alarm bells went off in my head at the same time, but I hung on despite the grey pall that was simultaneously passing over my eyes and my mind.

"I finally reached the top of the loop, a point where all the forces were in equilibrium. Suddenly, the G forces relaxed. I was not quite weightless, but neither was I my full body weight. There was a moment of grogginess, then the grey pall totally cleared. I noticed that the horizon was upside down and that the Zero was in my sights!

"It was now or never. I squeezed the gun-button beneath my right index finger. The eerie silence in my cockpit was broken by the steady roar of my machine-guns. The Zero never had a chance. It flew directly into the cone of deadly half-inch bullets. I was easily able to stay on it as the stream of tracer first sawed into the leading edge of the left wing. I saw little pieces of metal fly away from the impact area and clearly thought I should nudge my gunsight – which is to say, my entire Corsair – a hair to the right. The stream of tracer worked its way to the cockpit. I clearly saw the glass canopy shatter, but there was so much glinting, broken glass and debris that I could not see the pilot. The Zero wobbled, and my tracer fell into first one wing root, then the other, striking the enemy's unprotected fuel tanks. The Zero blew up, evaporated."

Left: Perhaps the greatest piston-engined naval fighter of all, the F4U (and Goodyear-built FG) Corsair took some time to develop, some of the first going to VF-71. Here early F4U-1s are returning to the USS Yorktown in 1943.

Saipan and Guam

FEBRUARY – JULY 1944

A combat formation of Vought F4U-1 Corsair fighters of the celebrated US Marine Corps 'Black Sheep' squadron (VMF-124) banks over the island of Bougainville in the Solomons. Corsairs were found to be highly effective at ground attack and were widely used in this role.

Inset: Nearly all of the American Corsairs in the Pacific theatre were flown by the US Marine Corps, accounting for 2,140 enemy aircraft. The 'Black Sheep' squadron was based in the Marianas, where 'Pappy' Boyington leads his men out to their aircraft.

Key to the US Navy's success in the Gilberts, Marshalls and Carolines had been the inability of the Japanese to bring into action any significant numbers of naval aircraft to contest air superiority over the landings. Indeed, following earlier heavy losses, the Japanese had been hard at work reorganising their depleted carrier forces. By mid-May the Japanese fleet at Tawi Tawi off the coast of Borneo included the surviving veterans *Zuiho*, *Shokaku* and *Zuikaku*, the new *Taiho*, the *Hiyo* and *Junyo*, and the light carriers *Chitose*, *Chiyoda* and *Ryuho*. These nine vessels constituted the largest force of carriers ever assembled under a Japanese task force commander. Although a new generation of aircraft, such as the improved A6M5 'Zeke' fighter-bomber, the D4Y3 'Judy' and the B6N1 'Jill' torpedo/attack bombers, were joining the fleet in growing numbers in 1944, the real weakness lay in a chronic shortage of experienced fliers. Two years of heavy fighting had taken a huge toll of Japan's naval airmen, and the replacements would now be pitted against vastly improved US aircraft, notably the F6F Hellcat and F4U Corsair.

Furthermore, following the assault on Truk in February 1944, the American carriers withdrew to reorganise, re-equip and re-crew. By June Task Force 58 had grown to five task groups with 15 carriers, the fleet carriers *Bunker Hill*, *Enterprise*, *Essex*, *Hornet*, *Lexington*, *Wasp* and *Yorktown*, and the light carriers *Bataan*, *Belleau Wood*, *Cabot*,

The Mitsubishi J2M-5 Thunderbolt (Allied codename 'Jack') naval interceptor fighter had a supercharged engine and could reach 20,000 ft in less than six minutes from take-off. It was used to intercept high-flying USAAF B-29s.

Cowpens, *Langley*, *Monterey*, *Princeton* and *San Jacinto*; between them they embarked no fewer than 480 Hellcat day and night fighters, 199 Avengers, 222 Helldiver and Dauntless dive-bombers and three Corsair night-fighters.

In Marianas skies

The Mitsubishi Ki-46 'Dinah' was one of the best reconnaissance aircraft of the war and was active until the end of hostilities over the Marianas' B-29 bases. About five times as many Curtiss SB2C

Helldiver carrier-based dive-bombers were produced as were 'Dinahs', but the type's development was protracted and it was never very popular with its air or ground crews, unlike the sleek Mitsubishi.

Mitsubishi Ki-46-III
With the capture or destruction of air bases in the Marianas, the long-ranged Ki-46s based elsewhere came into their own for tracking Allied movements. In 1944, the main service version was the improved Ki-46-III.

Curtiss SB2C Helldiver
The Curtiss SB2C was nicknamed the 'Son of a Bitch 2nd Class' by pilots and ground crew alike, as its handling and stability were so poor. It went on to achieve a useful war record and played a large part in the raids on Truk, Saipan, Tinian and Guam

Fighting 'boats

The Japanese Kawanishi H8K 'Emily' is generally acknowledged as the best four-engined flying-boat to see service in World War II. The H8K2 variant had sea search radar and armament of five 20-mm cannon and one machine-gun. The closest US equivalent was the twin-engined Martin PBM Mariner, which was comparitvely lightly-armed (eight machine-guns), faster but shorter-ranged.

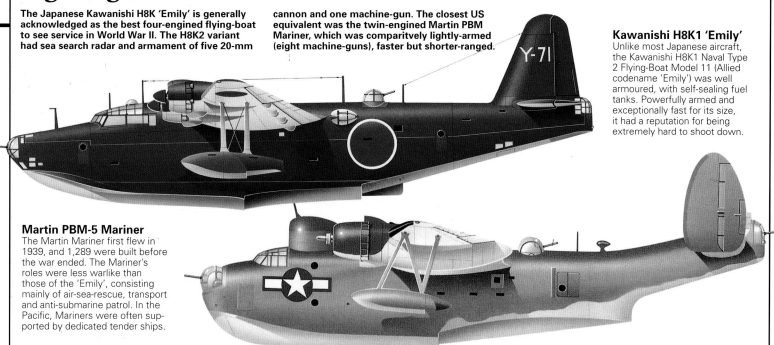

Kawanishi H8K1 'Emily'
Unlike most Japanese aircraft, the Kawanishi H8K1 Naval Type 2 Flying-Boat Model 11 (Allied codename 'Emily') was well armoured, with self-sealing fuel tanks. Powerfully armed and exceptionally fast for its size, it had a reputation for being extremely hard to shoot down.

Martin PBM-5 Mariner
The Martin Mariner first flew in 1939, and 1,289 were built before the war ended. The Mariner's roles were less warlike than those of the 'Emily', consisting mainly of air-sea-rescue, transport and anti-submarine patrol. In the Pacific, Mariners were often supported by dedicated tender ships.

Left: A formation of 18 Grumman TBF Avengers returns to the carrier USS Enterprise after a mission. Due to its range, the Avenger was the most widely used type for air patrols to counter the constant threat of submarines to vital Allied convoys.

Below: Throughout the war in the Pacific, the Nakajima B5N 'Kate' took its toll of Allied shipping. This excellent torpedo-bomber figured in all the naval engagements after Pearl Harbor until superseded by the same company's B6N.

BUILD-UP IN THE MARIANAS

The newly appointed Japanese commander-in-chief, Admiral Soemu Toyoda, recognised that the American operations in the Central Pacific were but a prelude to a major and sustained thrust either westwards or southwestwards, and that such a thrust would pose a serious threat to their forces in New Guinea and the East Indies. He decided on a plan, Operation A-Go, to seek a decisive battle with the US 5th Fleet, his own forces being spearheaded by his carriers. In order to be close to the fuel source of the Borneo oil fields, Toyoda chose to base his fleet at Tawi Tawi (accepting the risk of using their characteristically highly volatile fuel in his ships).

As soon as US reconnaissance aircraft exposed the Japanese naval concentration at Tawi Tawi, US Navy submarines flocked to the area and by mid-June had torpedoed four oilers and five destroyers.

The presence of these submarines prevented the Japanese from going to sea for training, so that many new aircrews had to remain without adequate experience of operations with the fleet. The Americans, on the other hand, while failing to entice the Japanese out of Tawi Tawi, sailed for Marcus and Wake in order to gain 'controlled' combat experience for their new airmen, flying strikes during the last 10 days of May with relatively light losses.

The US plans now included the capture of Saipan and Guam, respectively at the north and south

Left: A P-47D-20-RA Thunderbolt of the 19th Fighter Squadron, 318th Fighter Group in the Marianas prepares for a dive bombing mission to Pagan Island, Saipan. Airfields were quickly established once an island was captured.

Below: The kamikaze attack became the biggest threat to US sailors in the latter part of the war, beginning initially when pilots of mortally crippled aircraft aimed to crash their damaged aircraft on ships. The practice was to become highly organised.

Northrop P-61 Black Widow

Illustrated here is one of the most famous P-61s operated in the Pacific Theatre. P-61B-1-NO 42-39403 was almost unique in having the dorsal gun barbette fitted. Other features of the B model included a slightly longer nose and four external pylons.

Armament
The P-61 carried four 20-mm M-2 cannon, each with 200 rounds; its dorsal barbette had four 12.7-mm Colt-Browning M-2 machine-guns, each with 560 rounds; four external pylons were each capable of carrying 726 kg (1,600 lb) and able to carry bombs or other stores up to this weight.

Powerplants
The P-61 was powered by two 1491-kW (2,000-hp) Pratt & Whitney R-2800-65 Double Wasp 18-cylinder radial engines.

Performance
The P-61 enjoyed a maximum speed of 589 km/h (366 mph) at 6096 m (20,000 ft), with an initial climb rate of 637 m (2,090 ft) per minute, and a range of 2172 km (1,350 miles) at 368 km/h (229 mph).

Dimensions
The wing span of the P-61B-1-NO was 20.11 m (66 ft 0¾ in), with a total wing area of 61.53 m² (662.36 sq ft), a length of 15.11 m (49 ft 7 in) and a height 4.47 m (14 ft 8 in).

---

ends of the Mariana chain, and the stage was now being set for what was to be the greatest-ever carrier battle, the Battle of the Philippine Sea, in which the once-vaunted Japanese carrier force would be crushingly defeated and suffer huge losses in aircraft.

The preliminary actions of Operation Forager against Saipan and Guam opened on 11 June as the American carriers launched strikes against Saipan and Tinian with 208 Hellcats and eight Avengers, destroying about 36 enemy aircraft on the ground. On the following day a small Japanese convoy was attacked from the air as it sailed from Saipan, losing 10 merchant ships, a torpedo boat and three sub-chasers. On 15 June US Marines landed on Saipan.

TACTICAL ERROR

Two days earlier, however, now warned of the presence of the American 5th Fleet, the Japanese navy sortied from Tawi Tawi, a sailing immediately reported by the submarine *Redfin* to Admiral

Left: US Marine Corps pilots on a Pacific island before embarking for a mission. Although a standard pilots uniform was issued, few pilots wore it as only the inflatable Mae West, helmet and goggles were deemed essential.

The Mitsubishi A6M5 Naval Type 0 Carrier-borne Fighter Model 52 was an advanced version of the A6M with strengthened wings, and could be dived at speeds in excess of 400 mph. The A6M5a (above) was fitted with a long-barrel, belt-fed cannon.

Left: A large group of 7th US Air Force personnel watch a B-24J take-off from an airstrip in the Marianas. Following in the wake of the liberation forces, the USAAF was eager to get bases nearer to the Japanese mainland.

Above: By 1944, security measures resulted in unit insignia no longer being painted on aircraft, only individual aircraft numbers within the unit. These SBD-3s are described as 'returning to their carrier after a dive-bombing mission'.

Spruance. This admiral then made one of the few major controversial decisions of the American naval campaign in the Pacific. He cancelled the imminent invasion of Guam and ordered most of the assault and supply ships off Saipan to disperse; he also ordered all five task groups of TF 58 to concentrate to meet the Japanese threat. It has been argued that he should have allowed the fast battleships of Task Group 58.7 under Vice Admiral Willis Lee to remain independent. With the subsequent decimation of the Japanese carrier forces, in which the battleships would take little or no part during the Battle of the Philippine Sea, such a powerful force of ships could have been deployed in readiness to destroy the remaining Japanese fleet without fear of air attackr. While the gruesome naval battle was being fought, the island of Saipan eventually fell on 9 July after 14,000 Americans had fallen dead or wounded; Japanese dead totalled 30,000.

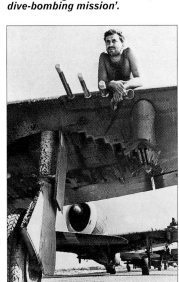

Right: Perched on the wings of P-47Ds of the 19th Fighter Squadron, 218th Fighter Group, Saipan, crew chiefs guide pilots along a taxiway to the runway. Without this guidance, the pilot would be forced to zig-zag to keep the route ahead in view.

A Mitsubishi G4M Betty naval attack bomber in a semi-derelict state on an island in the Marianas. Probably the best known Japanese bomber, the G4M had considerable range capability, achieved by lightweight structure and a total lack of armour protection.

Right: The guns are manned and ready as an F6F Hellcat lands on the deck of the USS Lexington (CV-16, part of CVAG-16) during a Japanese air attack in the Battle of Saipan. On 19 June, Dauntless dive-bombers flew their last major combat operation from the carrier.

The Marianas Turkey Shoot

JUNE – AUGUST 1944

Left: Outbound Republic P-47 Thunderbolts on island patrol have the right of way as they flash across the end of the runway at a strategic base in the Marianas in August 1944.

Below: Despite its unpopularity in service, resulting in the re-interpretation of its designation as 'Son of a Bitch, 2nd Class', some 7,000 Curtiss SB2C Helldivers were built. These aircraft are returning to a carrier of Task Force 58.1 following a bombing mission over Chici-Jima on 7 June 1944.

The June of 1944 found the American forces heavily committed in their 'island-hopping' advance through the central Pacific, and the US forces were by that time far inside the original empire defence perimeter declared by the Japanese some two years previously. The success that attended this bloody advance was rendered possible by the steady build-up of powerful American naval forces, not least in carriers, in the Pacific. On 15 June 20,000 US Marines supported by US carrier aircraft and a heavy naval bombardment, went ashore on Saipan.

BATTLE FLEETS PREPARE

As soon as the Japanese supreme command learned of this landing, it ordered the 'destruction' of the US Pacific Fleet by the Japanese Mobile Fleet. In effect the American force then located in the Philippine Sea comprised Task Force 58, commanded by Vice-Admiral Marc A. Mitscher, with seven fleet carriers (the *Bunker Hill*, *Enterprise*, *Essex*, *Hornet*, *Lexington*, *Wasp* and *Yorktown*), eight light carriers, seven fast battleships, eight heavy cruisers, 12 other cruisers and 66 destroyers. Embarked in the carriers were 199

TBF/TBM Avenger torpedo bombers, 222 SB2C Helldiver and SBD Dauntless divebombers and 483 F6F Hellcat fighters. Against them the Japanese Mobile Fleet under Vice-Admiral Jisaburo Ozawa, consisted of five fleet carri-

ers (the *Hiyo*, *Junyo*, *Shokaku*, *Taiho* and *Zuikaku*), four light carriers, five battleships, seven heavy cruisers, two light cruisers and 23 destroyers; embarked were 99 B5N and B6N torpedo bombers, 206 dive-bombers and 145 A6M Zero

Left: P-38L-1 Lightning 'Little Red Head II' of the 318th Lightning Provisionals, being fitted with large drop tanks for a long-range mission from Isley Field, Saipan, Marianas in mid-1944. With two 1136-litre (300-gallon) drop tanks the 'L' had a range of 4184 km (2,600 miles).

Above: No aircraft was to have greater impact on the Japanese than the Grumman F6F Hellcat. The type formed the backbone of the US Navy's fighter defences throughout the offensive stages of the war. This aircraft awaits its next mission on board CV-10 USS Yorktown in June 1944.

Day and night fighters

Immensely powerful and heavily-built, P-47's served the USAAF in Europe and the Pacific and the RAF in the Far East. The primary production variant was the P-47D, later examples of which had a bubble canopy, which greatly improved visibility. The first purpose-built night fighter in the USAAF was the radar-equipped P-61. In service from 1944, these aircraft filled a secondary ground-attack role.

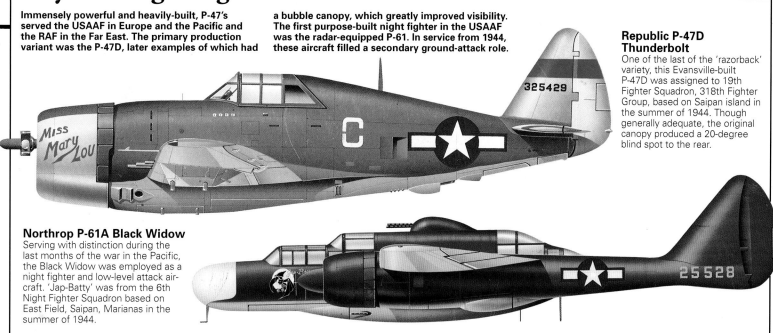

Republic P-47D Thunderbolt
One of the last of the 'razorback' variety, this Evansville-built P-47D was assigned to 19th Fighter Squadron, 318th Fighter Group, based on Saipan island in the summer of 1944. Though generally adequate, the original canopy produced a 20-degree blind spot to the rear.

Northrop P-61A Black Widow
Serving with distinction during the last months of the war in the Pacific, the Black Widow was employed as a night fighter and low-level attack aircraft. 'Jap-Batty' was from the 6th Night Fighter Squadron based on East Field, Saipan, Marianas in the summer of 1944.

Right: The Vought OS2U Kingfisher was to prove the most useful of the observation and scout aircraft available to the US Navy at this time. Easily recognised by its large centreline and smaller under-wing floats, deliveries totalled 1,006 when production ceased in 1944.

fighters.

After sightings of the units of the Japanese fleet by US submarines, Admiral Spruance, commanding the American 5th Fleet, ordered Task Force 58 to assemble on 18 June, when it was located by a Japanese carrier search aircraft. That night the Mobile Fleet also assembled for battle and was spotted on radar by a PBM Mariner patrol flying-boat. By early on 19 June Task Force 58 was some 160-km (100-miles) west of Guam in the Marianas, the Japanese Mobile Fleet about 320 km (200 miles) farther west. Sporadic air fighting occurred around dawn as Hellcats were launched to investigate radar reports of enemy aircraft; these proved to be search aircraft from the Japanese battleships and cruisers. Soon afterwards the first powerful strikes were launched by the Japanese carriers, and just after the *Taiho* had flown off 42 aircraft the carrier was struck by a torpedo from the US submarine *Albacore* (a second torpedo would have hit had its track not been spotted by a Japanese pilot who dived his aircraft on to the missile and exploded it).

Warned by radar of the

Below: A Nakajima Ki-49 Donryu (Storm Dragon) – Allied codename 'Helen' – being strafed on an air-field in the Marianas. The Ki-49 was intended to replace the Mitsubishi Ki-21 'Sally', but units equipped with them suffered heavy losses during the Allied advance from the Philippines.

Above: Lt Cdr Kiyokuma Ikajima (seated) in front of his Mitsubishi A6M5 of the 203 Flying Group in the Marianas. The A6M was known to the Japanese airmen as the 'Rei Sentoki', or Zero fighter, a term commonly abbreviated to 'Reisen'.

Left: A somewhat later design than the Catalina, the Martin PBM Mariner was a larger aircraft and superior in performance, although it served in smaller numbers. Here a Mariner is operating from a mobile seaplane tender on patrol bombing missions and protective cover flights for the Pacific Fleet.

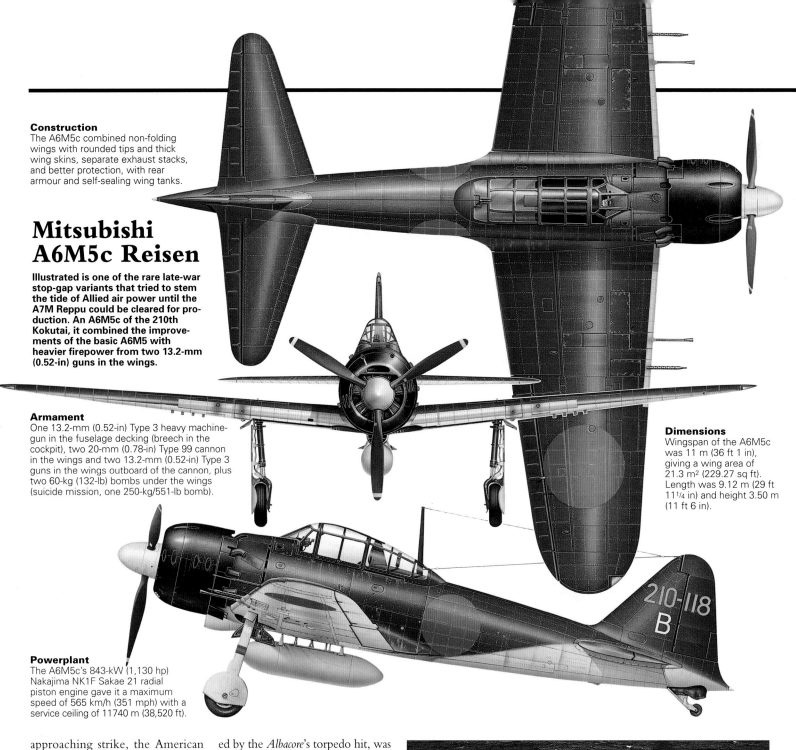

Construction
The A6M5c combined non-folding wings with rounded tips and thick wing skins, separate exhaust stacks, and better protection, with rear armour and self-sealing wing tanks.

Mitsubishi A6M5c Reisen

Illustrated is one of the rare late-war stop-gap variants that tried to stem the tide of Allied air power until the A7M Reppu could be cleared for production. An A6M5c of the 210th Kokutai, it combined the improvements of the basic A6M5 with heavier firepower from two 13.2-mm (0.52-in) guns in the wings.

Armament
One 13.2-mm (0.52-in) Type 3 heavy machine-gun in the fuselage decking (breech in the cockpit), two 20-mm (0.78-in) Type 99 cannon in the wings and two 13.2-mm (0.52-in) Type 3 guns in the wings outboard of the cannon, plus two 60-kg (132-lb) bombs under the wings (suicide mission, one 250-kg/551-lb bomb).

Dimensions
Wingspan of the A6M5c was 11 m (36 ft 1 in), giving a wing area of 21.3 m² (229.27 sq ft). Length was 9.12 m (29 ft 11¼ in) and height 3.50 m (11 ft 6 in).

Powerplant
The A6M5c's 843-kW (1,130 hp) Nakajima NK1F Sakae 21 radial piston engine gave it a maximum speed of 565 km/h (351 mph) with a service ceiling of 11740 m (38,520 ft).

approaching strike, the American carriers launched every available fighter. The US Navy and US Marine pilots destroying 42 of the 69 attacking aircraft. Apart from a single bomb hit on the battleship *South Dakota*, little damage was done and the raiders failed to reach the carriers. Shortly after 11.00 a second strike by 109 aircraft was spotted on radar. Again the Hellcats were launched and this time only about 15 of the raiders returned to their carriers. A third strike by 47 aircraft followed, and this time about half of them failed to find the American ships; of the others, seven were shot down. Yet one more strike, by 82 aircraft, was launched before midday on 19 June, no fewer than 73 of them being destroyed, many of them by the ships' guns as well as some caught by Hellcats as they tried to land on Guam.

Meanwhile the *Taiho*, whose seaworthiness had been little affect-ed by the *Albacore*'s torpedo hit, was in trouble as her crew fought to get the fires under control; these efforts were succeeding when the ship's ventilating system was opened to dissipate the fumes of leaking fuel; suddenly in mid-afternoon a tremendous explosion occurred in

Above: An F6F Hellcat landing on the new USS Hornet (CV-11), after a raid over the Marianas in June 1944. During what became known as 'The Great Marianas Turkey Shoot', the Japanese lost 346 aircraft, while the US lost 130.

Left: Seen on 26 June 1944, this Thunderbolt 'Hed up 'N locked' fell victim to a Japanese sniper's bullet on Saipan. Some usable parts have been salvaged, including the four 12.7-mm (0.5-in) machine-guns from the starboard wing.

back on their carriers in the darkness and short of fuel. A total of 130 American aircraft were lost during the day, compared with three Japanese carriers, two oilers and 346 aircraft.

Little wonder the Battle of the Philippine Sea earned the gruesome nickname among the US Navy of 'The Great Marianas Turkey Shoot'. By 10 August Saipan had

the big carrier and she eventually capsized, Ozawa and his staff having been transferred to a destroyer; 13 aircraft went down with her.

Disaster had overtaken another Japanese carrier, this time the Pearl Harbor and Coral Sea veteran *Shokaku* being hit by three torpedoes from the American submarine *Cavallo* soon after midday. Once more volatile gases spread through the ship from ruptured fuel tanks and three hours later she blew up and sank, taking with her 1,263 men and nine more aircraft.

THE 'TURKEY SHOOT'

It was now the turn of the Americans to launch strikes against the Japanese fleet. Starting at 18.40 a total of 216 aircraft were flown off, split into half a dozen groups, one of which sank two Japanese fleet oilers. Another attacked the Japanese 2nd Carrier Division, two torpedo hits being made on the *Hiyo*, which later sank; the *Junyo*

was hit by two bombs but escaped. Elsewhere the *Zuikaku* was struck by one bomb, as was the light carrier *Chiyoda*. Although the Japanese fighters reacted strongly and shot down about 20 of the American aircraft, far more were destroyed in accidents as their pilots tried to land

Left: A Japanese Navy B6N 'Jill' succumbs to anti-aircraft fire while attacking the USS Yorktown (CV-10). Air-to-air attack was another hazard, especially when escorting A6M Reisen fighters fell to American Hellcats.

Above: The islands of the Pacific were littered with crashed aircraft. This wrecked Mitsubishi A6M is symbolic of the devastating firepower brought to bear upon Japan's air forces, mainly by the US Navy's F6F Hellcats.

Nakajima's dive-bombers

Nakajima's B5N dive-bomber was the most modern aircraft of its type in any of the world's navies at the time of the Pearl Harbor attack. A specification for a replacement for the type had been drawn up as early as 1939. The result was the B6N Tenzan (Heavenly Mountain), the chief difference being a considerably more powerful engine. Both types were operational in the Marianas campaign.

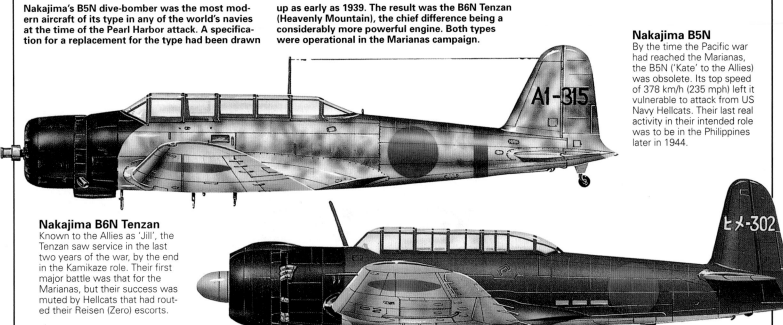

Nakajima B5N
By the time the Pacific war had reached the Marianas, the B5N ('Kate' to the Allies) was obsolete. Its top speed of 378 km/h (235 mph) left it vulnerable to attack from US Navy Hellcats. Their last real activity in their intended role was to be in the Philippines later in 1944.

Nakajima B6N Tenzan
Known to the Allies as 'Jill', the Tenzan saw service in the last two years of the war, by the end in the Kamikaze role. Their first major battle was that for the Marianas, but their success was muted by Hellcats that had routed their Reisen (Zero) escorts.

Philippine Landings

NOVEMBER 1944 – MARCH 1945

Above: The invasion of Luzon began with a fiercely opposed landing at Lingayen Gulf. Here a Kamikaze is diving on the USS Columbia on 6 January 1945. The aircraft hit the main deck of the ship, causing extensive damage.

Left: The 5th and 13th Air Forces were placed in the new Far East Air Forces (FEAF) under General Kenney, putting around 500 P-38s at his disposal. Here P-38Js drop napalm bombs near Ipo Dam, Luzon.

After the great carrier battle of the Marianas, American forces went on to complete the capture of Saipan, thereby providing an important base for subsequent B-29 attacks on Japan. They landed on Guam on 21 July, and on Tinian four days later. The final capture of Guam on 10 August marked the end of the American campaign in the Central Pacific and the end of organised Japanese carrier warfare. The *Hiyo* had been sunk by air action, and the *Taiho* and *Shokaku* had been sunk by US submarines, while no fewer than 1,223 Japanese naval aircraft had been destroyed in the two-month campaign.

Four further Japanese carriers, the *Zuikaku, Chitose, Chiyoda* and *Zuiho*, went to the bottom during the battles of Leyte Gulf. On 30 November, only 11 days after her commissioning, the huge ex-battleship aircraft-carrier *Shinano* (69152 tonnes/68,060 tons) was sunk by the submarine USS *Archerfish* in Tokyo Bay. Before the end of the year the carriers *Unryu,* *Shinyo, Taiyo, Chuyo* and *Unyo* had been sunk and the *Junyo* was permanently crippled. During the same period the US Navy lost but one carrier, the light-carrier *Princeton*.

UNEXPECTED ENEMY

Although the initial landings on Leyte marked the start of the Philippines campaign, the invasion of the main island, Luzon, did not take place until 9 January 1945, four divisions being put ashore in Lingayen Gulf. Already Task Force 38 had to contend with a powerful new enemy: atrocious weather. On 18 December a fully-fledged typhoon struck the fleet; three destroyers capsized with the loss of more than 800 men; aircraft tore loose in the carriers, starting fires as they ripped up electric cabling; the *Cowpens, Monterey* and *San Jacinto* between them lost 33 aircraft, 19 others were swept off the battleships and cruisers, and the smaller escort carriers lost a further 94. Such losses and the search for survivors in the mountainous seas delayed the ultimate assault on Luzon.

As pre-emptive strikes against Japanese air bases on Formosa were being flown by the carriers of TF 38 in the first week of 1945, the Lingayen Gulf assault force, carried by the US 7th Fleet under Vice-Admiral Thomas C. Kinkaid. came under heavy Japanese suicide attacks as it approached the landing area. The escort carrier *Ommaney Bay* was hit and sunk on 4 January,

Above: A Curtiss SB2C Helldiver is flagged off on a mission from USS Hancock (CV-19) on 25 November 1944. On the same day, a Kamikaze exploded directly over the ship, and burning debris started several fires.

Right: B-24M Liberators, including examples from the 494th Bomb Group nearest the camera, at an airstrip on Angaur Island in the Carolines. From here raids were made against the Philippines.

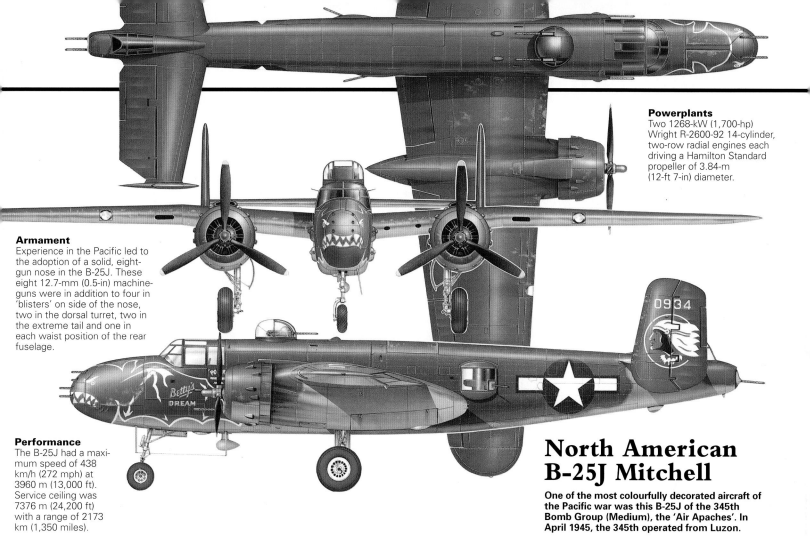

Powerplants
Two 1268-kW (1,700-hp) Wright R-2600-92 14-cylinder, two-row radial engines each driving a Hamilton Standard propeller of 3.84-m (12-ft 7-in) diameter.

Armament
Experience in the Pacific led to the adoption of a solid, eight-gun nose in the B-25J. These eight 12.7-mm (0.5-in) machine-guns were in addition to four in 'blisters' on side of the nose, two in the dorsal turret, two in the extreme tail and one in each waist position of the rear fuselage.

Performance
The B-25J had a maximum speed of 438 km/h (272 mph) at 3960 m (13,000 ft). Service ceiling was 7376 m (24,200 ft) with a range of 2173 km (1,350 miles).

North American B-25J Mitchell

One of the most colourfully decorated aircraft of the Pacific war was this B-25J of the 345th Bomb Group (Medium), the 'Air Apaches'. In April 1945, the 345th operated from Luzon.

Above: TF 38 returned to Ulithi Atoll without hitting Luzon again in December 1944 because of a typhoon. Taken from the USS Essex (CV-9), this picture shows the Task Group as it enters Ulithi.

and the following day the *Manila Bay* was damaged and suffered more than 70 casualties; on 8 January both the *Kitkun Bay* and the *Kadashan Bay* were badly damaged and had to retire from the battle.

On 9 January, as the American forces went ashore in Lingayen Gulf, Admiral William F. Halsey's 3rd Fleet (including TF 38), with eight fleet carriers, five light carriers, two escort carriers, six battleships, 11 cruisers and 61 destroyers,

Above: View from the USS Essex on 25 November 1944 as a 'Banzai' suicide bomber heads towards the carrier after being hit by flak. It landed on the edge of the port side of the deck forward of the No. 2 elevator.

entered the South China Sea, its main task being to locate and destroy the two battleship carriers, *Hyuga* and *Ise*, and also to prevent the Japanese from sending reinforcements to Luzon. Although the giant carriers were not found, the American carrier aircraft flew wide-ranging strikes over French Indochina, China proper and Formosa; few targets were found.

BLOODY ADVANCE

Suicide attacks around Luzon continued to increase, the Australian cruiser *Australia* being hit five times. Fighting on the ground grew fiercer and, despite an order from General Yamashita to evacuate Manila, a Japanese admiral organised resistance by 20,000 men in the naval base. Bataan fell on 16 February, and Corregidor (in Manila Bay) on 28 February. By then, however, the bulk of the American carrier forces had moved

on to prepare for the invasion of Iwo Jima. Indeed, with the steady but bloody advance through Luzon, and the over-running or building of airstrips on the island, it now fell to the fighter and fighter-bomber squadrons of the USAAF and US Marine Corps to provide cover over the battlefield, and to the guns of the fleet to create a curtain of fire

against the suicide attacks.

On 4 March 1945, after 173 days ashore on Luzon, American forces finally captured the shattered city of Manila, having lost more than 40,000 in dead and wounded, and more than 360 aircraft. Ten days later Iwo Jima also fell to the Americans. The US 10th Army, and the 16 carriers of Task Force 58 in support, were poised for assault on the last stepping stone to Japan: Okinawa.

Below: The Philippines played host to the Vought F4U-1 Corsairs of the US Marine Corps. These excellent aircraft were soon found to be highly capable at ground attack and were widely employed in this role.

The Battle of Leyte Gulf

SEPTEMBER – OCTOBER 1944

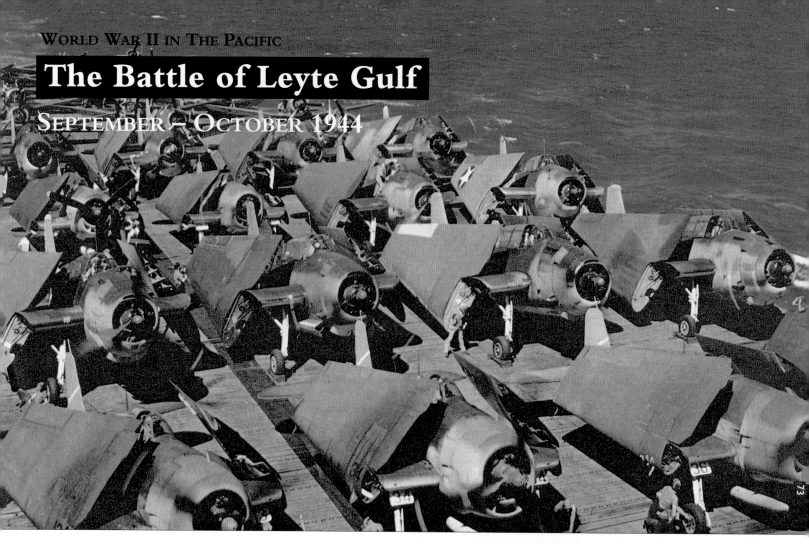

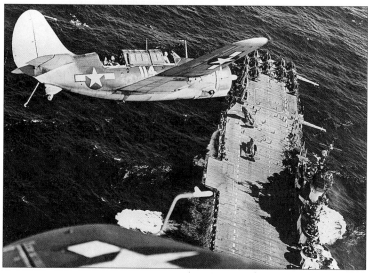

Mid-1944 found the US forces in the Pacific engaged in two main offensives towards the Philippines, one under the direction of Admiral William F. Halsey north-west from Guadalcanal along the northern coast of New Guinea, the other through the Gilberts, Marshalls and Marianas led by Admiral Raymond A. Spruance's 5th Fleet. Between the two thrusts Task Force 38 with 16 carriers struck the major Japanese bases in the Palaus and at Yap early in September, expecting to

Above: Hellcats, Avengers and Dauntlesses on Lexington's deck before the massive three-day series of air strikes was launched against Japanese air power on Formosa from 12/14 October 1944.

encounter heavy Japanese resistance in the air. In the event opposition was very light and the American ships and aircraft went on the rampage, destroying 58 aircraft and sinking 15 supply ships.

Surprised by the relatively weak defences, Halsey changed his plans and initiated air attacks on the central Philippines, the islands of Bohol, Cebu, Leyte, Negros, Panay and Samar. In two days the American carrier aircraft destroyed 478 aircraft and sank some 60 small ships, all for the loss of nine aircraft. Moving his sights up, Halsey now attacked the main island of Luzon and on 22 September his carrier aircraft destroyed 300 more Japanese aircraft. He went further, putting forward a proposal for the invasion of Leyte two months earlier than planned. As General MacArthur was at sea and observing radio silence the proposal went before Roosevelt and Churchill, who were in conference at Quebec, and approval for the plan was given without any delay. By the time

Left: Leyte marked the end of the Imperial Japanese Navy as an effective force. This destroyer in Ormol Bay is being attacked by a gunship version of the B-25, 'skip-bombing' two 454-kg (1,000-lb) bombs.

Halsey had been forced by bad weather to leave Luzon waters on 24 September his pilots had destroyed more than 1,000 aircraft and about 150 ocean-going ships for the loss of 72 aircraft.

COMBINED FLEET

At the time of these preliminaries to the invasion of the Philippines, the Japanese still possessed eight completed carriers with a total theoretical complement of 400 aircraft; however, neither the pilots nor aircraft existed to equip them fully. Recognising that the naval and air forces remaining in the Philippines stood no chance of withstanding the combined strength of Task Force 38 and Task Group 77.4

Above: Curtiss SB2C Helldivers return to USS Hornet (CV-12) following strikes over the Philippines. Admiral Halsey's intention was to destroy any potential opposition prior to the invasion of the islands.

under Rear Admiral Thomas L. Sprague with 18 escort carriers and 500 aircraft, the Japanese decided to assemble the Combined Fleet with four of their carriers and two battleship carriers (the *Ise* and *Hyuga*).

On 17 October US Army Rangers began going ashore on the islands in the mouth of Leyte Gulf, covered by Task Group 77.4. Meanwhile, uncertain of the ultimate invasion point, the Japanese Combined Fleet had split into three groups, two diversion attack forces

Once mighty 'Zeke'

First flying in 1939, the Mitsubishi A6M Reisen (Zero Fighter) became the symbol of Japanese air power; more were produced than any other Japanese type. When it entered service in 1942 it matched the speed, armament and protection of Allied fighters and despite being judged obsolete in 1943, continued in production. Allied types like the Hellcat ultimately challenged its superiority.

Mitsubishi A6M2 Reisen
The Mitsubishi A6M was still providing the main fighter assets of the Japanese navy at the time of Leyte Gulf. This A6M2 of the 402nd Chutai, 341st Kokutai was land-based at Clark Field, Manila in the Philippines, for many years an American air base. 'Zeke' was the Allied codename.

Right: Aircraft on the USS Intrepid *prepare to launch strikes against the Philippines after spending a quiet Thanksgiving Day at sea. Those closest to the camera are Hellcats, with Helldivers beyond.*

being despatched to the Lingga Roads and the Ryukyu Islands, 640 km (400 miles) and 480 km (300 miles) respectively to the west of Leyte. As reports came in of the American landings the main Japanese naval force sailed from Formosa.

INTO BATTLE

The first battle involved Task Force 38, whose northern-most carrier group, with the carriers *Essex*, *Lexington*, *Langley* and *Princeton*, was attacked by about 160 land-based aircraft (hurriedly moved from Formosa to the Philippines) on 23 October. When seven F6F Hellcats intercepted the attackers one American pilot, Commander David McCampbell, shot down at least nine within one hour. The *Princeton* was hit by two bombs and after internal explosions had reduced her to a hulk she was sent to the bottom by American torpedoes. Following the location of the first Japanese diversion attack force, 259 American carrier aircraft took off to attack the enemy ships which now included the 46-cm (18.1-in) gunned battleships *Musashi* and *Yamato*. The former was hit by no fewer than 19 torpedoes and about 10 bombs before the 65027-tonne (64,000-ton) ship sank, taking with her more than 1,000 of her crew. In another battle, this time involving Vice-Admiral Nishimura's force of two battleships, a heavy cruiser and four destroyers, Vice-Admiral

Kinkaid's force sank both the Japanese capital ships and two destroyers in history's last battleship-versus-battleship engagement, in Surigao Strait.

The next phase opened when carrier aircraft from TF 38 spotted the Japanese carriers approaching on 25 October. Strikes were sent off, hitting and sinking the *Chitose*, and damaging the *Zuiho* and *Zuikaku*; later that day another strike sank the *Zuiho*. In another action involving the American escort carriers 320 km (200 miles) to the south-west, the US ships

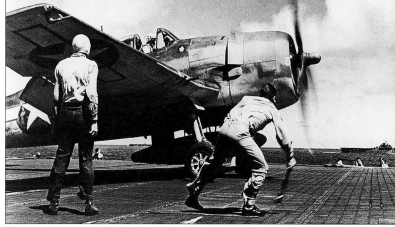

Right: Almost all the major air combats in the Pacific theatre from August 1943 onwards were dominated by the F6F-5 Hellcat. Here a Hellcat gets the take-off flag aboard USS Randolph.

were less fortunate when four Japanese heavy cruisers engaged them, damaging the *Kalinin Bay*, *Fanshaw Bay* and *White Plains*, and sinking the *Gambier Bay*.

It was at this point that the Japanese first introduced their Kamikaze (suicide) aircraft, the first to achieve success being a Zero pilot who struck and damaged the escort carrier USS *Santee*, another

damaged the *Suwannee*, and then the *St Lo* was hit and sunk, the first American warship to be sunk by suicide aircraft.

The Battles of Leyte Gulf marked the end of the Imperial Japanese Fleet as a powerful and balanced fighting force, its losses of four carriers, three battleships, nine cruisers and eight destroyers comparing with the American loss of three carriers and two destroyers. The fighting on Leyte continued until the spring of 1945 but, with Japanese naval power virtually eliminated, the final outcome was never in any doubt.

Left: The Yokosuka D4Y 'Judy' was a naval carrier-borne reconnaissance aircraft to replace the Aichi D3A2 'Val'. About 140 D4Y1s and 35 D4Y1-Cs took part in the Battle of the Philippine Sea. Nearly all were lost.

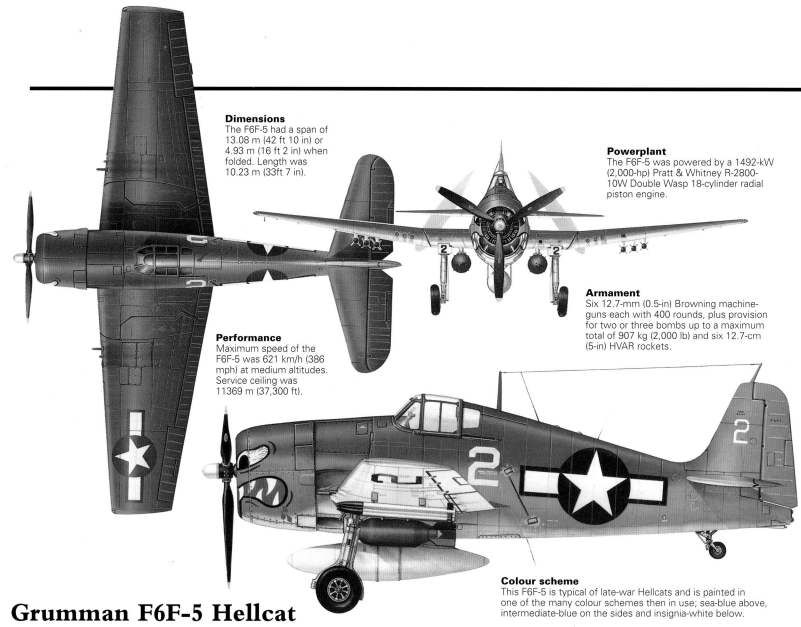

Dimensions
The F6F-5 had a span of 13.08 m (42 ft 10 in) or 4.93 m (16 ft 2 in) when folded. Length was 10.23 m (33ft 7 in).

Powerplant
The F6F-5 was powered by a 1492-kW (2,000-hp) Pratt & Whitney R-2800-10W Double Wasp 18-cylinder radial piston engine.

Performance
Maximum speed of the F6F-5 was 621 km/h (386 mph) at medium altitudes. Service ceiling was 11369 m (37,300 ft).

Armament
Six 12.7-mm (0.5-in) Browning machine-guns each with 400 rounds, plus provision for two or three bombs up to a maximum total of 907 kg (2,000 lb) and six 12.7-cm (5-in) HVAR rockets.

Colour scheme
This F6F-5 is typical of late-war Hellcats and is painted in one of the many colour schemes then in use; sea-blue above, intermediate-blue on the sides and insignia-white below.

Grumman F6F-5 Hellcat

The F6F-5 was the major production version of the Hellcat with over 6,300 built. This example flew with VF-27 aboard USS *Princeton* in 1944.

Above: The Wildcat was in the twilight of its career by the end of 1944. Some remained in use aboard escort carriers (CVEs), specifically FM-2s. The FM-2 was an F4F-8 built by the Eastern Aircraft division of General Motors and was distinguished by its taller tailfin.

Left: Japanese battleship carrier Ise *or* Hyuga *in action off Engano on 25 October. Smoke from anti-aircraft guns is evident as the vessel comes under air attack. As 'decoy' carriers at Leyte Gulf, neither ship operated aircraft in action.*

Above: Intrepid *opened the aerial part of the battle just after 08.00 on 24 October 1944 when one of its Helldivers spotted the Japanese Force in the Sibuyan Sea. This Helldiver just made it back to the* Intrepid *as it ran out of fuel.*

The Kamikaze threat

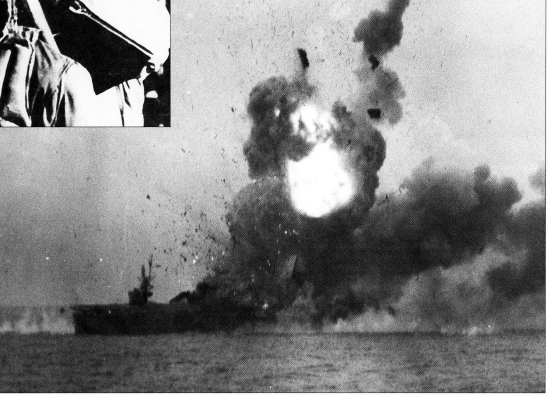

Above: A comrade tightens the 'Hachimaki' for a Japanese Kamikaze pilot ready for a mission in late-1944. The 'Hachimaki' was a Samurai symbol of courage and composure before the battle and was worn by all Kamikaze pilots. A number of different aircraft types were used in the role, including fighters and dive-bombers.

Right: The Japanese Southern Force was routed during the night of 25 October 1944 in Surigao Strait, but TF-38 was decoyed to attack the Northern Force off Cape Engano. This gave the Center Force a golden opportunity to disrupt the Leyte landings, a chance that was lost when they attacked escort carriers off Samar. Here an explosion on USS St Lo (VC-65) of Carrier Unit One following a Kamikaze hit, sinking within the hour.

Left top: The Battle of Leyte Gulf saw the first widescale use of Kamikaze aircraft. Here a pilot is cheered off by groundcrew as he sets off in his bomb-laden Mitsubishi A6M. These attacks caused major problems for the Allied fleets.

Left: Dramatic picture of a Kamikaze manoeuvring his Zero to crash on the deck of the USS Missouri. Fortunately on this occasion the aircraft went into the sea. Many of the Kamikazes ended their mission by being shot down.

Above: A damaged Japanese dive-bomber plunges towards the escort carrier USS Kitkun Bay (CVE-71) off Leyte, October 1944. After the failure of the Sho operation, flights of up to five suicide aircraft with one or two escorting fighters became the principal weapon of the Imperial Navy whose ships were no longer able to operate as a fleet. In the foreground are Grumman Avengers aboard another of the carriers of Task Force 38.

Burma and China

MARCH 1944 - AUGUST 1945

After months of limited advance and counter-offensive in northern Burma, the Japanese embarked on their last major offensive in March 1944, thrusting towards Assam in the northwest. Now reformed as Long-Range Penetration Groups (LRPs), the Chindits were para-chuted into the jungle behind enemy lines at Indaw on 5 March and, after overland reinforcement, began construction of a number of landing strips (of which 'Broadway' was the most important); within a week 9,000 Allied troops had been flown deep into enemy-held terri-tory. However, when the Japanese launched an attack against the air-fields being used to fly supplies over 'the Hump' into China, they also destroyed 'Broadway', togeth-er with most of the RAF fighters based there.

RAF Hurri-bombers make a low-level attack on a Japanese-held bridge on the Tiddim Road in Burma in October 1944. Hurricane Mk IIs and Mk IVs remained in front-line service in the Far East until 1945.

In May 1944, No. 42 Squadron moved into the Imphal fighting, where its Hurricanes were highly active on army close-support bombing and strafing. In addition, they flew a large number of Rhubarb sorties in search of targets of opportunity.

Above: A Short Sunderland Mk III with full ASV Mk III radar seen serving with No. 230 Squadron when it returned to the Far East and operated in the Burma cam-paign in 1944. The Sunderland is in Pacific theatre markings, and is pictured after landing on a jungle river for the first time.

Below: The flight crew of C-46 Commando Polly the Queen turns the propellers prior to start-up at Chenyi in China on 6 January 1945. The two engines are 2,100-hp (1566-kW) Pratt & Whitney Double Wasp 18-cylinder radials, driving four-bladed Hamilton Standard propellers.

In the course of the Japanese advance the defended towns of Kohima and Imphal were sur-rounded and besieged. By June it seemed that Imphal would be forced into surrender but, in the nick of time, General Slim's 14th Army managed to reach and break through the Japanese perimeter. Within days the withdrawal of the enemy had turned to rout, as RAF, SAAF and USAAF fighters and fighter-bombers began a year-long operation to destroy the Japanese forces in Burma.

By that time (July 1944), Air Command, Southeast Asia, com-manded by Air Chief Marshal Sir Richard Peirse, had grown to a total of 90 squadrons, of which 26 were American (flying P-38s, P-40s, P-51s, B-24s, B-25s and C-47s), four were Indian (flying Hurricanes), one a Canadian squadron with Catalinas and one a South African squadron with Venturas. The remaining 58 were of the RAF, flying Thunderbolts, Spitfires, Hurricanes, Beaufighters, Mosquitos, Wellingtons, Liberators, Sunderlands and Catalinas.

As the new advance (somewhat cautious at first) began, and the Allied forces found abundant evi-dence that the Japanese army was

Below: This is a Mitsubishi Ki-51, Allied codename 'Sonia'. With over 1,500 built, it was used as a ground-attack and tactical reconnaissance aircraft and was so successful that it remained in production for most of the war.

Japanese attackers

Although the best Allied aircraft enjoyed a small qualitative edge by 1944, the gap was slight, and the Japanese forces based in China included some highly effective aircraft types. However, the biggest change since the start of the war in the Far East lay in the fact that the Allies no longer regarded the Japanese as being invincible, and morale was much higher.

Nakajima Ki-44
Lacking the agility of other Japanese fighters, the Nakajima Ki-44 followed a more Western approach and proved fast and stable, with excellent climb and dive capabilities. This is a Ki-44-IIb, flown by the commanding officer of the 85th Sentai from Canton, China, during 1944.

Mitsubishi Ki-46
Illustrating one of the many colour schemes applied to Japanese aircraft in World War II, this Mitsubishi Ki-46-II 'Dinah' displays the leaping tiger motif of the 18th Chutai, 82nd Sentai operating in China in 1944. The Ki-46 proved particularly effective in the recce role.

Nakajima Ki-49
The Nakajima Ki-49-I 'Helen', Army Type 100 Heavy Bomber, was underpowered, and more powerful engines were introduced on the Ki-49-II. Its performance was little improved and the type was easy prey for Allied fighters over Burma and China. This is a Ki-49-IIa of the 3rd Chutai, 95th Sentai.

Right: An Australian-built Bristol Beaufighter Mk 21 of No. 22 Squadron, with whom it served during the final year of the war in the Far East. The Beaufighter's arsenal of bombs, rockets and guns wrought widespread havoc among river and jungle targets throughout the Burma campaign until the final liberation of Rangoon.

Below: Often confused with the similarly shark-mouthed 23rd FG, the 51st Fighter Group painted all its Mustangs with the aggressive decoration, while within the 23rd FG only the 76th Squadron aircraft were so adorned. The P-51B was a mainstay of the USAAF in the Far East.

far from invincible, a heightened morale gripped the Allied aircrews. Combat procedures and weapons, hitherto confined to the European war, were adopted. The dreadful napalm weapon, found so effective in the jungle, came into use, as did Air Support Signals Units for the control of 'cab ranks', the patrols by fighters over the battlefield.

ADVANCE SOUTH

When the 1944 monsoon season arrived in July all effective operations by the Japanese air force in Burma ceased. By then the Allies were closing up to the Irrawaddy, and their air forces, particularly the long-range Liberators, concentrated on the enemy supply lines to prevent a build-up of reinforcements. By the end of the rains in November, when the advance southwards resumed, the Japanese

Below: A Waco CG-4A Hadrian glider on tow behind a C-47. In March 1944, the second Wingate Chindit operation in Burma involved Hadrians landing in a jungle clearing by night, 150 miles behind the main Japanese lines. The CG-4A could carry 15 equipped troops, including two acting as pilots.

Markings

The Sentai markings on the tail are stylised renderings of the digits 4 and 8; the numeral 21 is the individual aircraft number within the unit. Standard identification markings include a white band around the rear fuselage and orange-yellow inboard wing leading-edge panels.

Nakajima Ki-43

When it entered service during the last year of the war, the Ki-43-III-Ko version of the Nakajima fighter possessed all the external characteristics of contemporary fighter-bombers, but lacked adequate performance and armament.

Wing span

Wing span of the Ki-43 was 35 ft 6.75 in (10.84 m) with a wing area of 230.4 sq ft (21.4 m²).

Powerplant

The Ki-43-II was powered by one 1,150-hp (858-kW) Nakajima Ha-115 14-cylinder air-cooled radial piston engine.

Performance

Maximum speed of the Ki-43 was 329 mph (530 km/h) at 13,125 ft (4000 m). It could climb to 16,405 ft (5000 m) in 5 minutes 49 seconds and had a service ceiling of 36,750 ft (11200 m). Normal range was 1,095 miles (1760 km).

Armament

The Ki-43 had two 0.5-in (12.7-mm) Type 1 (Ho-103) machine-guns in the upper fuselage decking, and could carry two 66-lb (30-kg) or 551-lb (250-kg) bombs.

could muster no more than 125 aircraft in the entire theatre. In the North Shan States efforts were made to open the Burma Road from Mandalay to China as a Chinese Expeditionary Force fell on and captured Wangting on 21 January 1945, supported by aircraft of the USAAF in China. Exactly two months later the northern capital of Mandalay fell to the 14th Army as the Chinese fought their way southwards through Lashio and Hsipaw. Throughout this campaign the needs of more than 350,000 fighting men were supplied by the Dakotas of the Combat Cargo Task Force, an achievement which, having regard to the harsh weather conditions, hazardous terrain and a desperate enemy, was acknowledged by Slim as the vital component of the 14th Army's victory. Even when a sudden Japanese thrust menaced Kunming in distant China, the Dakotas were quickly switched to fly 25,000 Chinese troops, their guns and pack animals across the 'Hump' to meet the threat.

The advance southwards from Mandalay was double-pronged along the great rivers, the Irrawaddy and the Sittang, while XV Corps advanced down the

Right: The B-24 Liberator was much sought after due to its endurance. Range was often of paramount importance in air attacks on Japanese targets. This B-24 is attacking positions at Armapura in Burma in January 1945.

Left: Thunderbolt Is of No. 134 Squadron transferred from India to Burma in December 1944. One of the leading American fighters of WWII, the Thunderbolt did not enter operational service with the RAF until August 1944, and it was then used exclusively by SE Asia Command against the Japanese.

coast, leapfrogging islands until Taungup was reached and captured on 28 April. Occasionally Ki-43 fighters tried to interfere, but these were always quickly overwhelmed by the ever-present Spitfires, Hurricanes and Thunderbolts. Soon there was no remaining usable base or airstrip available to the Japanese aircraft, and all air opposition evaporated.

TRAPPED

The great seaport of Rangoon was itself captured after a landing by XV Corps from the sea on 2 May, and four days later a link-up was

Known by the Japanese as 'Whispering Death', the Bristol Beaufighter Mk X was supremely effective in the low-level strike role, especially against jungle river traffic. Here a 'Beau' lands between others of the type.

achieved with IV Corps advancing down the Sittang. Trapped in the Burmese hinterland lay some 20,000 Japanese troops, sick and hungry yet fanatically determined to break eastwards across the Sittang into the mountains of Indo-China. In 10 days' concerted action by Allied tactical aircraft, the RAF

alone flew more than 3,000 sorties and dropped 1,500,000 lb (680400 kg) of bombs and napalm, killing 10,000 of the enemy. By the end of July the Japanese had been defeated throughout Burma. Plans were already in hand to mount Operation Zipper, the invasion of Malaya and the capture of Singapore. It was never put into action. On 9 August the second atomic bomb, which fell on the city of Nagasaki, persuaded the Japanese to acknowledge final defeat.

A P-40K of the 23rd Fighter Group at Kweilin, China early in 1944. A C-46 Commando of the 14th Air Force can be seen on finals behind. Note the five victory emblems below the canopy and the pilot's personal emblem next to the fuselage star.

Above: Sqn Ldr G. Kerr DFC, CO of No. 152 Squadron, is seen with his strikingly decorated Spitfire Mk VIII. In July 1944, the squadron moved forward to landing strips around Imphal, from where it provided escorts for supply-dropping C-47s.

Allied fighter-bombers

The Allied air forces in Burma and China were primarily engaged in supporting the army. Tactical operations were more common than strategic, and air transport and close air support duties assumed a huge importance. The P-51 Mustang, the Hawker Hurricane and the P-47 Thunderbolt were among the most important types.

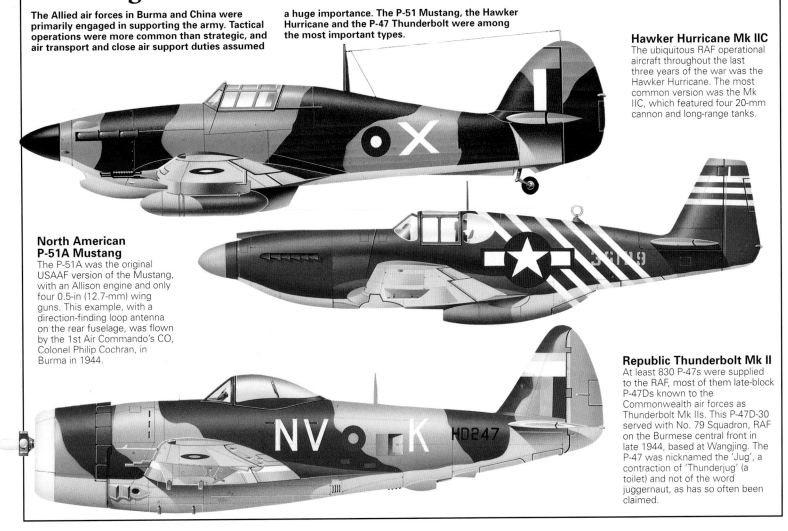

Hawker Hurricane Mk IIC
The ubiquitous RAF operational aircraft throughout the last three years of the war was the Hawker Hurricane. The most common version was the Mk IIC, which featured four 20-mm cannon and long-range tanks.

North American P-51A Mustang
The P-51A was the original USAAF version of the Mustang, with an Allison engine and only four 0.5-in (12.7-mm) wing guns. This example, with a direction-finding loop antenna on the rear fuselage, was flown by the 1st Air Commando's CO, Colonel Philip Cochran, in Burma in 1944.

Republic Thunderbolt Mk II
At least 830 P-47s were supplied to the RAF, most of them late-block P-47Ds known to the Commonwealth air forces as Thunderbolt Mk IIs. This P-47D-30 served with No. 79 Squadron, RAF on the Burmese central front in late 1944, based at Wangjing. The P-47 was nicknamed the 'Jug', a contraction of 'Thunderjug' (a toilet) and not of the word juggernaut, as has so often been claimed.

The Aleutians and Kuriles

DECEMBER 1941 – AUGUST 1945

A CATALINA, NAVY 'DUMBO', PATROLS ALONG ALEUTIAN COAST.

Above: A US Navy PBY-5A pictured over the Aleutians in 1944. In areas such as this, with consistently bad weather, the range of these reliable amphibians brought many crews to safe landings on land or water.

Below: The P-40K Warhawk had a dorsal fin which made it the ugliest of the type. Here one with a long-range fuel tank attached is preparing to taxy across a pierced steel planking (PSP) surface.

Among the lesser-known war theatres in the war against Japan was the North Pacific, an ill-defined geographical area that embraced the chain of Aleutian Islands which extend westwards from Alaska, and the Kurile Islands that run north-east from Japan towards the Kamchatka peninsula.

At the time of Pearl Harbor the air defence of Alaska and the northern Pacific was vested in the USAAC's 28th Composite Group which had recently been trained to operate in Arctic conditions and had its headquarters at Elmendorf, Alaska. It possessed two pursuit squadrons, the 18th and 34th with P-40Bs, plus the 36th, 37th and 73rd Squadrons with a miscellany of aircraft, including a small number of bombers. However, it was

Above: North American B-25B or C Mitchells of the 77th Bomb Squadron, 28th Bomb Group, flying in close formation over waters south-east of Attu, Aleutian Islands in September 1943.

beyond the scope of this group to perform long-range reconnaissance, and although the Japanese task force which attacked Pearl Harbor from the north had sailed from Hittokappu Bay in the Kuriles it was not detected by the American air force.

ALEUTIANS VULNERABLE

It was part of the Japanese overall war strategy to create an outer defence perimeter stretching from Kiska in the Aleutians southwards through Midway, and the capture of the islands of Attu, Adak and Kiska were intended to divert

American attention from the major attack on Midway. This part of the plan did not succeed and the American commander, Rear Admiral Frank Fletcher, concentrated his naval forces (including all his available carriers) to win the great Battle of Midway; by so doing he was forced to leave the Aleutians exposed to attack from the air and

sea. By June 1942 American air forces in the immediate area of the Aleutians comprised some 100 USAAF P-40s, 12 B-17s, 24 B-26s and 20 US Navy PBY flying-boats.

The Japanese launched a strike/invasion force which included the carrier *Junyo* and *Ryujo* with 30 Mitsubishi A6M fighters, 24 dive-bombers and 20 torpedo-bombers.

American aircraft in the north

Over 2,300 P-40E Warhawks were built, the most numerous varaint until the P-40N. Powered by the ubiquitous Allison V-1710, the Curtiss designation was Model 87-A3 Hawk. As the Lockheed Hudson was a development of the Model 14 Super Electra passenger transport, the Ventura was derived from the larger Model 18 Lodestar. Venturas introduced better armament and performance.

Curtiss P-40E Warhawk
Displaying distinctive 'tiger's head' cowling markings, this P-40E of the 11th Fighter Squadron, 343rd Fighter Group, was based at Fort Glenn, Alaska in late-1942. The unit saw action in the Aleutian Islands during 1943-45 with frequent detachments to Amchitka. The 'tiger's head' nose art was adopted as a tribute to Claire Chennault, leader of the 'Flying Tigers'.

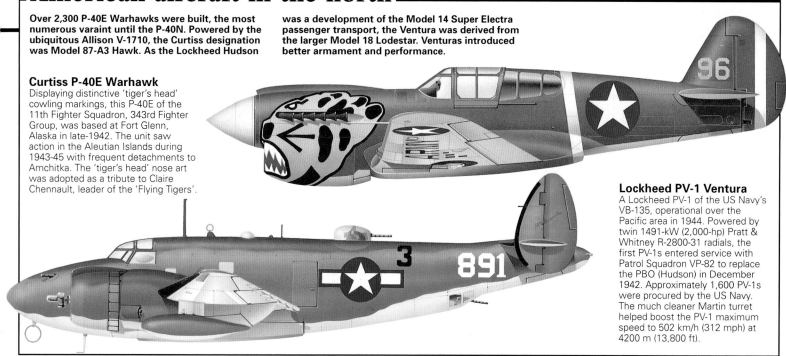

Lockheed PV-1 Ventura
A Lockheed PV-1 of the US Navy's VB-135, operational over the Pacific area in 1944. Powered by twin 1491-kW (2,000-hp) Pratt & Whitney R-2800-31 radials, the first PV-1s entered service with Patrol Squadron VP-82 to replace the PBO (Hudson) in December 1942. Approximately 1,600 PV-1s were procured by the US Navy. The much cleaner Martin turret helped boost the PV-1 maximum speed to 502 km/h (312 mph) at 4200 m (13,800 ft).

As carrier strikes were launched against Dutch Harbor in the eastern island of Unalaska, 2,500 troops would land and seize the three western islands. The air strike on Dutch Harbor was duly carried out on 3 June and achieved the destruction of three PBY flying-boats for the loss of four aircraft. One of these was an A6M which force-landed on Akutan Island, the first such aircraft to fall into American hands in a repairable state; its recovery and subsequent testing by the USAAF was to prove of inestimable value to the Allies.

The following day the Japanese launched a further strike against Dutch Harbor, causing considerable damage to shore installations, losing five further aircraft. The B-17s located and attacked the Japanese carriers but failed to hit them and lost one of their own number. Meanwhile the invasion of the western islands was postponed while Admiral Yamamoto sent the carrier *Zuiho* (and later the *Zuikaku*) north as reinforcements lest the Americans should now attempt to reinforce the Aleutians by diverting carriers. No such carriers could be spared and the Japanese duly went ashore on Kiska and Attu, to find them occupied by just 10 unarmed men. To have attempted to defend and sustain these islands at that stage of the Pacific war would have overtaxed the USA's air and naval forces beyond their strength. As it was the Japanese retained their toehold on a tiny part of the American continent (sic) for just one year.

DIVERSIONARY TACTICS
Meanwhile the 28th Composite Group was joined in Alaska by the newly constituted 343rd Fighter Group whose 11th, 18th, 54th and 344th Fighter Squadrons were equipped with P-38s and P-40s, initially at Elmendorf and Fort Glenn in Alaska, and later at Adak. It was largely this move forward by these squadrons that prompted the Japanese to withdraw hurriedly from Kiska, only just before a joint US-Canadian assault force landed. Both this island and Attu were reoccupied by the Americans in July and August 1943, aircraft of the 28th and 343rd Groups moving into bases there almost immediately.

In particular the 28th Group's B-24s flew long-range reconnaissance and bombing missions over the Kuriles, latterly 'trailing their coat' to attract Japanese fighters and thereby weaken their forces in the south, a strategy that earned the Group a Distinguished Unit Citation. The 343rd Group, which had been heavily engaged in strafing attacks on Kiska prior to American re-occupation, flew no further combat missions after October 1943.

The presence of some 50 B-24

Above: Kawasaki's Ki-45 KAI Toryu (Dragon Killer) or Army Type 2 two-seat fighter had the Allied code-name 'Nick'. This is a KAId cannon fighter version introduced before the end of the war for anti-shipping strikes.

Liberators, which flew sporadic raids over the Kuriles during the last 16 months of the war, caused the Japanese to divert two Sentais of Ki-45 'Nick' heavy-fighters to the north of the Japanese homeland, a force of some 40 aircraft that would otherwise have been a useful element in the defence against the disastrous raids by the American B-29 Superfortresses.

Below: A group of P-38Gs between missions in the Aleutians in 1943. The first P-38 victory over a Japanese aircraft came as early as 4 August 1942 when two Lightnings shot down a pair of 'Mavis' flying-boats.

Right: US Navy PV-1s operated in all weathers on anti-shipping strikes and attacks on the Japanese bases at Paramushiro and Shimushu, and fought off attacks by defending Mitsubishi A6M3 Reisens.

Iwo Jima

JANUARY – FEBRUARY 1945

By January 1945 US fleet dispositions were being made for an assault on and capture of the island of Iwo Jima, just 1223-km (760-miles) south of Tokyo itself, and roughly the same distance north of Saipan. Principal covering naval force under Vice-Admiral Mitscher was Task Force 58 (the Fast Carrier Force) comprising five task groups sailing a total of 11 fleet carriers and five light carriers plus 100 battleships, cruisers and destroyers. The assault force destined for Iwo Jima itself, a force of more than 1,000 ships, included Rear Admiral Durgin's Task Group 52.2 with 12 escort carriers, embarking a total of 226 F4F Wildcats and 138 TBM Avengers, some of whose pilots were trained in gunnery spotting.

The importance of Iwo Jima lay in its location almost directly in the path of B-29 Superfortress heavy bombers flying from Saipan on raids over Japan, enabling the Japanese observation posts to alert interceptor fighters both on Iwo Jima and in the homeland. Once captured the island could be used by the USAAF as a base for fighters to escort the B-29s.

To cover the approach by Task Group 52.2, Task Force 58 sailed to within 97 km (60 miles) of Tokyo and launched a number of strikes in the area of the Japanese capital, attracting some 100 enemy aircraft into the air and shooting down about 40. On the following day, 17 February, Mitscher carried out searches for Japanese shipping and failing to find any, turned the great fleet south for Iwo Jima.

THE END IN SIGHT

On 19 February the Fast Carrier Force struck the island with both big-gun bombardment from two of the eight battleships and strikes by Helldivers, Avengers and Corsairs. Meanwhile, evidently believing the US fleet still to be close to Tokyo, the home-based Japanese aircraft did not interfere with the invasion force off Iwo Jima until the evening of 19 February, by which time no fewer than 40,000 US Marines had gone ashore under cover of fighters from the carriers *Enterprise* and *Saratoga*. When the Japanese aircraft did arrive they failed to get through to the invasion transports and were heavily engaged by the naval fighters which, with gunfire from the fleet joining in, shot down a dozen of the attackers. On 21 February the *Saratoga* was detached from

Above: A USAAF Consolidated B-24M Liberator of the 7th Air Force over the flaming beachhead of Iwo Jima, with Suribachi Mountain in the background. The last B-24 model to be built in large quantities, the 'M' variant was distinguished by a lightweight tail turret. By the beginning of 1945, over 6,000 Liberators were in operational strength with the USAAF, equipping 45 Groups.

Above: A group of young Japanese Kamikaze pilots are briefed the night before a mission, early in 1945. The Americans experienced Kamikaze attacks for the first time during the Battle of Leyte Gulf in October 1944, when five carriers off Saman were attacked by Japanese suicide pilots.

Left: In the closing months of the war, Allied air power was overwhelming. Here a US Marine Corps TBM-3E from the USS Essex, with a 227-kg (500-lb) bomb under each wing, accompanies a formation of Curtiss SB2Cs over the Japanese mainland, with Mount Fujiyama beyond.

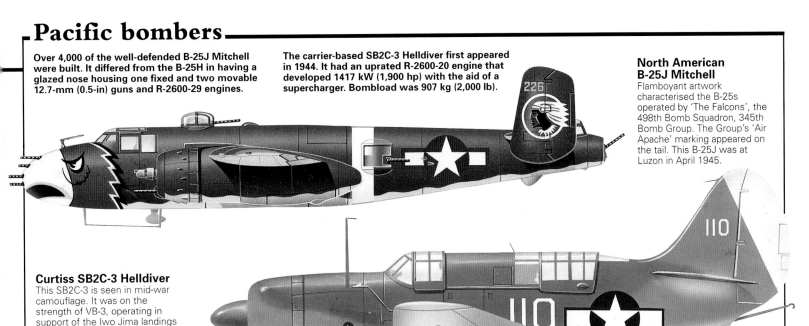

Over 4,000 of the well-defended B-25J Mitchell were built. It differed from the B-25H in having a glazed nose housing one fixed and two movable 12.7-mm (0.5-in) guns and R-2600-29 engines.

The carrier-based SB2C-3 Helldiver first appeared in 1944. It had an uprated R-2600-20 engine that developed 1417 kW (1,900 hp) with the aid of a supercharger. Bombload was 907 kg (2,000 lb).

North American B-25J Mitchell
Flamboyant artwork characterised the B-25s operated by 'The Falcons', the 498th Bomb Squadron, 345th Bomb Group. The Group's 'Air Apache' marking appeared on the tail. This B-25J was at Luzon in April 1945.

Curtiss SB2C-3 Helldiver
This SB2C-3 is seen in mid-war camouflage. It was on the strength of VB-3, operating in support of the Iwo Jima landings with Task Force 58 from the carrier USS *Yorktown* (CV-10) in February 1945. Underwing APG-4 radar is fitted.

Above: The capture of Iwo Jima's airfield allowed these USAAF P-51D Mustangs of the 21st FG to operate on long-range escort missions with B-29 Superfortresses of the 20th Air Force to bomb mainland Japan. The following month, they penetrated to Tokyo for the first time.

February, but poor weather curtailed the carrier strikes and few combats ensued; instead Mitscher turned his attention against Okinawa to the west but, apart from securing useful reconnaissance of the island, found little in the way of targets. Within a fortnight the capture of Iwo Jima had been completed, no further significant air attacks having troubled the land or naval forces, while aircraft from the escort-carrier *Anzio* had sunk two Japanese submarines on 26 and 27 February.

During the Iwo Jima operations the guns and pilots of the Fast Carrier Force and Task Group 52.2 were estimated to have destroyed 393 enemy aircraft in the air and a further 200 on the ground. Task Force 58 had, however, lost 95 aircrew and 143 aircraft. Far more significant, a key base had been secured within fighter range of Japanese airspace and without any irreplaceable losses among the vital American carrier task forces.

Left: Task Force TF-58, consisting of 166 ships, sailed on 12 February 1945 and was the first carrier strike to hit the Japanese mainland since Doolittle's raid three years earlier. With Japan itself under attack, the assault on Iwo Jima began. US troops are seen raising the Stars and Stripes on the island.

Below: The aftermath of a direct hit by a Kamikaze aircraft on the USS Saratoga on 21 February 1945. A total of 123 men were killed and 192 injured; 42 aircraft were either destroyed or had to ditch as they were left with nowhere to land.

Task Force 58 with three destroyers to cover the amphibious forces, and at about 17.00 hours that afternoon was attacked by six Japanese aircraft manned, as it transpired, by suicide pilots. Two were hit by the carrier's guns but struck the ship's side where their bombs exploded; the bomb from a third aircraft struck the forward end of the flight deck, a fourth also struck the flight deck and a fifth hit the starboard side of the ship; the sixth aircraft was shot down. Two hours later the *Saratoga* was again attacked, this time by five suicide aircraft, one of which struck the flight deck but bounced overboard, its bomb causing further damage. Yet the old carrier survived; with 123 dead or missing and 192 injured, and 42 of her aircraft destroyed or jettisoned, she was ordered to retire from the area, returning to active duty after only two months under repair.

Later on that same evening the escort-carrier *Bismarck Sea* was hit by two suicide aircraft, and soon afterwards became a raging inferno; her captain ordered her to be abandoned and just as the survivors got clear a torpedo hit blew the carrier apart. She went down with 218 of her crew, 19 Wildcats and 15 Avengers.

In an effort to prevent further attacks by suicide aircraft, the Fast Carrier Force was detached north towards Japan once more on 23

Okinawa

MARCH – JULY 1945

Left: USS Randolph (CV-15) was hit by a Japanese suicide attack on 11 March with the loss of 27 men, but by the first week of April it had been repaired and returned to operations off Okinawa. F6F-5 Hellcats of Fighter Squadron 12 (VF-12) leave Randolph's deck on a ground-attack sortie.

their home waters, causing some damage, particularly to the light carrier *Ryuho*. Pre-occupation with these attacks on the Japanese naval vessels allowed a number of Japanese bombing raids to take off, the aircraft making for Task Group 52.2, whose *Wasp* was hit and badly damaged; 102 men were killed and 269 injured, but her crew managed to extinguish the fires and within an hour she was recovering her aircraft. Almost simultaneously the fleet carrier *Franklin* suffered two bomb hits which started massive fires in her hangar and set off explosions that continued to rock the ship for hours. In an epic of a sea rescue only 90 kilometres (55 miles) from Japan, the carrier was saved, although 832 of her crew perished. In attacks over Japan the Task Force pilots claimed the destruction of 432 enemy aircraft during

The invasion of Okinawa, an island which lies almost midway between Formosa and the southernmost point in the Japanese homeland, involved an assault and support force second only in size to that thrown against the Normandy coast in Europe 10 months previously, but far exceeded that great operation in the distances and logistics involved. If the American naval forces had been fortunate to escape serious losses in the Iwo Jima assault, the Japanese were about to react with the utmost force and ferocity at Okinawa. Once more the 5th Fleet Task Force 58 would provide the naval muscle in the assault and its protection.

JAPAN ATTACKED

Before the fleet sailed from Ulithi to the south-west of the Marianas, the fleet carrier *Randolph* was hit by a suicide aircraft flying from Minami Iwo, and put out of action with 27 men killed. On 14 March 1945 Task Force 58 sailed north to attack airfields in Japan where the majority of suicide units were

thought to be based; warned of the Americans' approach many of the Japanese aircraft were withdrawn out of range of the carrier aircraft. Fifty aircraft did take-off to attack the Task Force, however, but only caused superficial damage. Meanwhile the carrier aircraft had found and attacked Japanese warships in

Above: P-38L Lightnings routinely carried drop tanks for long-range missions. This P-38L of the 475th Fighter Group at Lingayen Airstrip, Luzon, is equipped with two auxiliary tanks; one of 1173-litres (310 US gallons) capacity and the other 625 litres (165 US gallons).

Left: Two Nakajima B5N2 carrier-borne attack-bombers (Allied code-name 'Kate') flying over the Yamato. This Naval Type 97 was one of the most successful torpedo-bombers ever built and had the ability to remain airborne for over four hours. Production of the 'Kate' totalled some 1,150.

Below: The TF 58 strike against mainland Japan came under very heavy air attack. The most serious raid on 19 March damaged the Wasp and Intrepid and nearly sank the Franklin, whose entire complement of aircraft was lost, along with 832 men killed and 270 wounded.

the opening of Operation 'Ten-Go', a concerted suicide assault by surface and air forces. No fewer than 4,500 aircraft would be involved in suicide and conventional attacks on the Americans. Of all the extraordinary elements of this operation was the sailing of the super-battleship *Yamato* (65027 tonnes/64,000 tons) from Japan on 6 April, it being intended to penetrate right to the Okinawa invasion beaches and destroy as many transport ships as possible before being overwhelmed by American bombs and guns. Fortunately the huge ship was detected on her departure from

18/19 March, and the following day the American ships withdrew as further attacks, now by suicide pilots, were aimed at the carriers, causing some damage to the *Enterprise*. Two days later the *Franklin*, *Enterprise* and *Wasp* left the combat area for repairs.

On 23 March the assault on Okinawa opened with air strikes by TF 58's carrier aircraft and a bombardment by 10 battleships, which lasted a week. The invasion was to be supported by the 13 remaining fast carriers, by six light carriers and by no fewer than 18 escort carriers, between them embarking more than 1,000 aircraft. A further 10 escort carriers were loaded with replacement aircraft and the US Marine fighters which would be based on Okinawa.

MASS SUICIDE ATTACKS

When the landing assault on Okinawa was launched on 1 April the Japanese responded by ordering

Left: Two B-25J Mitchells of the 345th Bomb Group (Medium) of the 5th Air Force attack a Japanese warship on 29 March 1945. The Group adopted the name 'Air Apaches' and carried a Red Indian head on the fins of their aircraft and at war's end was based off Okinawa.

Right: A Japanese Kawasaki Ki-61 Swallow (Allied codename 'Tony') makes a suicide dive on the escort carrier USS Sanganon (CVE-26) at Kerama Retto in the Okinawa Group on 4 May 1945, missing the carrier by less than 7.6 m (25 ft).

From Okinawa to Japan

The last stepping stone on the way to Japan was the island of Okinawa. Once established there, bombing raids on the mainland could begin. B-24s had served in many theatres and took on this role from spring 1945. While the most important operators of the type were the Marines (in a fighter-bomber role), the F4U was conceived as a carrier-based fighter for the US Navy.

Consolidated B-24J Liberator
One of the last B-24s to see action, this B-24J-CO was given a particularly flamboyant paint scheme by the 43rd Bomb Group operating against the Japanese mainland from Ie Shima in the Spring of 1945.

Vought F4U-1D Corsair
From the 4,100th F4U-1 and 2,602nd Goodyear-built FG-1, zero-length launchers were added under the outer wings for eight 12.7-cm (5-in) rockets. Added to many Corsairs already delivered, this feature was widely used during the attack on Okinawa. This F4U flew from the carrier *Essex*.

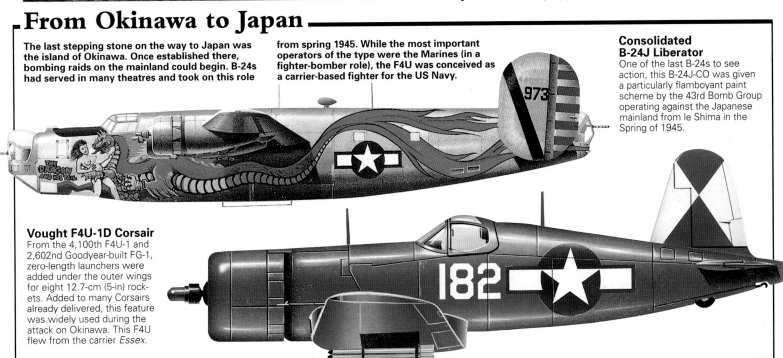

home waters, shadowed by Mariner flying-boats and ultimately attacked by a strike of 280 carrier aircraft from Task Force 58, including 98 Avenger torpedo aircraft. Inevitably the *Yamato* succumbed, but only after being hit by 10 torpedoes and five bombs, taking to the bottom 2,498 of her crew; with her went an accompanying light cruiser with almost 450 men, hit by seven torpedoes and 12 bombs.

A HARD BATTLE

The reduction of Okinawa itself occupied three months and involved one of the greatest naval/air campaigns ever fought. The early part of April was marked by sustained conventional and suicide attack. On the same day that the *Yamato* was sunk the American carrier *Hancock* was badly damaged by a suicide aircraft; on 11 April the *Enterprise* (recently rejoined after repairs) was again hit, as was the carrier *Essex*. On 11 May the fast carrier *Bunker Hill* (Mitscher's flagship) was hit by bombs and suicide aircraft, but was saved after losing 389 of her crew.

When the Okinawa campaign was officially declared ended on 2 July 1945, it was calculated that the Japanese had launched some 34,000 sorties by 6,000 aircraft, many of them suicide attacks. US pilots and gunners claimed 2,336 shot down, losing a total of 790 aircraft. American naval losses amounted to 33 ships sunk (including 13 destroyers) and 119 severely damaged, including nine fleet carriers, one

Left: Japanese aircrew on standby with a Mitsubishi G4M 'Betty'. This aircraft was one of a batch modified to carry the Ohka piloted missile and was designated G4M2e. It reduced top speed and poor handling made it an easy target.

Below: The tailplane of this Mitsubishi A6M6c Zero fighter breaks away after being hit whilst attacking the USS Essex (CV-9) on 14 May 1945. This dive-bomber version had special bomb racks.

Unique Swallow

Known to the Allies as 'Tony', the Hien (Swallow) was unique in the Japanese air forces in having a liquid-cooled engine, long tapered nose and high aspect-ratio wings. It was initially thought to be a licence-built Messerschmitt Bf 109 or an unknown Italian design. Its service was not extensive, but during the mid-war years it was the only Japanese aircraft able to engage fast Allied fighters.

Kawasaki Ki-61 Hien
Crudely applied green paint was an attempt to tone down the natural metal finish on this Ki-61-I KAI of the 3rd Chutai, 19th Sentai. This group fought over Leyte Gulf in the Philippines as well as Okinawa and Formosa.

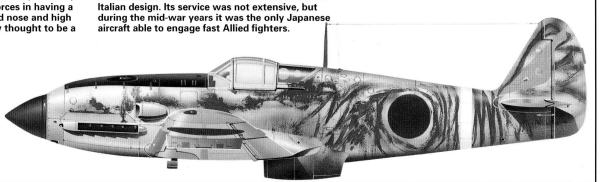

Following the early Pacific carrier battles, when the myth of the supremacy of the Japanese Zero had been shattered, and with the introduction of new US fighters such as the Hellcat and Mustang, the victory tallies of Allied pilots began to mount. There was intense competition to see who would become the top ace of the theatre. As it was, the two top scorers flew P-38 Lightnings, a type that had a checkered career elsewhere, but which was ideal for the long-range overwater missions common in the Pacific.

Major Gregory 'Pappy' Boyington

Leader of the most famous of all USMC squadrons, VMF-214 'Black Sheep', 'Pappy' Boyington (left) had scored six victories over Burma while serving with the American Volunteer Group before returning to the Marine Corps as commander of the 'Black Sheep' over the Solomon Islands. Boyington had scored 25 victories by the time he was shot down in January 1944 (after scoring three more times) and was captured by a Japanese submarine. With 28 kills, he was the top pilot in the Marine Corps.

Major Richard I. Bong

With 40 kills confirmed, Richard Bong (right) was the top-scoring US pilot of the war, and remains to this day the highest ranking American ace of all time. Dick Bong flew P-38 Lightnings with the 5th Air Force in New Guinea. By April 1944, he had surpassed Eddie Rickenbacker's World War I score of 28 (the first US pilot to do so) and was sent home on leave. Continuing to increase his score on his return, Bong was awarded the Medal of Honor later in 1944 and scored his 40th and final victory on 17 December.

Lt Cdr David McCampbell

David McCampbell (above) was the commander of Air Group 15 on USS *Essex* (CV-9) in 1944. On 19 July 1944, he shot down seven Japanese aircraft in two sorties and on 24 October a further nine (a record for a US pilot). In addition, McCampbell was credited with 21 aircraft destroyed on the ground. All McCampbell's kills were scored in F6F Hellcats, which were usually named 'Minsi' after a ladyfriend. With 34 victories, McCampbell was the leading Navy ace.

Major John C. Herbst

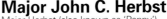

Major Herbst (also known as 'Pappy') flew the A-36A Apache version of the P-51 Mustang (right) with the 23rd Fighter Group in China. Prior to his arrival in the China Burma India (CBI) theatre in late-1944 he had scored one kill over Europe. At war's end John Herbst had taken his total to 19, and was by then the relatively advanced age (for a fighter pilot) of 35 years. Like Richard Bong, 'Pappy' Herbst was killed in the crash of a P-80 Shooting Star in 1946.

Lt Col Robert E. Westbrook

Leading ace of the 13th Air Force, USAAF, Westbrook (left), shot down his 17th Japanese aircraft on 30 September 1944 over Japanese-held Kendari Field in the southern Celebes. His eventual total was 20 kills, of which 13 were accomplished while flying a P-38. Westbrook was killed on 22 November 1944 while with the 18th Fighter Group, in a strafing attack on enemy shipping, the first mission of his eighth combat tour.

Major Robert W. Moore

With a total of 12 victories, Robert W. Moore (left) was not one of the top-ranking Pacific aces, but was the top scorer of the 7th Air Force. In the last few months of the war, Moore, aged 23, commanded the 45th Fighter Squadron of the 15th Fighter Group. All his kills were scored against fighters over the Japanese home islands while flying P-51s from Okinawa on gruelling round-trip missions of 2575 km (1,600 miles).

light carrier and three escort carriers, nine battleships and 37 destroyers. Obviously the Japanese suicide attacks posed a serious threat in all the operations of 1945, but such were the enormous reserves and resources now available to the Americans that the losses, grievous though they were, could be shrugged aside, and never in fact endangered the success of the campaign.

Left: P-47D 'Little Rock Ette' is seen being used by pilots and ground-crew of the 19th Fighter Squadron, 318th Fighter Group at Ie Shima on 11 July 1945 to hang a scoreboard showing the number of Japanese aircraft shot down.

Above: The Hellcat was developed to counter the Japanese Zero, the dominant fighter during early Pacific actions. It proved so effective that recorded a 9:1 kill ratio. Here a Hellcat waits a mission from USS Randolph in March 1945.

The Bombers finish Japan

JANUARY – AUGUST 1945

Boeing B-29s drop incendiaries high over Japan. Although the atomic bomb raids caused greater emotional and political fallout, the firestorms at Yokohama caused far greater casualties. Seven square miles of the city were completely razed by the B-29s.

If controversy still rages about the effect of bombing on Germany in World War II, there is no questioning the effect of the American Superfortress campaign in the Far East. The USAAF's B-29s literally burned and blasted the heart out of Japan. The cost in dollars was prodigious, yet without the big bombers the cost in American lives, in an invasion of the Japanese homeland, would have been horrifying.

Plans to produce a 'super bomber' had been laid in January 1940, long before the USA entered the war, calling for a 400-mph (644-km/h) aircraft capable of delivering 2,000 lb (907 kg) of bombs over a range of 5,300 miles (8530 km). Initial development was leisurely by later standards, and only after Pearl Harbor was the utmost priority afforded to the new aircraft,

Ground crews of the 500th BG ready a B-29 for action. This posed scene compresses the activity involved to launch a mission, but gives an idea of the effort required for each of hundreds of bombers.

and on 21 September 1942 the first XB-29 was flown. By that time orders for 1,664 production examples had been placed.

THE B-29 GOES TO WAR

On 1 June 1943 the 58th (Very Heavy) Bombardment Wing was activated in the USA for initial service trials and B-29 crew training. The future pattern of the war in the Pacific had been decided and, with fortunes running in the Allies' favour in Europe, the big bomber was henceforth only considered in the context of the war against Japan. With four 2,200-hp (1641-kW) engines, the service version, with a span of 141 ft 3 in (43.05 m), had a speed of 358 mph (576 km/h) at 25,000 ft (7620 m), a maximum range of 4,100 miles

Faced with an increasing air threat against the home islands, the Japanese were forced to develop new interceptor fighters. One such design was the Nakajima Ki-44 Army Type 2 Shoki (Demon), known to the Allies as 'Tojo'.

(6600 km) and a maximum bombload of 20,000 lb (9072 kg). In every respect it eclipsed all other in-service aeroplanes anywhere in the world; in an unparalleled feat of engineering a total of 3,970 of these very large bombers was built by Boeing, Bell and Martin in just three years.

The first B-29s to arrive in the Far East were those of the US 20th Air Force which landed at Kwanghan in China on 24 April 1944. No fewer than nine huge bases had been constructed by 700,000 Chinese labourers in India and China to accommodate the new bomber force. It flew its first raid on 5 June, attacking Bangkok in Thailand, and on 15 June 50 aircraft were sent against Yawata in Japan, the first American raid on the

Last ditch defence

The Japanese fighters of the early war period were tailored to long-range escort and designed for manoeuvrability at the expense of armour protection and armament. The arrival of modern US fighters and bombers made the 'Zero' and 'Oscar' obsolete, although these types remained in production until late in the war. New types were introduced, but too late to make a difference.

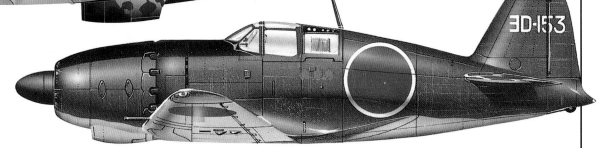

Kawasaki Ki-61-I KAlc
The Ki-61 was a departure from all previous Japanese fighters in having an inline engine (a Kawasaki-built Daimler-Benz DB 601A), and significant armour protection. This aircraft belonged to the 244th Sentai, one of four assigned to the defence of Tokyo. Unable to reach the B-29s, the Ki-61 was more successful against US Navy fighters.

Mitsubishi J2M3 Raiden
The Mitsubishi Raiden (Thunderbolt) was originally designed as a Naval interceptor. Dogged by technical problems, service test pilots complained about poor visibility. Production progressed at a very slow rate from 1943. The J2M3, fitted with six cannon, was the most important model and once in service was extremely popular with pilots in the bomber-destroyer role.

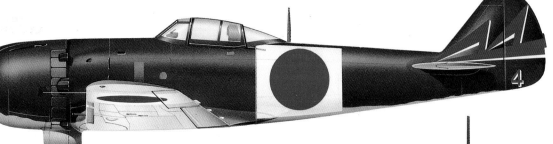

Nakajima Ki-84-la Hayate
Designed by Nakajima as a replacement for its own Hayabusa ('Oscar'), the Ki-84 Hayate (Gale), with the Allied reporting name 'Frank', was the best fighter produced in quantity in 1944-45. The white around the national insignia on this 7th Sentai Ki-84 indicates its home defence assignment.

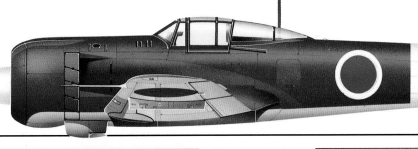

Kawasaki Ki-100-lb
When the supply of Ha-140 engines for the Ki-61-II KAI dried up due to teething and production troubles, Kawasaki fitted the 14-cylinder Mitsubishi Ha-112-II radial to spare Ki-61-II KAI airframes. The resulting Ki-100 was a superb interceptor, much feared by the B-29 crews.

The nose of this B-29 of the 881 BS, 500 BG sheared off in a crash landing on Saipan. All the crew survived, shocked but uninjured, despite the runaway bomber demolishing another B-29 and a tractor before stopping. Captain James Pearson had flown over 2400 km (1,500 miles) from Musashino with only two good engines following a fighter attack.

Left: Another mission over, a B-29 of the 40th Bomb Group slips in to Kadena in the last few days of the war. The 40th BG was part of the 58th BW and flew missions over the 'Hump' from India before moving to West Field on Tinian in February 1945 for the final assault on Japan.

There have been few aerial campaigns as intense as that flown against Japan at the end of the Pacific war. The super base at Tinian had seven parallel runways. Isley Field on Saipan had only two, and there are 145 B-29s lined up on one of them in this August 1945 photo.

Below: The Kawasaki Ki-61 Hein (Swallow) was the only Japanese fighter with an inline engine to see service. Despite many engine and production difficulties, the 'Tony' was the only Army fighter able to fight at the B-29's altitude.

The Superfortress was the most sophisticated and most powerful bomber of the war. Four Wright R-3350 engines provided enough power for a B-29 to reach most of Japan's industrial centres and return, sometimes on only three.

Japanese mainland since Doolittle's B-25 raid back in April 1942.

The great distances from the Indian and Chinese bases to Japan severely limited the bombloads of the B-29s, while bad weather rendered such raids of only limited effect. However, the capture of the Marianas in mid-1944 was followed by another marathon feat as American service engineers built five vast new bases (two on Guam, two on Tinian and one on Saipan), each capable of handling 180 B-29s. On 24 November 111 B-29s, led

by General Emmett O'Donnell, took off to raid the Nakajima engine works at Musashi; however, only 24 bombers found their target.

NIGHT ATTACKS

On 20 January 1945 Major General Curtis E. LeMay assumed command of XXI Bomber Command, USAAF, and at once announced a radical change of bombing policy and tactics by the B-29s. Henceforth the bombers would attack with incendiary bombs by night, individually and from below 10,000 ft (3050 m), and with reduced defensive armament in the

B-29s of the 497th and 498th Bomb Groups form up on the way to Japan. Formations were not as tight as those flown by the 8th Air Force over Europe, but the flak and fighter defences were not as tough at B-29 altitudes, either.

interests of increased bombloads.

The first such attack was made on 9/10 March by 302 aircraft against Yawata and Tokyo; for the loss of 14 aircraft, over 16 sq miles (41.4 km²) of the Japanese capital were reduced to ashes. In 10 days, five raids on Tokyo, Yawata, Nagoya, Osaka and Kobe — 29 sq miles (75.1 km²) of Japan's main industrial centres — were destroyed

Decorated B-29s

Nose art was a feature of both Allied and Axis aircraft, especially bombers. Masters of this form of expression were the Americans, and the 'Superfort' provided the biggest canvas of all for the cartoon

characters and pinups close to the hearts of men far from home. In March 1945, an order came down to remove the paintings, whether suggestive or not, although examples remained until war's end.

B-29 Superfortress

Crew
The B-29 had an 11-man crew for most missions. The forward compartment housed pilot, bombardier, engineer, navigator and radar/radio operators. The gunners were seated in the aft compartment.

Weapons load
The B-29 had capacity for up to 9075 kg (20,000 lb) of bombs in two huge bays, each of which had its own bomb-loading winch. Bomb release was sequenced to maintain centre of gravity.

Bombs
The main weapon used aginst Japanese cities was the incendiary bomb, such as the M-47, filled with napalm and loaded in clusters tied together with cord.

Markings
Dina Might belonged to the 421st BS, 504th BG. The rear fuselage bands denoted a bombing formation lead aircraft.

Fire control
The four rotating turrets were controlled by three gunners and the bombardier, and sighted through the various glass domes. A simple computer control system allowed one gunner to direct any or all of the guns depending on the threat.

by 10,100 tons of bombs. On 25/26 May the hardest-hitting raid was flown when 464 B-29s, led by pathfinders, attacked Tokyo, destroying 18.9 sq miles (48.95 km²) of the city for the loss of 26 aircraft. In these great fire raids (and others, including a raid on Yokohama where 85 per cent of the city was gutted) well over half a million Japanese civilians were killed and 13 million others rendered homeless.

Many historians have averred that continuation of the B-29 fire raids could by themselves have smashed the Japanese nation into surrender. It fell, however, to the delivery of two atomic bombs against Hiroshima and Nagasaki by the B-29s *Enola Gay* and *Bock's Car* of the USAAF's 509th Composite Group on 6 and 9 August 1945 respectively to convince the Japanese of the futility of continuing the war. Apart from special

Compared to the bases in India and China, the facilities in the Marianas were all that could be desired. Much of the islands' area was consumed by massive parking areas to disperse hundreds of B-29s from the threat of air attack.

training and the strictest security, the delivery of these awesome weapons posed no major operational problems and the bombs duly detonated above the doomed Japanese cities, killing more than 100,000 persons instantly; thousands were to die the next day, and the next.

ABRUPT ENDING
The B-29s' atomic bombs ended the war, quickly and surgically. As already suggested they may well have been superfluous having regard to the systematic destruction being achieved by the 'conventional' fire raids on Japanese cities and industry. Apart from almost certainly avoiding even greater carnage and destruction that would have accompanied such raids, the demonstration of those diabolical weapons was the convincing prelude to the post-war policy of 'peace by deterrent', and the deterrent to world war was to be the threat of nuclear weapons. Had Hiroshima and Nagasaki not been sacrificed someone, somewhere, would have attempted a more horrifying demonstration.

Above: No. 356 Squadron, RAF, Liberator ground crews celebrate the Japanese surrender, which was formally signed on 2 September 1945. RAF and USAAF B-24s played a pivotal role in the war against Japan.

Below: Phosphorous bombs dropped by a fighter explode above 7th Air Force B-24s over Okinawa. Despite its fearsome appearance, this weapon was mostly ineffective, as was the Japanese secret weapons programme in general.

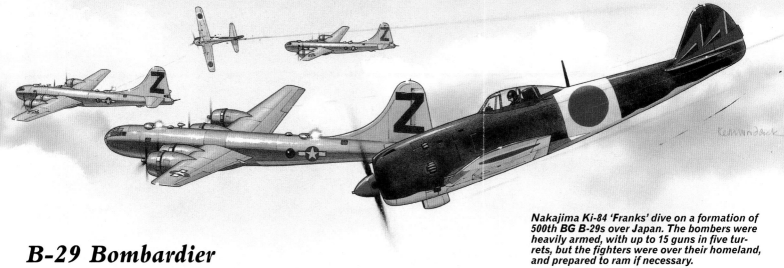

Nakajima Ki-84 'Franks' dive on a formation of 500th BG B-29s over Japan. The bombers were heavily armed, with up to 15 guns in five turrets, but the fighters were over their homeland, and prepared to ram if necessary.

B-29 Bombardier

The B-29 ushered in a new era, operating at extreme ranges and vast heights. Pressurised, carrying a huge ordnance load, and with their supercharged engines, the B-29s were the first of a new generation.

"I inspected the 28 500-lb bombs in the Superfortress. This was the heaviest bomb load we had ever carried. The bombs were wired together, two to a shackle. I had never seen bombs loaded that way and I didn't feel comfortable with it. My job was to aim and drop the bombs.

"I walked back from our Superfortress to join Major Tom Vaucher and the rest of the crew.

"This was my first operation as lead bombardier of the formation. We expected heavy flak and Japanese interceptors. I would have been nervous without the extra weight.

"I had been selected for special training as lead bombardier. That I had passed the course didn't make me any more confident than I had been when I had first been told of the new tactic.

"As we approached the coast, I spotted two innocent-looking ships lying offshore. Next moment the sky around us filled with bursts. The bursts were so close I could see the red flashes as the shells exploded. The sides of the plane

Whereas high explosives were needed to level the cities of Europe, incendiaries were more effective against the paper houses of Japan. This photograph was used in a leaflet, itself dropped to warn a city of an impending fire raid.

echoed with the explosions. Flak ships! And we were flying straight on in.

"'The target's clear,' I called to Vaucher.

"'You take the turn,' Vaucher responded. I grabbed the turn knob on the stabiliser and slowly turned the aeroplane. The effort of concentration temporarily blotted out my awareness of the continuing flak.

"I looked over the sight to check we were on line for the target, then switched to the telescope and used the turn knob to bank the plane until the vertical hair in the telescope split the target. I felt the drama of the moment, knowing that 14 B-29s depended on my work.

"We were drifting off. I made a slight course correction. It looked good. My hands trembled slightly as I adjusted the rate knobs until the crosshairs stayed steady on the aiming point

"Ten more seconds and I could do nothing more. I glanced anxiously back at the sight.

"'Bombs away!' I yelled, and salvoed quickly.

"'Rear bomb bay clear,' the tail gunner reported.

"I waited for Carmona to announce the front bomb bay clear so I could close the doors.

"'Eight bombs hung up and the

arming wires pulled out,' came Carmona's nervous report. 'They are hanging nose-down with the arming vanes backwards and forwards.

"If the arming vanes spun off and the bombs dropped, they would explode when they collided with each other. The Superfortress, with us in it, would be blown to pieces. In desperation I pressed the salvo switch several times but nothing happened.

"Vaucher said, 'How dangerous is it leaving them that way?'

"I said, 'Dangerous. Once we're back over the sea I'll try kicking them free.'

"For the last 10 minutes I had been oblivious to the flak. Now I could feel it again, bursting close. I looked over the bomb sight to spot the bombs. Twenty-three thousand feet below us the Japanese aircraft plant stood out in stark relief. Then tiny puffs of smoke spotted the buildings. The smoke spread and the plant seemed to rise up, then disintegrate. After so many misgivings now, finally, I could relax, sure of myself.

"'How are the bombs holding?' I called back to Mike Egan. 'The arming vanes still on?'

"'Same position, Captain Morrison.'

"'Fighter at nine o'clock!'

"I put the bombs out of my mind and searched the sky. Two fighters, one on each side of the formation, circled waiting for an opening. Suddenly the fighter to our right dived at us. I tracked him and when he was in range let go a long burst, but still he came on.

"As he passed right over the top of us, a huge, blossoming, yellowish-white mass descended in a shower of streamers.

"'What's that?' yelled Todd from the top turret.

"'Phosphorus bomb,' Vaucher told him.

"'I'm going back in the bomb bay to see if I can pry the bombs loose,' I told Vaucher.

"I edged my way out of the cabin and into the navigator's compartment. My Mae West and parachute made movement difficult. And I had to carry a portable cylin-

der of oxygen for my mask.

"'I waited a minute or two for my breathing to steady before crawling out along the narrow catwalk on the left side of the bay. I didn't want to look down but couldn't avoid doing so – 23,000 feet of nothing, then the white caps of the ocean. I shuddered and looked away quickly.

"I pulled some cotter pins out of my pocket, leaned far over into the bomb bay, left hand clutching the rack, and felt for the nose fuse of the first bomb. Fingers stiffening with the cold, I fumbled the cotter pin into the fuse.

"Fourteen to go. The longer I took the colder I'd get, and the more clumsy. My arms were shaking both with fear and from the extreme exertion of reaching down into the bay from the 10-inch-wide catwalk while gripping desperately to the rack.

"At last it was done. I was so exhausted I had to stand on my narrow perch for a minute or two to get my breathing steady and my nerves back under control before trying to push the bombs free.

"I struggled with a screwdriver to pry loose the wires that were holding the bomb in place. It was no use. Finally I gave up and edged my way back into the forward cockpit.

"We all felt as if we were riding a keg of dynamite as we approached the field.

"'Land her like a case of eggs,' the co-pilot told Vaucher. 'This is no time to go bouncing 10 feet in the air.'

"The wheels hit and ran. Egan yelled, 'They're still in place.'

"I wiped the sweat off my face and grinned back at Vaucher. He taxied over to the parking area, cut the engines, and shouted down to the ground crew to stand clear. 'We've got bombs hung up in the front bay.'

"'I'm going to open the bomb bay doors,' I said.

"The bomb doors snapped open. Eight 500-lb bombs smashed onto the crushed-stone parkway. Time stood still for a second.

"'I told you I didn't think they'd go off,' I told Vaucher."

Above: Enola Gay was a B-29-45-MO built by Martin at Omaha. On 6 August 1945 it was to become the single most famous aircraft of the war, and change the face of warfare forever. This is pilot Paul Tibbets (with pipe) with his crew.

Below: By mid-1944, Japan's empire had shrunk enough for B-29s to attack the homeland from bases in China. With the construction of five huge bases on the Marianas at the end of the year, all the major centres came under threat of bombing.

Above: 'Little Boy' was the code-name of the atomic bomb that exploded over Hiroshima at 9.30 a.m. on 6 August 1945. Made with uranium 235 and developed in great secrecy, the bomb exploded with the force of 20,000 tons of TNT.

Below: Hiroshima after the bomb: it was not just the scale of destruction or number of casualties that was so shocking, as worse had been caused by the firebomb raids, but the sheer power of a single weapon and the lingering effects of fallout.

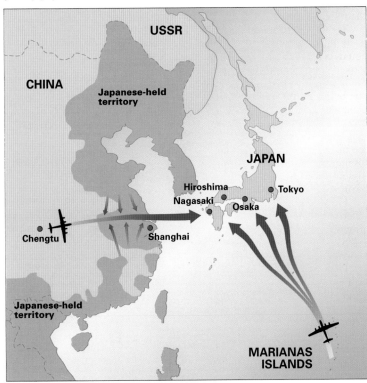

B-29 Superfortress

Bockscar was the Boeing B-29 which dropped the atomic bomb on Nagasaki on 9 August 1945, effectively ending the war. It, and *Enola Gay* which had dropped the first bomb three days earlier on Hiroshima, were flown by the 509th Bomb Group, based on Tinian. The special B-29s, codenamed 'Silverplate', were painted in the markings of regular B-29 units operating from the Marianas, in this case the 444th Bomb Group

INDEX

INDEX

Picture acknowledgments

The publishers would like to thank the following
organisations for their help in providing photographs for
this volume:

Imperial War Museum
Royal Air Force Museum
Bundesarchiv
US Air Force
US Navy
US Marine Corps
MacClancy Collection
Aerospace Collection